Caring for the Elderly in Diverse Care Settings

Caring for the Elderly in Diverse Care Settings

Charlotte Eliopoulos, RNC, MPH

Consultant, Author, and Educator
Glen Arm, Maryland

J. B. Lippincott Company

Philadelphia

Grand Rapids
New York
St. Louis
San Francisco
London
Sydney
Tokyo

Sponsoring Editor: Patricia L. Cleary
Production: P. M. Gordon Associates
Production Coordination: Lori J. Bainbridge
Compositor: Achorn Graphic Services
Printer/Binder: R. R. Donnelley and Sons

6 5 4 3 2

Library of Congress Cataloging-in-Publication Data

Caring for the elderly in diverse care settings / [edited by]
   Charlotte Eliopoulos.
          p.   cm.
      Includes bibliographical references.
      ISBN 0–397–54671–8
      1. Geriatric nursing. I. Eliopoulos, Charlotte.
      [DNLM: 1. Geriatric Nursing.   WY 152 C27723]
RC954.C375   1989
610.73′65—dc20
DNLM/DLC
for Library of Congress   89–12978
                                                          CIP

Any procedure or practice described in this book should be applied by the health-care practitioner under appropriate supervision in accordance with professional standards of care used with regard to the unique circumstances that apply in each practice situation. Care has been taken to confirm the accuracy of information presented and to describe generally accepted practices. However, the authors, editors, and publisher cannot accept any responsibility for errors or omissions or for consequences from application of the information in this book and make no warranty, express or implied, with respect to the contents of the book.

Every effort has been made to ensure drug selections and dosages are in accordance with current recommendations and practice. Because of ongoing research, changes in government regulations, and the constant flow of information on drug therapy, reactions, and interactions, the reader is cautioned to check the package insert for each drug for indications, dosages, warnings, and precautions, particularly if the drug is new or infrequently used.

Dedicated to the memory of Ray Johns,
a special influence in my life,
who did not have the opportunity to grow old.

Contributors

LuRae Ahrendt, RN
Nurse Consultant
Co-owner, Adaptive Equipment
  Specialists, Inc.
Tucker, Georgia

*Chapter 22: Adaptive Equipment
  Specialists: A Nurse-Owned
  Business to Promote Independent
  Living in the Community*

Beverly A. Baldwin, RN, PhD
Associate Professor
School of Nursing
University of Maryland
Baltimore, Maryland

*Chapter 15: Family Caregiving:
  Education and Support*

Judy Bobb, RN, MSN
Critical Care Nurse Coordinator
Maryland Institute for Emergency
  Medical Services Systems
Baltimore, Maryland

*Chapter 7: Injuries in the Elderly,
  Section Two: Strategies for Care*

Susan K. Brock, RPT
Registered Physical Therapist
Denver, Colorado

Chapter 8: Geriatric Rehabilitation

Lynne R. Crouch, RN, MSN
Clinical Nurse Specialist
Southeast Mental Health Center
Baltimore, Maryland

*Chapter 21: Putting Widowhood in
  Perspective: A Group Approach
  Utilizing Family Systems
  Principles*

Bridget Doyle, MPH, RS
Director of Dietetic Services
Lenoir Life Care Community
Columbia, Missouri

*Chapter 5: Nutritional
  Considerations in the Care
  of the Elderly*

James Eastham, Jr., ScD
Chairman
Emergency Health
  Services/MIEMSS
University of Maryland Baltimore
  County
Catonsville, Maryland

*Chapter 7: Injuries in the Elderly,
  Section Two: Strategies for
  Care*

Mary Edwards, RN, MSN
Director of Senior Care
Columbia Regional Hospital
Columbia, Missouri

*Chapter 19: Support Groups
for Caregivers of Alzheimer's
Disease Victims: The Nurse's
Role*

Charlotte Eliopoulos, RNC, MPH
Consultant, Author, and Educator
Glen Arm, Maryland

*Chapter 1: The Older Population
and Nursing*
Chapter 2: Aging and Wellness
*Chapter 3: Assessing Normal from
Abnormal in the Elderly*
*Chapter 4: Nursing Diagnosis in
Gerontological Care*
*Chapter 6: Safe Drug Use with the
Elderly*
Chapter 11: Quality Assurance
*Chapter 12: Promoting Positive
Attitudes toward the Aged*
*Chapter 26: Selecting and
Adjusting to Nursing Home
Care*
*Chapter 27: Nursing Administra-
tion in the Nursing Home
Setting*

Sheryl A. Feutz
Attorney and Counselor at Law
Shugart, Thomson, Kilroy
Kansas City, Missouri

*Chapter 9: Legal Aspects of
Gerontological Nursing*

Melinda D. Fitting, PhD
Licensed Psychologist and Physical
Therapist
Baltimore, Maryland

Chapter 8: Geriatric Rehabilitation
Chapter 10: Ethical Issues

Lacy Flynn, RNC
Geriatric Assessment Team Nurse
Greater Baltimore Medical Center
Baltimore, Maryland

*Chapter 23: A Hospital-Based
Geriatric Assessment Team*

Patricia Grodin, RN, MSN
Geropsychiatric Nurse Specialist
Private Practice
Silver Spring, Maryland

*Chapter 28: The Role of the Psy-
chiatric Clinical Nurse Specialist in the Nursing Home Setting*

Sharon Kern, RN, MSN
Director of Staff Development
Meridian Healthcare Corporation
Baltimore, Maryland

*Chapter 16: The Geriatric Nurse
Practitioner in a Multipurpose
Senior Center*

Kay Kness
Director of Psychosocial Programs
Manor Health Care
Ruxton, Maryland

*Chapter 26: Appendix: Family
Support in the Nursing Home
Setting: The "In Touch" Program*

Monica Koshuta, RN, MSN
Director, Hospice of Washington
Washington Home and Hospice
Washington, D.C.

Chapter 20: Hospice Care

Mary Jane Lucas-Blaustein, RNC
Codirector, Dementia Research
Clinic
Alzheimer's Disease Center for
Excellence
Johns Hopkins University
Baltimore, Maryland

*Chapter 25: Psychiatric
Emergencies of the Elderly*

Kay Mehlferber, RN
Director
Queen Anne Adult Day Care
  Center
Queen Anne's County, Maryland

*Chapter 18: The Role of the Nurse
  in Adult Day Care*

Ann H. Myers, ScD
Assistant Professor
School of Hygiene and Public
  Health
Johns Hopkins University
Baltimore, Maryland

*Chapter 7: Injuries in the Elderly,
  Section One: Risks and
  Prevention*

Martha Anne Palmer, RNC, BA, MA
Coordinator of Aging
Department of Gerontology and
  Geriatrics
Bon Secours Hospital
Baltimore, Maryland

*Chapter 24: Care of the Older
  Surgical Patient*

Barbara Santamaria, RN, MPH, CNP
Nurse Practitioner
Hospital-Based Home Care
Veterans Administration Medical
  Center
Baltimore, Maryland

Chapter 14: Home Health Care

Kay Seiler, RN, MS
Director, Department of Aging
Greater Baltimore Medical Center
Baltimore, Maryland

*Chapter 13: Effective Communica-
  tion with the Elderly*
*Chapter 17: Continuing Care
  Retirement Living: The Nurse's
  Role*

Amy Sharpe, MHS
Research Assistant
American National Red Cross
Washington, D.C.

*Chapter 7: Injuries in the Elderly,
  Section One: Risks and
  Prevention*

Georgia Stevens, RN
Assistant Research Professor
School of Nursing
University of Maryland
Baltimore, Maryland

*Chapter 15: Family Caregiving:
  Education and Support*

Preface

The graying of America has touched the nursing profession. Be they employed in psychiatric hospitals, surgical services, acute medical units, home health agencies, health maintenance organizations, private physicians' offices, clinics, rehabilitation centers, shock trauma stations, or long-term care facilities, nurses can be sure that they will be caring for increasing numbers of older persons.

The growing involvement of nurses with older adults is an exciting opportunity for nursing. Most of the health problems possessed by elderly persons fall within the domain of nursing for independent diagnosis and treatment; thus nursing can assume leadership in this growing area of specialization and demonstrate new models of care delivery. This opportunity can be exciting for nursing, true, but it challenges nurses to gain increased expertise in gerontological care to assure that a high quality of service is delivered to the elderly.

Formal preparation in the specialty of gerontological nursing is something that few nurses currently possess. Gerontological nursing role models are relatively scarce, and new services and programs for the elderly challenge nurses to create roles in territory new to nursing. Gerontological nursing theory and knowledge of practical application are essential to guide nurses in working with older adults.

This book is intended to serve as a resource to nurses in a variety of settings along the health care continuum. It presents an overview of the following:

The unique characteristics of older persons and their service needs.

Services that aid the elderly in maintaining independent living in the community.

Complexities of long-term care.

Acute care problems and risks of the elderly.

Emerging nursing roles to meet the diverse needs of older adults in a variety of settings.

Core knowledge of gerontological care, universal to every setting, is provided through chapters on nursing and the elderly, the nursing process, pharmacology, legal aspects, nutrition, rehabilitation, quality assurance, and ethical issues. In addition, nursing interventions and considerations in a variety of settings, including support groups, life care communities, adult day care, assessment clinics, trauma centers, home health, nursing homes, surgical units, and private business, are described by nurse-contributors' own experiences. The content can serve as a stimulus and guide to nurses for service development in their own communities.

CHARLOTTE ELIOPOULOS

Contents

Caring for
the Elderly
in Diverse
Care Settings

PART ONE

Essentials of Gerontological Nursing

Gerontological nursing has burgeoned in virtually every practice setting. Older persons are using primary care clinics, home health agencies, outpatient surgery departments, adult day-care centers, emergency rooms, long-term care facilities, and other services in growing numbers, and nurses who never anticipated practicing gerontological nursing are being challenged to increase their competencies in the nursing care of the elderly. The population trends assure that the demand for nursing services for the elderly will increase.

Nurses who are involved with older persons soon learn that there are some unique features to the elderly and their service needs. Age-related changes create a unique set of norms by which assessment data must be interpreted. Health status and the prioritization of care needs are influenced by a wide range of psychosocial factors. The aged's altered metabolism, detoxification, and excretion of drugs, combined with the interactions from multiple drugs consumed, heighten the risks associated with medication use. Issues such as competency, use of life-sustaining measures, and rationing of resources more frequently cloud service delivery. Nurses must be aware of normal aging and the needs and risks in old age to deliver gerontological services competently.

This unit presents core knowledge to guide gerontological nursing practice in any setting. The unit begins with an overview of the aging population to enable nurses to separate myth from reality and understand the issues facing gerontological nursing practice today and in the future. The meaning of and requisites for health are discussed with consideration of the unique factors that influence health and health-related choices in late life. Components of a nursing assessment are presented with an outline of normal and pathological findings, followed by a discussion of how assessment findings are used to form nursing diagnoses. The topics of nutrition, medication use, and injuries in old age are explored to aid in reducing risks associated with these areas. Philosophies and practices that promote positive treatment of the elderly are found in chapters that discuss rehabilitation, communication, and attitudes. Chapters also are devoted to quality assurance, legal aspects, and ethical issues to acquaint nurses with principles that promote safe, high-quality gerontological care. The general knowledge reviewed in this unit should serve as a foundation for nurses in the many roles they can assume in gerontological nursing.

CHAPTER 1

The Older Population and Nursing

Charlotte Eliopoulos

Chapter Objectives
At the completion of this chapter the reader will be able to:

1. Describe the dramatic growth of the elderly population in the United States.
2. Discuss the older population's marital, employment, financial, educational, and health status.
3. Identify future characteristics and trends regarding the aging population.
4. Trace the history of gerontological nursing, which has influenced the current problems of the specialty.

Gerontological nursing, once thought to be limited to nursing homes and nurses who were less competent than their colleagues in other settings, is undergoing a major change in image. Nurses in emergency rooms, medical-surgical hospitals, intensive care units, mental health clinics, health maintenance organizations, outpatient surgical centers, home health agencies, and other practice sites are confronting increasing numbers of older adults and realizing the unique and multifaceted aspects of caring for this population. The different norms, altered symptomatology and response to therapy, increased likelihood of possessing psychological problems that complicate their physical care, and wide range of service needs are causing nurses to appreciate how complex the care of the aged really is. Historically, schools of nursing have not prepared nurses for this area of specialization, resulting in many nurses having to learn by trial and error. Increased competency and knowledge in gerontological nursing are seriously needed now that growing numbers of nurses in a variety of settings are confronting more elderly people in their caseloads.

The Aging Population

The fact that nurses are seeing greater numbers of elder adults in their practices should come as no surprise when demographic data are taken into account. In the United States the population over age 65 years grew twice as fast as the general population in the past two decades and now represents

During the past two decades the older population has grown at a rate twice that of the general population, with the most dramatic increase in the group over age 75 years.

more than 27 million individuals. Whereas only 4% of the population was over the age of 65 in 1900, that segment of the population represents more than 12% now. Not only are more people than ever reaching their senior years, but they are living longer once they do: A child born in 1986 can expect to live nearly 27 years longer than someone born at the turn of the century. The elderly population is becoming an older one. The fastest growing segment of the population is the 75-year-and-over group. The 75 + group, now less than 5% of the population, will increase to 10% of the population by 2030, when members of the "baby boom" generation reach their senior years. The portion of persons 85 + years will rise from its current level of 1% of the total population to 5% by 2050. Of course, as will be discussed later in this book, the older the individual, the greater the prevalence of frailty, chronic illness, and need for physical, psychological, and social support.

Among the elderly, most men are married, and most women are widowed (79% of older males are married compared to 40% of older women; 13% are widowers, and 50% are widows). There are three women for every two men over age 65, and with each advancing decade the ratio is increased. These statistics have meaning for health and social well-being. Older men have a greater likelihood of living with a family member who can assist and support them (87% live in family settings). Slightly more than half of all older women live in family settings, and the number of older women living alone has doubled in the past 15 years. Older widows have significant adjustments to face, such as a reduction in income or loss of intimate partner. Many of today's older women relied on their husbands for home repairs, financial matters, and transportation, and are handicapped when they must assume these responsibilities alone. A majority of older people have children with whom they have regular contact. People in older age groups have surviving parents in the proportions shown in the following list (NRTA-AARP, 1981):

40% of people in their late 50s

20% of people in their early 60s

10% of people in their late 60s

3% of people in their 70s

As more people survive to later years, families will be faced with growing responsibility for the care of their elder members.

If the present trend continues, more older adults will have surviving parents for whom they may need to assume a caregiving responsibility.

Most of the older population reside in metropolitan areas. The states of California, New York, Florida, Illinois, Ohio, Pennsylvania, and Texas possess 45% of the older population. Only a minority of persons relocate in old age, and, if they do, most will move within the same state. Florida, believed to be the state to which most retirees flee, receives 25% of all elderly who move. Most older adults own their own homes.

Less than 12% of the elderly are employed, and approximately one-half of that employment consists of part-time work. Older workers constitute only a small percentage of the total labor force. More than one-fourth of the elderly employed are self-employed—about three times the rate as for younger age groups. Social Security, originally intended to be a supplement to other sources of income in old age, is the major means of support for most elderly, followed by earnings, investment income, and pensions. There are significant differences in income among the sexes and races in old age. Per capita annual income is

$9,766 for males

$5,599 for females

$9,555 for whites

$4,105 for nonwhites

Although the economic status of the elderly has been steadily improving over the years, minorities and women who live alone are at risk of poverty in old age.

Whereas 12% of white senior citizens fell below the poverty level, minorities fared worse: 36% of older blacks and 23% of elderly Hispanics had poverty-level incomes. Persons living alone were poorer than those living with families. Although the median income of the old has increased over past years at a rate faster than that of younger age groups, many individuals find that reduced income in later life necessitates significant changes in life-style.

The elderly are the least educated members of society. Less than 50% completed high school, and of those approximately 10% completed college. However, this situation has been steadily improving, and educational level can be expected to improve with each future generation of elderly. Poor educational status has implications for health education and self-care capacity (as will be discussed later in this book).

The cry to control rising costs of health and social programs has been loud and clear in recent years, requiring a hard look at the funds spent on the older population. The total cash benefits to the elderly have more than quadrupled, and in-kind benefits have experienced nearly a sevenfold increase (Table 1-1). Thirty-one percent of all health care expenditures are for the elderly, and this expenditure is three times what is spent on younger persons. When health, social programs, housing, and other expenditures are

TABLE 1-1. Growth of Federal Expenditures
for the Elderly, 1971–1984 (billion dollars)

	1971	1984
Social Security	27.1	132.2
Federal civilian employees	2.3	12.4
Supplemental security income	1.4	2.5
Veterans' pensions	0.9	4.6
Medicare	7.5	56.4
Medicaid	1.9	6.9
Food stamps	0.2	0.6
Subsidized housing	0.2	4.2

Data from U.S. Department of Commerce, Bureau of the Census: Statistical Abstract of the United States, 1987.

TABLE 1-2. Acute Illness in Adults
(rates per 100 population)

	17–44-Year-Olds	45–64-Year-Olds	65+ Years
Infections and parasites	21.6	8.9	6.3
Upper respiratory	51.5	28.5	25.7
Other respiratory	59.7	44.2	29.5
Digestive system	10.6	5.0	5.3
Injuries	38.0	22.1	20.0

Data from U.S. National Center for Health Statistics, series 10, and unpublished data, 1981.

combined, 51% of all local, state, and federal dollars are spent on the elderly. There is reason for concern as the number of elderly increases: Continued support of these programs is not compatible with society's desire to reduce taxes. Nurses may find themselves in the dilemma of, as nurses, wanting to provide all the services they can for patients, while, as taxpayers, resisting any further erosion of their incomes. (This and other ethical dilemmas will be discussed in a later chapter.)

Health problems and disability increase with advancing age. Tables 1-2 and 1-3 show the rates for different illnesses. The elderly average 40 days of restricted activity yearly as a result of health problems. Seven percent of 65–74-year-olds, 16% of 75–84-year-olds, and 39% of persons over age 85

TABLE 1-3. Chronic Illness in Adults (rate per 1,000 population)

	17–44-Year-Olds	45–64-Year-Olds	65+ Years
Heart conditions	37.9	122.7	277.0
Hypertension	54.2	243.7	378.6
Varicose veins	19.0	50.1	83.2
Hemorrhoids	43.7	66.6	65.9
Chronic bronchitis	28.1	40.9	46.1
Asthma	29.0	33.6	28.6
Chronic sinusitis	158.4	177.5	183.6
Hay fever	100.2	77.5	51.9
Eczema, dermatitis	39.3	29.8	30.9
Sebaceous gland diseases	38.5	10.0	7.0
Arthritis	47.7	246.5	464.7
Diabetes	8.6	56.9	83.4
Migraine	38.7	33.7	17.2
Urinary system diseases	25.8	31.7	56.1
Visual impairments	27.4	55.2	136.6
Hearing impairments	43.8	142.9	283.8
Deformities or orthopedic impairments	90.5	117.5	128.2

Unpublished data from U.S. National Center for Health Statistics.

TABLE 1-4. Hospital and Physician Visits by Elderly
Compared to Other Age Groups

	Age < 15	Age 15–44	Age 45–64	Age > 65
Physician visits (per person)	2.1	2.2	3.1	4.3
Hospital discharges (per 1,000 population)	70.8	140.3	192.2	412.7
Inpatient surgeries (per 1,000 population)	44.5	139.8	193.5	358.5

Data from U.S. Department of Health and Human Services, National Ambulatory Medical Care Survey, 1981, Summary, Vital and Health Statistics, Advance Data, No. 88, March 16, 1983; U.S. Department of Health and Human Services, National Hospital Discharge Survey, 1983, Summary, Advance Data, No. 101, September 28, 1984.

who live in the community need assistance with their activities of daily living. The elderly have a higher rate of hospital and physician visits than the general population (Table 1-4). Although Diagnostic Related Groups (DRGs) have brought about a slight decline in hospital admissions, the elderly hospitalized patient has a longer length of stay: 9 days compared to 5.6 days for those under age 65. The U.S. Census Bureau projects that the demand created by the elderly for hospital services will increase by 40% from 1987 to 2000.

Less than 5% of the elderly are in nursing homes and other institutional settings. Although the percentage of institutionalized elderly is not expected to change, that 5% will represent greater numbers; thus an increase in nursing home beds will be needed. There is a trend, as many nursing homes have noted already, for nursing home patients to possess more complex medical and nursing problems. In addition, deinstitutionalization efforts and the increased survival of persons with lifelong psychiatric problems will result in a larger proportion of mentally impaired persons in the nursing home population. The demand for nursing home staff will increase by 220% by the year 2000 (ANA, 1986).

Some predictions can be made concerning future generations of elderly:

- *They will be more knowledgeable about health care.* The "blind obedience" to health professionals will be replaced with a demand for high-quality, convenient, cost-effective services.
- *They will be wiser and more demanding consumers of health care services* as they are faced with paying for more services out of their own pockets; thus they may be open to new, creative ways of having their needs met.
- *Families will be providing more direct care to elderly members for longer periods of time* than ever before. Most of this responsibility will continue to fall on a daughter, and in light of the trend of women increasingly working outside the home, creative ways to aid families in their caregiving responsibilities will be needed.

One can see that a majority of the future needs of the elderly will be in the areas of prevention, restoration, support, and self-care of chronic problems—areas within the realm of independent nursing practice.

Nursing and the Aged

In the future the older population will demand health care that focuses on prevention, restoration, support, and promotion of self-care; these are areas that fall within the scope of independent nursing practice.

Why have most nurses been reluctant to embrace the specialty of gerontological nursing? Even home health and acute care nurses who have primarily older persons in their caseloads are hesitant to admit they are engaged in gerontological care. Perhaps the historically poor image of the specialty contributed to the aversion that so many nurses feel toward it. Nurses have been involved in the care of the aged for a long time, but—as was typical for nurses in the past—they were a rather passive, subservient group with minimal influence over geriatric care. Nursing's lack of power and leadership is well exemplified by the profession's lack of influence over the nursing home industry when Medicaid and Medicare reimbursement emerged.

Medicine was not enthusiastic about the passage of Medicare, believing it would cause hospitals to be flooded with older patients. The strong lobbying efforts of the AMA caused the House Ways and Means Committee to develop the concept of the ECF, "Extended Care Facility," to provide reimbursement for short-term posthospital care. The AMA was involved with drafting this concept and worked to keep the ECF standards weak, arguing that high standards would prohibit most facilities from qualifying for reimbursement (these standards included 24-hour licensed nursing coverage and individualized nursing care plans—conditions less than 6% of the existing facilities could meet!). Rather than use the incentive of reimbursement to improve standards, the Social Security Administration yielded to the AMA's pressure and waived those basic requirements. Although these weakened standards directly affected the quality and quantity of nursing services, the nursing community's voice was absent, or insignificant, during this process. (U.S. Congress, Senate Subcommittee on Long-Term Care of the Special Committee on Aging, 1974)

Thus the nursing profession allowed its name to be used to describe this type of facility, that is, *nursing* home, when it had no influence in the development, operation, or quality control of this form of care. Unfortunately, the weak standards led to the many scandals witnessed throughout the 1960s and 1970s, further discouraging nurses from entering long-term care facilities. As critics from the sidelines, nurse colleagues in other specialties did little to improve this situation, and the stigma associated with gerontological nursing was perpetuated.

Finally in 1961 the ANA sensed the need to address the needs of those nurses working with older adults and recommended that a special-interest group for geriatric nurses be formed. A small group of nurses convened the following year for the first national meeting of the ANA's Conference Group on Geriatric Nursing Practice. In 1966 this group formally became the Geriatric Nursing Division, later to change its name (in 1976) to the

The American Nurses' Association formed the Geriatric Nursing Division in 1966. The division later replaced "Geriatric" with "Gerontological" in its title to reflect nursing's broader role with the elderly.

Gerontological Nursing Division to reflect the fact that nurses' roles with the elderly involve more than the care of the sick elderly. Standards of practice and certification in the specialty soon followed, further enhancing its credibility. The literature dedicated to this nursing specialty experienced a rapid growth also: In 1956 the Cumulative Index of Nursing Literature listed 32 topics on the care of the aged; 10 years later twice that number were listed; and every year thereafter there has been a doubling of the number of articles published. Increasing numbers of nursing schools are offering undergraduate and graduate courses in gerontological nursing. Fine nurse researchers, clinicians, administrators, educators, and other leaders are not only making this specialty competitive with the more traditional ones, but in some ways demonstrating independence, creativity, and innovation that surpass them. (Perhaps the benefit of being a relatively new specialty is that one can learn from other specialties' successes and not make the same mistakes.)

The demographics reviewed earlier support the realization that nurses in a variety of settings will be involved with more complex geriatric care and increasing amounts of it. Be it the older patient in the recovery room who demonstrates a greater risk of hypothermia and respiratory problems, the senior citizen in the health maintenance organization who asks for help in managing his Alzheimer's victim wife at home, the retiree who comes to the mental health clinic because he has lost interest in life, or the nursing home patient who suddenly becomes confused from any one of a dozen different causes, the older patients whom nurses will confront will force nurses to draw from a specialized body of knowledge. The elderly's interdependence of physical, emotional, and social health will necessitate that nurses practice truly holistic care to be effective. New settings and health concerns will challenge nurses to be creative in developing new roles.

Gerontological nursing's history is heavily laced with lost opportunities for nursing power and influence over the care of older adults. Nursing is now at a challenging crossroads where leadership opportunities abound. A majority of the problems presented by the elderly fall within the domain of nursing to diagnose and treat; thus nurses can assume a major role in upgrading the health and well-being of this patient population. This role is further enhanced by the growing body of knowledge that delineates appropriate, effective care. Armed with a strong knowledge base and problems they can manage independently, gerontological nurses can develop independent nursing practices and new models of care delivery—opportunities that few other nursing specialties afford. The time is right for nurses to demonstrate leadership in the care of older adults.

REFERENCES

ANA (American Nurses' Association): The American Nurse looks at councils: Council on Gerontological Nursing. American Nurse, May 1986, p. 10.
NRTA-AARP (National Retired Teachers Association–American Association of Retired Persons): National Survey of Older Americans. Washington, DC, American Association of Retired Persons, 1981.

U.S. Congress, Senate Subcommittee on Long-Term Care of the Special Committee on Aging: Nursing Home Care in the U.S.: Failure in Public Policy. Washington, DC, Government Printing Office, 1974.

BIBLIOGRAPHY

American Association of Retired Persons: A Profile of Older Americans. Washington, DC, AARP, 1988.

Brock AM: The necessity of change. Gerontol Nurs 14(1): 7, 1988.

Brody JA, Brock DB, Williams TF: Trends in the health of the elderly population. Annu Rev Public Health 8: 211–234, 1987.

Burnside I: Nursing and the Aged: A Self-care Approach, 3rd ed. New York, McGraw-Hill, 1988.

Ebersole P, Hess P: Toward Healthy Aging: Human Needs and Nursing Response, 3rd ed. St. Louis, CV Mosby, 1987.

Eliopoulos C: Gerontological Nursing, 2nd ed. Philadelphia, JB Lippincott, 1987.

Gunter LM: Nomenclature: What is the name "gerontic nursing?" J Gerontol Nurs 13(12): 7, 1987.

Howie C: Helping the aged. Nurs Times 83(5): 40–42, 1987.

Rosenwike I, Logue B: The Extreme Aged in America: A Portrait of an Expanding Population. Westport, CT, Greenwood Press, 1985.

Schick FL: Statistical Handbook on Aging Americans. Phoenix, AZ, Oryx Press, 1986.

Snape J: Nurses' attitudes to care of the elderly. J Adv Nurs 11(5): 569–572, 1986.

Wells DL: Gerontological nurse specialists: Tomorrow's leaders today! Role implementation strategies. J Gerontol Nurs 11(5): 36–40.

Wolinsky FD, Mosely RR, Coe RM: A cohort analysis of the use of health services by elderly Americans. J Health Soc Behavior 27(9): 209–219, 1986.

CHAPTER 2
Aging and Wellness
Charlotte Eliopoulos

Chapter Objectives
At the completion of this chapter the reader will be able to:

1. Describe the meaning of health.
2. Outline the variables that influence the fulfillment of self-care requirements.
3. Discuss age-related differences and related interventions in the fulfillment of universal self-care requirements.

The high prevalence of chronic illness among the elderly, coupled with the reality that the major employment settings for nurses are hospitals, nursing homes, and home health settings where a majority of nursing efforts fall within the realms of secondary and tertiary care, causes most nurses to be involved with the *ill* elderly. However, gerontological nurses must appreciate that they have a significant responsibility in the promotion and maintenance of older adults' *health*. This responsibility is important, considering the following factors:

Most elderly are not impaired, but are functional in the community, thereby benefiting from wellness-oriented interventions.

The elderly are more vulnerable to physical, emotional, and socioeconomic problems than other age groups and may require special attention to health promotion and maintenance.

Gerontological nursing as a profession advocates a strong role for nurses in assisting persons toward a healthy aging process.

What Is Health?

There has long been an awareness that health implies more than the absence of disease, reflected in these popular definitions of health:

"A state of complete physical, mental and social well-being, and not merely the absence of disease or infirmity" (WHO, 1947).

"An integrated method of functioning which is oriented toward maximizing the potential of which the individual is capable" (Dunn, 1959).

TABLE 2-1. Universal Self-care Requirements for Maintaining Health

Ventilation and circulation
Nutrition
Excretion
Activity and rest
Solitude and social interaction
Safety
Normality

"The state of optimum capacity of an individual for the effective performance of his roles and tasks" (Parsons, 1972).

An important component of nursing practice is the assessment of health status so that interventions that will improve and sustain health can be planned and implemented. One of the major ways nurses determine physical, emotional, social, and spiritual well-being of clients is through an evaluation of the degree to which basic human needs or universal self-care requirements are met. For the purpose of this discussion, a modification of the universal self-care requirements used by Orem (1985) will be used as a framework for presenting those needs which must be fulfilled to maintain a healthy state (Table 2-1). The nursing process begins by using assessment findings to determine how each need is satisfied. Although this evaluation seems basic, there are many complex variables that influence the fulfillment of these universal self-care requirements:

> Requirements for a healthy state include ventilation, circulation, nutrition, excretion, activity, rest, solitude, social interaction, safety, and normality. The fulfillment of these requirements is influenced by the person's desire and decision to take actions consistent with good health, as well as the physical, mental, and socioeconomic ability, knowledge, and skills to engage in good health practices.

Desire and decision to take action. Many persons know they should eat a well-balanced diet, exercise, obtain adequate sleep, not smoke cigarettes, and engage in other healthy practices, but they choose not to do so. Personal values, attitudes, and beliefs influence health care decisions: "I'd rather enjoy life's vices, even if it means I won't live as long." Crises and circumstances affect the decision to take actions that promote wellness: "I know I should give up smoking, but there are too many problems in my life right now"; "The surgery I need will have to wait because I will not place my ill spouse in the care of anyone else." Depression, anxiety, and other emotional states can cause persons to seek or avoid healthy actions, as can alterations in physical status. Cognitive disorders can impair judgment to make sound health-related decisions. Of course, some persons may rather spend their money on items that yield more immediate pleasure than health examinations, good nutrition, and home maintenance. Although nurses can attempt to influence clients' motivation to engage in good health practices through education, counseling, and support, all competent persons have the right to make their own decisions about health practices—even if those decisions run contrary to health promotion and maintenance.

Physical, mental, and socioeconomic means. In order to engage in healthy practices people must be able to afford and obtain good food and safe housing; have the energy and mobility to ingest food, ambulate, bathe, dress, and toilet themselves; and have the cognitive function to remember and make competent choices about self-care activities.

Knowledge, experience, and skills. People must possess correct information about good nutrition, exercise, stress management, safe medication use, and other actions consistent with good health. Likewise, acts such as meal planning, grooming, and household management and cleaning require a certain degree of expertise that is learned. Misinformation or inexperience can be factors in deficits in self-care ability.

When self-care requirements are not being met, nurses must explore for the specific variable that is responsible in order to select the appropriate nursing intervention. For example, an older woman may be found to be obese and deficient in vitamins, minerals, and proteins in her diet. The reasons for this problem could include the following:

Desires and decisions

Cultural belief that plumpness reflects health.

Perception that she looks good.

Pressure from partner to be plump.

Preference for high-carbohydrate snack foods.

Enjoyment from eating at fast-food restaurant.

Overeating as a result of depression, anxiety, or loneliness.

Feeling that at her age she shouldn't deprive herself of foods she likes.

Physical, mental, and socioeconomic factors

No transportation to grocery store; therefore, must get food supply from local convenience store.

Insufficient finances to purchase meats, fish, fruits, and vegetables.

Becomes too fatigued from cooking; therefore, relies on prepared foods or carry-out items.

Eats excessive sweets to compensate for reduced taste sensation.

Poor condition of teeth.

Indigestion, food intolerances.

Altered cognitive state.

Misperceptions about food resulting from paranoia.

Knowledge, experience, and skills

Believes bacon, tea, cheese crackers, and fruit punches supply good nutrition.

Now must cook for herself since death of spouse who had done all the cooking.

Recently moved to studio apartment that has a microwave oven rather than a stove and is having difficulty learning to use appliance.

Age is one of the many factors that affect clients' ability to maintain a healthy state. In addition to advocating practices that facilitate wellness for persons of all ages, gerontological nurses must also promote actions that take into account the unique norms, challenges, and risks associated with advanced age. The discussion that follows reviews the universal self-care requirements, highlighting age-related differences and interventions that promote an optimal state of wellness.

Ventilation and Circulation

The cardiovascular and respiratory systems experience changes with age that can affect the exchange and transport of oxygen and carbon dioxide (Table 2-2). The potential for impaired gas exchange demands that actions be taken to promote good respiration and circulation.

Efforts to promote full expansion of the lungs should be incorporated into the daily activities of older adults, including walking, swimming, bicycling, dancing, singing, and other forms of exercise. Older adults can be instructed in deep breathing exercises (Figure 2-1) that can be performed several times throughout the day to improve respiratory activity.

Older adults should be instructed to recognize signs of respiratory infection and seek evaluation in a timely fashion. Altered cough response, pain sensation, and presentation of fever can cause delayed recognition of respiratory infection if persons are looking for the typical symptoms displayed by younger adults. The elderly need to be aware that a change in breathing pattern, fatigue, dizziness, confusion, tightness or heaviness over the chest, loss of appetite, and changes in the amount or characteristics of sputum production can indicate pneumonia. Caution must be taken that the older person doesn't self-medicate with cold remedies that could mask symptoms

TABLE 2-2. Age-Related Changes to Cardiovascular and Respiratory Systems

Increased rigidity and thickness of valves
Increased rigidity of heart muscle
Sclerosis and thickening of endocardium
Increased subpericardial fat
Increased prominence of superficial vessels
Decreased vasomotor tone
Increased vagal tone
Decreased elastic recoil of lungs
Decreased number and elasticity of alveoli
Weaker diaphragm and thorax
Decreased inspiratory reserve volume
Increased respiratory reserve volume
Reduced cough efficiency
Decreased thoracic expansion

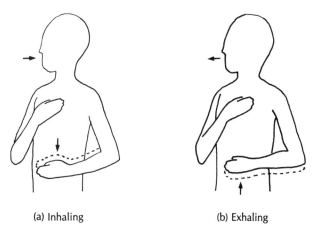

(a) Inhaling   (b) Exhaling

FIGURE 2-1. Breathing Exercises. Breathing exercises should emphasize forced expiration. (a) Inhaling. With one hand below the ribs, on the stomach, and the other over the middle anterior chest, the client should inhale to the count of one. The hand over the stomach should fall as the stomach moves downward; the hand over the chest should not move. (b) Exhaling. Expire air to the count of three. The hand over the stomach should rise as the stomach moves upward; the hand over the chest should not move. (Eliopoulos C: Gerontological Nursing, 2nd ed, p 85. Philadelphia, JB Lippincott, 1987.)

In late life there are many more reasons for mobility to be decreased, as well as many more complications resulting from immobility. Frequent position change and exercise based on activity tolerance must be built into the older adult's daily routine.

and delay diagnosis. "Colds" or respiratory changes that have existed for two weeks or more warrant evaluation.

Good oxygenation of all body tissue is facilitated by mobility. There are many problems that increase in prevalence with age that can impair the older person's mobility, such as symptoms associated with arthritis and cardiovascular disease. The nursing assessment must identify such threats to mobility so that interventions can be planned to promote adequate activity. Useful measures could include frequent position change, ambulation, and joint-range-of-motion and other exercises (depending on activity tolerance).

Older individuals should be advised to prevent obstructions to adequate circulation, as may result from garters, tight shoes or clothing, rings that are too small, and crossing legs. There should be caution about allowing the head to "bob" unsupported while napping in an upright position because this could interfere with cerebral circulation. Protecting body parts, particularly the hands and feet, from exposure to the cold can reduce the circulatory impairment that results from hypothermia.

Because older people may experience some drop in blood pressure when lifting to a sitting or standing position, they should be advised to change positions slowly. For instance, during night trips to the bathroom it can be a sound idea for older persons to sit on the side of the bed for a few minutes before rising.

Despite the cardiovascular changes that occur with age, most elderly persons have adequate function to engage in their activities of daily living. A major realization of the cardiac changes occurs when the elderly are faced with an unusual stress on the heart, such as that resulting from exer-

The older heart may require several hours to recover from stress. Activities should be planned to afford rest periods between events.

cise, fever, or emotional disturbances. Like the younger heart, the older heart responds to stress with tachycardia (although usually not the same degree of tachycardia as a younger heart would experience), but more time is necessary for the heart to recover from the stress and return to the baseline norm; sometimes several hours are required for the heart rate to return to normal. Consequently, it is important to rest several times during the day to provide an opportunity for the heart to recover from stress. Activities should be planned to afford rest between events; for example, a homemaker should rest between shopping for groceries and taking a walk, and a hospital patient should not be scheduled for several consecutive diagnostic tests in the same morning. When tachycardia is discovered in older adults, nurses need to ask about the events of the preceding several hours to differentiate possible cardiac pathology from normal cardiac response to stress.

Nutrition

Nutritional status largely impacts general health and function, and it is important in late life. A well-balanced diet, representing all food groups, remains important in old age. Slower metabolism and reduced energy expenditure require an adjustment to caloric intake. Body size, activity level, health status, and other factors influence differences in caloric needs; thus individual diet recommendations based on a sound nutritional assessment are advisable (see Chapter 5).

A variety of factors influence the nutritional status of older persons. Lack of transportation, fatigue, shortness of breath, and pain can make shopping for food difficult. Limited income can influence food selections that favor quantity instead of quality, resulting in a diet that lacks essential nutrients. Depression and anxiety can alter appetite. Persons who are accustomed to specific ethnic meals may be uninterested in eating if they are unable to enjoy the foods they prefer. All of the factors that impact food intake should be considered in assessing nutritional status. A wide range of resources can be utilized to assist older adults in improving and maintaining their nutritional status, including

Congregate eating programs

Home-delivered meals

Nutrition counseling and education

Food stamps

Grocery shopping and delivery services

Grocery stores and restaurants that offer senior citizen discounts

The changes to the gastrointestinal system (Table 2-3) can interfere with good food intake. Altered taste sensations can distort the flavor of foods, thereby reducing intake, and cause excessive amounts of salt and sugar to be added to food. Slower food motility along the gastrointestinal tract can

TABLE 2-3. Age-Related Changes to the
Gastrointestinal System

Thinner tooth enamel
Increased tooth brittleness
Reduction in taste buds, primarily for sweet and salt
Decreased esophageal motility
Decreased gastric acids and enzymes
Delayed gastric emptying
Reduced liver size and storage capacity
Weaker intestinal musculature
Slower peristalsis

---

cause a sense of fullness that discourages food intake. Indigestion can reduce intake or lead to the omission of necessary nutrients from the diet.

Although tooth loss is not a normal outcome of aging, many of today's
elderly lack teeth and use dentures, or if natural teeth are present, the person's oral health may be poor. An oral cavity assessment should determine
the condition of the teeth, fit of dentures, and presence of abnormal lesions
or masses. Annual dental examination remains important throughout life
and may be particularly crucial for older adults because of the rising incidence of benign and malignant oral health problems with age. The misconception that dentures eliminate the need for dental examination should be
corrected: The potential for oral health problems to exist and the changing
tissue structure that can alter the fit of dentures supports the need for regular visits to the dentist.

> Evaluation of oral health by a dentist remains important in old age, even if dentures are used.

Good nutrition is influenced by food preparation and presentation.
Bland foods of similar color, consistency, and flavor are unappealing to persons of any age. The use of Styrofoam dishes and plastic utensils can make
mealtime a less pleasant experience than the use of china and silverware for
dining. Eating alone or being seated at a dining table with persons who cannot communicate can discourage eating, as can being served meals in an environment that is dirty, odorous, and noisy. Attention should be paid to
making mealtime a pleasant, social experience.

Fluid intake must be considered in nutritional status. Unless medically
contraindicated, 2,500 to 3,000 ml of fluid should be ingested daily. The
lower fluid reserves of the elderly make inadequate fluid intake and fluid
loss more problematic and increase the risk of dehydration. Fluid needs can
be met through fruit juices, fruit shakes, Jello, soups, ices, and diet sodas.
Consideration should be given to factors that can limit fluid intake, such as
inability to obtain or drink fluids independently, home environment without
running water and refrigeration, and cognitive impairment. Older persons
who restrict fluid intake as a means of reducing urinary frequency should be
counseled as to the dangers of this practice.

> Gerontological nurses should advocate for older adults by assuring that prescribed dietary restrictions do not remove the enjoyment from eating. Compromise may be needed to achieve a diet that meets therapeutic needs while respecting the patient's unique preferences.

There are many geriatric conditions that necessitate special diets. Although special diets have a therapeutic benefit, they can have a negative influence on food intake: Having to eat unseasoned foods or eliminating eth-

nic foods that have been enjoyed for a lifetime can take the pleasure from eating. Food preferences and patterns are deeply ingrained and difficult to change. Compromise may be necessary when special diets are prescribed that drastically change the food intake of the older person. Better compliance and good nutritional intake can be facilitated by making provisions for certain restricted foods to be included in the diet. Assuring that special diets do not remove the pleasure from eating is an important advocacy function of the gerontological nurse.

Excretion

Age-related changes in the urinary and lower gastrointestinal systems affect elimination patterns in late life (Table 2-4). Slower peristalsis can make regular bowel elimination more difficult; this difficulty can be compounded by inactivity, constipating medications, and a diet low in fiber and fluid. Older persons should be instructed to promote bowel elimination through good fluid intake, diet, activity, and establishing a regular time for bowel movements. Laxative and enema use should be strongly discouraged; not only can a dependency on these substances develop, preventing normal bowel excretion without their aid, but they can also lead to the development of a new set of problems (e.g., diarrhea, dehydration, electrolyte imbalances, interactions with medications).

Urinary frequency and nocturia can be bothersome outcomes of changes in the urinary tract. Most older people need to void approximately every two to three hours during the day and once during the night. Frequent toileting needs must be taken into account in the planning of environments, trips, and activities for the elderly. Older adults should be advised that increased frequency of voiding (e.g., every 30 minutes instead of one's usual pattern of every two hours) could indicate a urinary tract infection, the most common infection of the elderly, or other urinary disorders and should be evaluated. The elderly also may need to be advised that reducing fluid intake to control urinary frequency can not only result in complications such as dehydration, but also make the urine more concentrated and increase the frequency of voiding.

Although incontinence is not normal in old age, many people mistakenly believe it to be a consequence of aging and do not report it as a prob-

TABLE 2-4. Age-Related Changes to the Urinary Tract

Reduced number of nephrons
Reduced renal filtration
Lower renal threshold for glucose
Altered tubular reabsorption of glucose
Decreased bladder capacity
Weaker bladder muscles

Some older adults may not admit being incontinent because they believe that incontinence is a normal expectation in old age.

lem to health care professionals. The high prevalence of this misconception demands that nurses ask specifically about incontinence during their assessment.

Most elderly men have some degree of prostatic hyperplasia, which can result in urinary retention and hesitancy, as well as dribbling. These symptoms need to be reviewed and the importance of regular evaluation of the prostate gland emphasized.

Waste excretion through the skin necessitates bathing; however, age-related skin changes alter the bathing pattern for the elderly. The decreased hydration, vascularity, and thickness of the skin make it drier and more fragile. Perspiration and oil production are reduced. Frequent bathing is not only unnecessary, but it can rob the skin of protective oils and cause drying. Unless there is reason to the contrary, complete baths should be restricted to every three to four days, with daily partial cleansing. Moisturizers should be used regularly to prevent drying and irritation. (Petroleum jelly and other inexpensive lubricants are just as effective as highly expensive products.)

Activity and Rest

The importance and need for activity and rest have been discussed earlier. Activity can improve circulation, respiration, digestion, elimination, mobility, appetite, socialization, and self-image. Many physical activities offer the opportunity for mental stimulation, as well.

The way the elderly feel about themselves and their beliefs about the roles and functions of older people can strongly influence the activities in which they will engage.

Self-concept and expectations can greatly influence activity. Some older adults may believe they are "too old" to dance, enroll in educational courses, hike, swim, or join a club. One person with an illness may adopt sick role behaviors that cause unnecessary restrictions in activity, while another individual with a similar illness will see the illness as an inconvenience that will not be allowed to interfere with living. Messages from family, friends, and society can define expected behaviors; for instance, the widow who enjoys dating, dancing, and traveling with friends may be asked by her family why she is not satisfied with doing crafts at home and making Sunday dinner for her grandchildren. Nurses must assess both the activity pattern of the elderly and the beliefs held about activity in old age.

Naps and periods of rest during the day are beneficial to the elderly, but long blocks of night sleep can have detrimental effects. Extended sleep periods cause the body to be immobile for a lengthy time and increase the risk of secretions pooling in the lungs, intestinal motility being reduced, joints stiffening, and pressure sores developing, as well as other problems related to immobility. Five to seven hours of night sleep should be sufficient for most older adults. Nurses should encourage the use of nonpharmacological sleep inducers, such as warm milk, soft music, and backrubs, and caution the elderly against indiscriminate use of sedatives.

Changes in activity tolerance, functional ability, rest requirements, and sleep pattern can indicate a variety of physical and mental health problems and warrant comprehensive evaluation.

Solitude and Social Interaction

Both periods of relating to other human beings and being alone serve important functions throughout life and are therapeutic in terms of the psychological challenges, or developmental tasks, of old age. Many adjustments and losses are faced by the elderly, such as death of significant others, retirement, chronic illness, relocation, reduced income, reduced dependency of children, and increased dependency on children. Support, guidance, and the sincere concern of others can aid the elderly in coping with these changes.

Reminiscence enables older adults to put their lives in perspective, resolve conflicts, and recognize that their lives have had meaning.

Erik Erikson described eight challenges facing persons during different stages of life that had to be resolved in order to achieve psychological satisfaction (Erikson, 1963). The challenge in old age that Erikson identified was to achieve a sense of ego integrity versus despair. Reminiscence is a psychosocial process that nurses can use to aid older adults in achieving a sense of integrity (Table 2-5). Through reminiscence the unfinished business of the past can be confronted and resolved; also, the accomplishments and meaning of one's life can be identified.

The ability to communicate effectively affects the fulfillment of socialization needs. Chapter 13 explores the many factors that can influence communication in old age.

Safety

Age-related changes in the sensory organs (Table 2-6) have a significant impact on the ability of older adults to protect themselves from injuries. Directions and warnings may not be seen as a result of presbyopia. The inability to accurately see the height of stairs and curbs can promote falls. Reduced peripheral vision can lead older drivers to traffic accidents from failure to yield right of way. Presbycusis can prohibit warnings and directions from being heard. Poor olfaction can prevent gas leaks, smoke, and other environmental hazards from being detected. Decreased sensitivity to pressure can lead to skin breakdown. Not only are the elderly at greater risk of in-

Sensory changes can cause misperception of the environment and limit older adults' ability to detect hazards.

TABLE 2-5. Highlights of Reminiscence Therapy

- Reminiscence is a psychosocial activity in which the nurse guides the elderly in recalling past events or experiences.
- Topics for reminiscence can include special experiences with a parent or sibling, first friend, school days, home town, hobby, favorite people, immigration experience, first home, best time in life, most devastating experience.
- Reminiscence can be conducted through a free-flowing discussion or a structured activity (e.g., writing a poem, making a scrapbook, interview).
- Old newspapers, magazines, records, photographs, movies, and field trips can be used to stimulate reminiscence.
- Reminiscence can serve as a social activity, provide education for the young, give caregivers insight into the client and help the client resolve conflicts and understand the significance of his or her life.

TABLE 2-6. Age-Related Sensory Changes

Development of farsightedness (presbyopia)
Decreased peripheral vision
Increased light perception threshold
Yellowing of lens
Distorted depth perception
Development of presbycusis (degeneration of nerve cells)
Decreased number of taste buds
Reduced olfactory ability
Decreased tactile sensations

curring injuries due to sensory deficits, but they may also be less likely to protect themselves with quick response because of the slower movement of impulses along the nervous system.

Knowing that the risk of injury is high, gerontological nurses must act to eliminate or minimize safety risks. Prevention begins with identifying the individual's specific risks through the nursing assessment and planning interventions to address those risks. Eyeglasses, hearing aids, and other assistive devices should be obtained and used by persons with deficits. Safety education can be provided that instructs older adults in ways to protect themselves, such as measuring water temperature before getting into the bathtub, using night-lights, changing positions slowly, and wearing well-fitting shoes and clothing. Hazards in the home environment can be corrected and modifications made to promote safety and independence (Table 2-7).

TABLE 2-7. Components of a Safe Environment for the Elderly

Telephone
Smoke detector on every level of home (ideally connected to central monitoring system with direct signal to local fire station)
Fire extinguisher on every level of home
Vented heating system
Refrigeration and storage units for food
Lighting in hallways and stairways
Handrails on stairs
No clutter on floors, scatter rugs, or extension cords
Unobstructed doorways, painted a color that contrasts with walls
Nonslip bathtub or shower surface
Grab bars in bathtub or shower
Screened windows that are easy to open and close
Ample number of safe electrical outlets, preferably three feet higher than floor for easy reach
Safe stove with burner control in front
Easy-to-operate faucets with clear hot and cold designations
Covered garbage disposal container

Modified from Eliopoulos C: Gerontological Nursing, pp 129–130. Philadelphia, JB Lippincott, 1987.

The many health problems of the elderly contribute to the use of a large number of prescription and nonprescription drugs by this population. The inappropriate use or administration of drugs, along with the potential interactions and adverse reactions that may develop, presents significant safety risks. Careful evaluation and supervision of medication use is a major gerontological nursing responsibility. Chapter 6 presents a comprehensive review of medication use in the elderly and should assist the nurse in identifying interventions that promote safe drug use.

A thorough discussion of the causes, prevention, consequences and care of injuries in the elderly is offered in Chapter 7.

Normality

Living an average, normal life can be challenging for older persons because of the stereotypes, expectations, and prejudices of society. In a country obsessed with youth, the aged seem misfits. Most advertisements feature the young; successful marketing often hinges on a product's association with a young market. Clothing styles respond to the tastes and builds of younger buyers. Automobile designs emphasize youthful sex appeal over safety. The noise, glare, and physically taxing layout of modern structures give little consideration to environmental needs of an older population.

Health professionals sometimes reflect the ageism displayed in society as a whole, as in these examples:

- The status and needs of a perfectly coherent older person may be discussed with family members rather than directly with the client.
- Staff may approach all older clients with the assumption that mental competency is questionable.
- The impact of disease and medications on sexual function may be omitted from the education and counseling provided to an older person.

There may be differences in how staff treat the young and old in regard to privacy, aggressiveness of treatment, and other aspects of care.

Gerontological nurses must be sensitive to negative attitudes and treatment of the aged, and they must be advocates for respect to the unique needs of the older population. In addition to being role models of positive attitudes in the workplace, gerontological nurses should be active in the community at large, for example, giving advice to builders on how environments can be user-friendly for an older population and recommending to department stores product lines that would appeal to older consumers.

The gerontological nurse must learn about the client's unique preferences and patterns to identify that which is normal for the individual.

It must be remembered that, in some ways, what is normal is in the eyes of the beholder. Some older adults may be satisfied reflecting on fond memories while others want each day to bring new adventure; some may find special pleasures in caring for grandchildren, while others are satisfied with a relationship with grandchildren at a distance; and some persons are comfortable showing the physical signs of advanced age, while other individuals strive to maintain a youthful appearance. Patterns and styles will be diverse. Thus there can be no universal standard for normality in old age. Nurses are challenged to learn what is normal for individual clients and develop care strategies to maintain that normality.

REFERENCES

Dunn H: What high level wellness means. Can J Public Health, 50(11): 447–457, 1959.

Erikson E: Childhood and Society, 2nd ed. New York, WW Norton, 1963.

Orem D: Nursing: Concepts of Practice, 3rd ed. New York, McGraw-Hill, 1985.

Parsons T: Definitions of health and illness in the light of American values and social structure. In Jaco EG (ed), Patients, Physicians, and Illness, 2nd ed. New York, Free Press, 1972.

WHO: Constitution of the World Health Organization. Chronicle of WHO 1: 1–2, 1947.

BIBLIOGRAPHY

Beck CK, Rawlins RP, Williams SR: Mental Health–Psychiatric Nursing: A Holistic Life-Cycle Approach, 2nd ed. St. Louis, CV Mosby, 1988.

Black S: The needs of the well elderly. Health Visit 60(8): 266–267, 1987.

Butler FR: Minority wellness promotion: A behavioral self-management approach. J Gerontol Nurs 13(8): 23–28, 1987.

Buturusis B: The well elderly: Assessing health needs. J Gerontol Nurs 12(6): 11–14, 1986.

Clark CC: Wellness Nursing: Concepts, Theory, Research, and Practice. New York, Springer, 1986.

Dychtwald K (ed): Wellness and Health Promotion for the Elderly. Rockville, MD, Aspen Systems, 1986.

Eliopoulos C: A self-care model for gerontological nursing. Geriatr Nurs 5(8): 366–368, 1984.

Horgan PA: Health status perceptions affect health-related behaviors. J Gerontol Nurs 13(12): 30–33, 1987.

Neville K: Promoting health for seniors. Geriatr Nurs 9(1): 42–43, 1988.

Orem D: Nursing: Concepts of Practice, 3rd ed. New York, McGraw-Hill, 1985.

Parsons MT, Levy J: Nursing process in injury prevention. J Gerontol Nurs 13(7): 36–40, 1987.

Rauckhorst LM: Health habits of elderly widows. J Gerontol Nurs 13(8): 19–22, 1987.

Shannon MD: Health promotion for new older Americans. J Gerontol Nurs 13(8): 7, 1987.

Slimmer LW, Lopez M, LeSage J, Ellor JR: Perceptions of learned helplessness. J Gerontol Nurs 13(5): 33–37, 1987.

Stanhope M, Lancaster J: Community Health Nursing: Process and Practices for Promoting Health. St. Louis, CV Mosby, 1986.

CHAPTER 3

Assessing Normal from Abnormal in the Elderly

Charlotte Eliopoulos

Chapter Objectives

At the completion of this chapter the reader will be able to:

1. Describe factors that should be considered in interviewing older adults, such as timing, consent, environmental disturbances, sensory deficits, language barriers, and the client's ability to recall significant data.
2. List the changes that accompany normal aging throughout the body.
3. Describe the type of data to collect and skills to utilize in performing a comprehensive nursing assessment.
4. Identify abnormal assessment findings and their potential causes.

The foundation of care in any practice setting rests upon an accurate, comprehensive assessment. Effective assessment is particularly significant to gerontological nursing practice because of the multitude of problems that are likely to be present in advanced age, the elderly's unique manifestations of alterations in health status, and the changes in normal physiology and responses to therapy resulting from the aging process.

Implicit in skilled assessment of the older adult is the knowledge of the outcomes of the normal aging process. Of course, what is known about "normal" aging is changing all the time. For example, consequences of growing old that were once believed to be normal, such as incontinence and dementia, are now understood to be pathologies in need of attention. Likewise, glycosurias and blood pressures exceeding middle-aged norms are not necessarily cause for immediate intervention. Part of the difficulty and challenge of gerontological care is that the body of knowledge regarding normal and abnormal aging is still being formed, requiring nurses to constantly stay abreast of new findings. Not only must nurses understand age-related differences in the older population compared to other age groups, but also they must recognize the diversity that exists among the elderly themselves. Perhaps more than at other ages, in later life individuals of similar age can display wide differences in their health status and function. Hereditary factors, diet, life-style, stress management, activity pattern, and exposure to pollutants and disease are among the reasons for individual variation.

The usual methods of collecting data are applicable to assessing older

> Not only does the older population have norms different from other age groups, but also there can be much diversity among elderly individuals of the same age.

adults. However, the following paragraphs describe some special factors that should be considered.

Time. With the wealth of history possessed by most older adults, more time must be allocated for the assessment process. In addition, fatigue, discomfort, and other problems may limit the amount of time during which clients will participate meaningfully. Realistically, several one-hour time blocks may need to be planned. Before the assessment is initiated, clients should be made aware of how long the process will last, both to assure that they have the available time and energy, and to avoid taking them by surprise with abrupt finishes because allocated time has expired.

Consent. All components of the assessment should be reviewed, and it should be explained that the client has a right to refuse to answer any question or participate in any part of the process. Accompanying this explanation should be a review of how the information will be used and who it will be shared with. (For example, clients may not be willing to openly share that an adult child resides in the same household if they feel that this information, if shared with another agency, could jeopardize their subsidized care.)

Environment. A room temperature of 75°F is usually comfortable for older persons. Cooler temperatures that may be fine for staff who are more active may be excessively cold for the elderly who have less insulation. Bright fluorescent lighting or direct sunlight can produce uncomfortable glare for older eyes. Passing foot traffic, televisions and radios, paging systems, ringing telephones, and employee conversation may be blocked out by staff accustomed to them, but such sounds can be significantly distracting to the elderly.

Sensory Deficits. Hearing and vision losses, highly prevalent among older adults, can interfere with the collection of accurate data. Clients may not hear questions, or misinterpret what they did hear; incorrect or inappropriate responses can result. (In fact, these inappropriate responses mistakenly can be attributed to altered mental status.) Ascertain early in the assessment process if sensory deficits exist and compensate appropriately. During the interview allow a distance of 3 feet between you and the client: close enough to facilitate communication while allowing the comfort of a normal social distance. Be sure the client is wearing eyeglasses and hearing aids if they are normally used.

Language. Language needs to be tailored to the individual client. Obviously, interpreter assistance may be needed if the client speaks a foreign language, but it is also important to ascertain if an English-speaking person uses a foreign language. In stressful situations English may be blocked and the foreign tongue resorted to. Sensitivity must be paid to the use of jargon, not only the complex medical terms, but also the terms assumed to be universally understood (e.g., clean caught specimen, expectoration, lesions, urinary frequency). Until the client's level of understanding is determined, it may be advantageous to offer explanations and to couple medical terms with related lay ones.

Recall. The long histories they possess, coupled with the commonly found short-term memory deficits, make the elderly more likely to forget significant pieces of data. Carefully structured questions can be crucial in unveiling this information. For example, rather than ask if the client has any allergies, invest the time in reviewing specific allergic reactions and asking if any food, drug, or article of clothing has caused them. Similarly, with medications, don't assume the client remembers all the prescription *and* nonprescription drugs being administered. Instead, name a variety of drugs commonly used by older adults—aspirin, antacids, laxatives, topical rubs, sleeping pills—to trigger recall.

At the close of the interview it is beneficial to summarize findings and provide an opportunity for the client to form and ask questions.

A variety of physical and mental health problems can be identified by keen observation during the interview.

While interviewing clients, one can learn a great deal about their physical and mental status. For example, observation of limited mobility, inappropriate speech, or edematous ankles indicates problems in need of further evaluation. A systematic approach will make the assessment process more efficient and reduce the risk of omitting certain portions of data. One possible framework for organizing the assessment process is outlined on the following pages, accompanied by normal and abnormal findings.

Assessment of Physical Status

Head and Neck

Hair and Scalp

Age-related changes: Manifestations of the aging process are apparent in the graying and whitening of scalp hair. There is a reduction in scalp hair growth and a thinning of the hair. Various degrees of baldness are present in most men, and some women may experience excess hair growth over the lip and chin area. The hair over the rim of the ears and in the nostrils becomes more coarse in males. Like the skin over the entire body, scalp hair becomes drier.

Assessment	Abnormal Findings	Possible Cause
Note consistency, texture, amount, distribution, and grooming of hair.	Coarse, dry, brittle hair	Hypothyroidism
	Excessively oily hair	Poor grooming practices, parkinsonism
Inquire as to hair-care practices.	Irregular patches of hair loss	Fungal infections of scalp
	Loose, scaling scalp	Seborrhea
Ask about soreness, itching, hair loss or change.	Areas of redness and tenderness near hairline, accompanied by pulsations of superficial temporal arteries	Giant cell arteritis
Inspect entire scalp; use comb to part hair into rows.	Smooth, round nodules	Sebaceous cysts
	Nodular, ulcerative, raised, glossy, painless growths that bleed easily	Melanomas, basal cell carcinoma
	Wartlike, flesh-colored lesion	Squamous cell carcinoma
	Reddish patches of dry skin with silver-white, light gray, or brown scale, less than 1 cm	Solar (actinic) keratoses (premalignant)

Neck

Age-related changes: Cervical range of motion decreases with age, although motion is sufficient to allow normal function in the activities of daily living. There is increased resistance to passive neck movements, as well as more prominent pulsations of the carotid arteries and jugular veins.

Assessment	Abnormal Findings	Possible Cause
Perform active and passive range of motion of head and neck.	Limited range of motion	Spinal arthritis, muscle stiffness or soreness
Ask client to lie down and resist your efforts to turn his or her head with your hand.	Inability to resist force of examiner's hand	Weakness or damage of sternocleidomastoid muscle, disorder of spinal accessory nerve
Ask client to tilt head back and swallow.	Prominence of thyroid gland	Enlarged thyroid gland
Observe and palpate carotid pulse, inspect jugular veins.	Large, strong carotid pulse with rapid upstroke or downstroke	Fever, stress, anemia, hyperthyroidism, aortic insufficiency, complete heart block
	Weak carotid pulse with diminished stroke volume	Left ventricular failure (secondary to myocardial infarction, aortic valvular stenosis, constrictive pericarditis)
	Double carotid pulsation	Aortic stenosis with insufficiency
	Jugular veins distended above normal when client erect or in 45° angle position	Congestive heart failure, pericarditis
	Unilateral jugular vein distension	Kinking of innominate vein

Face

Age-related changes: Flattening of the epidermis, stiffening and reduced solubility of collagen, and increased branching and thickening of elastin fibers cause the dryness, fragility, and decreased elasticity of the skin. Loss of subcutaneous fat and elasticity result in the development of lines and wrinkles. Skin pigmentation ("age spots," "liver spots") may occur in light-skinned persons because of the clustering of melanocytes. The thinning, sagging subcutaneous tissue can give the face a more angular look and cause the nose to sag and protrude. Benign skin tags may develop.

Assessment	Abnormal Findings	Possible Cause
Observe face for symmetry, rashes, scars, lesions. (It is preferable to use nonfluorescent lighting; fluorescent lighting can mask fine rashes.)	Raised, yellowish, shiny growth, 1–5 mm in diameter	Senile sebaceous adenoma
	Raised, well-marginated nodular lesion, ranging from a few mm to more than 1 cm, waxy-looking skin	Basal cell epithelioma
	Circumscribed pigmentation, peripheral enlargement, raised, papules within lesion	Malignant melanoma
	Flat, pigmented macular lesion	Melanotic freckle
Ask about facial pain, numbness. Test the function of the trigeminal nerve (cranial nerve V). Have the client close eyes while examiner gently touches forehead, cheek, and chin with a cotton wisp and then a pin. Repeat on other side of face. Test muscles of mastication (also associated with trigeminal nerve function) by asking client to open mouth and resist examiner's efforts to close client's mouth.	Paralysis on upper and lower face of one side	Bell's palsy
	Asymmetry and paralysis around mouth, upper portion of face unaffected	Upper motor neuron lesion associated with stroke

Eyes

Age-related changes: The eyes experience a variety of changes with age that affect the ability to function, protect oneself from hazards, and enjoy a high quality of life. The aging eye loses efficiency in the ability to accommodate and focus for near vision (presbyopia); most persons over age 40 require corrective lenses for this purpose. Vision in dim areas or at night is more difficult because of an increased light perception threshold. Sclerosis of the pupil sphincter and a decrease in pupil size make the pupil less responsive to light. There is opacity of the lens and decreased tolerance for glare. A gradual narrowing of the visual field may occur. A slight drooping of the eyelid can result from a loss of tissue elasticity. A reduction in tear production can lead to less lustrous eyes and clients' complaints of having dry eyes. A grayish white ring at the margin of the cornea can be noted in some older adults.

Assessment	Abnormal Findings	Possible Cause
Inspect eyes. Note drooping of eyelids (normally they should not cover pupil), tearing, discharge, unusual movements, discoloration of sclera. (Black-skinned persons may have a yellow discoloration, not necessarily associated with jaundice.)	Ptosis	Impairment of oculomotor nerve (cranial nerve III), edema
	Edematous eyelids	Allergy, infection, nephrosis, heart failure
	Infected eyelid with sty (hordeolum)	Infection of sebaceous glands of lid
	Protruding eyes (exophthalmos)	Hyperthyroidism (although ocular signs of hyperthyroidism occur less frequently in aged)
Palpate eyes; with client's lids closed gently palpate eyeball.	Soft, spongy feeling eyeball	Dehydration
	Extremely hard feeling eyeball	Increased intraocular pressure
Ask about visual capacity, pain, discomfort, sensations, seeing spots in visual field.	Eye pain, perception of halo around lights, dilated pupils	Acute glaucoma
	Complaint of "smeared" vision, unclear vision, tearing, headaches	Chronic glaucoma
	Hazy vision, progressive loss of vision	Cataract
	Complaint of having black spots float through visual field	Early indication of detached retina
	Blind area in visual field (scotoma)	Glaucoma
	Blindness in same half of both eyes (homonymous hemianopsia)	Cerebrovascular accident
Test visual acuity with use of Snellen chart or newspaper.	Inability to see small print	Presbyopia
Test extraocular movements by having client follow examiner's finger with eyes as finger moves to different horizontal and vertical points.	Irregular, jerking movements of eyes	Disturbance of cranial nerves III, IV, and VI
Ask about last ophthalmologic examination, including tonometry. Arrange examination if one has not been done within past year.		

Ears

Age-related changes: A deterioration of the cochlea and neurons of the higher auditory pathways leads to a sensorineural hearing loss (presbycusis); initially the high-frequency sounds (particularly s, sh, f, ph) are impaired, progressing to the middle and low frequencies.
An atrophy of the tympanic membrane can give it a white or gray appearance on inspection.
A stiffening of the cilia of the ear, combined with the higher keratin content of cerumen, causes ear wax to impact easily, further decreasing the ability to hear. Ears may protrude more in late life owing to the loss of supporting cartilage.

Assessment	Abnormal Findings	Possible Cause
Ask about pain, itching, discharge, tinnitus, hearing deficits, care of ears.	Hearing deficit	Sensorineural or conductive hearing loss, cerumen accumulation, upper respiratory infection, ototoxic drugs, diabetes

Assessment	Abnormal Findings	Possible Cause
	Tinnitus	Destructive process in hearing pathway, hypertension
	Itching in ears	Cerumen, dry ear canal, chronic external otitis
	Small, crusted ulcerated lesion on pinna	Basal or squamous cell carcinoma

Nose

Age-related changes: Some reduction in olfaction is believed to occur with age. The nasal mucosa becomes drier.

Assessment	Abnormal Findings	Possible Cause
Ask about pain, feeling of obstruction, nosebleeds, excessive dryness.	Nosebleeds	Irritation from picking, hypertension, vitamin C deficiency
Inspect nares for lesions, masses, perforated septum. Test patency of each naris by obstructing one at a time and asking client to inhale with mouth closed.	Obstructed nasal breathing	Dried crusts, mass, polyp
Determine client's ability to smell by asking him/her to differentiate or acknowledge various scents (e.g., orange peel, coffee, rose). Avoid using irritating substances such as ammonia or oil of wintergreen.	Inability to smell	Impairment of olfactory nerve, local irritation or bleeding

Mouth and Throat

Age-related changes: A loss of elasticity of perioral skin causes a vertical wrinkling of the skin surrounding the mouth. The buccal mucosa is thinner, less vascular, and drier. Taste sensations are altered because of a reduction in taste buds, especially those for sweet and salty flavors. Varicosities may develop on the ventral surface of the tongue. The secretion of salivary ptyalin is decreased. Tooth loss is *not* a normal outcome of growing old, although many elderly individuals are edentulous. Teeth are often more brittle and break easily because of increased calcification. There may be some reabsorption of gum tissue at the base of the teeth. Edentulous persons lose bone in their lower jaw at a faster rate than persons with teeth; also, dentures may facilitate bone destruction.

Assessment	Abnormal Findings	Possible Cause
Evaluate voice tone and quality, articulation.	Aphasia	Neurological disease
	Monotonous, soft, slurred speech	Parkinsonism
	Slurred speech	Hypoglycemia, intoxication, neurological disease
Note color, symmetry, position, and moisture of mouth. (Dark-skinned persons may have a bluish hue to the lips as a normal finding.)	Blue lips	Anoxia, anemia
	Dryness of lips, oral cavity	Dehydration
	Sore, lesion on lip	Infection, cancer
	Fissure at corner of mouth	Vitamin B complex deficiency, infection, overclosure due to missing teeth or poorly fitting dentures
Inspect oral cavity with light and tongue depressor. (Dark-skinned persons may possess a brownish line along the gum and brownish markings as a normal finding.) Examine tongue.	Bluish, black line along gumline	Lead, arsenic, or mercury poisoning
	Smooth, red tongue	Iron, niacin, or vitamin B_{12} deficiency
	White patches resembling dried milk	Moniliasis infection
	Thick, white patch on tongue, present for several weeks	Leukoplakia (precancerous)
	Lesions, masses on undersurface of tongue	Carcinoma

Assessment	Abnormal Findings	Possible Cause
	Brown pigmentation of buccal mucosa in light-skinned persons	Addison's disease
	Bright red spots encased by hyperkeratotic epithelium found on hard palate	Nicotine stomatitis (associated with cigarette smoking)
Palpate (with gloved hand) tongue and gums for evidence of masses, pain, bleeding.	Lesions, masses	Oral cancer (90% of all oral cancers occur after age 40)
Test gag reflex, rise of soft palate when client says "ah."	Failure of soft palate to rise	Vagus nerve paralysis
Note unusual breath odors.	Sweet, fruity smelling breath	Ketoacidosis
	Breath odor of urine	Uremic acidosis
	Breath odor of clover	Liver failure
	Foul breath odor	Halitosis, lung abscess

Respiratory System

Age-related changes: With advanced years there is less elastic recoil of the lungs during expiration and more energy expenditure required to achieve full respirations. Skeletal muscle strength and function are reduced, and there is increased rigidity of the thorax and diaphragm. Some calcification of the costal cartilage occurs. The number of and diffusion in the alveoli are reduced. Vital capacity decreases while residual volume increases; a slight decrease in arterial oxyhemoglobin saturation is experienced. Cough efficiency is reduced. Some increase in anterior-posterior chest diameter may occur, although that diameter normally does not exceed transverse diameter.

Assessment	Abnormal Findings	Possible Cause
Ask client about coughing, sputum production and characteristics, chest pain, orthopnea, dyspnea, and other respiratory symptoms. Determine when last tuberculin test or chest X ray was performed. Record dates of last influenza and pneumonia vaccines. Inquire about frequency and pattern of respiratory problems and how they are managed. Obtain sputum specimen.		
Inspect bare chest: Note coloring, scars, structural abnormalities.	Ruddy, pink coloring of face, trunk, limbs	Chronic obstructive lung disease
Observe spinal curvatures. Evaluate respiratory rate, rhythm, depth, and length, and symmetry of chest expansion.	Bluish, gray hue to face and neck	Chronic bronchitis
	Barrel look to chest	Chronic obstructive lung disease
	Asymmetrical lung expansion	Acute pleurisy, pleural fibrosis, atelectasis, pulmonary emboli, pleural effusion, pain, fractured ribs
Palpate the posterior chest by placing both hands on the client's back (thumbs alongside spine and fingers over intercostal spaces). Feel depth of respirations and chest movement; be alert to areas of sensitivity, masses.	Crepitus (crunchy feeling to skin, resulting from air getting trapped under epidermis)	Recent tracheostomy
Evaluate tactile fremitus (vibratory tremors felt during palpation of chest wall): Using palmar bases of fingers or ulnar surface of hands, feel for vibrations as the client says "99."	Lack of fremitus in upper lobe	Chronic obstructive lung disease, pneumothorax
	Increased fremitus in lower lobe	Pneumonia, mass

Assessment	Abnormal Findings	Possible Cause
Fremitus is best heard in upper lobes of lungs.		
Percuss lungs: Start at upper lobe and percuss downward; alternate from one side to the other to compare sounds. Normal lung sounds are resonant (clear and low pitched).	Dull sound	Consolidation, pleural effusion, atelectasis
	Hyperresonant sound (hollow, high pitch)	Emphysema, pneumothorax
Auscultate to assess pitch, intensity, quality, and duration of breath sounds. *Bronchial breath sounds* are normally heard at the trachea and characterized by short inspirations and long expirations; *vesicular breath sounds* are heard over the entire lung field and have long inspirations and short expirations; *bronchovesicular sounds* are heard over the sternum and scapula, and have equal inspirations and expirations.	Diminished breath sounds	Emphysema, shallow respirations, pleural thickening
	Increased breath sounds	Extensive lung damage
	Rales (crackles): crackling sound at the end of inspiration, disappears with coughing or suctioning	Extra interstitial fluid, as in congestive heart failure, pulmonary edema, bronchitis, pneumonia
	Rhonchi: rattling sounds at the end of expiration, can disappear with coughing or suctioning	Increased mucus production and partial airway obstruction as in severe bronchitis or bronchiectasis
	Wheezes: groaning sounds that do not clear with coughing or suctioning	Presence of large amounts of thick mucus or airway narrowing as in asthma, pulmonary stenosis

Cardiovascular System

Age-related changes: A variety of profound changes are experienced in this major system. Heart valves become thick and rigid. The endocardium experiences thickening and sclerosis, and subpericardial fat increases. There is a thickening in the region of the SA node and a dilation of the aorta and aortic branches. A slight kinking of the carotid arteries may occur. The heart muscle is more rigid, making dilation and contraction more problematic. The resting heart rate is unchanged, as is the resting cardiac output. However, when extra demands are placed on the heart, the heart rate and stroke volume are decreased. The less efficient cardiovascular stress response causes the aged heart to achieve lower tachycardia rates than younger persons and to remain elevated for extended periods of time. Increased peripheral resistance and more rigidity of vessels lead to a higher diastolic blood pressure, while decreased ability of the aorta to distend affects an increase in systolic blood pressure. Vagal tone increases, and the heart is more sensitive to carotid sinus stimulation.

Assessment	Abnormal Findings	Possible Cause
Observe generalized coloring, tortuous looking vessels, energy level, shortness of breath, mental status.	Lower extremity cold to touch, pale, missing hair, edema, shiny and taut skin	Poor circulation
	Thick, rigid nails	Chronic arterial insufficiency
Inquire about symptoms of cardiovascular problems: light-headedness, coughs, blackouts, confusion, edema, fatigue, cold extremities.	Confusion, blackouts, fatigue, dizziness	Decreased carotid blood flow, aortic stenosis, reduced cardiac output, digitalis toxicity
	Coughs, wheezes	Left-sided heart failure
	Hemoptysis	Pulmonary embolus, heart failure
	Chest pain, pressure	Myocardial infarction (can occur without severe chest pain)
Palpate the PMI (point of maximal impulse) in the apical or left ventricular area (fifth left intercostal space or slightly medial to the midclavicular line). It should be 2 cm or less and last about one-half second.	Displaced PMI	Left ventricular hypertrophy, marked kyphoscoliosis
Palpate the *right ventricular area* at the lower left sternal border, the *pulmonary area* at the second left	Thrills in apical area	Mitral valve disease
	Thrills in right ventricular area	Ventricular septal defect
	Thrills in pulmonary area	Pulmonic stenosis

Assessment	Abnormal Findings	Possible Cause
intercostal space at the base of the heart, the *aortic area* at the second right intercostal space, and the *epigastric area* at the fifth intercostal space near the sternum. Note *thrills* (palpable vibrations similar to the feeling of a cat during purring).	Thrills in aortic area	Aortic stenosis
Auscultate the entire heart. The bell portion of the stethoscope will aid in hearing low-frequency sounds (e.g., diastolic murmur of mitral stenosis).	Bruits (transmitted cardiac murmurs)	Local obstruction
The diaphragm portion of the stethoscope will reveal higher frequency sounds (e.g., murmurs associated with aortic and mitral regurgitation, pericardial friction rub). Note rate, rhythm, extra sounds, murmurs.	Although many elderly persons have functional systolic murmurs, this finding should be referred for evaluation	
Measure jugular venous pressure: Expose neck and chest. If pressure is significantly elevated, have client sit erect; if pressure is moderately elevated, elevate client to 45° angle; if pressure is normal or slightly elevated, have client lie flat. Support head and neck to relax sternocleidomastoid muscle. Turn client's head slightly away and shine light tangentially across client's sternocleidomastoid muscle. Observe pulsations. Repeat for other side. Normally full neck veins disappear when client is supine; pulsations are less than 2 cm above clavicle when client is in 45° angle elevation.	Bilateral jugular vein distention Unilateral jugular vein distension	Congestive heart failure, pericarditis, superior vena cava obstruction Kinking of left innominate vein
Inspect carotid arteries for abnormally large, bounding pulses. Palpate pulse at medial edge of sternocleidomastoid muscle. To avoid carotid sinus massage, palpate only one side at a time. Listen for bruits by auscultating the arteries with the bell portion of the stethoscope as the client holds his or her breath.		
Evaluate blood pressure in lying, sitting, and standing positions. The elderly can have significant changes in blood pressure when changing positions. Obtain the palpatory systolic pressure before auscultating to promote accuracy and client comfort. Note *ausculatory gap* (a silent period between systolic and diastolic).	Blood pressure exceeding 160/95 on repeated measurements	Hypertension
Inspect peripheral vessels. Note color and temperature of extremities. Ask about pain or other symptoms.	Dilated tortuous vessels Intermittent claudication, neuropathy Edema, warmth, pain of calf muscle Ulceration on lower extremity, skin cold to touch, reddened, becomes pale when extremity elevated	Varicose veins Arteriosclerosis obliterans Venous thromboembolism Stasis ulcer

Gastrointestinal System

Age-related changes: The changes to the gastrointestinal system often affect the older individual's general health and comfort. Decreased salivary gland activity and a drier oral mucosa can cause the swallowing and mixing of food to be problematic. Decreased esophageal motility and delayed esophageal and gastric emptying result in food remaining in the upper gastrointestinal system for a longer period of time. The gastric mucosa is thinner, increasing the risk of irritation and ulceration. The risk of indigestion increases owing to reduced secretion of gastric acids and pancreatic enzymes. Hunger contractions are reduced, and insulin is released at altered rates. The intestinal mucosa atrophies, and the intestinal musculature weakens. Peristalsis is slower, contributing to constipation.

Assessment	Abnormal Findings	Possible Cause
Ask about swallowing difficulties, indigestion, regurgitation, pain, nausea, vomiting, flatus, constipation; review client's management of these problems. Review dietary intake.	Bleeding and irritation of esophagus	Esophageal varicosities
	Excessive salivation, hiccups, dysphagia, anemia, chronic bleeding, thirst	Esophageal cancer
	Gastric pain, painless vomiting, anemia, weight loss	Gastric ulcer or cancer
	Heartburn, dysphagia, belching, vomiting, regurgitation, pain, symptoms more pronounced in recumbent position	Hiatus hernia
Prepare client for examination: Assure comfortable room temperature, have client void, place client in supine position. Inspect the abdomen: Sides should be symmetrical, rounded abdomen with adipose tissue normal. Note discoloration, asymmetry, dilated vessels, bulges, distension, rashes, scars, strong contractions. Have client raise head and note any herniations which may then become noticeable.	Striae (stretch marks)	If blue or pink, recent stretching of abdominal wall due to tumors, ascites, obesity; if silver or white, old stretching due to weight changes, pregnancies
	Jaundice	Cirrhosis, gallstones, pancreatitis
	Abdominal rashes	Drug reactions, irritation
	Small painless nodules on abdomen	Skin cancer
	Symmetrical distension of abdominal wall	Tumor, hernia, obesity, ascites
	Central, lower quadrant distension	Enlarged bladder, ovarian or uterine tumor
	Central, upper quadrant distension	Gastric dilatation, pancreatic cysts or tumor
Auscultate abdomen before percussing or palpating: Listen over intestines for bowel sounds. Warm stethoscope first and use diaphragm portion. Peristaltic sounds should be heard every 5–15 seconds, irregularly. If sounds are not heard, listen for a full 5 minutes and then flick finger against client's abdominal wall to stimulate intestinal motility. Continuous sounds are heard if food has been ingested within past several hours.	Absent or reduced bowel sounds	Peritonitis, late bowel obstruction, handling of bowel during surgery, electrolyte imbalances
	Increased bowel sounds	Gastroenteritis, diarrhea, early bowel obstruction
Auscultate vascular sounds: Place bell portion of stethoscope over the major arteries, above the umbilicus. Normally a heartbeat can be heard. Note irregular sounds.	Murmurs over abdominal aorta	Aneurysm
Auscultate over the liver and spleen for *friction rubs* (grating sound similar to shoes rubbing on cement) indicating enlarged organ coming in contact with peritoneum.	Friction rub	Enlarged organ

Assessment	Abnormal Findings	Possible Cause
Percuss all quadrants of abdomen: *Tympany* (a drumlike, musical sound) is heard over air-filled areas; *dullness* is heard over organs or air-filled areas containing solid masses. Percuss to identify borders of liver and spleen.	Dullness in air-filled areas	Ascites, masses
Palpate lightly in all quadrants, followed by deeper palpation. Note rigidity, pain, masses.	Bulge	Hernia
	Lumps, masses	Nodules, cancer
	Palpable spleen	Enlarged spleen
Examine rectum: Lie client in left-lateral position with right hip and knee flexed. Inspect perianal area and note rashes, hemorrhoids, fissures, and masses. Have client pant as examiner inserts lubricated gloved finger into anal canal. Rotate finger and palpate rectal wall for masses.	Rectal mass	Tumor, fecal impaction
	Varicosities in rectal area	Hemorrhoids
	Absence of normal bowel movement, oozing of liquid fecal material (resembling diarrhea), abdominal distension, palpable rectal mass	Fecal impaction
	Bright red rectal bleeding	Hemorrhoids, lower GI cancer, diverticulitis
Obtain a stool specimen.	Dark, tarry stools	Upper GI bleeding, iron supplements
	Gray, tan, unpigmented stool	Obstructive jaundice
	Pale, fatty stool	Absorption problems
	Mucus in stool	Inflammation
	Small worms in stool or rectal area	Pinworms

Reproductive System

Age-related changes: As they age, women will notice decreased vascularity, elasticity, and subcutaneous fat of the vulva. Pubic hair is lost, and the labia flatten and become thin and shiny. The vaginal canal becomes thinner, drier, and less vascular; the vaginal environment is more alkaline. The cervix and uterus shrink, and estrogen production and ovulation cease. Breasts atrophy and sag.

Men also note a loss of pubic hair. There is reduced size and firmness of the testes. Sperm production decreases, as does the viscosity of the semen. The achievement of an erection requires more direct stimulation and takes more time, as does the achievement of orgasm. Ejaculations will be slower and less forceful, and may not occur with every intercourse. Some degree of prostatic enlargement exists in most older men.

Assessment	Abnormal Findings	Possible Cause
For females:		
Obtain history of pregnancies, menstrual pattern, gynecological problems, and gynecological care.	Postmenopausal bleeding	Cancer, estrogen therapy
Ask about current problems with sexual function.	Painful intercourse	Age-related changes to vaginal canal, infection, prolapsed uterus, mass
Inspect genitalia: Note inflammation, irritation, discharge, lesions, prolapse.	Vaginal discharge, odor, irritation, soreness, itching	Vaginitis, moniliasis, trichomoniasis
	Protrusion of uterine wall outside vulva, pelvic pressure or heaviness, urinary tract symptoms	Prolapsed uterus, cystocele, rectocele
	White patches on membrane of vulva	Leukoplakia (can be precancerous)
Palpate genitalia for masses, tenderness. Obtain a Pap smear.	Palpable mass	Carcinoma (clitoris and Bartholin's glands common sites in older women)
Ask about breast changes, pain, tenderness, nipple discharge. Inspect	Dimpling, retraction, nontender, nonmovable hard mass.	Carcinoma

Assessment	Abnormal Findings	Possible Cause
breasts while client is supine, sitting erect, and leaning forward. Note dimpling, asymmetry, discoloration. Minor variation in the size of each nipple is not uncommon. Palpate each breast in clockwise manner from the outer tissue, moving toward nipple. Note masses, pain. Squeeze the nipple and note discharge. Since breast cancer is highest among older women, it is essential that they know how to perform a self-examination of their breasts. Access their knowledge and skill in performing this procedure.	Painful, edematous, reddened breasts	Inflammatory carcinoma, chronic irritation (e.g., from restraints)
For males:		
Inspect genitalia for lesions, edema, discharge, deformity, masses.	Discharge	Urethritis, prostatitis, venereal disease
	Crooked, painful erection	Peyronie's disease
Palpate scrotum for symmetry of testicles, tenderness, masses.	Mass	Carcinoma
	Scrotal pain, swelling	Epididymitis, orchitis, carcinoma (scrotal swelling can occur with renal or cardiac disease)
Review history of sexual function.	Impotency	Psychological stress, depression, medications (e.g., reserpine), alcohol ingestion, fatigue, overeating, neuropathy, long period of sexual inactivity
Obtain rectal examination of prostate.	Enlarged prostate gland	Benign prostatic hypertrophy, cancer
	Urinary frequency, hesitancy, dribbling, nocturia	Prostatic disease
Inspect breast tissue and nipples; ask about pain, changes.	Painful, edematous, reddened breasts	Irritation from suspenders, restraints
	Disk-shaped, firm, movable, tender mass under areola	Fibroadenosis (needs to be differentiated from malignancy by further evaluation)
	Noninflammatory breast enlargement	Obesity, side effect from drug (e.g., digitalis, phenothiazines, isoniazid), liver dysfunction, testicular tumor, bronchogenic cancer

Urinary Tract

Age-related changes: The loss of nephrons that occurs with aging reduces glomerular filtration. In addition, the kidneys have less tubular reabsorption and a lower threshold for glucose and creatinine clearance. Urinary frequency and nocturia are outgrowths of the smaller bladder capacity, and weaker bladder muscles contribute to urinary retention, dribbling, and stress incontinence.

Assessment	Abnormal Findings	Possible Cause
Ask about pattern and frequency of voiding.	Incontinence	Urinary tract infection, prostatic enlargement, neurogenic bladder, tumor, cerebral cortex lesion, calculi, medications (e.g., diuretics), altered mental status
	Increase in episodes of urinary frequency	Urinary tract infection, diuretic therapy, increased fluid intake, diabetes, hypocalcemia, anxiety

Assessment	Abnormal Findings	Possible Cause
Obtain urine specimen for evaluation.	Cloudy, alkaline, odorous urine; temperature elevation; frequency	Urinary tract infection
	Hematuria, pain, signs of urinary tract infection	Renal calculi
	Painless hematuria, signs of urinary tract infection	Bladder cancer
	Yellow-brown or green-brown urine	Jaundice, obstructive bile duct
	Pink, red, rust-colored urine	Presence of blood
	Cloudy urine	Presence of sperm or prostatic fluid, infection
	Dark brown or black urine	Hematuria, carcinoma
	Orange urine	Presence of bile, ingestion of pyridium

Musculoskeletal System

Age-related changes: Over the years muscle fibers, bulk, and strength are reduced. Muscles are more rigid and become fatigued with greater ease. Resting tremors may be present in some individuals. Bone mass and strength are also reduced, and older bones fracture with less stress than do younger bones. Cartilage decreases, contributing to some discomfort with joint mobility and shortening of the vertebral column. There is a decrease in tendon reflexes.

Assessment	Abnormal Findings	Possible Cause
Ask about joint pain, restricted movement, tremors, spasms. Place all joints through active and passive range of motion. Palpate all muscles for tenderness, contractions, masses. Test muscle strength.	Back pain	Degenerative arthritis, muscle strain, osteoporosis, osteomalacia
	Joint pain, stiffness, crepitus bony nodules (Heberden's nodes)	Osteoarthritis
	Joint pain, stiffness, redness, warmth, subcutaneous nodules over bony prominences, atrophy of surrounding muscle, flexion contractures	Rheumatoid arthritis
	Calf cramps during exercise, relieved by rest	Intermittent claudication
	Red, dry, thickened piece of skin over bony prominence	Corn
	Medial allocation of first metatarsophalangeal joint	Digiti flexus (hammer toe)

Assessment of Mental Status

Age-related changes: A loss of mental function is not a normal outgrowth of growing old, nor is a significant change in personality. Poor mental function must be evaluated in terms of the individual's lifelong pattern and potential health problems. Intelligence remains stable throughout the life span, and the potential to learn is unchanged, although more time may be necessary for older adults to learn new and difficult tasks. Short-term memory becomes poorer, but long-term memory is good. Psychomotor activity occurs at a slower rate. The incidence of mental health problems increases with age.

Assessment	Abnormal Findings	Possible Cause
Observe general appearance: appropriateness of dress, grooming and hygienic practices, posture, body language, facial expressions.	Rapid onset of confusion, normal level of consciousness	Reversible disturbance to cerebral circulation (e.g., drug reaction, malnutrition, congestive heart failure, hypotension, infection, trauma, stress)
Determine level of consciousness: lethargic, stuporous, semiconscious, unconscious. Ask about feelings of	Progressive decline in cognitive function, misidentification of people, loss of social courtesies, inattention to personal care, aphasia, ataxia, agnosia	Dementia (e.g., Alzheimer's disease, arteriosclerosis)

Assessment	Abnormal Findings	Possible Cause
self-worth, relationships, mood changes, fears, hallucinations, delusions, phobias, suicidal thoughts and plans. Test cognitive function: orientation, memory, retention, calculations, judgment, ability to follow three-stage command. (Standardized mental status evaluation tools can be used.)	Sadness, hopelessness, helplessness, insomnia, anorexia, constipation, self-depreciation, apathy, guilt, no alteration in intellectual function (Note: Persons in early stages of dementia who realize they are experiencing cognitive losses may become depressed; depressed persons who suffer insomnia, malnutrition, and poor self-care practices may develop signs mimicking dementia. Skilled psychiatric evaluation is crucial to differentiate.)	Depression
	Nervousness, hyperventilation, palpitations, rigidity in thinking, insomnia, pacing, somatic complaints, possible confusion	Anxiety
	Suspiciousness, insecurity	Paranoid disorder, sensory deficit, abuse, disability that increases dependency
	Continuous complaints/preoccupation with health, no organic basis for complaints	Hypochondriasis
	Hyperactivity, euphoria, hostility, paranoia, feelings of grandiosity	Mania
	Sadness, lack of interest in activities, anorexia, crying, anger, recent or anticipatory loss	Grief reaction

Problems identified during the assessment must be prioritized and described in nursing diagnostic statements to facilitate effective care planning and delivery.

Findings during the assessment process mean little if merely stored in a chart. Data must be transferred to caregivers in a relevant manner. Most likely, there will be numerous problems and needs discovered while assessing older adults—often more than caregivers realistically can address simultaneously. Priorities must be set, therefore, both in terms of the most urgent problems in need of intervention and the nonurgent but important problems that can create risks if given low priority. Once needs have been ranked from the assessment data, they must be articulated according to the problems they create for *nursing*, that is, nursing diagnosis (see Chapter 4).

BIBLIOGRAPHY

Bower F, Patterson J: A theory-based nursing assessment of elderly clients. Topics Clin Nurs 8(1): 22–32, 1986.

Bowers AC, Thompson JM, Miller M: Manual of Health Assessment, 3rd ed. St. Louis, CV Mosby, 1988.

Burnside I: Nursing and the Aged: A Self-Care Approach, 3rd ed. New York, McGraw-Hill, 1988.

Busse EW, Maddox GL: The Duke Longitudinal Studies of Normal Aging, 1955–1980. New York, Springer, 1985.

Carnevali DL, Patrick M: Nursing Management for the Elderly, 2nd ed. Philadelphia, JB Lippincott, 1986.

Downey KK, Davis BK: Measuring blood pressure via sensory detection. J Gerontol Nurs 12(11): 8–11, 1986.

Eliopoulos C (ed): Health Assessment of the Older Adult, 2nd ed. Menlo Park, CA, Addison-Wesley, 1989.

Gioiella EC, Bevil CW: Nursing Care of the Aging Client: Promoting Healthy Adaptation. Norwalk, CT, Appleton-Century-Crofts, 1985.

Jessup L: The health history. In Steffl BM (ed): Handbook of Gerontological Nursing. New York, Van Nostrand Reinhold, 1984.

Jones D: Health Assessment Manual. New York, McGraw-Hill, 1986.

Mace N: Facets of dementia: Using mental status tests. J Gerontol Nurs 13(6): 33, 1987.

Remondet JH, Hansson RO: Assessing a widow's grief—A short index. J Gerontol Nurs 13(4): 30–34, 1987.

Rossman I (ed): Clinical Geriatrics, 3rd ed. Philadelphia, JB Lippincott, 1986.

Struble LM, Sivertsen L: Agitation behaviors in confused elderly patients. J Gerontol Nurs 13(11): 40–44, 1987.

Tynan C, Cardea JM: Community service home health hazard assessment. J Gerontol Nurs 13(10): 25–28, 1987.

CHAPTER 4

Nursing Diagnosis in Gerontological Care

Charlotte Eliopoulos

Chapter Objectives

At the completion of this chapter the reader will be able to:

1. Define nursing diagnosis.
2. Form a nursing diagnosis statement.
3. Identify potential nursing diagnoses presented by the elderly and the causes or contributing factors for these diagnoses.

The term *nursing diagnosis* was first used in 1953 to describe the analytic process that preceded the development of the nursing care plan (Fry, 1953). Although there were efforts to develop theoretical foundations of nursing practice that clearly differentiated nursing from other professional practices, little was done to promote the concept of nursing diagnosis for the next two decades. It was not until 1973 that a group of nurses met and formed the National Classification Group for the Classification of Nursing Diagnosis (now called the North American Nursing Diagnosis Association) and published the first list of nursing diagnoses. The understanding, acceptance, and development of nursing diagnosis have increased considerably since that time (see Table 4-1).

A nursing diagnosis can be defined as "an actual or potential health problem which nurses, by virtue of their education and experience, are capable and licensed to treat" (Gordon, 1982, 3). This definition has been further developed by Carpenito, who describes nursing diagnosis as "a statement that describes a health state or an actual or potential alteration in one's life processes (physiological, psychological, sociocultural, developmental, and spiritual)" (Carpenito, 1983, 4). Typically, there are two major elements to the diagnostic statement:

Nursing diagnoses are problems or conditions that nurses can independently identify and manage.

1. *Health state.* The terms that describe the health state are those found on the list of acceptable nursing diagnoses, such as "alterations in thought processes" or "sleep pattern disturbance." Sometimes, the term *potential* or *possible* is placed in front of the health state to offer a clearer description (*potential* implying that the problem is at risk of occurring if

TABLE 4-1. Nursing Diagnoses Accepted by the North American Nursing Diagnosis Association

Pattern 1: Exchanging
Altered nutrition: more than body requirements
Altered nutrition: less than body requirements
Altered nutrition: potential for more than body requirements
Potential for infection
Potential altered body temperature
Hypothermia
Hyperthermia
Ineffective thermoregulation
Dysreflexia
Constipation
Perceived constipation
Colonic constipation
Diarrhea
Bowel incontinence
Altered patterns of urinary elimination
Stress incontinence
Reflex incontinence
Urge incontinence
Functional incontinence
Total incontinence
Urinary retention
Altered (specify type) tissue perfusion (renal, cerebral, cardiopulmonary, gastrointestinal, peripheral)
Fluid volume excess
Fluid volume deficit
Potential fluid volume deficit
Decreased cardiac output
Impaired gas exchange
Ineffective airway clearance
Ineffective breathing pattern
Potential for injury
Potential for suffocation
Potential for poisoning
Potential for trauma
Potential for aspiration
Potential for disuse syndrome
Impaired tissue integrity
Altered oral mucous membrane
Impaired skin integrity
Potential impaired skin integrity

Pattern 2: Communicating
Impaired verbal communication

Pattern 3: Relating
Impaired social interaction

Social isolation
Altered role performance
Altered parenting
Potential altered parenting
Sexual dysfunction
Altered family processes
Parental role conflict
Altered sexuality patterns

Pattern 4: Valuing
Spiritual distress

Pattern 5: Choosing
Ineffective individual coping
Impaired adjustment
Defensive coping
Ineffective denial
Ineffective family coping: disabling
Ineffective family coping: compromised
Family coping: potential for growth
Noncompliance (specify)
Decisional conflict (specify)
Health seeking behaviors (specify)

Pattern 6: Moving
Impaired physical mobility
Activity intolerance
Fatigue
Potential activity intolerance
Sleep pattern disturbance
Diversional activity deficit
Impaired home maintenance management
Altered health maintenance
Feeding self-care deficit
Impaired swallowing
Ineffective breastfeeding
Bathing/hygiene self-care deficit
Dressing/grooming self-care deficit
Toileting self-care deficit
Altered growth and development

Pattern 7: Perceiving
Body image disturbance
Self-esteem disturbance
Chronic low self-esteem
Situational low self-esteem
Personal identity disturbance
Sensory/perceptual alterations (specify: visual, auditory, kinesthetic, gustatory, tactile, olfactory)
Unilateral neglect

TABLE 4-1. (*Continued*)

Hopelessness	Anticipatory grieving
Powerlessness	Potential for violence: self-directed or directed at others
Pattern 8: Knowing	Post-trauma response
Knowledge deficit (specify)	Rape-trauma syndrome
Altered thought processes	Rape-trauma syndrome: compound reaction
Pattern 9: Feeling	Rape-trauma syndrome: silent reaction
Pain	Anxiety
Chronic pain	Fear
Dysfunctional grieving	

there is no nursing intervention and *possible* conveying that the problem may be present but additional data are needed to confirm it).

2. *Causative or contributing factors.* Causative or contributing factors can be numerous and include pathophysiological states, situational circumstances, and age-related conditions.

These two elements are linked by the term *related to;* for example:

- Impaired physical mobility related to missing limb.
- Anxiety related to hospitalization.
- Impairment of skin integrity related to edema.

Many of the problems and needs of older adults fall within the realm of nursing for independent diagnosis and management. The use of nursing diagnoses, therefore, is logical and relevant to gerontological nursing practice.

Nursing Diagnoses

Skill in the use of nursing diagnoses comes with practice.

The following section reviews nursing diagnoses and discusses some of the unique causative and contributing factors in older adults to which the health state can be related. Nurses will find that their training in nursing diagnosis is like learning a new language—skill in its use comes with practice.

Activity Intolerance

Definition: A limitation in the capacity to withstand physical or mental activity.

Causative or Contributing Factors

Pain. There is a greater prevalence of chronic conditions in late life that can cause basic activity to be more uncomfortable. In addition, situations such as surgery and the stress of losing a loved one can limit activity endurance.

Immobility. Be it from pain, convalescence, or self-imposed limitations, immobility can lead to a loss of motivation and strength to engage in activity.

Sleep disturbances. Nocturia, muscle spasms, and joint discomfort are among the factors that interfere with the elderly's sleep. Insufficient sleep can leave older adults too fatigued to tolerate activity.

Reduced muscle strength and endurance. Age-related changes to the muscles can cause muscles to tire and ache easily.

Prolonged recovery from cardiac stress. When placed under a stress, the older heart requires more time to return to a normal rate. Tachycardia can reduce activity tolerance.

Congestive heart failure. Hypertensive heart disease, coronary artery disease, bronchitis, and pneumonia are among the conditions influencing a higher incidence of CHF in advanced age. Associated edema, shortness of breath, and orthopnea reduce activity tolerance.

Anginal syndrome. The fear of instigating an attack or the weakness and discomfort experienced when one occurs can limit activity.

Myocardial infarction. Hardly an unusual problem in old age, MI has a higher incidence in persons with a history of hypertension and arteriosclerosis. Symptoms may be atypical in older adults (e.g., the absence of crushing chest pain) and result in a delayed diagnosis. The direct effects on heart muscle and the patient's fear of causing additional damage can pose limitations on activity.

Arrhythmias. Impaired circulation from conduction disturbances can cause fatigue, pain, and other symptoms that interfere with an active state. Arrhythmias can be caused by anginal syndrome, hypokalemia, coronary insufficiency, and acute infections, but the most common cause is digitalis toxicity, emphasizing the importance of close monitoring when the patient is using this medication.

Varicose veins. The dull pain and cramping of legs that have varicosities can make physical activity a highly uncomfortable experience. This discomfort can be compounded by dizziness when rising from a lying position (caused by a pooling of blood in the lower extremities).

Respiratory disease. Bronchitis, emphysema, and asthma rank as the eighth leading cause of death in persons over age 65, demonstrating the prevalence of chronic respiratory diseases in old age. Insufficient oxygen transport limits activity tolerance.

Malnutrition. Poor nutrition can result from a variety of physical, psychological, and social factors, ranging from insufficient intake of needed nutrients to excessive intake of calories, carbohydrates, or sodium. Fatigue, obesity, edema, and other outcomes will hamper an active state.

Chronic illness. A majority of older individuals possess at least one chronic disease. Activity intolerance can be related to the fatigue, functional impairment, or psychological factors secondary to the disease.

Defining Characteristics

Confusion

Weakness

Excessive fatigue

Inability to engage in self-care activities

Increase or decrease in respiratory rate

Dyspnea

Tachycardia lasting more than three hours after activity

Change in heart rhythm or strength

Increase in diastolic blood pressure >15 mm Hg

Reluctance to engage in activities

Anxiety

Definition: A feeling of nervousness and emotional uneasiness as a result of a perceived threat.

Causative or Contributing Factors

New or worsening health problem. Concern regarding the unknown physical, mental, and socioeconomic consequences of health problems can understandably cause anxiety.

Death. With each advancing year there is greater awareness of the mortality of loved ones and oneself. There may be anxiety about how one will be affected by the death of a family member, or how one's own dying process will be managed.

Retirement. Although seen by many to be a wonderful period of freedom and leisure, retirement is accompanied by many losses—role, social world, income, activity—that can be quite anxiety provoking.

Increased vulnerability. The recognition that one cannot independently change a tire on a car or protect oneself against a purse snatcher can cause an uneasy awareness of how vulnerable the elderly are in society.

Change in caregiver's status. The inability of the caregiver to continue providing services can cause anxiety as the patient wonders who, if anyone, will replace those services. There may be an underlying fear of institutionalization.

Relocation. Be it a move to a new apartment or admission to a nursing home, adjusting to a new environment produces anxiety, particularly to the elderly, who may have sensory deficits, limited mobility, or other problems that make the adjustment more difficult.

Losses. Any threat to the status of personal health and function, family health and function, residence, income, role, or life-style can cause anxiety.

Defining Characteristics

Confusion

Impaired memory

Poor concentration abilities

Irritability

Easily frustrated

Hostility

Withdrawal

Pacing, restlessness

Increased or decreased appetite

Increased pulse, respirations, blood pressure

Insomnia

Fatigue

Palpitations

Increased frequency of voiding

Constipation

Definition: A limitation in the ability to expel feces manifested by reduced frequency of bowel movements, abdominal distension and discomfort, difficulty in expelling feces, and feces of a hard, dry consistency.

Causative or Contributing Factors

Age-related changes. The slower peristalsis that occurs with aging increases the risk of constipation.

Inadequate roughage and fluids. Poor appetite, limited finances, painful gums, loose dentures, inability to market and prepare foods, or personal preferences can limit the intake of fruits, vegetables, and other fiber-containing foods. Likewise, poor motivation to drink, inability to obtain fluids, and self-imposed fluid restrictions to control urinary frequency can reduce the fluids necessary to promote regular bowel elimination.

Immobility. Many of the health problems possessed by the elderly produce fatigue, discomfort, functional impairments, and other consequences that limit the activity necessary to promote good elimination.

Medications. Antacids, analgesics, psychotropics, and many of the other drugs of which the elderly are major consumers cause constipation. Also, the habitual use of laxatives can create a dependency on these drugs for bowel elimination to occur.

Hemorrhoids. One in seven older adults is troubled by hemorrhoids that can make defecation extremely painful and, therefore, postponed as long as possible.

Toileting dependency. Traveling to and remaining on the toilet for a sufficient amount of time are difficult when one must depend on others. This problem can be compounded if an altered mental status prevents expression of toileting needs.

Defining Characteristics
Decreased frequency of bowel movements

Hard, formed, difficult to pass stool

Reduced bowel sounds

Abdominal and rectal fullness

Possible palpable impaction

Diarrhea

Definition: The frequent passage of liquid or unformed stool.

Causative or Contributing Factors
Diet. A high intake of caffeine, fruits, bran, or foods to which the individual is sensitive can cause diarrhea. Some tube feedings also have this effect.

Gastrointestinal disorders. Gastritis, diverticulitis, ulcerative colitis, spastic or irritable colon, and cancer of the stomach, pancreas, and intestines are among the conditions that can cause diarrhea.

Medications. Antibiotics, certain antacids, and laxatives are among the drugs that can cause diarrhea.

Fecal impaction. The oozing of soft fecal matter around the impaction can mimic diarrhea.

Bacteria. Lack of knowledge, altered mental status, improper storage or cooking, and reluctance to throw away old food items can cause the elderly to ingest foods and fluids that contain harmful bacteria.

Other. Stress, fear, anxiety, and warm weather are among the additional factors that can lead to diarrhea.

Defining Characteristics
Loose, watery stools

Increased frequency of bowel movements

Abdominal discomfort, cramps

Decreased Cardiac Output

Definition: A reduction in the heart's ability to meet the body's circulatory demands.

Causative or Contributing Factors
Age-related changes. Aging can cause valves to become thicker and more rigid; the endocardium can thicken and become sclerotic; the heart muscle

can lose elasticity; and the aorta can become dilated. An associated reduction in cardiac output may occur.

Cardiac disease. Arrhythmias, hypertension, myocardial infarction, and congestive heart failure are among the diseases of the elderly that can damage heart muscle and impair normal heart function.

Hypokalemia. The elderly are susceptible to hypokalemia because of thiazide and loop diuretic therapy; inadequate dietary intake; intracellular shifting of potassium due to alkalosis, glucose, and insulin; renal disorders; and excessive loss from vomiting or diarrhea.

Hyperkalemia. Less common than hypokalemia, hyperkalemia in the elderly can be caused by excessive potassium intake, spironolactone or triamterene diuretic therapy, severe acidosis, and oliguria.

Hypocalcemia. In addition to its effects on the bones, hypocalcemia can irritate the heart muscle.

Hypercalcemia. Excessive intake of calcium supplements may be among the factors that lead to hypercalcemia and subsequently to a decrease in cardiac muscle strength and tone.

Overhydration, dehydration. Changes in body fluids and the subsequent changes in electrolyte concentrations can reduce cardiac function.

Vagal stimulation. Straining to have a bowel movement (Valsalva's maneuver) is one cause of vagal stimulation that can induce bradycardia and reduce cardiac output.

Medications. Any drug that has the potential to alter heart rate, blood pressure, or fluid balance can adversely alter cardiac output.

Anemia. The elderly have a higher prevalence of anemia-producing conditions, such as blood loss, chronic liver disease, antibiotic therapy, leukemia, metastatic cancer, and deficiencies of iron, vitamin B_{12}, folic acid, and vitamin C. Anemia has a profound effect on the cardiovascular system and can decrease output.

Defining Characteristics
Increased pulse rate

Decreased blood pressure

Edema

Cyanosis

Fatigue, activity intolerance

Restlessness, apprehension

Scanty or no urine output

Dysrhythmia

Pain

Definition: A negative or uncomfortable feeling in response to physical or psychological stimuli.

Causative or Contributing Factors

Arthritis. Approximately one-half of the elderly population has arthritis. This condition can cause even the most basic movements to be painful.

Injury. The poor coordination, vision, and mobility of many elderly individuals increases their risk of falls, burns, and other potentially painful injuries.

Diseases. Cardiovascular, respiratory, gastrointestinal, musculoskeletal, neurological, and renal disease, as well as cancer, are more prevalent among the elderly.

Poor positioning. Dependent and frail elderly may be placed in uncomfortable positions or not be able to move independently from a painful position. Pain is among the adverse consequences.

Defining Characteristics

Facial grimaces

Protecting or favoring specific body part

Retracting from touch

Crying, groaning, moaning

Lack of interest in activities of daily living

Increased pulse, respirations, blood pressure

Diaphoresis

Dilated pupils

Impaired Verbal Communication

Definition: A limitation in the ability to receive or understand speech, or correctly select, form, or express oneself through spoken words.

Causative or Contributing Factors

Language barrier. Many of today's elderly are first- or second-generation immigrants for whom English is a foreign language. Even if there is an ability to communicate in English, full comprehension and expression can be limited.

Aphasia. Although infections, trauma, and tumors can cause aphasia, the most common cause in the elderly is a cerebrovascular accident. Most patients will show both an expressive and receptive aphasia.

Breathing impairments. Severe respiratory disease can cause normal speech to be exerting and cause shortness of breath. Speech may be avoided as a consequence.

Hearing deficit. A high-frequency hearing loss, presbycusis, affects many older adults and can distort the sound of normal speech.

Medications. Some drugs, particularly those that depress CNS function, can cause the reception and expression of speech to be altered.

Altered mental status. Acute confusional states, dementias, depressions, and other changes in mental state can interfere with communication.

Defining Characteristics

Withdrawal

Slurring

Delayed responses

Extended time to select or form words

Failure to understand conversation

Weak voice tone

No speech

Shortness of breath, wheezing

Ineffective Individual Coping

Definition: A limitation in the ability to manage stress.

Causative or Contributing Factors

Health problems. The effects of changes in body function associated with chronic illnesses can weaken the ability to manage stress.

Reduced finances. Adequate economic resources afford one a sense of security and power. For many persons, income is reduced in old age, limiting the ability to control stressors.

Relocation. In late life, when physical and emotional reserves are decreasing, the ability to adapt to a new environment or life-style can be a major challenge.

Ageism. Prejudicial treatment by others can be a source of uncontrollable stress for the elderly.

Defining Characteristics

Reduced ability to engage in self-care activities

Increased or inappropriate use of defense mechanism

Increased injuries

Confusion

Poor judgment and decision-making ability

Expressed hopelessness and helplessness

Diversional Activity Deficit

Definition: An insufficient quantity or quality of stimulating, recreational, or other types of pleasurable activities.

Causative or Contributing Factors

Functional impairment. Sensory deficits, pain, impaired mobility, and other health problems may limit the activities in which the elderly may engage.

Depression. A variety of physical, emotional, and socioeconomic factors can create a mood that is not conducive to seeking diversional activities.

Institutionalization. Long-term hospitalization or nursing home placement can prohibit patients from engaging in favorite diversions.

Retirement. Often, one's interests are affiliated with one's job, for example, company bowling leagues or dances. The loss of the work role can be an obstacle to continued participation in these functions.

Defining Characteristics
Restlessness

Irritability

Fatigue

Increase or decrease in weight

Complaining

Expressions of boredom

Altered Family Processes

Definition: A disruption to the family unit's usual roles and functions.

Causative or Contributing Factors
Illness. The effects of a family member's illness on the entire family unit can be devastating in terms of altered roles and functions. The high prevalence of disease and disability with advancing years creates a considerable risk to aging families in their ability to function effectively.

Death. Coping with and readjusting to the loss of a family member or significant other can create disruption in normal family processes.

Relocation. Family stress can arise from an elderly relative moving in with family members or being institutionalized.

Retirement. The usual household routines and life-style may be altered when a family member retires (e.g., adjusting to reduced income, invading the territory of the homemaker-spouse).

Conflict. Family members may have different positions concerning decisions that must be made. Should an ill relative live with a child or be institutionalized? Should a spouse divorce her husband who has a dementia in order to protect assets? How aggressive should treatment measures be for a terminally ill relative?

Defining Characteristics
Arguing among family members

Poor or ineffective communication

Unmet physical, emotional, or spiritual needs of family members

Inability to maintain normal patterns of living

Fear

Definition: A feeling resulting from the belief that there will be negative consequences from a real or perceived threat.

Causative or Contributing Factors

Change in body structure or function. Poor vision, reduced hearing, slower movements, and decreased strength often accompany aging and can give rise to concern over the inability to protect oneself adequately.

Chronic illness. There may be legitimate fear concerning the potential discomfort, disability, dependency, and death that chronic diseases can bring.

Crime. Living in a high-crime district or recognizing one's own vulnerability to crime can create a sense of fear.

Defining Characteristics

Feeling of powerlessness, lack of control

Suspiciousness

Reluctance to be alone

Increased use of defense mechanisms

Increased pulse, respirations, blood pressure

Diaphoresis

Fluid Volume Deficit

Definition: Insufficient fluid to meet the body's requirements for fluid.

Causative or Contributing Factors

Age-related changes. With age there is a reduction in total body fluids; consequently, the lower fluid reserve makes it harder to withstand any fluid loss or reduction in intake. Dehydration occurs more easily. There also is a reduced sensation of thirst that can threaten the ability of older adults to protect themselves from dehydration.

Excess fluid loss. Vomiting, diarrhea, excessive perspiration, continuous nasogastric suctioning, diuretic therapy, dialysis, uncontrolled diabetes, and excessive wound drainage are among the factors that can cause a negative fluid balance.

Insufficient fluid intake. The elderly may not consume enough fluid because they may be unable to obtain a drink independently; thirst sensation may be decreased; motivation to drink may be reduced (e.g., owing to depression); there may be pain associated with drinking; they may be fatigued; they may choose to restrict fluid intake to control urinary frequency; and there may be NPO restrictions.

Defining Characteristics

Fluid output exceeding intake

Decreased volume and increased concentration of urine

Weight loss

Increased pulse, body temperature

Poorer skin turgor

Dry skin, mucous membranes, eyes

Confusion

Weakness, lethargy

Thirst

Nausea

Fluid Volume Excess

Definition: An excess of fluid in relation to the body's requirement.

Causative or Contributing Factors

Age-related changes. Decreased cardiac output, poor circulation to extremities, and reduced renal function can cause the circulation of fluids to be impaired.

Immobility. Insufficient movement can cause venostasis.

Health problems. The aged are at greater risk of congestive failure, myocardial infarction, cirrhosis, renal failure, cancer, and other pathologies that cause fluid retention.

Defining Characteristics

Fluid intake exceeds output

Edema

Weight gain

Increased blood pressure

Grieving

Definition: A reaction to a real or perceived loss of person, object, role, or function characterized by extreme sadness and a disruption of daily life or lack of interest in daily life.

Causative or Contributing Factors

Age-related changes. Decline in body function and the structural changes experienced with aging are constant reminders to the elderly that they are not able to function or look as they once did.

Health problems. Changes in life-style and restrictions that accompany many chronic diseases often result in a loss of role, function, or independence.

Death of significant other. With each advancing decade the risk of losing loved ones increases.

Retirement. A profound emotional emptiness can accompany the loss of role, identity, relationships, and activities when the work role is forfeited.

Relocation. Leaving a familiar environment, the source of fond memories, can be difficult. This problem can be compounded if the elderly move from a situation of independence to one in which they are dependent or a member of someone else's household.

Terminal illness. The elderly more than any other age group confront the reality that life will soon be ended—perhaps the greatest loss a human being must face.

Changes. Changes in the status of a caregiver, income, friendships, and responsibilities are among the factors that can precipitate grief as the older adult anticipates such personal losses.

Defining Characteristics
Anticipated, perceived, or actual loss

Sadness, crying, hopelessness

Increased use of defense mechanisms

Change in sleep pattern

Poor appetite

Lack of interest in grooming, social activities

Altered Health Maintenance

Definition: A limitation in the ability to take actions to promote wellness and prevent illness.

Causative or Contributing Factors
Age-related changes. Greater ease of skin breakdown, reduced respiratory activity, slower peristalsis, and delayed excretion of drugs are among the outcomes of the aging process. These changes demand special effort to prevent disruptions to health.

Lack of knowledge. The elderly may not understand how to use medications properly or to distinguish between pathology and normal outcomes of age.

Poor self-concept. Persons who have negative self-images may not be motivated to take positive actions in their own behalf.

Religious or cultural beliefs. Restrictions or special practices (e.g., fasting, refusing medical treatment, using home remedies) may be contrary to good health practices.

Altered mental status. The individual with a cognitive deficit may not have the ability to engage in good self-care practices. The paranoid individual's suspicions may promote unsound health practices, while the depressed person may not be motivated to sustain a healthy life.

Insufficient income. Annual ophthalamologic, audiometric, gynecologic, and other preventive health care examinations may seem like luxuries when one barely has the funds to pay monthly utility bills. Likewise, fresh fruits and vegetables and proteins may be less affordable than filling carbohydrates.

Caregiving responsibilities. Caregivers who invest considerable physical, emotional, and socioeconomic resources on dependents may have little left to invest in their own health practices.

Defining Characteristics
Poor hygiene and grooming

Frequent infections

Frequent injuries

Excess or low body weight

Bowel irregularity

Fatigue, malaise, weakness

Impaired thinking or behavior

Impaired Home Maintenance Management

Definition: A limitation in the ability to keep one's home environment safe and sanitary.

Causative or Contributing Factors
Age-related changes. The ability to maintain a home and prevent and recognize safety hazards can be hampered by visual and hearing deficits, reduced range of joint motion, slower response and reaction time, and other changes associated with the aging process.

Health problems. The fatigue, dizziness, mobility limitations, shortness of breath, and other effects of illness can prevent individuals from maintaining a safe home environment.

Altered mental status. Persons without the cognitive ability to know or engage in functions that keep their environments safe are at risk. Depressed individuals may lack the motivation or energy to maintain their households.

Insufficient funds. With reduced income in retirement the elderly may put home maintenance expenditures low on their priority list.

Defining Characteristics
Poor condition of home environment
    Insects, rodents
    Odors

Accumulated garbage
Lack of cleanliness
Limited or no support system

Potential for Injury

Definition: A limitation in the ability to protect oneself from harm.

Causative or Contributing Factors

Age-related changes. The aging process may result in less acute pain and pressure sensations, decreased olfactory ability, poor vision, hearing deficits, slower reactions, and other outcomes that can promote or interfere with one's ability to prevent injury.

Health problems. Various diseases can cause fatigue, edema, dizziness, shortness of breath, reduced mobility, pain, or alterations in mental status, thereby increasing the risk of injury.

Mobility aids. Improperly fitted or incorrectly used walkers, canes, crutches, and wheelchairs can lead to falls and other injuries.

Unsafe use of medications. The large number of drugs used by the elderly causes considerable risk. Problems can result from using outdated drugs, administering drugs incorrectly, self-medicating in an unsound manner, combining drugs with foods or other drugs with which they interact, and not recognizing adverse reactions.

Unsafe environment. Slippery surfaces, unsafe wiring, excessively hot water temperatures, malfunctioning appliances, and poor lighting are among the factors that can increase the elderly's risk of accidents.

Altered mental status. Persons with dementias may not have the ability to recognize dangers or protect themselves from hazards. Depressed persons risk injury through suicide attempts.

Defining Characteristics

Frequent falls, accidents

Unsafe environment

Sensory deficits

Weakness, immobility

Altered mental status

Knowledge Deficit

Definition: A limitation in knowledge or skill required to take actions to promote and maintain health or care for health problems.

Causative or Contributing Factors

Misunderstanding of age-related changes. Misinformed health care providers as well as the aged themselves may interpret normal age-related changes (e.g., some glycosuria, blood pressure increases) to mean absolute pathology in need of intervention, while abnormalities (e.g., sexual dysfunction, confusion, incontinence) may be accepted as normal.

Therapeutic demands. There may be inadequate knowledge concerning the special diets, medications, treatments, and restrictions that accompany health problems.

Lack of motivation. Persons who are depressed or have a pattern of being unmotivated may not be interested in obtaining knowledge that can aid them in maintaining health.

Barriers to learning. Anxiety, sensory deficits, and poor command of the English language are among the variables that can have an impact on the learning process.

Defining Characteristics
Verbalized or displayed lack of knowledge or skill

Noncompliance

Impaired Physical Mobility

Definition: A limitation in the ability for independent physical movement.

Causative or Contributing Factors
Age-related changes. With age, muscles atrophy and lose agility and strength, the cartilage between joints decreases and interferes with full range of motion, and vision becomes poorer, all potentially limiting movement.

Health problems. Reduced mobility can be caused by many of the diseases that are highly prevalent in late life including arthritis, congestive heart failure, cerebrovascular accident, hypertension, and Parkinson's disease.

Bedrest, inactivity. Not only are many risks associated with immobility increased when one is in an inactive state, but the ability to resume full activity can be impaired by the potential weakness, stiff joints, and other consequences of inactivity.

Mobility aids. Although intended to improve mobility, improperly used walkers, canes, wheelchairs, and crutches can cause problems that can further limit mobility.

Defining Characteristics
Reduced ability to move, transfer, walk

Weakness

Presence of casts, splints, restraints

Poor coordination

Noncompliance

Definition: Lack of adherence to health promotion or maintenance activities, or therapeutic plan of care.

Causative or Contributing Factors

Illness-imposed limitations. The ability to follow special protocol or engage in specific self-care practices can be affected by weakness, pain, altered mental status, or other consequences of illness.

Attitude toward health professional. The patient may dislike the health care professional and reject the advice given by that person, or have limited faith in the advice given.

Insufficient funds. Older adults with limited funds may try to stretch their dollars by not returning for follow-up clinic visits, not refilling prescriptions, or discontinuing health care services. It is not unusual for persons to create other reasons for their noncompliant behavior rather than confess to having financial problems.

Family circumstances. The burdens of being a caregiver to someone else, a family crisis, or pressure from family members to reject the plan of care can cause patients to be noncompliant.

Choice. A conflict in values between what the patient desires and what the professional feels is best may result in noncompliant behavior.

Altered mental status. Persons who are too confused to retain or follow directions, or unmotivated because of depression may not adhere to the plan of care.

Defining Characteristics

Lack of adherence to good health practices or plan of care

Expressed refusal to follow advised practices or activities

Altered Nutrition: Less Than Body Requirements

Definition: Insufficient intake of nutrients to meet body's requirements.

Causative or Contributing Factors

Age-related changes. Reduced saliva production and taste sensations for salty and sweet flavors, slower esophageal motility and gastric emptying, less secretion of digestive juices, fewer hunger contractions, and decreased peristalsis are changes experienced by many older persons that contribute to poor appetite, indigestion, a sense of fullness, and constipation—all of which threaten to reduce food intake.

Health problems. Anorexia, nausea, vomiting, and fatigue accompany many of the illnesses experienced by the aged.

Dentures. Missing or poorly fitting dentures can restrict the foods the elderly are able to ingest.

Medications. The side effects of drugs (e.g., anorexia, nausea, confusion, increased excretion, or blocked absorption of nutrients) can affect nutritional status.

Insufficient funds. To manage within the constraints of a limited budget the elderly may reduce the quantity or quality of food eaten.

Deficits in obtaining, preparing food. No transportation to the grocery store, insufficient energy to shop for and carry groceries, inadequate kitchen facilities, and lack of cooking skill are among the variables affecting food intake.

Social isolation. The motivation to prepare a nutritious meal and eat properly can be limited if one is alone.

Altered mental status. Demented persons may not recognize the need to eat or know the proper foods to consume. Appetite can be hampered by depression and anxiety. A paranoid individual may ingest insufficient nutrients because of suspicions concerning the food.

Defining Characteristics
Confusion

Weight loss

Weakness

Decreased serum albumin, transferrin, and lymphocytes

Altered Nutrition: More Than Body Requirements

Definition: Nutrient intake in excess of body's requirements.

Causative or Contributing Factors
Age-related changes. Slower metabolism and a less active state reduce caloric needs in late life. Altered taste sensations can cause excess salt and sugar to be ingested.

Ethnic or cultural practices. Food is an important part of life to many persons; most family and social functions involve food intake. Some ethnic diets may be rich in calories and exceed the caloric requirements of older adults. Attempts to alter a lifelong pattern of eating are often met with resistance.

Lack of knowledge. There may be a misunderstanding of the caloric content of various foods or a lack of knowledge of recommended dietary allowances.

Inactivity. Lack of motivation, bedrest, pain, fatigue, and frailty can contribute to a reduced expenditure of calories.

Altered mental status. Persons with dementia may select foods unwisely or not have the ability to control their food intake. Some persons respond to depression and anxiety by overeating.

Defining Characteristics
Weight gain of 10% above ideal weight

Inactivity

Observed poor dietary practices

Altered Oral Mucous Membrane

Definition: An irritation or break in integrity of the oral mucosa.

Causative or Contributing Factors

Age-related changes. There is a greater risk of drier oral mucosa in late life.

Teeth, dentures. Teeth with jagged edges, food accumulations beneath dentures, and poorly fitting dentures can cause irritation and breakdown of the mucosa.

Health problems. Periodontal disease, cancer, diabetes, malnutrition, dehydration, and the effects of cancer therapies can cause infections and irritations of the oral mucosa.

Medications. Irritation and dryness of the oral cavity can be side effects of drugs. Likewise, irritation can result from a tablet or capsule dissolving in the mouth rather than being swallowed.

Poor oral hygiene. Patients may not have the functional ability, mental status, or strength to attend to their oral health care needs independently.

Defining Characteristics

Dry, coated tongue

Leukoplakia

Stomatitis

Oral lesions, tumors, abrasions

Powerlessness

Definition: A real or perceived lack of control over activities that affect one's life.

Causative or Contributing Factors

Age-related losses. Changes in function and appearance, retirement, relocation, death of loved ones, and other losses that are prevalent among the elderly cause them to feel very vulnerable.

Health problems. Restricted mobility, impaired vision, deafness, aphasia, pain, fatigue, and other outcomes of pathologies can cause a sense of powerlessness.

Institutionalization. The ability to control one's schedule, meals, and lifestyle can be severely restricted when one must conform to institutional routines.

Dependency. The loss of functional abilities forces persons to forefeit to caregivers varying degrees of control over their lives.

Insufficient funds. Money can help even the most debilitated individual exercise some control.

Crime. Being robbed, burglarized, or assaulted or knowing that one is highly vulnerable to such crimes intensifies feelings of powerlessness.

Defining Characteristics

Anxiety, anger, depression over inability to control situation or make decisions

Dependence on others for decisions

Ineffective Breathing Pattern

Definition: A limitation in the ability to inhale, exchange, or eliminate gases (O_2, CO_2).

Causative or Contributing Factors

Age-related changes. Changes to the respiratory system occurring with age that can alter respiratory function include reduced elastic recoil of lungs, stretching and loss of alveoli, increased residual volume, reduced cough efficiency, and weaker thoracic and diaphragmatic muscles.

Inactivity, immobility. Decreased lung expansion and exchange of gases occurs when the body is less active.

Cigarette smoking. Smoking has destructive effects to the structure and function of the respiratory system.

Improper use of oxygen. Since the elderly are at high risk for carbon dioxide retention, high levels of oxygen (which in turn produce high levels of carbon dioxide) can cause carbon dioxide narcosis and threaten adequate respirations.

Medications. Many of the drugs widely used by the elderly (e.g., sedatives, analgesics) can depress respiratory activity.

Poor positioning. Full lung expansion can be impaired by a flexion of the trunk that can occur while the patient is in bed or sitting in a chair.

Pain. Fractured ribs, cardiac pain, spinal arthritis, and fear of causing injury or discomfort at an incisional site can cause one to limit chest movement.

Defining Characteristics

Change in depth, rate, or pattern of respirations

Abnormal lung sounds (wheezes, crackles, rhonchi)

Cough

Dyspnea

Orthopnea

Shortness of breath

Asymmetrical chest expansion

Cyanosis

Confusion

Apprehension

Restlessness

Self-care Deficit

Definition: A limitation in the ability to feed, bathe, dress, toilet, ambulate, or transfer.

Causative or Contributing Factors

Health problems. The elderly have a high prevalence of diseases that cause stiff joints, fatigue, dizziness, edema, vision and hearing impairments, and other effects that limit the ability to engage in self-care. The U.S. National Center for Health Statistics (1985) reports that 26% of persons over age 65 have activity limitations due to arthritis and rheumatism, 24.8% due to heart conditions, 11.7% due to hypertension, 5.8% due to impairments of the lower extremity and hip, and 4.6% due to impairments of the back and spine.

Altered mental status. The dementias are notorious for producing self-care deficits. Minor activities of daily living become major obstacles for the affected individuals.

Immobility. The inability to move about one's environment independently or fully creates a need for assistance in meeting the activities of daily living.

Defining Characteristics
Unable or unwilling to bathe, dress, eat, or toilet

Self-esteem Disturbance

Definition: The possession of negative attitudes or feelings about oneself.

Causative or Contributing Factors

Age-related changes. The loss of firm muscle tone; the appearance of lines, wrinkles, and gray hair; the new aches and pains; and a less efficiently functioning body can change the positive image that one formerly held of oneself.

Retirement. The work role is accompanied by an identity, status, and responsibilities that give one a sense of worth. Loss of that role can be traumatic, particularly if there are no new roles or functions to substitute for the lost work role.

Deaths of significant others. The realization of one's own mortality becomes acute when one witnesses increasing numbers of deaths within one's peer group and family.

Health problems. Living with a chronic disease often requires an adjustment to signs and symptoms, life-style limitations, and care activities. These impositions on one's life can cause a negative feeling about oneself.

Dependency. The loss of independence can have profound effects. Having to rely upon others or feeling that one is a burden to others changes self-concept.

Societal attitudes. The elderly may be victimized, scolded for moving too slowly in a fast-paced society, and treated as incompetents just because they are old. They may begin to see themselves as others see them—negatively.

Defining Characteristics

Change in roles or functions

Refusal to care for self, learn care techniques, discuss health problems

Hostility toward well, functional persons

Denial of health problems

Self-destructive behaviors

Grieving

Increased dependency on others

Sensory-Perceptual Alterations

Definition: A disruption in the ability to obtain or interpret visual, auditory, gustatory, olfactory, or tactile sensations.

Causative or Contributing Factors

Age-related sensory changes

Sight. The aging eye experiences farsightedness (presbyopia), altered depth perception, reduced visual field, distortion of low tone colors, lens opacity, and a higher risk of glaucoma.

Hearing. A gradual sensorineural hearing loss (presbycusis) occurs with age, first affecting the high-frequency sounds and then progressing to the middle and low frequencies. The *s, sh, ch, f,* and *ph* sounds become filtered from normal speech.

Taste. There is a reduction in the number of functioning taste buds with age, primarily affecting the receptors for sweet and salty flavors.

Smell. Although this area has not received significant research attention, there is believed to be a less acute sense of smell with age.

Touch. There is a reduction in the perception of pressure, contributing to a higher risk of skin breakdown; older persons do not sense the need to change positions. Pain sensations are altered, and it may take more time for the elderly to sense and react to extremes in temperatures; they may burn themselves as a result.

Neurological disease. Cerebrovascular accidents and neuropathies diminish sensory function.

Impaired homeostasis. Fluid and electrolyte disturbances and reduced oxygenation to tissues can reduce the reception of sensory input.

Medications. Psychotropics and sedatives are among the drugs that can dull sensations or cause hallucinations or other sensory distortions.

Hospitalization. The isolation, disruption to normal routine, and 24-hour stimulation that can occur during hospitalization can cause serious misperceptions of the environment.

Stress. Feeling overwhelmed in a new environment, confronting a crisis, and having to adapt to new self-care behavior are among the stressors that can contribute to sensory overload or a distortion of incoming sensory stimuli.

Defining Characteristics
Confusion

Disorientation

Suspiciousness

Restlessness

Anxiety

Fear

Misperceptions

Sexual Dysfunction

Definition: A limitation in the ability to engage in or derive satisfaction from sexual activity.

Causative or Contributing Factors
Age-related change. With age, men find it necessary to have more direct physical stimulation to achieve an erection and will be less likely to regain an erection following intercourse. An aging woman's drier, more delicate vaginal canal can make penile penetration more difficult. For both sexes, changes in general body appearance may cause a negative self-concept that can interfere with sexual function.

Impotence. A variety of factors affect a man's ability to achieve or sustain an erection, including alcohol, drugs (e.g., antidepressants, antihypertensives, anticholinergics, sedatives, tranquilizers), diabetes, severe anemia, arteriosclerosis, prostatectomy, and psychological factors (e.g., retirement, financial problems).

Effects of health problems. Arthritic pain, vaginal infections, and shortness of breath can make sexual activity undesirable or uncomfortable.

Fear of aggravating health problems. After a myocardial infarction there may be fear that sexual activity will tax the heart and cause another attack. There may be concern that intercourse will harm a repaired hip fracture.

Partner. The partner may be uninterested or unwilling to engage in sexual activity or may have physical or mental limitations that alter his or her sexual appeal or function.

Lack of partner. Most older women are widowed and of a generation that adhered to strict standards regarding sex without marriage; therefore, they may not have a partner for their sexual activity. Even if a partner exists, that person may be institutionalized or not available.

Lack of privacy. In a hospital or nursing home setting the opportunities for visiting uninterrupted may be limited, and if they do exist there can be concern as to "what others may think." Likewise, the elderly who live with family members may not be afforded privacy or may feel embarrassed to have sexual activity.

Misconceptions. Aging persons may believe that sexual function should cease in old age or that normally they should not expect to be sexually functional.

Medications. In addition to the effects of impotence, medications can cause drowsiness, dizziness, and other problems that interfere with sexual interest or activity.

Defining Characteristics
Lack of sexual interest or activity

Dissatisfaction with sexual activity

Disturbance in relationship with sexual partner

Impaired Skin Integrity

Definition: A break in the integrity of the skin.

Causative or Contributing Factors
Age-related changes. The aging process shows its effects by causing the skin to become drier and thinner. This increased fragility increases the ease of skin breakdown. Likewise, the reduced ability to sense pressure may contribute to a greater risk of decubitus ulcers (bedsores).

Health problems. Anemia, diabetes, cirrhosis, cardiovascular disease, obesity, and skin infections are among the disorders that make the skin more susceptible to injury.

Immobility. Reduced activity imposed by physical or mental illnesses, medications, pain, or restraints can threaten adequate circulation to the tissues.

Incontinence. Urine and feces have a very irritating effect on the skin.

Defining Characteristics
Pruritus

Lesion

Erythema

Ulcer

Incision

Fistula

Burn

Blister

Stoma

Sleep Pattern Disturbance

Definition: A limitation in the ability to obtain sufficient sleep to meet the body's requirements.

Causative or Contributing Factors

Age-related changes. Nocturia, muscle cramps, and an increased ease of being awakened contribute to sleep interruptions in late life.

Misconceptions about sleep needs. Although rest periods throughout the day are beneficial to the elderly, there is less need for nighttime sleep: five to seven hours should be adequate for most older adults. The older person who naps on the sofa after dinner may have obtained several hours of sleep before going to bed and, consequently, may have met his or her full quota of sleep by 2 or 3 A.M. If this situation is not understood, the elderly person or a caregiver may have concern that insomnia exists and inappropriately administer a sedative. Since drugs take longer to filter from the older adult's body, the effects of the sedative can persist throughout the morning and early afternoon; a reversal in the normal sleep cycle can occur.

Depression. Insomnia or excessive sleeping may indicate a depressed state.

Health problems. The limitations, discomfort, manifestations, and anxiety associated with an illness can interfere with sleep.

Environment. It may be difficult for persons to sleep comfortably in a new environment. In health care settings, the patient can be awakened by noise, lights, or the need for interventions.

Medications. Excess sleeping can be caused by tranquilizers, antidepressants, and antihypertensives. Sleep can be interrupted by the effects of diuretics and laxatives. There may be a need to awaken to take an antibiotic or other medications during the night.

Inactivity. The lack of exercise can hamper sleep.

Stress. Financial worries, health problems, retirement, caregiving responsibilities, and a variety of other concerns can threaten sleep.

Defining Characteristics

Difficulty falling asleep

Sleep easily disrupted

Fatigue upon awakening

Mood or behavior changes

Use of alcohol or medications to induce sleep

Social Isolation

Definition: An inability to have human contact.

Causative or Contributing Factors

Mobility problems. Paralysis, arthritis, and other difficulties in independent mobility can limit one's environment.

Sensory deficits. People may have trouble traveling to social contacts when they have visual or hearing problems. Even if they can reach these situations, their ability to communicate effectively can be limited.

Health problems. The effects of illnesses can cause the elderly to lack the energy, functional capacity, or self-concept to socialize.

Insufficient funds. A limited budget can prevent older adults from going to the movies, shopping, golfing, or taking trips with others. Some persons may avoid group participation altogether rather than be embarrassed by admitting to their financial limitations.

Loss of social contacts. The elderly often have older friends and relatives who may be too ill to socialize. If institutionalized or relocated themselves, the elderly may lose touch with friends and social activities.

Attitudes of others. Younger friends and family members may not want to be associated with an older person, may be uninterested in the things that interest a senior, or may be uncomfortable with the physical or mental deficits of the elderly individual. People may have stereotypical views that certain social functions are specific to certain age groups (e.g., dancing for the young, knitting for the old).

Defining Characteristics
Expressed feelings of being alone, wanting more social contact

Depression

Apathy

Anxiety

Irritability

Decreased physical or mental function

Excess or insufficient sleep

Excess or insufficient food intake

Spiritual Distress

Definition: A limitation in the ability to adhere to beliefs and practices consistent with one's religious views or value system.

Causative or Contributing Factors
Health problems. The effects and care requirements of illnesses can interfere with the practice of religious rituals or attendance at religious services.

Hospitalization, institutionalization. Inaccessibility to one's religious organization, restrictions imposed by the plan of care, confinement, isolation, and embarrassment at practicing spiritual rituals in front of others can create barriers to fulfilling religious needs.

Attitudes of others. There may be conflict between the patient's beliefs and what others see as good or reasonable. The patient, for example, may refuse medication that a physician feels would correct the problem, or the family may oppose the patient's choosing prayer with a spiritual healer over surgical intervention.

Defining Characteristics
Threat to or feeling of uncertainty about belief system

Alterations in Thought Processes

Definition: A limitation in memory, judgment, reasoning, problem solving, orientation, calculation, and comprehension capabilities.

Causative or Contributing Factors
Disruption to homeostasis. Alterations in body chemistry can alter a person's mental state. Confusion is often an early clue to a variety of physiological disorders in the elderly.

Mood disorders. Depression, anxiety, and other mood changes can threaten cognitive function.

Medications. Drugs commonly consumed by the elderly (e.g., antihypertensives, hypoglycemic agents, sedatives) can alter mental functioning.

New environment. Admission to a health care facility or relocation to a new apartment can require an overwhelming adjustment by the elderly person to new objects and routines, forfeiture of special possessions or pets, and the loss of control.

Hospitalization. Particularly in critical care settings and isolation rooms it may be easy to lose orientation to time or experience sleep disruptions that can alter cognitive function.

Mental illness. Dementias, schizophrenias, and other psychiatric disorders disrupt normal mental function.

Crisis, trauma. The sudden death of a family member, an unexpected increase in expenses, or being burglarized are some of the situations that can present an overwhelming emotional burden to the elderly and affect cognitive function.

Defining Characteristics
Confusion

Disorientation

Poor memory

Misperception of environment

Misidentification of people

Short attention span

Poor judgment

Altered Tissue Perfusion

Definition: Insufficient capillary circulation to meet cellular requirements for nutrients and the exchange of O_2 and CO_2.

Causative or Contributing Factors

Age-related changes. The aging process can result in reduced cardiac output, poor peripheral circulation, orthostatic hypotension, and capillary fragility.

Health problems. Circulation can be impaired by a variety of conditions that are highly prevalent in advanced age, such as congestive heart failure, angina, pulmonary edema, arteriosclerosis, cerebrovascular accident, myocardial infarction, hypertension and hypotension, hyperglycemia and hypoglycemia, anemia, renal failure, and cancer.

Medications. Any drug that can affect blood pressure or fluid and electrolyte balance can alter circulation.

Immobility, inactivity. Poor circulation results from insufficient exercise or relief of pressure.

Defining Characteristics

Tachycardia

Tachypnea

Confusion

Altered level of consciousness

Decreased urinary output

Edema

Cool, pale skin

Decreased motor and sensory function

Altered Patterns of Urinary Elimination

Definition: A change in the frequency, quantity, or control of urinary elimination.

Causative or Contributing Factors

Age-related changes. Weaker bladder muscles can cause urinary retention; decreased bladder capacity can cause urinary frequency and nocturia.

Urinary tract disorders. Urinary tract infections, calculi, strictures, bladder-neck contractures, and other abnormalities can alter voiding patterns.

Health problems. Urinary elimination can be affected by diabetes, cerebrovascular accident, prostatic hypertrophy, vaginitis, obesity, dehydration, fecal impaction, and altered mental status.

Medications. Diuretics, antihistamines, and anticholinergics are among the drugs affecting urinary elimination.

Altered mental status. The confused individual may not recognize cues that voiding is necessary.

Stress. Anxiety and stress can increase urinary frequency.

Indwelling catheters. Catheterization can be devastating because of the significant risk of infection that accompanies it, as well as the loss of muscle tone that occurs over the long run.

Toileting deficit. The inability to toilet independently or to communicate one's needs can be a cause of unnecessary incontinence.

Defining Characteristics
Increased frequency of voiding

Incontinence

Anuria

Hesitancy

Dribbling

Potential for Violence

Definition: Aggressive behavior that threatens harm to oneself or others.

Causative or Contributing Factors
Medications. Behavioral problems can be manifestations of adverse drug reactions.

Dementia. The lack of behavioral control and the use of violent behavior as a response to overwhelming stimuli are not uncommon with brain disease.

Altered cerebral function. Impaired oxygenation of cerebral tissue, hormonal or biochemical imbalances, or trauma can alter brain function and behavior.

Alcohol abuse. Intoxication can cause an elderly person to exhibit violent or uncontrolled behavior.

Suicide. Suicidal behavior encompasses overt or covert hazardous acts to oneself.

Reactions to stress, fear. Violence may be a response to unique situations, such as being restrained or forced to do something contrary to one's wishes.

Defining Characteristics
Expressed or demonstrated hostility, aggression

Agitation

Anxiety

Fear

Delusions, hallucinations

Paranoia

With the preceding discussion serving as a foundation, the following case example will demonstrate how problems and needs identified during the assessment process can be expressed as nursing diagnoses.

CASE EXAMPLE

Seventy-six-year-old Mrs. C. is visiting the assessment clinic of the senior center for the first time, accompanied by her 77-year-old husband. She is of Italian descent with a heavy accent, although she speaks English fluently. Her husband speaks very little English and relies on Mrs. C. for translation.

Mrs. C. and her husband live in the same three-story, five-bedroom home they purchased nearly 50 years ago. The house requires considerable upkeep. Although Mr. C. is not well, he refuses to hire assistance in maintaining the property. Mrs. C. states, "He will probably kill himself trying to keep that old place up." She admits that the neighborhood is changing for the worse, and that she worries frequently about her home being burglarized or vandalized. Although she and her husband no longer need the space—they live primarily on the first floor—they are comfortable in their home and want to preserve the "family home" for their children and grandchildren.

Both Mr. and Mrs. C. receive social security checks; in addition, Mr. C. has a small pension from the factory in which he worked. They have $12,000 in savings. Their monthly income exceeds their expenses by $200, and they do not have to use their savings unless a major repair to their home is required.

Mrs. C. has three living children: a daughter, 57, and two sons, 54 and 52. All are married and live in other states; they telephone their parents weekly and visit at most holidays. Although Mrs. C. states that her children are good to her, she emphasizes that she would never want to live with any of them. Mrs. C.'s youngest child died four years ago of cancer, and Mrs. C. tearily describes missing her deeply. Mrs. C. has insomnia, is not interested in activities, and cries frequently about her dead daughter; she talks about her so much that her family becomes annoyed.

Mrs. C. has a limited social world. She has never belonged to clubs, and only has an occasional visitor to her home. Her husband no longer drives, and she has never learned how; consequently, she is not able to attend church regularly, about which she expresses regret. She does try to pray at home daily, but does not feel she is adequately fulfilling her religious obligations.

PHYSICAL EXAM

Mrs. C. is prepared for the physical examination. Her height is 5'2"; she claims to have been 5'3" in younger years. She admits her weight has gradually increased over the past several years; she now weighs 165 pounds.

Physical examination revealed the following:

Head and Scalp. *Her gray hair is clean and well-groomed. There are no breaks or abnormalities in the scalp.*

Face. *Her facial skin is extremely dry and wrinkled; she claims to have always spent a great deal of time in the sun. A ½" scar is present under the exterior edge of her right eyebrow; she says it is from a childhood injury.*

On the chin is a raised, waxy-looking nodular lesion. Mrs. C. reports she stopped using makeup several years ago, commenting that she is "no longer a pretty lady, so why bother?"

Eyes. *There is no ptosis, unusual tearing, or discharge; the sclera are white. She complains of occasionally seeing spots before her eyes. With eyeglasses she is able to read the small print of a newspaper. The visual field in her left eye is decreased. Her pupils constrict to light.*

Ears. *Mrs. C. complains of itching in her ears; otoscopic inspection reveals large amounts of cerumen bilaterally. She states she sometimes has trouble hearing but is able to hear adequately during the examination. The Rinne test reveals that bone sound is superior to air sound in her left ear.*

Nose. *There is no nasal obstruction or deviation. She is able to differentiate various odors.*

Mouth and Throat. *Mrs. C. says she has not seen a dentist for more than 10 years. She has complete upper and lower dentures, the same set for the past 12 years. The lower dentures fit poorly, and Mrs. C. sometimes removes them while she eats. The last three teeth on the left side of her upper dentures are chipped, causing friction against the oral mucosa. Further examination reveals crepitus of the jaw, a red, smooth tongue, decreased sensitivity to sweet flavors, and a good rise of the soft palate. There are no lesions or unusual odors of the mouth.*

Respiratory Exam. *Respirations occur at a rate of 18 per minute. Shallow breathing is present, with reduced breath sounds bilaterally. Mrs. C. claims to awaken at night with dyspnea and wheezing. Sputum is clear, and Mrs. C. denies having a cough. She says she received pneumonia and influenza vaccines last year.*

Cardiovascular Exam. *The heart rate is 86 per minute with no apical-radial difference. Pulses are palpable and equal at all sites except the left pedal pulse, which is weaker than the right. Blood pressure is 180/80 lying, 180/80 sitting, 170/70 standing. Mrs. C. takes 1,000 mg methyldopa daily and 500 mg hydrochlorothiazide daily; she denies knowing that hydrochlorothiazide is a diuretic. The veins in both legs are tortuous. Mrs. C. complains that her legs ache when she walks more than several blocks or stands more than one hour. The skin temperature in her left lower extremity is cooler than in her right. There is a purple-bronze discoloration near her left ankle; she denies having been injured and does not know when the discoloration appeared.*

Breasts. *The breasts are large and pendulous; there is minor excoriation under both. Mrs. C. does not examine her own breasts, nor does she know the procedure for doing so. A firm mass is palpated in the upper right quadrant of her right breast; there is no pain, skin changes, or nipple discharge.*

Gastrointestinal System. *Mrs. C. reports her typical daily diet to be as follows:*

Morning

    6:00   *Coffee and Danish*
    7:30   *Two fried eggs, bacon or sausage, two slices of toast, juice*
   10:00   *Coffee, one or two cookies*

Afternoon

   12:00   *Sandwich, soda*
    2:00   *Tea or soda, three or four peanut butter crackers*

Evening

    5:00   *Beef or chicken, pasta with tomato sauce, green vegetable, roll with
             butter, tea or soda, ice cream or pie*
    8:00   *Pretzels, cheese crackers or nuts, soda*
   10:00   *Milk (one glass)*

May awaken during the night and drink a glass of milk with several cookies.

Mrs. C. complains of indigestion, regurgitation, and frequent belching; she takes antacid tablets for symptoms. She has occasional (less than once per month) pain over the sigmoid area, which is relieved by bowel movement. She does not have a daily bowel movement, and uses castor oil daily for what she believes to be constipation. Bowel sounds are normal: there are no palpable masses. Stool is normal.

Genitalia. *Mrs. C. has not had a gynecologic exam for 10+ years. She states she has not been sexually active for more than five years, never found sex pleasurable, and does not miss it. Pubic hair is thin; labia are flat. There is vaginal redness, white discharge, odor, and itching. No masses, tenderness, or bleeding are found.*

Urinary System. *Mrs. C. voids every two hours and twice during the night. Once she feels the urge to void she has difficulty retaining urine and is incontinent if she doesn't void within two to three minutes after the signal. She is incontinent during sleep approximately three times each week and has stress incontinence almost daily. Mrs. C.'s urine appears cloudy and concentrated; a specimen is sent to the lab.*

Extremities and Skin. *Mrs. C.'s fingers are painful; she complains of difficulty moving them in the morning, which improves by afternoon. Hip mobility is restricted. There is hallux valgus of the left foot and corns on all toes. Mrs. C.'s toenails are long and brittle; she claims she has difficulty bending to cut them. Mrs. C. has "age spots" on her forearm.*

OTHER FINDINGS

No dysfunction of cranial nerves is evident. Mrs. C. is oriented to person, place, and time; she denies having hallucinations, delusions, suicidal thoughts, and paranoia. She perceives herself as a good person. Mrs. C. is preoccupied with her daughter's death and feels guilty that she should live to old age while her daughter died young. Throughout the examination she repeatedly mentions how much she misses her daughter.

Mental and Emotional

Oriented to person, place, time

Denies hallucinations, delusions, suicidal thoughts, paranoia

Perceives herself as good person

Preoccupied with daughter's death; feels guilty that she should live to old age while her daughter died young; repeatedly mentions how much she misses daughter

From the assessed data the following nursing diagnoses can be derived. These nursing diagnoses have been prioritized, recognizing that there may be different opinions as to how various nurses view the significance of various problems presented. In some instances, several diagnostic titles can be associated with one problem or need; examples of these are demonstrated using a diagonal slash mark (/) to separate the various diagnostic titles stemming from the same problem or need.

Problem or Need Identified	Expressed as Nursing Diagnosis
Palpable breast mass	*Anxiety related to unknown etiology of mass*
Excoriation beneath breasts	*Pain/potential for infection/impaired skin integrity related to excoriation*
Shallow respirations, decreased breath sounds	*Ineffective breathing pattern related to reduced depth of respirations*
	Impaired physical mobility related to shallow respirations
Night dyspnea and wheezing	*Activity-intolerance-related sleep disruption secondary to respiratory symptoms*
	Possible decreased cardiac output related to symptoms of congestive heart failure
Incontinence	*Activity intolerance/anxiety/potential for injury/potential for infection/impaired skin integrity/sleep pattern disturbance/social isolation/altered pattern of urinary elimination related to incontinence*
	Knowledge deficit related to accepting incontinence as normal for age
Spots before eyes; decreased visual field; use of eyeglasses	*Sensory-perceptual alteration/potential for injury related to vision problems*
Red, smooth tongue	*Altered oral mucous membrane related to irritated tongue*

Problem or Need Identified	Expressed as Nursing Diagnosis
Misinformation concerning actions of antihypertensives	*Knowledge deficit/potential for injury related to medication misinformation*
Symptoms of hiatal hernia and diverticulosis	*Pain /potential altered nutrition: less than body requirements, related to gastrointestinal symptoms*
Nodular lesion (possible basal cell epithelioma)	*Impaired skin integrity related to lesion*
	Possible anxiety related to unknown diagnosis of lesion
Unresolved grief associated with daughter's death	*Dysfunctional grieving/ineffective individual coping related to maladjustment to daughter's death*
	Sleep pattern disturbance related to unresolved grief
	Potential for altered thought processes related to unresolved grief
Hallux valgus, corns, long toenails	*Activity intolerance/pain/possible impaired home maintenance management/potential for infection/potential for injury/impaired physical mobility/potential self-esteem disturbance potential social isolation related to hallux valgus, corns, long toenails*
Symptoms of vaginitis	*Pain/potential impaired skin integrity related to vaginal irritation, itching, and discharge*
No GYN exam for 10+ years	*Knowledge deficit related to need for continued GYN exam*
Poor fit and condition of dentures	*Pain/potential altered oral mucous membrane related to poor condition of dentures*
12 + years since last dental exam	*Altered health maintenance related to lack of regular dental exam (secondary to knowledge deficit? noncompliance?)*
Varicose veins	*Activity intolerance/pain/possible impaired home maintenance management/possible impaired physical mobility/potential for injury/altered tissue perfusion related to effects of varicosities*

Problem or Need Identified	**Expressed as Nursing Diagnosis**
Leg pain with exercise	*Activity intolerance/pain/potential impaired home maintenance management/impaired physical mobility/social isolation related to leg pain*
Cerumen in both ears	*Pain/sensory-perceptual alteration related to cerumen accumulation*
Rinne test: bone sound superior to air	*Sensory-perceptual alteration related to possible conductive hearing loss*
Poor dietary habits	*Altered nutrition: more than body requirements related to high caloric and carbohydrate intake*
	Altered nutrition: less than body requirements related to insufficient vitamin and mineral intake
Decreased hip mobility	*Activity intolerance/pain/potential impaired home maintenance management/potential for injury/impaired physical mobility/potential social isolation related to restricted use of hip*
Crepitus of jaw	*Pain related to crepitus of jaw secondary to possible arthritis*
Laxative dependency	*Constipation and diarrhea related to adverse effects of laxative use*
	Knowledge deficit related to unawareness of nonpharmacological means to facilitate bowel elimination
Weight of 165 pounds	*Activity intolerance/pain/potential self-esteem disturbance related to excess body weight*
Dry skin	*Potential impaired skin integrity/related to skin dryness*
Lack of knowledge of self-exam of breasts	*Knowledge deficit related to inability to self-examine breasts*
Inability to attend church	*Spiritual distress related to inability to maintain usual religious practices*
Limited social world	*Potential diversional activity deficit/social isolation related to minimal contact with other persons*

Problem or Need Identified	Expressed as Nursing Diagnosis
Husband's dependency on her for translation and assistance with health problems	*Anxiety related to husband's well-being*
	Altered family processes related to changes in husband's capabilities
Large home	*Anxiety related to decreasing ability to manage home*
	Impaired home maintenance management related to declining health status of self and husband
Changing neighborhood	*Anxiety/fear related to high risk of being victim of crime*
	Powerlessness related to decreased ability to protect self
Bilingual	*Potential for impaired verbal communication related to blocking of English language secondary to stress*

REFERENCES

Carpenito LJ: Nursing Diagnosis: Application to Practice. Philadelphia, JB Lippincott, 1983.

Fry, VS: The creative approach to nursing. Am J Nurs 53:301–302, 1953.

Gordon M: Historical perspective: The National Group for classification of nursing diagnoses. In Kim, MJ, Moritz, DA (eds): Classification of Nursing Diagnoses. New York, McGraw-Hill, 1982.

US National Center for Health Statistics: Vital and Health Statistics, series 10, and unpublished data, 1985.

BIBLIOGRAPHY

Caine RM, Bufalino PM: Nursing Care Planning Guides for Adults. Baltimore, Williams & Wilkins, 1987.

Carpenito LJ: Nursing Diagnosis: Application to Clinical Practice, 2nd ed. Philadelphia, JB Lippincott, 1987.

Eliopoulos C: A Guide to the Nursing of the Elderly. Baltimore, Williams & Wilkins, 1987.

Gordon M: Manual of Nursing Diagnosis, 1986–1987. New York, McGraw-Hill, 1987.

Gordon M: Nursing Diagnosis: Process and Application, 2nd ed. New York, McGraw-Hill, 1987.

Hallah J: Nursing diagnosis: An essential step to quality care. J Gerontol Nurs 11(9): 35–38, 1985.

Hannah KJ, Reimer M, Mills WC, et al.: Clinical Decision Making: The Future with Nursing Diagnosis. New York, Wiley, 1987.

Tucker SM, Canabbio MM, Paquette EV, et al.: Patient Care Standards: Nursing Process, Diagnosis, and Outcome, 4th ed. St. Louis, CV Mosby, 1988.

Ulrich SP, Canale SW, Wendell SA: Nursing Care Planning Guides: A Nursing Diagnosis Approach. Philadelphia, WB Saunders, 1986.

CHAPTER 5

Nutritional Considerations in the Care of the Elderly

Bridget Doyle

Chapter Objectives
At the completion of this chapter the reader will be able to:

1. List the nutritional requirements for an older adult.
2. Identify factors that can interfere with good nutrition in late life, such as poor dental condition, sensory deficits, illness, and socioeconomic factors.
3. Describe the components of a comprehensive nutritional assessment.
4. Discuss problems that can result from or cause poor nutritional status.

Nutrition plays a significant role in the aging process. Not only is nutrition one of the determinants of the number of years one will live, but it also affects the quality of those years: The level of energy, function, and comfort is greatly influenced by nutritional status.

Nutrition is no less significant to the elderly than it is to younger persons. With the exception of caloric requirements, nutritional requirements remain relatively unchanged throughout adulthood. Food preferences and the psychosocial dynamics related to food and eating experiences continue. Alterations in nutritional status are as much of a threat to the old as the young and could have even greater consequences because of the reduced ability of older bodies to manage physiological disturbances. If anything, good nutrition becomes more important in later life.

Achieving and maintaining a good nutritional status can be more problematic for the older adult, however. A variety of physical, mental, social, and economic factors can pose serious obstacles. Knowing that such threats to nutritional status are highly prevalent in later years, nurses must be prepared to identify and assist the elderly in correcting nutritional problems.

Nutritional Requirements

There are a variety of age-related changes that impact nutritional needs in old age. Throughout adult life there is a loss of cells. The proportions of various types of body tissue change, resulting in a reduction in lean body mass and an increase in adipose tissue. The fact that adipose tissue has a

Although caloric requirements decrease with age, the calories that are consumed need to reflect a high-quality diet.

slower metabolic rate than lean body tissue, combined with the overall reduction in basal metabolic rate, causes the caloric requirement to decline with age. More times than not persons are less active in their later years, thereby further reducing caloric needs. Many individuals begin to note a tendency to gain weight in their middle years if they attempt to ingest the same number of calories as they did in their younger life. Although the recommended daily allowances (RDA) for calories are reduced in senior years, daily caloric requirements need to be individually determined based on body size, activity level, and general health status.

Protein requirements remain unchanged throughout adult life: 0.8 gram per kilogram of body weight. It is important that there be an adequate protein intake even though fewer calories are ingested. In essence, fewer calories must be packed with good sources of protein.

Fats are important to the diet because they supply fat-soluble vitamins (A, D, K, and E) and essential fatty acids. The intake of fats should constitute no more than 35% of the total caloric intake.

The requirements for vitamins and minerals are relatively unchanged for older adults (Table 5-1). After menopause, iron requirements for men and women become the same. The overall quality of the diet will influence the degree to which vitamin and mineral needs are fulfilled, again reinforcing the importance of calories being loaded with good nutrients. With a nutritious diet, vitamin and mineral supplements are not necessary; the elderly should be guided toward ingesting sufficient vitamins and minerals through their diets rather than taking vitamin and mineral supplements (Table 5-2).

Risk Factors

Aging

Although nutritional needs in late life seem basic and simple, there are many factors interfering with the older adult's ability to fulfill these requirements. One of the factors affecting nutrition is the aging process itself. Salivary secretions are reduced, causing the chewing, mixing, and swallowing of food to be more difficult. The breakdown and absorption of food are less efficient because of decreased secretions of digestive acids and enzymes. Altered glucose metabolism can affect the body's ability to manage high levels of simple carbohydrates in the diet. Reduced peristalsis can promote constipation.

Tooth Loss

Although tooth loss is not a normal outcome of the aging process, today's older generation has suffered severe tooth loss as a result of poor diet, insufficient attention to tooth care, and limited access to dentists. The edentulous status of today's elderly will be less prevalent in future generations.

(*Text continues on page 80*)

TABLE 5-1. Recommended Daily Dietary Allowances for Adults (Revised 1980)

Nutrient	Men[a] Age 23–50	Men[a] Age 51+	Women[b] Age 23–50	Women[b] Age 51+
Protein, g	56	56	44	44
Fat-soluble vitamins				
Vitamin A, μg retinol equiv.[c]	1,000	1,000	800	800
Vitamin D, μg[d]	5	5	5	5
Vitamin E, mg α-tocopherol equiv.[e]	10	10	8	8
Water-soluble vitamins				
Vitamin C, mg	60	60	60	60
Thiamine, mg	1.4	1.2	1.0	1.0
Riboflavin, mg	1.6	1.4	1.2	1.2
Niacin, mg niacin equiv.[f]	18	16	13	13
Vitamin B_6, mg	2.2	2.2	2.0	2.0
Folacin, μg	400	400	400	400
Vitamin B_{12}, μg	3.0	3.0	3.0	3.0
Minerals				
Calcium, mg	800	800	800	800
Phosphorus, mg	800	800	800	800
Magnesium, mg	350	350	300	300
Iron, mg	10	10	18	10
Zinc, mg	15	15	15	15
Iodine, μg	150	150	150	150

[a] Relates to reference man weighing 70 kg and 178 cm in height.
[b] Relates to reference woman weighing 55 kg and 163 cm in height.
[c] 1 retinol equivalent = 1 μg retinol or 6 μg β-carotene.
[d] As cholecalciferol; 1 μg cholecalciferol = 40 IU.
[e] 1 α-tocopherol equivalent = 1 mg D-α-tocopherol.
f 1 niacin equivalent = 1 mg niacin or 60 mg dietary tryptophan.

Source: Reprinted from *Recommended Dietary Allowances*, 9th ed., 1980, with permission of the National Academy Press, Washington, DC.

TABLE 5-2. Nutrients for Health

Nutrients are chemical substances obtained from foods during digestion. They are needed to build and maintain body cells, regulate body processes, and supply energy.

About 50 nutrients, including water, are needed daily for optimum health. If one obtains the proper amount of the ten "leader" nutrients in the daily diet, the other 40 or so nutrients will likely be consumed in amounts sufficient to meet body needs.

One's diet should include a variety of foods because no *single* food supplies all the 50 nutrients, and because many nutrients work together.

When a nutrient is added or a nutritional claim is made, nutrition labeling regulations require listing the ten leader nutrients on food packages. These nutrients appear in the chart below with food sources and some major physiological functions.

Nutrient	Important Sources of Nutrient	Some Major Physiological Functions Provide Energy	Some Major Physiological Functions Build and Maintain Body Cells	Some Major Physiological Functions Regulate Body Processes
Protein	Meat, poultry, fish Dried beans and peas Eggs Cheese Milk	Supplies 4 calories per gram	Constitutes part of the structure of every cell, such as muscle, blood, and bone; supports growth and maintains healthy body cells	Constitutes part of enzymes, some hormones and body fluids, and antibodies that increase resistance to infection

TABLE 5-2. (*Continued*)

Nutrient	Important Sources of Nutrient	Some Major Physiological Functions		
		Provide Energy	Build and Maintain Body Cells	Regulate Body Processes
Carbohydrate	Cereal Potatoes Dried beans Corn Bread Sugar	Supplies 4 calories per gram Major source of energy for central nervous system	Supplies energy so protein can be used for growth and maintenance of body cells	Unrefined products supply fiber— complex carbohydrates in fruits, vegetables, and whole grains—for regular elimination Assists in fat utilization
Fat	Shortening, oil Butter, margarine Salad dressing Sausages	Supplies 9 calories per gram	Constitutes part of the structure of every cell Supplies essential fatty acids	Provides and carries fat-soluble vitamins (A, D, E, and K)
Vitamin A (retinol)	Liver Carrots Sweet potatoes Greens Butter, margarine		Assists formation and maintenance of skin and mucous membranes that line body cavities and tracts, such as nasal passages and intestinal tract, thus increasing resistance to infection	Functions in visual processes and forms visual purple, thus promoting healthy eye tissues and eye adaptation in dim light
Vitamin C (ascorbic acid)	Broccoli Orange Grapefruit Papaya Mango Strawberries		Forms cementing substances, such as collagen, that hold body cells together, thus strengthening blood vessels, hastening healing of wounds and bones, and increasing resistance to infection	Aids utilization of iron
Thiamine (B_1)	Lean pork Nuts Fortified cereal products	Aids in utilization of energy		Functions as part of a coenzyme to promote the utilization of carbohydrate Promotes normal appetite Contributes to normal functioning of nervous system
Riboflavin (B_2)	Liver Milk Yogurt Cottage cheese	Aids in utilization of energy		Functions as part of a coenzyme in the production of energy within body cells Promotes healthy skin, eyes, and clear vision
Niacin	Liver Meat, poultry, fish Peanuts Fortified cereal products	Aids in utilization of energy		Functions as part of a coenzyme in fat synthesis, tissue respiration, and utilization of carbohydrate Promotes healthy skin, nerves, and digestive tract Aids digestion and fosters normal appetite
Calcium	Milk, yogurt Cheese Sardines and salmon with bones Collard, kale, mustard, and turnip greens		Combines with other minerals within a protein framework to give structure and strength to bones and teeth	Assists in blood clotting Functions in normal muscle contraction and relaxation, and normal nerve transmission
Iron	Enriched farina Prune juice Liver Dried beans and peas Red meat	Aids in utilization of energy	Combines with protein to form hemoglobin, the red substance in blood that carries oxygen to and carbon dioxide from the cells Prevents nutritional anemia and its accompanying fatigue Increases resistance to infection	Functions as part of enzymes involved in tissue respiration

Source: "Guide to Good Eating," courtesy of the National Dairy Council.

Teeth that are missing or in poor condition and the presence of dentures alter the ability to ingest and enjoy a wide range of food.

Sensory Changes

Sensory changes directly and indirectly affect food intake. Poor vision can impair food shopping, preparation, and enjoyment. The loss of taste buds with age, primarily affecting the sweet and salty flavors, can cause less enjoyment of food or excessive intake of sugar and salt as a means of compensation. Reduced olfaction can limit the interest in food generated from scents, while hearing losses may affect the desire of the person to combine eating with a social experience.

Reductions in the taste buds for sweet and salty flavors can reduce appetite and lead to excessive consumption of sugar and salt.

Chronic Illness

A majority of older adults possess a chronic illness, the effects of which can have an impact on nutrition. Disease-related weakness and fatigue can make marketing and cooking major tasks; eating a full meal can be a tiring experience. Pain can reduce appetite and the ability to prepare and ingest food. The restrictions imposed by special diets can lead to a loss of interest in eating.

Mental Illness

Mental health problems can jeopardize nutritional status. Lack of interest in food often accompanies the depression that is highly prevalent in old age. Insufficient or excessive nutrient intake can be associated with anxiety. Paranoid individuals' suspicions surrounding food can seriously limit food intake, and demented persons may lack the ability to remember to eat or ingest food safely.

Drugs

The high consumption of drugs by the elderly has an effect on nutritional status. Many drugs have anorexia, gastrointestinal upset, and constipation as side effects. Others interact with food in deleterious ways (see pages 92–94).

Social Factors

The saying that "mealtime is a social time" exemplifies the influence of social factors on nutrition. Widowed or single persons who live alone may not be motivated to prepare full meals. These persons may snack or rely on high-carbohydrate fillers from the local fast-food restaurant. Ethnic or cultural preferences can cause a rejection of diets that differ from one's native eating habits. Likewise, special dietary practices or preferences may cause people to consume food that contributes to health problems. For example, a person who must restrict sodium intake may continue to consume the high-sodium meats of a kosher diet.

Income

An ideal diet depends on adequate income, another problem in the lives of many older adults. Persons with limited incomes may not have the funds to purchase the food they need. Medical care, prescriptions, household repairs, and other expenses may compete with the food budget. Elderly individuals may find that their food dollar goes further on high-carbohydrate fillers than on high-quality meats and fresh fruits and vegetables.

Alcohol

Alcohol consumption also challenges nutritional status by depleting the resources available to purchase food, reducing appetite, and impairing vitamin metabolism.

Knowledge Deficits

Not to be overlooked are knowledge deficits related to diet. Some persons may not understand what is meant by a protein, or they may hold erroneous beliefs concerning the nutritional content of certain foods, like believing bacon to be a good source of protein. Individuals who have never learned to cook will be at a loss when the people they depended on for meal preparation are no longer available. Others have lived under certain misconceptions for years—for example, it is all right to skip a meal if you take a vitamin; one needs to fast a few days each month; it is necessary to take a laxative once a week to "clean out one's system."

Assessing Nutritional Status

A comprehensive nutritional assessment includes anthropometric and biochemical measurements, evaluation of clinical status, and review of dietary intake.

Nutritional assessment is a multifaceted process that explores a variety of sources of nutritional data, including

anthropometric measurement

biochemical measurement

clinical status

dietary intake

Anthropometric Measurement

Anthropometric measurement involves the evaluation of height, weight, and thickness of triceps and subcapsular skinfold. Weight references for the over-65 population have been sorely lacking and criticized for their inability to distinguish between body size and composition. Based on their work at the Gerontology Research Center, Andres et al. (1985) have developed a valid weight table that deletes sex and body frame as variables (Table 5-3). The standards they propose are lower for young adults and increase with age. When assessing weight, factors such as age-related declines in height and fluid retention must be considered.

Biochemical Measurement

Biochemical measurements are usually easy to obtain and offer valid data on nutritional status. Included in this screening would be serum levels of iron (total iron binding capacity, transferrin saturation), protein, albumin, urea nitrogen, and glucose. Serum or urine vitamin levels may be misleading, since significant deficiencies must be present before low levels occur and some levels can be altered by recent intake of the vitamin; screening is use-

TABLE 5-3. Comparison of the Weight-for-Height Tables from Actuarial Data (Build Study): Non-Age-Corrected Metropolitan Life Insurance Company and Age-Specific Gerontology Research Center Recommendations[a]

Height (ft–in.)	Metropolitan 1983 Weights (pounds) for Ages 25–59[b]		Gerontology Research Center Weight Range for Men and Women (pounds)[c]				
	Men	Women	Age 25	Age 35	Age 45	Age 55	Age 65
4–10	—	100–131	84–111	92–119	99–127	107–135	115–142
4–11	—	101–134	87–115	95–123	103–131	111–139	119–147
5–0	—	103–137	90–119	98–127	106–135	114–143	123–152
5–1	123–145	105–140	93–123	101–131	110–140	118–148	127–157
5–2	125–148	108–144	96–127	105–136	113–144	122–153	131–163
5–3	127–151	111–148	99–131	108–140	117–149	126–158	135–168
5–4	129–155	114–152	102–135	112–145	121–154	130–163	140–173
5–5	131–159	117–156	106–140	115–149	125–159	134–168	144–179
5–6	133–163	120–160	109–144	119–154	129–164	138–174	148–184
5–7	135–167	123–164	112–148	122–159	133–169	143–179	153–190
5–8	137–171	126–167	116–153	126–163	137–174	147–184	158–196
5–9	139–175	129–170	119–157	130–168	141–179	151–190	162–201
5–10	141–179	132–173	122–162	134–173	145–184	156–195	167–207
5–11	144–183	135–176	126–167	137–178	149–190	160–201	172–213
6–0	147–187	—	129–171	141–183	153–195	165–207	177–219
6–1	150–192	—	133–176	145–188	157–200	169–213	182–225
6–2	153–197	—	137–181	149–194	162–206	174–219	187–232
6–3	157–202	—	141–186	153–199	166–212	179–225	192–238
6–4	—	—	144–191	157–205	171–218	184–231	197–244

[a]Values in this table are for height without shoes and weight without clothes. To convert inches to centimeters, multiply by 2.54; to convert pounds to kilograms, multiply by 0.455.
[b]The weight range is the lower weight for small frame and the upper weight for large frame.
[c]Data from Andres R: Mortality and obesity: The rationale for age-specific height-weight tables. In Andres R, Bierman EL, Hazzard WR (eds): Principles of Geriatric Medicine. New York, McGraw-Hill, 1985, 311–318.
Source: Reprinted with permission from Andres R, Elahi D, Tobin JD, Muller DC, Brant L: Impact of age on weight goals. Ann Intern Med 103(6): 1032, 1985.

ful, however, to detect serious deficiencies. Prothrombin time and the urine's specific gravity are beneficial to evaluate as well.

Clinical Status

During the physical assessment and throughout care activities clinical signs of malnutrition should be noted. Among the factors to consider are hair and skin condition, vision, muscle strength, neurological function, and mental status (Table 5-4). It should be kept in mind that health problems, as well as the consequences of normal aging, can contribute to some of the changes observed; thus careful evaluation is essential.

Dietary Intake

Dietary assessment includes interviews, direct observation, and indirect data gathering of food intake, food patterns, cultural and ethnic variables, and impact of socioeconomic and environmental factors. The food intake of institutionalized individuals can be determined through direct observation and evaluation of intake. The assessment of the community-based elderly can require more creativity and effort, since it relies on the recall and compliance of the clients themselves. Techniques that can be employed include

Food records, in which the client documents the amount and type of food and the time it is consumed.

Food-frequency checklists, whereby the client indicates the number of times foods from the four major food groups are consumed within a designated time period (day, week).

Dietary recall of all food consumed, usually during the past 24-hour period.

Findings are compared to recommended daily intakes of specific food groups. Care must be taken to assure that the data reflect typical eating patterns and that memory deficits are not distorting the information shared by the client.

Thorough dietary assessments can reveal specific nutritional disorders and give clues to other health and socioeconomic problems.

Nutrition-Related Problems

Obesity

Perhaps one of the most common nutritional disorders is obesity. As mentioned earlier, caloric requirements decrease with age, but some elderly may not adjust their diets accordingly. Obesity can result and lead to new health problems or a worsening of existing ones. The criterion for determining obesity has been a body weight 20% or more above the ideal weight; with the more specific, age-adjusted weight tables developed by Andres et al. (Table 5-3) the determination of obesity may be easier to derive. Modifica-

TABLE 5-4. Clinical Nutrition Examination

Clinical Findings	Consider Deficiency of	Consider Excess of
Hair, nails		
Flag sign (transverse depigmentation of hair)	Protein, copper	
Hair easily pluckable	Protein	
Hair thin, sparse	Protein, biotin, zinc	Vitamin A
Nails spoon-shaped	Iron	
Nails lackluster, transverse ridging	Protein-calorie	
Skin		
Dry, scaling	Vitamin A, zinc, essential fatty acids	Vitamin A
Erythematous eruption (sunburn-like)		Vitamin A
Flaky paint dermatosis	Protein	
Follicular hyperkeratosis	Vitamins A, C, essential fatty acids	
Nasolabial seborrhea	Niacin, pyridoxine, riboflavin	
Petechiae, purpura	Ascorbic acid, vitamin K	
Pigmentation, desquamation (sun-exposed area)	Niacin (pellagra)	
Subcutaneous fat loss	Calorie	
Yellow pigmentation spring sclerae (benign)		Carotene
Eyes		
Angular palpebritis	Riboflavin	
Band keratitis		Vitamin D
Corneal vascularization	Riboflavin	
Dull, dry conjunctiva	Vitamin A	
Fundal capillary microaneurysms	Ascorbic acid	
Papilledema		Vitamin A
Scleral icterus, mild	Pyridoxine	
Perioral		
Angular stomatitis	Riboflavin	
Cheilosis	Riboflavin	
Oral		
Atrophic lingual papillae	Niacin, iron, riboflavin, folate, vitamin B_{12}	
Glossitis (scarlet, raw)	Niacin, pyridoxine, riboflavin, vitamin B_{12}, folate	
Hypogeusesthesia (also hyposmia)	Zinc, vitamin A	
Magenta tongue	Riboflavin	
Swollen, bleeding gums (if teeth present)	Ascorbic acid	
Tongue fissuring, edema	Niacin	
Glands		
Parotid enlargement	Protein	
"Sicca" syndrome	Ascorbic acid	
Thyroid enlargement	Iodine	
Heart		
Enlargement, tachycardia, high-output failure	Thiamine ("wet beriberi")	
Small heart, decreased output	Calorie	
Sudden failure, death	Ascorbic acid	
Abdomen		
Hepatomegaly	Protein	Vitamin A
Muscles, extremities		
Calf tenderness	Thiamine, ascorbic acid (hemorrhage into muscle)	

TABLE 5-4. (*Continued*)

Clinical Findings	Consider Deficiency of	Consider Excess of
Edema	Protein, thiamine	
Muscle wastage (especially temporal area, dorsum of hand, spine)	Calorie	
Bones, joints		
Beading of ribs (child)	Vitamins C, D	
Bone and joint tenderness	Ascorbic acid (subperiosteal hemorrhage), Vitamin A (child)	
Bone tenderness (adult)	Vitamin D, calcium, phosphorus (osteomalacia)	
Bulging fontanelle (child)		Vitamin A
Craniotabes, bossing (child)		Vitamin D
Neurologic		
Confabulation, disorientation	Thiamine (Korsakoff's psychosis)	
Decreased position and vibratory senses, ataxia	Vitamin B_{12}, thiamine	
Decreased tendon reflexes, slowed relaxation phase	Thiamine	
Drowsiness, lethargy		Vitamins A, D
Ophthalmoplegia	Thiamine, phosphorus	
Weakness, paresthesias, decreased fine tactile sensation	Vitamin B_{12}, pyridoxine, thiamine	
Other		
Delayed healing and tissue repair (e.g., wound, infarct, abscess)	Ascorbic acid, zinc, protein	
Fever (low-grade)		Vitamin A

Source: Reproduced by permission from Weinsier RL, Butterworth CE: Handbook of Clinical Nutrition. St. Louis, 1984, The C.V. Mosby Co., p. 30.

tion of dietary intake combined with exercise is a beneficial approach to achieving weight reduction. The benefits of weight reduction must be weighed against the impact of dietary restrictions on the quality of life: If no ill effects are caused by a minor weight excess, it may not make sense to alter an accepted and enjoyed eating pattern.

Dehydration

Signs of dehydration can include confusion, weakness, poor skin turgor, increased body temperature, concentrated urine, and dry tongue, skin, and mucous membrane.

Good fluid intake is essential to health. However, the elderly may have special problems in achieving an adequate level of hydration. Health problems and disabilities can prevent persons from obtaining fluid independently. Some elderly, as well as their caregivers, may limit fluid intake to reduce the frequency of voiding. Indicators of dehydration include confusion; dry tongue, mucous membrane, and skin; poor skin turgor; weakness; and increases in body temperature, pulse, urine concentration, and serum sodium. Prompt correction is essential for this life-threatening problem. Active efforts to prevent dehydration should be promoted by assuring a fluid intake of six to eight glasses of fluid daily, assisting disabled persons in obtaining fluids, and educating clients against using fluid restriction as a means to control urinary frequency or incontinence.

Constipation

Constipation is a common problem of the elderly. Factors that contribute to this problem include age-related changes in the gastrointestinal system, a low intake of fiber and fluid, inactivity, certain medications (e.g., CNS depressants, some antacids), laxative dependency, and pain associated with bowel elimination, as occurs with hemorrhoids. The first step in assessing constipation is to determine how the client defines this problem: To some individuals, constipation means the lack of a daily bowel movement. Findings associated with constipation include less than three bowel movements per week, abdominal discomfort and distension, straining to pass stool, and the presence of hard, dry stool. Prevention of constipation through adequate fiber and fluid intake, activity, and a scheduled time allowance for bowel elimination is useful.

Iron Deficiency Anemia

Insufficient dietary intake of iron or health problems that cause blood loss or malabsorption of iron contribute to the common geriatric problem of iron deficiency anemia. Indicators of this problem include hemoglobin below 12 mg/100 ml for men and 10 mg/100 ml for women, hematocrit below 37 vol% for men and 31 vol% for women, and transferrin saturation below 15%. Increasing dietary intake of iron-rich food and use of ferrous sulfate are used to correct this problem; of course, correction of underlying medical problems that may be causing blood loss is essential. An adequate intake of vitamin C is encouraged, also, because it facilitates iron absorption.

Osteoporosis

Osteoporosis has received wide attention recently, and increasing numbers of persons are becoming more aware of the importance of calcium intake to avoid this disorder. In addition to insufficient calcium intake, factors contributing to this problem include lack of estrogen, inactivity, reduced parathyroid activity, and poor absorption of calcium that accompanies old age. With osteoporosis there is a reduction in the size and density of bones, causing them to fracture more easily. Prevention of osteoporosis should begin early in life. Although the recommended daily allowance of calcium is given as 800 mg, many practitioners are suggesting that postmenopausal women and men over age 60 consume 1,000–1,500 mg of calcium daily.

Community Considerations

Knowing that the elderly are vulnerable to nutritional problems, gerontological nurses must make every effort to promote good nutrition and to identify and correct nutritional disorders when they do exist. Education on the importance of good nutrition, dietary requirements, and the problems associated with poor nutritional status can be beneficial to the elderly. Such counseling can be given to individual clients or in group settings, such as in senior citizen centers.

Older adults should be made aware of the impact of medications on nutritional status. Drugs should be reviewed for potential food-drug interactions and adjustments made accordingly.

Low-income persons may benefit from Food Stamps and referral to a congregate eating program, the cost of which may be nominal. Local departments of social services and social workers can be valuable resources in obtaining assistance.

Ill or disabled elderly may benefit from having home-delivered meals (Meals on Wheels), grocery deliveries, home aides who can shop for and prepare food, and architectural modifications and assistive devices that can make independent cooking and eating possible.

Institutional Considerations

The public's interest in dining at restaurants that offer special atmosphere reinforces the reality that the dining experience entails more than eating food. The comfort and appearance of the restaurant and service provided can make or break a dining experience for us. Even in the home setting, mealtime is more pleasant if the dining table is set attractively and food presented in an appealing manner.

The fact that dining is an experience is sometimes minimized in the institutional setting. Dining rooms may be areas used for multiple purposes; Formica-topped tables that were used for arts and crafts may be cleared for mealtime use. Food is served in the most efficient manner, often using styrofoam and plastic. A person's dining companions may be individuals with no common interests or, worse still, with a significantly different level of mental function. There may be pressure to hurry through the meal to enable staff to complete feeding and cleaning responsibilities. This dining experience is hardly conducive to enjoying a meal. Persons may react to this situation by becoming agitated or depressed, or by trying to retreat to a less stressful and unpleasant area. The result can be poor food intake.

The Lenoir Life Care Community in Columbia, Missouri, observed some of the problems of institutional dining and implemented a project to improve the situation. A group of mentally alert residents of the nursing home unit were dissatisfied with their dining experience and not achieving optimal nutritional status as a result. These residents felt distressed with the eating environment, bored with the routine and monotony of dining, and powerless in their ability to effect a change.

The first step was to designate an activity room as their private dining area. Residents were given the opportunity to decorate the room with plants and pictures and began converting the room into an environment that reflected their personal styles. To reduce glare from the tabletops, tablecloths and place mats were obtained; the residents selected the color scheme they found most appealing. They were educated as to the importance of color contrast and made color selection that optimized their ability to see the outline of dishes and utensils against the cloth. Rather than serving the entire meal on a tray, dishes were served individually at the tables. Residents selected the dining group that they wished to join and maintained that table assignment. Also important, they became actively involved in meal selection, asserting their preferences to the dietician. The satisfaction voiced by residents has been significant since these modifications were made. Staff members have noted that residents consume a greater proportion of their meals and practice appropriate mealtime etiquette and socialization. Staff also report that more time is available to feed residents who need assistance, now that there has been a reduction of the problems that previously resulted from the integration of impaired residents with the more functional ones. There are multiple benefits to establishing a "homelike" dining experience in institutional settings.

A good nutritional status in old age results from sound dietary practices throughout one's entire life. Young persons need to be educated about the significance of nutrition to their aging process. It is far easier to prevent nutritional problems than to correct their consequences in old age.

Since the elderly are at risk of many problems that can have a negative impact on nutritional status, nurses must assure that their older clients receive comprehensive nutritional assessment and interventions as required. Be it financial aid to be able to afford nutritious foods, transportation to a congregate eating site where a daily balanced meal can be obtained, architectural modification to allow function within a kitchen, or more participation in meal selection in the institutional setting, every approach should be used to encourage a good nutritional status.

REFERENCE

Andres R, Elahi D, Tobin JD, Muller DC, Brant L: Impact of age on weight goals. Ann Intern Med 103(6): 1030–1033, 1985.

BIBLIOGRAPHY

Drugay M: Nutrition evaluation: Who needs it? J Gerontol Nurs 12(4): 14–18, 1986.

Eaton M, Mitchell-Bonair I, Friedman E: The effect of touch on nutritional intake of organic brain syndrome patients. J Gerontol 41(5): 611–616, 1986.

Green ML, Harry J: Nutrition in Contemporary Nursing Practice, 2nd ed. New York, Wiley, 1987.

Hatchett-Cohen L: Nasoduodenal tube feeding. Geriatr Nurs 9(2): 88–91, 1988.

Masoro EJ: Nutrition and aging: A current assessment. J Nutr 115(7): 842–848, 1985.

Moore MC: Pocket Guide to Nutrition and Diet Therapy. St. Louis, CV Mosby, 1988.

Stinson JK: Dietary professionals and politics in long term care. Contemporary Long Term Care 11(4): 104–106, 1988.

Yen PK: Easy-to-use nutritional supplements. Geriatr Nurs 8(6): 345, 348, 1987.

CHAPTER 6

Safe Drug Use with the Elderly

Charlotte Eliopoulos

Chapter Objectives

At the completion of this chapter the reader will be able to:

1. Describe the high volume of drugs consumed by the elderly and the problems it creates.
2. Outline age-related changes that influence how drugs act in the older adult.
3. List common drug-drug and drug-food interactions.
4. Discuss the gerontological nurse's role in advocating safe drug use with older adults.
5. Describe nursing considerations in the use of antacids, antianxiety drugs, anticoagulants, antidepressants, antidiabetics, antihypertensives, anti-inflammatories, antipsychotics, cardiac glycosides, diuretics, laxatives, and sedatives.

One of the most complicated and risky areas of therapeutic intervention with the elderly is that of medications. Drugs have contributed to longer, more comfortable lives for many older adults, and from this standpoint they have been beneficial. However, along with the benefits have come numerous risks from the elderly's unique reactions to drugs, polypharmacy, and other factors. Regardless of the practice setting, close monitoring of drug therapy is a high-priority nursing responsibility.

Problems Associated with Drug Therapy in the Aged

Volume of Drugs Consumed

It is estimated that the elderly experience as much as five times as many adverse reactions to drugs as younger age groups, and that 5–30% of all geriatric admissions to the hospital are associated with inappropriate drug therapy (Pagliaro and Pagliaro, 1986, 135). Recognizing these risks, it is important to understand the factors that promote them, one of which is the great number of medications being taken. The average older adult in the community has 11 prescriptions filled per year, and there are an average of eight drugs administered to each nursing home resident. Although they con-

TABLE 6-1. Interactions among Popular Drug Groups

	Antacids	Antianxiety	Anticoagulant	Antidiabetic	Antidepressant	Antihypertensive	Anti-inflammatory	Antipsychotic	Digitalis preparations	Laxatives	Salicylates	Thiazide diuretics	Tricyclic antidepressants
Antacids													
Antianxiety					↑								↑
Anticoagulants (oral)	↑	↑			↑		↑			↑	↑	↓	↑
Antidiabetics			↑			↑	↑				↑	↓	
Antidepressants												↑	
Antihypertensives		↑			↓							↑	↓
Anti-inflammatory	↓												
Antipsychotic													
Digitalis preparations	↓					↑				↓		↓	
Laxatives													
Salicylates	↓				↓								
Sedatives					↑		↑	↑					
Thiazide diuretics						↑					↓		
Tricyclic antidepressants													

Arrows indicate the effect of drugs listed in the left-hand column on those listed at the top.

stitute 12% of the population, the elderly consume 32% of all prescriptions. Frequently, an older adult with the medical diagnosis of diabetes mellitus, anemia, chronic bronchitis, and arthritis may be prescribed an antidiabetic agent, iron supplement, bronchodilator, and analgesic. In addition, the same client could be self-medicating with an antacid, antihistamine, cough suppressant, laxative, vitamins, and a topical anesthetic. In this not so atypical example, the potential for ill consequences from interactions is significant. (A sample of drug interactions among some of the more popularly prescribed drug groups is shown in Table 6-1.)

When multiple drugs are used, it is essential to check for potential interactions. The additional cost of using a pharmacy that maintains a drug profile on individual clients and checks for interactions is an investment that can potentially spare serious complications, not to mention unnecessary costs from inappropriate prescriptions. When this type of pharmacy service is not available, it becomes crucial for nurses to conduct a comprehensive review of all medications the client consumes and assess for interactions. Clients should be advised to remind health care providers of medications

TABLE 6-2. Impact of Age-Related Changes on Drug Therapy

Change	Impact on Drug Therapy
Less total body fluid	Higher blood level of water-soluble drugs
Increased adipose tissue	Greater accumulation of fat-soluble drugs (e.g., diazepam, barbiturates)
Decreased secretions in GI tract, lower gastric pH	Slight reduction in absorption
Reduced liver size, decrease in some forms of hepatic metabolism	Slower metabolism and longer half-life of some drugs (e.g., acetaminophen)
Reductions in number of nephrons, glomerular filtration rate, renal blood flow, creatinine clearance, tubular reabsorption	Slower elimination of drugs that are predominantly eliminated in unchanged form (e.g., digitalis, kanamycin, penicillin), increased competition of protein-bound drugs
Decreased albumin concentration	Delayed distribution and higher concentrations of protein-bound drugs (e.g., phenytoin, phenylbutazone, warfarin)
Drier oral mucosa	Difficulty swallowing tablets and capsules
Less muscle mass	Difficulty absorbing usual adult IM dose at single injection site
Reduced circulation to lower bowel and vagina	Prolonged melting time for suppositories

currently used when a new drug is prescribed; a written list of medications that can be carried in a wallet may prove more useful than depending on recall alone.

Physical Changes with Age

Some of the outcomes of the aging process alter the aged person's use and response to drugs (Table 6-2). For instance, the seemingly simple task of taking a medication can be a challenge for the older individual. Poor eyesight can limit the ability to differentiate various medication containers or to read how much of a medication should be taken at specific times. Memory deficits can make it difficult to remember whether or not a medication has been taken. Swallowing of tablets and capsules can be hampered by a dry oral mucosa.

Injectable forms of medications carry their set of problems, as well. The age-related reduction in muscle mass is particularly apparent in the arms and legs; thus the extremities are not the ideal location for intramuscular injections. Less muscle mass makes the absorption of large amounts of medications at a single site more difficult, necessitating that some injections be divided into two smaller injections at different sites to facilitate optimum absorption.

Suppository use creates problems for some individuals. A person with poor vision might not see the suppository's wrapping and insert it with the wrapping unremoved. Arthritic fingers may not be able to remove the tight covering from the suppository. If these administration problems are overcome, full value of the suppository can be threatened by the fact that the suppository can take longer to melt and therefore be expelled before it is fully melted.

Metabolism of drugs can be slower as a result of reduced liver size and mass. Likewise, a reduction in renal mass and function can delay the elimination of drugs. Responses to drugs are more individualized and less predictable. Many drugs need to be prescribed in dosages that are lower than the level recommended for the general adult population, and the appropriateness of the dosage has to be monitored over time in light of potential diminished organ function. Adverse reactions to drugs must be identified, recognizing that reactions can occur in response to drugs that the elderly individual has taken for years without problems.

Food and Drugs

Maintaining an adequate nutritional state can be problematic in late life for a variety of physiological, emotional, and socioeconomic reasons. Nutritional factors can compound the risks associated with drug therapy.

Nutritional problems can be caused by or contribute to drug problems. Many drugs can cause side effects such as anorexia, nausea, vomiting, gastric upset, or vitamin depletion, leading to nutritional risks (Table 6-3).

Various foods can alter the effectiveness of drugs (Table 6-4). For example, taking a medication with a meal high in fat content will cause the drug to be absorbed more slowly. Some drugs can interfere with the absorption or metabolism of certain nutrients, as is the case with phenytoin, which accelerates the liver's breakdown of vitamin D.

Cost

Prescriptions can be quite expensive, especially to someone living on a limited budget. Elderly persons may attempt to control prescription expenditures by

- Not having a prescription filled.
- Taking a friend's leftover supply of the drug.
- Using an old supply of the medication that has been stored in the medicine cabinet.
- Stretching the prescription by skipping dosages.

Affordability must be considered when drugs are prescribed. Patients who seem to be noncompliant or using poor judgment actually may be coping the best way they can with limited dollars.

Reducing Risks with Geropharmacology

The object of this discussion has not been to discourage drug use in the elderly, but to call attention to situations that could result in drug therapy being more harmful than beneficial. The cautious use of medications may

(Text continues on page 95)

TABLE 6-3. Examples of Potential Impact of Drugs on Nutritional Status

Drug	Nausea/vomiting	GI upset	Anorexia	Na retention	Reduced blood glucose	Iron deficiency	Vitamin A	Vitamin B1	Vitamin B6	Vitamin B12	Vitamin C	Vitamin D	Vitamin E	Vitamin K	Folacin	Zinc	Phosphate	Magnesium	Iodine	Sodium	Potassium	Diarrhea	Flatus
Acetaminophen		×																					
Acetohexamide	×																						
Allopurinol						×																	
Aluminum antacids							×				×	×											
Aspirin						×		×			×												
Benzodiazepines																							
Calcium carbonate antacids						×	×								×		×						
Calcium supplements			×																				
Chloral hydrate																							×
Cholestyramine							×						×										
Chlorpropamide				×																			
Cimetidine						×																	
Clonidine HCl				×																			
Digitalis								×							×	×					×		
Estrogen											×												
Furosemide															×	×					×		
Ibuprofen		×																					
Levodopa																					×		
Phenobarbital									×	×	×	×		×	×								
Phenylbutazone																			×				
Phenytoin											×	×	×	×									
Procainamide	×		×																			×	
Propranolol HCl		×																					
Spironolactone																				×	×		
Thiazides					×										×			×			×		

TABLE 6-4. Examples of Food and Drug Interactions

Drug	Potential Interactions
Acetaminophen	Accumulation to toxic level if more than 500 mg of vitamin C supplements are ingested daily
Allopurinol	Impairs iron absorption leading to iron deficiency anemia
	Combined with alcohol or simple carbohydrates can increase blood uric acid level
Aluminum antacids	Depletes phosphate and calcium
	Decreases absorption of vitamins A, C, and D, and magnesium, thiamine, folacin, and iron
Antihistamines	Ingestion of large amounts of alkaline foods (e.g., milk, cream, almonds, alcohol) can prolong action
Aspirin	Can cause iron deficiency anemia as a result of GI bleeding
	Causes vitamin C deficiency (12+ aspirin tablets daily)
	Causes thiamine deficiency
Calcium carbonate antacids	Cause deficiencies of phosphate, folacin, iron, thiamine
Calcium supplements	Combined with large doses of vitamin D can cause hypercalcemia
	Absorption decreased by foods rich in oxalate (e.g., spinach, rhubarb, celery, peanuts), phytic acid (e.g., oatmeal and other grain cereals), phosphorous (chocolate, dried beans, dried fruit, peanut butter)
Chlorpromazine HCl	Large amounts of alkaline foods can delay excretion
	Can increase blood cholesterol
Cimetidine	Reduces iron absorption
Clonidine HCl	Effectiveness reduced by tyramine-rich foods (e.g., chicken and beef livers, bananas, sour cream, meat tenderizers, salami, yeast, chocolate)
	Can cause sodium and fluid retention
Colchicine	Effectiveness decreased by caffeine
	Some herbal teas contain phenylbutazone, which can increase blood uric acid and decrease effectiveness of antigout drugs
Dicumarol	Effectiveness reduced by foods rich in vitamin K (e.g., cabbage, broccoli, asparagus, spinach, turnip greens)
Digitalis	Can cause deficiencies of thiamine, magnesium, and zinc
	Calcium supplements increase risk of toxicity
Estrogen	Hastens breakdown of vitamin C
Ferrous supplements	Absorption decreased by antacids, increased by vitamin C
Furosemide	Increases excretion of calcium, magnesium, potassium, and zinc
Hydralazine	Can cause vitamin B_6 deficiency
Levodopa	Effectiveness reduced by high-protein diet
	Can cause deficiencies of potassium, folacin, and vitamins B_6 and B_{12}
Magnesium antacids	Can deplete phosphate and calcium
Magnesium-based laxatives	30 ml contains nearly four times the average daily intake of magnesium; toxicity can result
Mineral oil	Decreases absorption of vitamins A, D, and K
Phenobarbital	Increases breakdown of vitamins D and K
	Impairs absorption of vitamins B_6 and B_{12} and folic acid
Phenylbutazone	Inhibits absorption of iodine
Phenytoin	Increases breakdown of vitamins D and K
	Reduces absorption of folacin
Potassium supplements	Absorption decreased by dairy products
	Impairs absorption of vitamin B_{12}
Probenecid	Effectiveness decreased by coffee, tea, or cola

TABLE 6-4. (*Continued*)

Drug	Potential Interactions
Spironolactone	Increases excretion of calcium
	Decreases excretion of potassium leading to potassium toxicity
Theophylline	Effectiveness reduced by high-carbohydrate diet
Thiazides	Increases excretion of calcium, potassium, magnesium, zinc
	Can decrease blood glucose level
Thioridazine	Excretion delayed by high-alkaline diet
Warfarin	Effectiveness reduced by large amounts of vitamin K in diet

Gerontological nurses serve an advocacy role for the elderly by advising nonpharmacological means to manage health problems, assuring that age-adjusted dosages are used, identifying interactions and adverse reactions, and regularly evaluating the effectiveness of drugs.

add not only years to life, but also an improved quality to the elderly's remaining years. Important guidelines to remember for safe geropharmacology include the following:

- Use nonpharmacological means to manage health problems whenever possible.
- Assure that the most appropriate dosage and route are used.
- Explore the possibility of drug-drug and drug-food interactions.
- Determine the knowledge base and physical and mental abilities of a patient self-administering a drug.
- Observe for adverse reactions, even from drugs that have been used over a long period of time.
- Periodically evaluate response and continued need for the drug.

Drug Profiles

The following section will review some of the drugs encountered in geriatric care. Trade names for the drugs are provided in parentheses.

Category: *Antacid*

Drugs
Aluminum carbonate gel (Basaljel)

Aluminum hydroxide gel (Amphojel, Alternagel)

Aluminum phosphate gel (Phosphajel)

Calcium carbonate (Alka-2, Tums, Chooz, Equilet)

Dihydroxyaluminum sodium carbonate (Rolaids)

Magaldrate (Riopan)

Magnesium hydroxide

Magnesium carbonate

Magnesium oxide (Par-Mag, Maalox)

Magnesium trisilicate

Sodium bicarbonate (Soda Mint)

Combinations, for example:

    Aluminum hydroxide, magnesium hydroxide, and simethicone (Di-Gel Liquid, Gelusil, Mylanta)

    Aluminum hydroxide and magnesium hydroxide (Maalox)

    Magnesium hydroxide and calcium carbonate (Bisodol Powder)

    Sodium bicarbonate, acetaminophen, citric acid (Bromo-Seltzer)

    Sodium bicarbonate and citric acid (Alka-Seltzer)

Nursing Considerations

- During the assessment ask about antacid use. Many patients fail to report that they chronically use baking soda or an over-the-counter antacid tablet.
- Explore the reason for antacid use. Chronic GI upset may indicate a problem more serious than indigestion. Antacid use may be masking a peptic ulcer or cardiac problem.
- Thoroughly shake liquid antacids before use. Tablets should be thoroughly chewed and followed by a glass of fluid. (Since thorough chewing of the tablet can be difficult for some elderly persons, the liquid form may be preferable.)
- Avoid administering other medications two hours before or after antacid administration. Antacids can impair absorption of other drugs.
- Monitor bowel movements. Diarrhea can result from magnesium-hydroxide combinations, constipation from aluminum hydroxide and calcium antacids. Chalky-looking streaks may normally appear in stool from antacid therapy.
- Consult with the physician before using sodium-based antacids for patients on sodium-restricted diets.
- Gastric hypersecretion (acid rebound) and hypercalcemia can occur when calcium carbonate antacids are taken with milk or foods rich in vitamin D. Adjust diet accordingly.
- Milk-alkali syndrome can occur when calcium carbonate or sodium bicarbonate is administered with milk or foods rich in vitamin D. Observe for nausea, vomiting, headache, and confusion.
- Patient teaching should reinforce the importance of using antacids only when absolutely necessary, not changing the brand of antacid used without consulting with health care provider, proper administration techniques, and observation for side effects.
- Prevent and identify drug and food interactions (see Tables 6-1 and 6-4).

Category: *Antianxiety*

Drugs

Benzodiazepines:

    Chlordiazepoxide (Librium)

    Chlorazepate dipotassium (Tranxene)

    Diazepam (Valium)

Halazepam (Paxipam)
Lorazepam (Ativan)
Oxazepam (Serax)
Prazepam (Centrax)
Barbiturates:
Amobarbital (Amytal)
Mephobarbital (Mebaral)
Phenobarbital

Note: Because of the profound depressant effects on the central nervous system and the risk of psychological and physical dependency, barbiturate use is discouraged for the geriatric population.

Nursing Considerations

- Assess for causes of anxiety and attempt to alleviate those factors before resorting to the use of an antianxiety medication.
- The longer biological half-life of these drugs warrants that lower dosages be prescribed for the elderly.
- The elderly are at greater risk of developing side effects from these drugs. Observe for and protect the patient from consequences of these side effects: drowsiness, confusion, slurred speech, poor coordination, dry mouth, GI upset, constipation, double vision, photosensitivity, impaired bladder control, and decreased resistance to infection.
- Advise patients not to ingest alcohol when taking these drugs.
- Periodically evaluate the patient's need to be on an antianxiety agent. Changes in life events or benefits from adjunct therapies may enable the patient to cope without the drug.
- Since a dependency to antianxiety drugs can develop, do not discontinue abruptly.
- The longer half-life of these drugs can cause their effects to be noted after discontinuation because of their continued presence in the blood.
- Prevent and identify drug and food interactions (see Tables 6-1 and 6-4).

Category: *Anticoagulant*

Drugs
Dicumarol

Phenprocoumon (Liquamar)

Warfarin potassium (Athrombin-K)

Warfarin sodium (Coumadin)

Nursing Considerations

- In the elderly, absorption of anticoagulants can be slow and erratic, and there is a greater risk of bleeding. Dosage must be highly individualized and effects closely monitored.

- After dosage is stabilized, prothrombin time should be evaluated every four to six weeks.
- Administer anticoagulants at the same hour each day to maintain a constant blood level.
- Patients on anticoagulant therapy should avoid eating turnip greens, broccoli, cabbage, spinach, and liver, since they are high in vitamin K and can have an antagonistic effect.
- Three grams or more of salicylates taken daily are sufficient to cause hemorrhage in an older adult who is on anticoagulants. Other analgesics should be used.
- Observe for signs of bleeding: headaches, bleeding gums, hemoptysis, bloody or tarry stools, fatigue, fever, chills.
- Provide patient education that reinforces proper administration (including not doubling dose if one is missed), dietary restrictions, observation for side effects, safe practices to avoid injuries, wearing Medic Alert bracelet to reveal anticoagulant use, consulting with health provider before starting or discontinuing any other medication.
- Prevent and identify food and drug interactions (see Tables 6-1 and 6-4).

Category: *Antidepressant*

Drugs

Tricyclic compounds (group of choice with elderly):
   Amitriptyline HCl (Elavil, Amitril, Endep)
   Amoxapine (Asendin)
   Desipramine HCl (Norpramin, Pertofrane)
   Doxepin HCl (Adapin, Sinequan)
   Imipramine HCl (Tofranil, Janimine)
   Imipramine pamoate (Tofranil-PM)
   Nortriptyline HCl (Aventyl)
   Protriptyline HCl (Vivactil)
   Trimipramine maleate (Surmontil)
Lithium carbonate:
   Lithium (Eskalith, Lithonate, Cibalith-S)
Monoamine oxidase (MAO) inhibitors:
   Isocarboxazid (Marplan)
   Phenelzine sulfate (Nardil)
   Tranylcypromine sulfate (Parnate)

Note: The use of MAO inhibitors is usually discouraged for older patients. These drugs can precipitate hypertensive episodes and interact with many other drugs.

Miscellaneous:
   Trazodone HCl (Desyrel)

Nursing Considerations

- Assess for all potential physical, emotional, or socioeconomic factors that could promote depression, and seek to alleviate those factors before resorting to medications. Review all medications being used to identify those that may cause depression, such as reserpine, methyldopa, propranolol, antiparkinson drugs, and hormones.
- Lower dosages are recommended for the elderly.
- Administration of antidepressants at bedtime is beneficial in that most of the uncomfortable effects can occur while the patient sleeps.
- Monitor patients carefully during the initial phase of treatment. Sedation may occur for the first few days of therapy.
- Several weeks of administration may be necessary before any positive effects are noted.
- Observe for side effects of drug: dry mouth, diaphoresis, urinary retention, indigestion, constipation, loose stool, hypotension, drowsiness, increased appetite, weight gain, blurred vision, photosensitivity, and fluctuating blood sugar level.
- Patient teaching should reinforce proper administration, observation for side effects, consulting with health provider before discontinuing or starting a drug, and promptly seeking help if depression worsens.
- Prevent and identify food and drug interactions (see Tables 6-1 and 6-4).

Category: *Antidiabetic*

Drugs [duration of activity]

Sulfonylureas:
  Acetohexamide (Dimelor, Dymelor) [intermediate, 12–16 hours]
  Chlorpropamide (Chloronase, Diabinese) [long, 36+ hours]
  Tolazamide (Tolinase) [intermediate, 8–12 hours]
  Tolbutamide (Orinase, Tolbutone) [short, 6–8 hours]
Second-generation sulfonylureas:
  Glipizide (Glucotrol) [short, 3–6 hours; 24+ hours with larger doses]
  Glyburide (DiaBeta, Micronase) [short, 4–6 hours; 24+ hours with larger doses]
Biguanides:
  Metformin (Diabexyl) [short, 3–6 hours]
Insulins:
  Insulin injection (Crystalline zinc, Regular) [short, 6–8 hours]
  Insulin zinc, prompt (Semilente) [short, 12–18 hours]
  Insulin isophane (Humulin-N, NPH) [intermediate, 22–24 hours]
  Insulin zinc (Lente, Monotard) [intermediate, 24–28 hours]
  Insulin globin zinc [intermediate, 16–18 hours]
  Insulin protamine zinc (PZI) [long, 24–36 hours]
  Insulin zinc, extended (Ultralente, Ultratard) [long, 24–36 hours]

Nursing Considerations

- Assure that age-adjusted gradients have been used in interpreting the glucose tolerance test. The elderly may normally possess a higher blood glucose level.
- Tolbutamide tends to be the oral antidiabetic agent of choice. Chlorpropamide has a prolonged half-life in the elderly and can be more hazardous. Close monitoring is important when second-generation sulfonylureas are used because they are extremely potent.
- Do not substitute different brand names of the same generic oral antidiabetic agent without consulting with the physician. Variations can exist among different brands.
- Initially, lower doses may be prescribed for the elderly. Monitor patients closely during this period.
- Administer acetohexamide, chlorpropamide, tolazamide, and tolbutamide with food. Glyburide is administered with the first main meal of the day. Glipizide is administered 30 minutes before a meal.
- Only regular insulin injections can be given intramuscularly or intravenously. All other forms must be given subcutaneously. Rotate injection sites, and do not reinject a site for at least six weeks.
- Insulin should be stored in a cool place, away from direct sunlight or extreme temperatures. Prefilled syringes of insulin may be stored in the refrigerator for as long as one week.
- Examine injection sites regularly. Insulin allergy is displayed by local redness, pain, swelling, and nodule development at the injection site. Insulin lipodystrophy, a harmless but unattractive condition, is displayed by a sunken area at the injection site.
- Assure that the diabetic patient is wearing a Medic Alert bracelet or other identifier to inform others of his or her condition in the event of an emergency.
- Patient teaching should reinforce realities of disease, proper administration and storage of drug, importance of not substituting drug (e.g., borrowing from a friend's supply when one's own supply is diminished), recognizing and reporting problems, maintenance of a regular diet and activity schedule, and the importance of reporting changes in health status and other medication changes to one's physician. It can be beneficial to include a family or a household member in the teaching activity.
- Hypoglycemia is a significant threat to the elderly. Symptoms include confusion, headache, slurred speech, blurred vision, irritability, tremor, increased perspiration, palpitations, tingling in extremities, and convulsions.
- Monitor the effectiveness of the drug. Be alert to indications of hyperglycemia, which could include thirst, excess voiding, weight loss, nausea, vomiting, dehydration, abdominal pain, Kussmaul's breathing, acetone on breath, and confusion.
- Prevent and identify drug and food interactions (see Tables 6-1 and 6-4).

Category: *Antihypertensive*

Drugs
Alpha-adrenergic blocking agents:
    Phentolamine (Regitine, Rogitine)
    Prazosin (Hypovase, Minipress)
Antiadrenergic/adrenergic neuron-blocking agents:
    Guanethidine (Ismelin, Visutensil)
    Reserpine (Eskaserp, Hydropres, Serpasil)
Beta-adrenergic blocking agents:
    Metopropol (Betaloc, Lopressor)
    Nadolol (Corgard, Corzide)
    Propranolol (Inderal, Panolol)
Central-acting alpha-adrenergic agonists:
    Clonidine (Catapres, Dixarit)
    Methyldopa (Aldomet, Dopamet, Presinol)
Vasodilators:
    Diazoxide (Hyperstat, Proglycem)
    Hydralazine (Apresoline, Lopress, Nor-press)

Nursing Considerations
- Support nondrug methods to control hypertension, for example, dietary modifications, weight reduction, improved stress-management techniques, relaxation exercises.
- Obtain three-position baseline blood pressure. When taking future blood pressures for evaluation, be sure to use the same arm and have patient in the same position.
- Drowsiness and postural hypotension are serious risks to elderly persons on antihypertensive therapy. Advise patients how to protect themselves from injury, for example, changing positions slowly, not driving during peak action of drug.
- The beta-adrenergic blocking agents tend to produce fewer side effects in the elderly than do other groups of antihypertensives. The extremities of patients on these drugs may feel cold as a result of the vasoconstrictive effects of these medications. The use of this drug group with diabetic patients warrants careful monitoring because beta-adrenergic blocking agents can mask the signs of hypoglycemia and increase sensitivity to tolbutamide.
- Reserpine carries a high risk of causing depression. Observe patient for signs of this mental state. Reserpine can also cause nightmares, increased appetite, weight gain, decreased libido, and impotence.
- Methyldopa can cause hemolytic anemia; regular evaluation of hematocrit and hemoglobin is important. It may also aggravate existing angina and cause the urine to darken when it is exposed to air. The elderly have a high incidence of hepatitis from this drug.
- The hypotensive effects of all antihypertensives can threaten adequate cerebral circulation and alter mental status.

- Effects of these drugs can persist for weeks after their discontinuation.
- Patient teaching should reinforce proper administration of the drug, recognition of side effects, precautions, importance of administering it at the same time each day and not discontinuing it abruptly or without medical advice, and need to take medication even in the absence of symptoms.
- Prevent and identify drug and food interactions (see Tables 6-1 and 6-4).

Category: *Anti-inflammatory* (nonsteroid)

Drugs
Indole acetic acid derivatives:
    Sulindac (Clinoril)
    Tolmetin (Tolectin)
Propionic acid derivatives:
    Fenoprofen (Fenopron, Nalfon)
    Ibuprofen (Advil, Motrin, Nuprin)
Pyrazolons:
    Oxyphenbutazone (Oxalid, Oxybutazone, Tandearil)
    Phenylbutazone (Azolid, Butazolidin, Phenbutazone)
Salicylates:
    Aspirin (Anacin, A.S.A., Bayer, Ecotrin, Zorprin)

Nursing Considerations
- Aspirin is inexpensive, available without a prescription, and an effective analgesic, anti-inflammatory, and antipyretic. For these reasons, it is a popular anti-inflammatory drug. Specific inquiry should be made as to the exact amount of aspirin consumed each day. Long-term use of high doses of aspirin can alter clotting time; signs of bleeding should be noted. Assess for salicylate toxicity, indicated by dizziness, vomiting, tinnitus, hearing loss, fever, sweating, burning in mouth and throat, confusion, convulsions, and coma.
- When combined with sulfonylureas, aspirin can cause hypoglycemia.
- Enteric coated aspirin should not be taken within one hour of ingesting milk or an antacid.
- Although the risk of GI upset and gastric ulcer formation is lower with nonsalicylate anti-inflammatories, the potential exists. Question patients about symptoms of these problems.
- Many anti-inflammatories are highly protein bound and may be displaced by other protein-bound drugs that the patient is taking (e.g., oral antidiabetics, oral anticoagulants, phenytoin). Review all drugs being used.
- Several weeks of therapy may be necessary before positive results are achieved. Regularly evaluate patient's pain and stiffness to determine effectiveness of drug.

- Patient teaching should reinforce proper administration of drug, need for periodic blood evaluations, identification of side effects, and the importance of consulting with a physician before changing the dose or taking a new medication.
- Prevent and identify interactions with food or other drugs (see Tables 6-1 and 6-4).

Category: *Antipsychotic*

Drugs
Butyrophenones:
  Haloperidol (Haldol, Serenace)
Phenothiazines:
  Acetophenazine (Tindal)
  Butaperazine (Repoise)
  Carphenazine (Proketazine)
  Chlorpromazine (Chlorprom, Thorazine)
  Fluphenazine (Dapotom, Permitil, Prolixin)
  Mesoridazine (Lidanar, Serentil)
  Perphenazine (Etrafon, Triavil)
  Piperacetazine (Actazine, Quide)
  Promazine (Atarzine, Norzine, Protactyl)
  Thiopropazide (Dartal)
  Thioridazine (Mellaril, Thioril)
  Trifluoperazine (Clinazine, Stelazine, Tripazine)
  Triflupromazine (Psyquil, Siquil, Vesprin)

Nursing Considerations
- Antipsychotics, also known as major tranquilizers, are started in small doses in the elderly and gradually increased if necessary. The longer half-life of these drugs in older adults makes the risk of adverse effects high.
- Antipsychotics can be very beneficial for psychotic patients; however, these drugs are not appropriate for patients suffering from dementias.
- Because most antipsychotics have a long half-life, they can be administered in a single dose. It is best for the drug to be administered at night so that its sedative and other effects can occur as the patient is sleeping.
- The elderly are more sensitive to the anticholinergic effects of antipsychotics; chlorpromazine and thioridazine carry a higher risk of this adverse effect and need to be used with caution. Monitor patients for confusion, agitation, dry or flushed skin, tachycardia, dilated pupils, dysarthria, and reduced bowel function.
- Orthostatic hypotension and severe sedation may occur. Protect patients from injury that could result from these side effects.
- After the first few weeks of therapy the anticholinergic effects, sedation, and orthostatic hypotension usually subside.

- Elderly men with prostatic hypertrophy are at greater risk of developing urinary hesitancy and retention; monitor urinary output.
- Constipation can be a serious adverse reaction while patients are receiving antipsychotics; bowel obstruction may result; monitor bowel elimination.
- Elderly individuals often develop extrapyramidal effects while on antipsychotics; signs include drug-induced parkinsonism, motor restlessness, agitation, severe muscle contractions, dyskinesias, and tardive dyskinesia. Tardive dyskinesia, the most serious of these adverse effects, is displayed through rhythmic involuntary movements of the tongue, mouth, and face, head and neck jerking, and jerking or swaying of the body. Early detection of symptoms is important, since a dosage change or discontinuation of the drug can reverse these problems. Prolonged tardive dyskinesia is not reversible.
- Drug holidays are recommended when antipsychotics are used on a long-term basis. Approximately every six months the patient should have drug-free periods (e.g., weekends). During these drug holidays behavior should be noted, as should indication of subtle dyskinesias that may have been masked during drug therapy.
- After clinical improvement is noted, the antipsychotic may be gradually decreased in dosage and discontinued. Abrupt withdrawal can cause a relapse.
- Monitor response to therapy. If one drug is not beneficial in controlling symptoms, another class of antipsychotic may prove more useful.
- Patient teaching should reinforce management of mild side effects (e.g., sucking on hard candy to combat dry mouth, including roughage in diet to avoid constipation, changing positions slowly to prevent falls from orthostatic hypotension), recognition and reporting of serious adverse reactions (e.g., tardive dyskinesia), proper administration, purpose of drug, and importance of consulting with health care provider before taking other medications.
- Prevent and identify food and drug interactions (see Tables 6-1 and 6-4).

Category: *Cardiac glycosides*

Drugs

Digitoxin (Cardidigin, Crystodigin, Purodigin)

Digoxin (Lanoxin, Natigoxine, Novodigoxin, Winoxin)

Nursing Considerations
- The elderly usually require lower, individualized doses of digitoxin and digoxin. Monitor response closely.
- Prior to initiating therapy, check blood values and evaluate for hypokalemia and hypercalcemia, conditions that can make the heart more sensitive to digitalis toxicity.

- Check apical pulse before administering drug. Patients should be instructed in taking radial pulse when self-administering a digitalis preparation.
- Digitalis toxicity is most commonly caused by low serum potassium, which causes the myocardium to be more sensitive to the drug. Blood levels of the drug may remain stable with this problem; thus clinical signs are important to note. Toxicity also can be caused by overdose or conditions that delay excretion of the drug (e.g., congestive heart failure). Signs of digitalis toxicity include nausea, vomiting, anorexia, blurred or yellow vision, sensation of seeing yellow or green halos around lights, fatigue, headache, altered heart rate, hallucinations, confusion, or psychosis. (Altered mental status is a common manifestation in the elderly.) The drug should not be administered until there has been medical evaluation of the problem.
- Patient teaching should reinforce proper administration, purpose, drug storage (in tightly closed container away from sunlight), the importance of checking pulse before administration, identification of adverse reactions, the importance of not changing dosage or brand used, and the importance of consulting with a health care professional before using new medication.
- Prevent and identify interactions with food or other drugs (see Tables 6-1 and 6-4).

Category: *Diuretics*

Drugs
Benzothiadiazines or thiazides:
    Bendroflumethiazide (Aprinox, Centyl, Naturetin)
    Chlorothiazide (Diupres, Diuril, SK-Chlorothiazide)
    Chlorthalidone (Hygroton, Igroton, Uridon)
    Hydrochlorothiazide (Esidrix, Hydrodiuril, Unipres)
    Quinethazone (Aquamox, Hydromox)
Quinazolines:
    Metolazone (Diulo, Zaroxolyn)
Loop diuretics:
    Ethacrynic acid (Edecrin, Hydromedin, Taladren)
    Furosemide (Lasix, Neo-Renal, Uritol)
Potassium-sparing:
    Amiloride (Midamor, Moduretic)
    Spironolactone (Aldactone)
    Triamterene (Dyrenium, Dytac)

Nursing Considerations
- Weight, vital signs, and laboratory evaluation of blood and urine should be done before initiating diuretic therapy and periodically reevaluated.
- Oral diuretics administered once a day are best taken in the morning so that peak effect is reached during daytime hours.

- Hypokalemia, hyponatremia, and hyperuricemia can result from taking loop and thiazide diuretics.
- Potassium-sparing diuretics can cause hyperkalemia with oliguria, impotence, decreased libido, and gynecomastia.
- Thiazide diuretics can cause photosensitivity.
- Thiazide, loop, and potassium-sparing diuretics can cause fluid and electrolyte imbalances, hyperglycemia, hypotension, and magnesium depletion.
- Patient teaching should reinforce proper administration, inclusion of additional potassium-rich foods in diet (unless potassium-sparing diuretics are being used), understanding of expected effects, recognition of adverse effects, and the importance of not changing the drug schedule or using a new drug without consulting with a health care professional.
- Prevent and identify food or drug interactions (see Tables 6-1 and 6-4).

Category: *Laxatives*

Drugs
Bulk-forming:
    Bran
    Methylcellulose (Cologel, Hydrolose)
Lubricants and stool softeners:
    Docusate sodium (Colace, Dual Formula Feen-A-Mint)
    Mineral oil (Agoral, Haley's M-O)
Saline laxative:
    Magnesium hydroxide (Milk of Magnesia)
    Magnesium sulfate (Epsom Salt, Mag-S)
Stimulant and irritant:
    Bisacodyl (Dulcolax)
    Cascara sagrada (Amlax, Biolax)
    Castor oil (Alphamul, Ricifruit)
    Glycerin (Agoral, Glyrol)
Miscellaneous:
    Senna (Senokot)

Nursing Considerations
- Do a physical assessment to validate patient's complaint of constipation.
- Try nondrug means to improve bowel elimination first (see Chapter 5).
- Ask specifically about laxative use during every assessment. Many patients fail to think of laxatives as drugs and may not contribute facts about laxative use during drug history.
- Laxative use on a chronic basis should be discouraged unless medically necessary. In addition to the risk of fluid and electrolyte imbalances, habituation can result.
- Patient teaching should include instruction about nondrug methods to prevent constipation, proper administration of laxatives, recognition of problems, and the importance of avoiding laxative dependency.

- Prevent and identify interactions with food or other drugs (see Tables 6-1 and 6-4).

Category: *Sedatives/Hypnotics*

Drugs
Chloral hydrate (Chloralex, Somnos)

Ethchlorvynol (Placidyl, Serensil)

Flurazapam (Dalmane, Novoflupam)

Nursing Considerations
- Evaluate patient's complaint of insomnia. The elderly require approximately five to seven hours of night sleep. The patient who falls asleep at 8 P.M. (including prebedtime napping in front of the television on a living room chair) may have met sleep requirements by 2 A.M. In this type of situation, awakening in the middle of the night is not true insomnia. A thorough sleep history is essential.
- Nondrug methods to promote sleep (e.g., warm milk, back rub, soft music, relaxation exercises) should be used before resorting to a medication.
- The effect of the drug on the central nervous system determines if it is a sedative or hypnotic. A higher dose of a sedative will produce a hypnotic effect.
- The continued need for the drug should be assessed. The central nervous system depressant effects of these drugs can produce serious risks if taken on a long-term basis.
- Monitor for daytime effects of drug, "hangover" effects, impairment of function, and tolerance to drug.
- Restlessness, insomnia, and nightmares that may occur after the drug is discontinued should gradually subside.
- Barbiturates are not recommended for older adults.
- Patient teaching should include proper administration, safety precautions related to central nervous system effects, recognition of adverse effects, and importance of not changing dosage or using new drug without consulting with a health professional.
- Prevent and identify interactions with food or other drugs (see Tables 6-1 and 6-4).

REFERENCE   Pagliaro AM, Pagliaro LA: Age-dependent drug selection and response. In Pagliaro AM, Pagliaro LA (eds): *Pharmacologic Aspects of Nursing*. St. Louis, CV Mosby, 1986.

BIBLIOGRAPHY   Benzoni T: Cost and compliance. Am Fam Phys 37(3): 55, 57, 59, 1988.
Fruncillo RJ: Drug therapy in the elderly. Am Fam Phys 35(2): 225–228, 1987.
Lamy PP: Drug interactions and the elderly. J Gerontol Nurs 12(2): 36–37, 1986.

Lamy PP: Geriatric drug therapy. Am Fam Phys 34(6): 118–126, 1986.

Pagliaro LA, Pagliaro AM (eds): Pharmacologic Aspects of Aging. St. Louis, CV Mosby, 1983.

Roberts J: Pharmacodynamic basis for altered drug action in the elderly. Clin Geriatr Med 4(1): 127–149, 1988.

Roberts PA: Extent of medication use in U.S. long term care facilities. Am J Hosp Pharm 45(1): 93–100, 1988.

Simonson W: Medications and the Elderly. Rockville, MD, Aspen Systems, 1984.

Thomas B, Price M: Drug reviews. J Gerontol Nurs 13(4): 17–21, 1987.

Thomas M: Directors of nursing speak out on long term care patients' drug therapy. Contemporary Long Term Care 11(8): 83–84, 89, 1988.

Todd B: Drugs and the elderly: Cigarettes and caffeine in drug interactions. Geriatr Nurs 8(2): 97–98, 1987.

Todd B: Newer antihypertensive agents. Geriatr Nurs 9(3): 187–188, 1988.

CHAPTER 7
Injuries in the Elderly

Chapter Objectives

At the completion of this chapter the reader will be able to:

1. Describe the three phases of injury and related nursing measures.
2. Outline the magnitude of the injury problem in the older population.
3. List factors associated with advanced age that contribute to injury.
4. Discuss the incidence, characteristics, prevention, and management of falls, burns, and automobile-related injuries in the elderly.
5. Describe how advanced age affects the treatment of injury victims.

Injuries among the elderly are a serious problem in terms of mortality, morbidity, changes in level of self-care, suffering, length of hospitalization, costs, and quality of life. Nurses working in every type of health facility and in the community can have a positive impact on the injury problems of the elderly.

At the heart of any prevention program is the need for thorough understanding of the risks associated with injury. Section One of this chapter will describe a conceptual framework for examining injuries among the elderly, the magnitude of the injury problem, and the major types of injuries among older persons. Section Two will present practical nursing strategies for caring for injured elderly persons and discuss some of the potential problems that may be encountered.

Risks and Prevention

Ann H. Myers and Amy C. Sharpe

Concept of Injury Control

The term *accident* implies a random event, one due to chance, fate, or misfortune. The term is being replaced by the term *unintentional event,* thus unintentional injury. (Intentional events resulting in injury or death include suicides and homicides.) Another concept associated with unintentional injuries is the notion of *injury control,* which emphasizes primary, secondary, and tertiary prevention (Haddon and Baker, 1981). A growing number of health professionals are being educated in, practicing, and becoming involved in injury control. In January 1987 the U.S. government, through the Centers for Disease Control, established and funded five centers for injury prevention, education, and research.

Injuries and their prevention and control by nurses may be conceptualized in three phases: the *preevent,* the *event,* and the *postevent* phases. An example of injury prevention and control in the preevent phase by a community health nurse or visiting nurse would be the identification of risk factors in the home such as cluttered stairs without handrails on both sides, poor and inaccessible lighting at night in the bedroom, the absence of handrails in the bathroom, or the absence of a workable smoke detector. Modification of these circumstances could reduce the risk of an injury event occurring. Once an event has occurred, reducing delays in seeking first aid and emergency care is important in reducing the extent of the injury and complications. In order to prevent delays a gerontological nurse could evaluate the patient's ability to move or leave the building in the event of a fire, develop and review an exit plan, and evaluate the ability to use telephones and their placement in the dwelling. In the postevent phase the hospital nurse's interventions emphasize the prevention of complications such as pneumonia. In discharge planning, the health team needs to evaluate how the injury event occurred and make changes in the environment or ameliorate a physical condition to prevent a recurrence.

Magnitude of the Problem

Much of the research in the area of injuries has concentrated on those of childhood and young adulthood, with the justification that the majority of injury deaths occur in these age groups. Injuries are the leading cause of death during ages 1–44. Numerous authors agree, however, that to examine injury rates or proportion of deaths due to injury masks the massive problem of injuries among the elderly (Hogue, 1980; Baker and Dietz, 1979). Table 7-1 lists the number of persons injured and rates of injury by sex and

TABLE 7-1. Number of Persons Injured and Rates of Injury per 100 Persons per Year, by Sex and Age Groups, United States, 1981

	Males		Females		Total	
Age Group	Number (millions)	Rate	Number (millions)	Rate	Number (millions)	Rate
Under 6 years	4.1	40.0	3.2	32.3	7.3	36.2
6–16 years	8.9	44.8	5.9	31.4	14.8	38.2
17–44 years	21.0	44.3	13.4	26.9	34.4	35.4
45–64 years	4.4	20.9	4.9	20.9	9.2	20.9
65 and older	1.7	16.9	2.8	19.2	4.5	18.3
Total	40.1	36.9	30.2	25.9	70.2	31.2

Source: National Center for Health Statistics, Collins JG: Persons injured and disability days due to injuries, United States, 1980–1981. Vital and Health Statistics Series 10, No. 149, DHHS Pub. No. (PHS) 85–1577. Public Health Service. Washington, DC, U.S. Government Printing Office, March 1985.

Injuries are the fifth leading cause of death among the young old, the seventh leading cause of death among the old old, and a major cause of disability.

age groups. Those over 65 years of age experience the lowest rates of injury. For all injuries combined, persons age 65 and older are less likely to be injured but more likely to have a fatal outcome if an injury occurs (Iskrant and Joliet, 1968). Injuries are the fifth leading cause of death among the elderly 65–74 years of age, the seventh leading cause of death among persons age 75 and over, and a leading cause of short- and long-term disability for the same age group. Table 7-2 compares the average number of restricted activity days, bed disability days, and work-loss days resulting from injury per 100 persons per year by age groups for both sexes.

TABLE 7-2. Average Number of Restricted Activity Days, Bed Disability Days, and Work-Loss Days per 100 Persons per Year, by Age Groups for Both Sexes, United States, 1980–1981

Age Group	Restricted Activity Days[a]	Bed Disability Days[b]	Work-Loss Days[b]
Under 6 years	44	14	—
6–16 years	179	34	—
17–24 years	314	72	
25–34 years	421	89	129
35–44 years	399	107	
45–54 years	465	143	
55–64 years	525	115	120
65–74 years	505	133	
75 years and older	664	194	84
Total	357	88	125

[a] Number of days per 100 persons per year.
[b] Number of days per 100 currently employed persons per year.
Source: National Center for Health Statistics, Collins JG: Persons injured and disability days due to injuries, United States, 1980–1981. Vital and Health Statistics Series 10, No. 149, DHHS Pub. No. (PHS) 85–1577. Public Health Service. Washington, DC, U.S. Government Printing Office, March 1985.

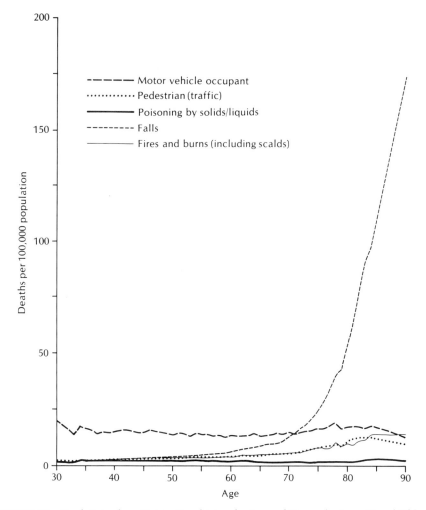

FIGURE 7-1. Death Rates from Unintentional Injury by Age and Cause, for Ages 30 and Older, 1977–1979. (Baker SP, Karpf RS, O'Neill B: The Injury Fact Book. Lexington, MA, Lexington Books, 1984, p. 43.)

Persons over age 55 have the highest average number of days of restricted activity. Although the average number of bed disability days decreases slightly after ages 45–54, the trend of increasing days of disability with rising age continues and reaches its highest point with the 75+ age group (National Center for Health Statistics, 1983b, 1985). Figure 7-1 depicts the death rates from unintentional injury by age and cause for persons over age 30. After age 60, the death rate from injuries continues to rise (Baker et al., 1984). Death rates due to injury are highest among persons over age 75. The rate of death from injury among 75–84 years of age is more than double that for all ages combined (Baker et al., 1984). The approximately 12% of the population who are 65 and over accounted for more than 25% of all injury fatalities in 1985 (National Safety Council, 1985a).

Elderly women tend to have more falls than men; older men have higher rates of burn and motor vehicle injuries (including pedestrian) than women. The death rates for elderly men are higher than those for women in all three categories. Before age 75 death rates from injury are highest among nonwhite males; after age 75 a crossover occurs and rates are highest among white males.

Differences in Risk: Amount and Exposure

Difference in injury incidence and mortality between the young and old arise from differences in risk among the elderly (Waller, 1985a). Risk of injury may be determined by several factors. Baker (1975) has described four determinants of injury incidence and severity: (1) differences in exposure, either in quality or quantity of exposure; (2) ability to respond to injury threat; (3) resistance to injury; and (4) probability of recovery from injury. The particular problems of injury among the elderly may be examined within this framework. Baker and colleagues (1984) list specific reasons for the high death rates from injury among the older population: The elderly have a decreased ability to perceive and avoid hazards; they experience both normal and pathologic musculoskeletal and proprioceptive changes; there is a greater likelihood that the older person will be injured when subjected to a given force; and the older trauma patient often has a poorer outcome following injury.

The elderly, consequent to their age, have different degrees of exposure to injury risk than young persons because their patterns of work, recreation, and operation of motor vehicles are different. The importance of different exposure patterns has been underscored by several authors (Baker et al., 1984; Waller, 1985b). For some causes death rates decline after age 70 or 80, such as for many occupational injury categories. There is a sharp decline in machinery-related deaths (farms, etc.) after age 75. As many elders independently restrict their driving, the elderly are more likely to be pedestrians than drivers. This fact is reflected in their high rates of pedestrian injuries.

Role of Normative and Pathologic Changes

In an analysis of the effect of medical impairments on injury exposure among a sample of injured elders, impaired men were underrepresented and impaired women overrepresented (Waller, 1985a). Impaired men are often less likely than other men to be exposed to occupational and recreational hazards, whereas impaired women may still have to cope with household chores and related hazards.

The combined effects of medical conditions and decrements of normal aging also influence injury exposure and incidence as well as the ability to respond to injury threat, the resistance to injury, and the probability of recovery. Such conditions have a magnified impact upon elderly people who are victims of numerous pathologies and decreases in functional capacities.

Almost half of all persons over age 65 experience some limitation of activity because of a chronic condition (National Center for Health Statistics, 1980a). About 70 out of every 1,000 persons over age 65 need the help of another person in performing at least one or more basic physical activities or home management activities (National Center for Health Statistics, 1983a). The reduction of the ability to perform self-care activities and carry out home maintenance caused by the presence of chronic disease and functional limitation increases the chance of exposure of elderly persons to injurious agents, and decreases their ability to escape harm from that exposure. Even normal facets of the biological aging process can limit the elder's capacity to prevent injury or to react in dangerous situations.

Waller (1985a, 1985b) provides a substantial review of both normative and pathologic changes that influence injury risk among the elderly.

Vision. Among the elderly the most significant change in vision is the development of presbyopia. The intensity of light required in order to see increases. With age, the lens of the eye becomes yellowed and opaque, filtering out light and increasing susceptibility to glare. The visual field narrows, and depth perception and the ability to distinguish color are decreased. Dynamic visual acuity, or the ability to identify and follow moving objects, is decreased. Consequently, more time is required for the aged eye to focus.

> Factors such as poor vision, decreased hearing, poor olfaction, weaker muscles, slower reflexes, orthostatic blood pressure, and the effects of disease and drug therapy can increase the risk of injury in the aged.

Hearing. Hearing is decreased, although this change is rarely implicated in injury events. Hearing deficits may, however, delay early warning by smoke alarms.

Smell. Older persons experience decreased acuity in the sense of smell.

Musculoskeletal changes. Mass and strength of bone and muscle are decreased, particularly among women. The increasing prevalence of osteoporosis among postmenopausal women contributes to the incidence of spinal compression fractures and fractures that occur even with minor activity such as sneezing or opening a window. Overall stature and stamina are decreased. As the gait becomes uncertain, there is often shuffling of the feet and a shifting forward of the center of gravity.

Physiological changes. Renal and hepatic function are decreased. Drug metabolism is slower, increasing sensory and psychomotor impairment. Tranquilizers may bring about excessive drowsiness, orthostatic drops in blood pressure, or uncoordination. Barbiturates often contribute to drowsiness and confusion. Digitalis may lead to arrhythmias and consequent loss of blood supply to the brain and myocardium.

Neurological and cognitive changes. Reflex reaction time, sensitivity to temperature change, and tactile and vibratory sensations are decreased; pain threshold may increase. The ability to learn and solve problems may decrease. Memory often deteriorates, and concentration becomes more difficult.

The burden of medical impairments or pathological changes that often accompany increasing age can place added strain on an older individual who faces an injurious scenario.

Certain cardiovascular conditions can cause either sudden or less acute impairment in abilities to resist or survive injury. Cardiac efficiency and rhythm may affect the amount of oxygen delivered to the brain without the individual's awareness.

Diabetes mellitus alters visual acuity, visual fields, and peripheral sensations in the later years. Visual impairment affects the incidence of falls, motor vehicle injuries (both pedestrian and crash-related), and burn injury. Peripheral vascular and nerve desensitization can prevent an individual from sensing a rapid temperature change when in contact with a hot surface or can delay awareness and treatment of a burn or other injury.

The frequency and severity of seizures may increase in those with seizure disorders, increasing the incidence of seizure-related falls and perhaps subsequent burn injury.

Prevalence of mobility disorders, specifically parkinsonism, multiple sclerosis, stroke, and advanced arthritis, can have a significant effect on the incidence of falls. Daily tasks requiring motor coordination, such as the handling of hot objects or flammable materials, become more risky in the impaired individual.

Additional visual deficits, like those resulting from cataracts, diabetic and hypertensive retinopathy, macular degeneration, and glaucoma, limit the capacity of the individual to avoid injury.

Alcoholism or excessive alcohol consumption, though a more infrequent contributor to serious injuries in the elderly, is the most important human cause of fatal highway crashes. It is also a common factor in fatal falls, home-related injuries, and drownings.

Other medical conditions that increase injury risk include the dementias, disorders of the parasympathetic nervous system, and disabilities secondary to previous trauma. The combined effects of more than one medical condition may be additive or multiplicative in increasing injury risk. Increased assessment of the elderly by health professionals for particular sensory deficits and medical conditions that have an effect on the incidence of injury may help to identify individuals who are at highest risk of injury and to target areas for intervention.

Social Factors

Advanced age places many older persons at a disadvantage in settings of rapid technological and social change. Reduced income in old age means that many elderly live in poor, unsafe housing with limited egress in case of fire and in neighborhoods with heavy traffic. In addition, many elderly are less financially able to maintain the safety of their environments through simple home repairs, installation of lifesaving devices such as smoke alarms, and provision of adequate heating fuel for the colder months. Many elderly are increasingly isolated socially and lack supportive life frameworks that might encourage them to seek medical care for correctable impairments, such as auditory or visual deficits. Thus the ability of the elderly to respond in situations of impending danger is impaired, often resulting in injury, a problem that significantly affects older people.

Rehabilitation of the elderly following injury is often complicated, for example, by fear of recurrence and loss of pride following reduction in mobility (Smith, 1976). Such complications increase the number of long-term care admissions, as even basic routine daily self-care activities become difficult and even dangerous, and create increased demands on Medicare and Medicaid funding. In a population with a large number of elderly, injuries in the aged place a disproportionate strain on hospital and social services (Smith, 1976). In this respect the problem of injuries among the elderly is not confined strictly to those injured but affects those family members who must directly provide for their needs, and it also affects those members of society who inevitably must bear an indirect financial responsibility for their care.

> The majority of injury deaths in the older population result from falls, burns, and motor vehicle accidents.

Among the elderly, three types of events account for three-fourths of all injury deaths: falls, fires and burns, and vehicular collisions (Waller, 1974). The following sections will discuss these three major injury problems among the older population, including descriptive epidemiology and proposed preventive strategies emphasizing the role of nursing professionals in injury prevention.

Falls and Fall Injuries

Of all types of injuries, those resulting from falls pose the most serious threat to the elderly (Baker and Harvey, 1985). While minor injuries such as lacerations, contusions, and abrasions occur most frequently, approximately 3% of falls result in major or serious injuries such as fractures (Myers et al., 1989).

Rates

> It is estimated that 30% of the elderly experience a fall each year and that a greater rate of falls exists among older persons who are experiencing acute episodes of illness.

There is a paucity of published community- or population-based research on falls and resulting injuries among the elderly; however, there are a half dozen such studies funded and currently under way. Table 7-3 shows the proportion of falls reported among the elderly living in the home/community environment. It is generally hypothesized that about 30% of the elderly experience a fall each year.

Most reported studies of falls among the elderly have taken place in a variety of institutional settings. Table 7-4 shows selected studies and suggests that the rate of falls is greater among the elderly experiencing acute episodes of illness.

The mortality rate from falls increases with age and is highest of all types of injuries (Figure 7-1). For ages 85 and older, one fatal fall out of every five occurs in a nursing home (Baker et al., 1984). In a nursing home study of falls and injuries, it was observed that 30% of the patients who sustained a hip fracture died within five months of the injury (Myers et al., 1989). Cummings and associates (1985) review reports that in the first year after a fracture the mortality rate in patients with hip fracture is about

TABLE 7-3. Studies of Falls in the Home Environment among the Elderly

Study	Proportion Who Fall (usually within one year)	Site
Sheldon (1960), England	40%	Random sample of residents in Wolverhampton
Droller (1955), England	36–45%	Random sample of elderly in Sheffield
Exton-Smith (1977), England	24–44%	Medical interviews of elderly
Prudham and Evans (1981), England	28%	Community survey
Wild et al. (1981), England	20/1,000	Physician-visits (case control)
Campbell et al. (1981), New Zealand	34% (at least one fall) 45% (80–89 years) 56% (90–99 years)	Community survey including hospitals and residential homes
Lucht (1971), Denmark	14/1,000 treated for fall	ER-hospital based
Waller (1974), U.S.A.	33% of controls _Cases_ 33%, 60–79 years 67%, 80 years	ER cases (many institutional matched with controls)
Perry (1982), U.S.A.	38%	High-rise apartments
Torbis et al. (1985), U.S.A.	34%, ≥ 60 20%, 60–69 36% 70–79 42%, 80–89 80%, 90–94	Independently living community older adults in California—three different groups
Hornbrook (1987), U.S.A.	30/100 person-years (intervention group) 37/100 person-years (control group)	10% of entire membership of Northwest Region of Kaiser Permanente age 65 and over

12–20% higher than in persons of similar age and gender who have not suffered a fracture, and that most of the excess mortality occurs within the first four months after the fracture.

Hip fractures are the most frequent of all serious injuries sustained by the elderly population, and repair of the fractures is the most common surgery for persons over 75 years of age (Birnbaum, 1978). The age-specific rates are highest for the elderly, ranging from 43 per 100,000 in 45–64-year-olds to 743 per 100,000 in the 65-and-over group (National Center for Health Statistics, 1980b). In 1980, among all diagnoses for the elderly population, only burns had a longer average hospital stay than hip fractures (25.8 days for burns, 20.5 for hip fractures) (National Center for Health Statistics, 1980b). In the oldest group (over 85), it is estimated that each year approximately 2% of all women and 1% of all men will suffer a hip fracture. Predictions of post-hip-fracture survival and independence are age (Cobey et al., 1976), prefracture ambulation status (Miller, 1978), prefracture social independence (Cobey et al., 1976; Jensen, 1984), physical

TABLE 7-4. Selected Studies of Falls among the Elderly (65+) in Institutional Settings

Study	Setting	Falls per 100 Patient-Years
Myers et al. (1989)	Nursing home	190
Rohde et al. (in press)	General hospital (metropolitan medical center)	182
Morgan et al. (1985)	Acute care specialty hospital	139
Gryfe et al. (1977)	Residential home	67

therapist assessment of physical function prior to hospital discharge (Cobey et al., 1976), and severity and type of other diseases (Dahl, 1980).

When patients with hip fracture return home, their needs change considerably. Of a group of patients admitted from home for hip fracture repair, 82% had returned to their homes at six-month follow-up. Of these, 29% were more dependent than before the fracture (Jensen et al., 1979). After 2.5 years of follow-up in this same group, 47% had deteriorated in their need for care and assistance (Jensen and Bagger, 1982). In another study of patients age 65 and older who were admitted from home with a femoral fracture, only one-fourth gained full recovery (Cobey et al., 1976). We found that of the 23 patients who sustained hip fractures in the nursing home, 19 (83%) did not return to the same level of care, but required additional or more skilled care upon discharge from the hospital (Myers et al., 1989). In 1980 there were approximately 200,000 persons with hip fractures at a median age of 79 years (Brody et al., 1987). According to Census Bureau projections, if the incidence rate for hip fracture remains the same, by the year 2000 the number of cases will have increased to almost 350,000 (Brody et al., 1987).

Among persons who have fallen there is a fear of falling again. This fear can affect their willingness to be active and mobile, thereby diminishing the quality of life.

A significant consequence among persons who have fallen is the fear of falling again, which can lead to decreased mobility, increased debility, decreased socialization, and a diminished quality of life (Granek et al., 1987; Tinetti, 1985; Mossey, 1985). Pawlson and associates' (1986) survey of nursing home residents revealed a substantial number of cognitively intact residents who walked but who also used a wheelchair. In addition to physical factors and multiple social and environment factors, fear of falling was related to the resident's decision to use a wheelchair.

Factors Related to a Fall

Following is a summary of the findings from several studies which identify factors associated with falling among elderly persons in a variety of settings:

- An acute illness or chronic health problem, a number of disabilities (Tinetti et al., 1986; Waller, 1978).
- Decreased or impaired mobility, ataxia (Brody et al., 1984; Tinetti et al., 1986; Janken et al., 1986; Sobel and McCart, 1983).

- Dizziness, vertigo (Stegman, 1983; Janken et al., 1986; Sobel and McCart, 1983).
- Orthostatic hypotension or change in diastolic blood pressure upon rising (Stegman, 1983; Rosen et al., 1985).
- Confusion, poor mental status (Tinetti et al., 1986; Janken et al., 1986; Sobel and McCart, 1983).
- History of falls (especially in those with medical impairment) (Wieman and Obear, 1986).
- Insomnia, increased agitation, management problem (Brody et al., 1984; Sobel and McCart, 1983).
- Psychoactive medications, sedative/hypnotics, diuretics (Sobel and McCart, 1983; Rosen et al., 1985).
- Decreased vision (Tinetti et al., 1986).
- Substance abuse (Waller, 1978; Janken et al., 1986).
- Increased depression, psychiatric diagnosis (Brody et al., 1984; Rosen et al., 1985).
- Environmental factors (especially in those without health problems).

Research has indicated that among nursing home residents ambulation status is the strongest predictor of a person's likelihood of falling (Myers et al., 1989). Among elderly ambulators, age (90+), vision status, history of falls, nonsteroidal anti-inflammatory agents, and sedative/hypnotics were significant predictors of persons likely to fall. Among nonambulatory residents, significant predictors of fallers included history of fall and use of antidepressants, sedative/hypnotics, and diuretics (Myers et al., 1989). From these studies and an additional analysis of medications and diagnoses in relation to falls (Granek et al., 1987), the risk of falling appears to increase with the use of selected medications.

Environmental factors contribute to falls and injuries and are important factors relative to prevention because they are potentially modifiable. Clark (1986), in reporting on a series of 450 women with fractures of the femur, estimated that one-quarter of the fractures were clearly preventable and one-half possibly preventable by alteration of the environment. Morfitt's (1983) work suggested that environmental modification at least up to the age of 75 would be relevant for the prevention of falls among the elderly at home. According to Ashley and colleagues (1977), the extrinsic or environmental factors may be the most readily identifiable and potentially modifiable element in a complex, multifactorial event.

Environmental factors refer to natural and manufactured environmental factors. Falling and resulting injuries have been attributed to icy winter conditions found in selected parts of the country (Waller, 1978). Reduced light or darkness has also been noted as contributing to falling, especially in the home environment at night (Czaja et al., 1982). A study of the hazardous products involved in injuries among the elderly treated at selected hospital emergency rooms in the United States revealed that stairs, steps, floors, and flooring materials were most frequently involved in injuries. Findings on how the injury occurred relative to stairs and steps revealed that the occurrence of stair injuries for women is three times that for men; 66% occurred at home, 9% in public places; 12% of the injuries occurred to the lower trunk, 9% to the head (Czaja et al., 1982). From the study descriptions of the circumstances cited below, the interaction of environmental factors and personal factors becomes apparent:

- *Loss of balance.* Victim suffers from sudden dizziness or loss of balance while using stairs and falls. Often there are no handrails on stairs to counteract the fall.
- *Inappropriate situational model.* Victim is unaware of stairway because surroundings are dark or unfamiliar and falls down stairs while en route to another location.
- *Misstep.* Victim misses a step on stairs because vision is obstructed by carried object or victim had inappropriate model of situation—thought he or she had reached the last step when in fact it was not the last step and fell.
- *Foot slipped.* While walking on stairs, foot slips on stair surface and victim falls.
- *Falls.* Victim is unable to exert enough force and limb "gives way"; unable to react quickly enough to counteract change in body position; victim falls (Czaja et al., 1982).

Findings related to floors and flooring materials suggest that the rate of occurrence for these falls among women is twice that for men; 67% occurred at home, 19% in public places; 29% of injuries occur to the lower extremity, 12% to the head. The circumstances involving floors, flooring materials, rugs, and carpets are as follows:

- *Tripping.* Victim trips over rug and falls. This type of accident occurs in the following circumstances:
  Change in floor surface. Victim, while walking, trips over edge of rug at rug-to-floor junction and falls, even though victim can see rug and is aware that it is there.
  Unperceived rug. Victim is in dark or unusual surroundings and fails to perceive rug, trips on it and falls.
- *Slipping.* Victim slips on rug or floor surface and falls. This type of accident occurs in the following circumstances:
  Bathroom rug slips. Victim walking or stepping into bath puts one foot on rug, which slips on shiny floor surface, causing the victim to fall.
  Change in flooring surface. Victim moves from one flooring surface to another and foot either slips or sticks, causing a fall.
  Friction force is exceeded. Victim's foot slips on flooring when friction force is exceeded, causing falls (Czaja et al., 1982).

The most frequent wheelchair-related fall occurred when an older adult pulled the wheelchair over on himself or herself. Other causes of wheelchair falls include transferring without locking the wheels, sliding from the chair, and missing the seat.

Numerous studies (Table 7-4) report that in institutional settings falls frequently occur around the bed and going to and from the bathroom. In the nursing home setting, our findings reveal that a wheelchair was involved in one fall in four. Of the 382 falls involving wheelchairs, 91 resulted in injuries. The most frequent known accident was pulling the wheelchair over on oneself. Other wheelchair falls involved getting out of protective devices, attempted transfers from or to unlocked wheelchairs, sliding from the chair, or missing the seat (Myers et al., 1989).

Burn Injuries

Burns among the elderly are a serious problem in terms of suffering, morbidity, mortality, medical and nursing care requirements, prolonged hospitalization, and health care costs. The burns of older persons have certain characteristics distinct from those in the young. Burn injury of the old has a different genesis, results in a different disease course, and requires a different therapeutic approach. This injury also carries different expectancies of

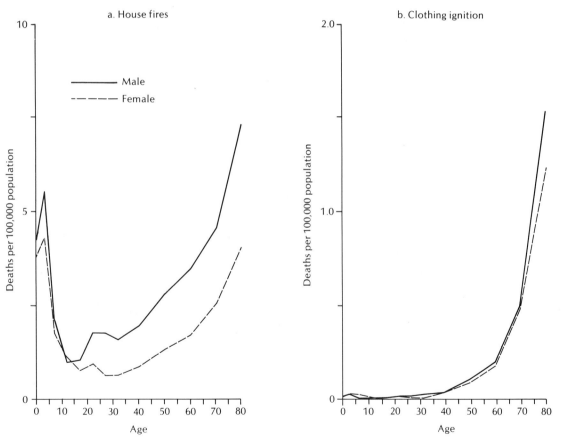

Note: Vertical scales differ

FIGURE 7-2. Death Rates from Housefires and Clothing Ignition by Age and Sex, 1977–1979. (Baker SP, Karpf RS, O'Neill B: The Injury Fact Book. Lexington, MA, Lexington Books, 1984, p. 140.)

Although the incidence of burns is lower in the older population, the mortality rate is higher. Older males have a higher rate of burns than older females.

survival. When death ensues, it usually follows at a later point in time, and the cause of death often differs from that of younger patients (Hajek and Peskova, 1974). Although the incidence of burns among the elderly is lower than that for younger persons, burn mortality among the aged is much higher. Even for minor burns, elderly persons are much more likely to be hospitalized and to remain longer because of the presence of other disabilities. The presence of chronic disease often complicates the severity of burn injury and recovery from its harm. Since many elderly have impaired senses and slow reaction time, their burns tend to be deeper. This factor, together with the reduced physiological ability of the older body to cope with the insult of injury, means that the elderly are more likely to die even from less severe burns.

An extensive literature review reveals that most research in the area of burns has examined burn incidence in all age groups combined, but that few works have concentrated on the older population (Beverley, 1976; Slater and Gaisford, 1981; Deitch and Clothier, 1983; Housinger et al., 1984; Rossignol et al., 1985). Thus, studies exploring the particular issues involved with elderly burns are much needed. In general, the studies reviewed do not discuss specific prevention strategies or modification of the current health care system to any extent, although some work in the area of treatment modalities for burns among the aged has been accomplished. Two of the more significant studies of older burn patients were completed outside the United States, in nations where medical technology differs (Hajek and Peskova, 1974; Maisels and Ghosh, 1968). Even a cursory glance at the literature dealing with burns in older persons indicates the necessity of additional research in this area.

Morbidity and Mortality

Within the elderly population there exist certain patterns of incidence of burn injury. Burn rates are generally higher among males than females. In the 65-years-and-older group, rates of burn tend to increase with age (Rossignol et al., 1985) (Figure 7-4).

Most of what is reported in the literature concerns basic epidemiology of burns in the elderly. Burns are the third largest contributor to death from injury among persons age 65–74, and the fifth leading cause of death from injury among those over 75. For deaths due to fire or burns only the death rates for those aged 0–4 years and for those over age 75 exceed that of the 65–74-year-old age group. Figure 7-3 illustrates the death rate from fires and burns by age and sex. About 1,400 fire/flame burn deaths per year occur among the approximate 12% of the population who are 65 years of age and older, accounting for more than one-third of all deaths due to burns of this type. Twelve hundred of these occurred in the home. This figure excludes burns caused by contact with a hot object or hot liquid scalds, most of which also occur in the home (National Safety Council, 1985a). In addition, burn injury among the elderly accounts for anywhere from 9% (Brodzka et al., 1985) to 20% (Slater and Gaisford, 1981) of all hospital

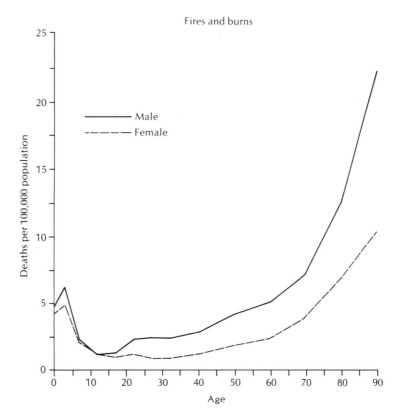

FIGURE 7-3. Death Rates by Age, Sex, 1977–1979. (Baker SP, Karpf RS, O'Neill B: The Injury Fact Book. Lexington, MA, Lexington Books, 1984, p. 41.)

admissions due to burns. (The Brodzka study, however, included only burn patients referred for rehabilitation, survivors, and a probable decreased proportion of elderly persons, and therefore may be a rather low estimate of aged burn admissions.)

Although the rate of burn incidence is about one and one-half times higher among the young than in the older age groups, 23.8 injuries per 100,000 person-years compared to 15.5 per 100,000 person-years, mortality among the elderly is roughly seven times higher than in the young (Rossignol et al., 1985).

Burn care has progressed greatly in the last four decades. Until the late 1940s there had been no report of a patient over 60 years of age who had survived a burn covering greater than 10% of the total body surface area (TBSA). By the early 1970s mortality was reported to be 100% for patients over 60 years with burns greater than 30% TBSA. More recently, in a review of 34,731 cases, Feller and Crane (1970) report a survival rate of 56.5% among geriatric burn patients.

In one study (Anous and Heimbach, 1986), four variables were shown to be significant in a comparison between deceased patients with the lowest

%TBSA burns and survivors of burn injury: (1) lower extremity burns were associated with lower mortality; they were not associated with higher total burn surface area, exposure to toxic fumes, or inhalation injury; (2) decedents required almost twice their calculated fluid needs within the first 24 hours after injury in order to maintain vital signs, thus setting the scene for respiratory complications; (3) pneumonia, frequently fatal in older persons; and (4) poor nutrition or particularly high caloric requirements due to presence of infection.

Common causes of burn mortality among the elderly include circulatory insufficiency, renal and pulmonary failure, lung and wound sepsis, and shock (Hajek and Peskova, 1974; Slater and Gaisford, 1981). As age increases there are fewer deaths from sepsis and more from circulatory insufficiency. Because older persons tend to die sooner from their burns there is less opportunity for sepsis to develop. The most frequently encountered organisms were *Staphylococcus aureus* and *Pseudomonas* (Anous and Heimbach, 1986).

It has been suggested that an age bias exists in the treatment of burns. In a study of emergency treatment of nonhighway injury, Waller (1975) reports that subjects under age 30 received preferential assistance by lay people and professionals. Linn (1980) reports that there was almost no difference between older and younger burn patients in treatments received, despite the higher severity of burns in older patients. A frequently accepted notion is that since most burns in the elderly are fatal, an aggressive approach toward early surgical wound coverage in these patients is not worthwhile, despite much evidence that the elderly can withstand and benefit from surgical intervention and rehabilitation (Slater and Gaisford, 1981; Deitch and Clothier, 1983). Rehabilitative efforts are often likewise thought to be unproductive, and any reconstructive plastic surgeries unnecessary in persons who are in the autumn of their lives.

Circumstances Surrounding Burn Incidence in the Elderly

There are several characteristic ways in which to describe a burn. Burns may be *structure related* (e.g., house fire) or *nonstructure related* (e.g., clothing ignition by cooking flames or smoking materials). Following the initial distinction, burns are described by *mechanism of injury*: contact (with hot item, including scalds), flame/flash, or electrical. Figure 7-4 shows the percent of hospital admissions for nonstructure-related burns by age and cause. Another important factor worthy of examination is the activity taking place at the time of the incident. Among the elderly, approximately 60% of burns occur while carrying out household chores, such as cooking or doing home repairs (Brodzka et al., 1985).

Smoking materials are often implicated both in house fires and other nonstructure-related burns (Mierley and Baker, 1983; Halpin et al., 1975; Birky et al., 1979). Flame burns as a result of smoking incidents and house fires are the leading cause of burn death for both sexes of elderly (Slater and Gaisford, 1981; Rossignol et al., 1985). Faulty heating equipment is the sec-

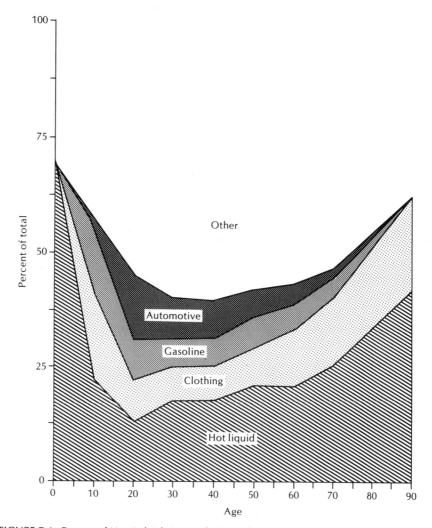

FIGURE 7-4. Percent of Hospital Admissions for Burns by Age and Cause, New York State Burn Study, 1974–1975. (Baker SP, Karpf RS, O'Neill B: The Injury Fact Book. Lexington, MA, Lexington Books, 1984, p. 148.)

ond leading cause of death from flame burns and house fires (Mierley and Baker, 1983; National Fire Data Center, 1978).

Scalds, the most common burn type among women, are a significant cause of injury among elderly females. Hot liquids are the most important cause of hospitalized burns among the elderly (Baker et al., 1984) (see Figure 7-3). Brodzka and colleagues (1985) suggest that as many as 50% of bathtub scalds occur among those 63–73 years of age. In another study 27% of hospitalized scalds were among those over 60 years of age (Feck and Baptiste, 1979; Baptiste and Feck, 1980). Older patients are often unable to remove themselves quickly from the tub or shower in order to avoid scalding and may fall or slip in the tub after being scalded. Seizures, cardiovascular accidents, or syncopal episodes can result in prolonged exposure to water hot enough to burn. Thirty seconds of exposure to water at 130° can cause a full thickness burn (Moncrieff, 1979; Moritz and Henriques, 1947).

Factors Related to Burn Injury and Mortality

Many authors refer to the existence of a burn-prone individual, one who is predisposed to burn injury (Maisels and Ghosh, 1968; MacArthur and Moore, 1975; Brodzka et al., 1985). The elderly are considered to be pre-disposed to burn injury, not strictly because of their advanced age and other normative biological factors related to aging, but because of limitations that frequently develop with increasing age that contribute to burn incidence and severity. The physical and mental limitations of many elderly persons hinder them from participating in primary personal injury prevention. These same limitations are considered to be risk factors for burns. Brodzka and others (1985) observed predisposing conditions such as substance abuse, cardiovascular disease, dementia, epilepsy, cerebrovascular disease, impaired mobility, mental illness, blindness, impaired sensation, peripheral neuropathy, and advanced age among burn survivors referred for rehabilitation. They found that these factors were present in 85% of those over age 60 but only in 48% of those younger.

> Cardiovascular and cerebrovascular disease, substance abuse, impaired mobility, mental illness, and blindness are among the factors that not only increase the risk of burn injury, but also complicate treatment and threaten survival.

In one study all complications except contractures were associated over-whelmingly with the elderly (Linn, 1980). The mentally ill, demented, or otherwise impaired patient may be less able to cooperate in care and may be more apt to die of a minor burn. Anous and Heimbach (1986) indicate a tendency for those with documented alcohol problems to live alone and have higher total burn surface area. The proportion of alcoholics, however, was similar in the highest and lowest burn groups. It is unclear whether these impairments and conditions truly increase the individual's probability of sustaining burn injury, since no study has compared burn patients with nonburned controls.

The same factors that may predispose to burn injury also complicate burn survival. The work of Feller and colleagues (1980) indicates that age, general disability, and significant underlying disease contribute to a mortality of 50% after full-thickness burns of 10–14% in the elderly.

As the body ages, there is a loss of dermal thickness, resulting in the paper-thin and almost transparent appearance of the skin. There is decreased sensitivity of the nerve endings in older persons; thus heat and cold are not readily appreciated. The skin has a decreased growth and repair rate, slowing down the process of wound closure and increasing the chance of infection. The injury response rate is slowed, masking the initial severity of burn wounds. In the elderly, owing to decreased circulation, burn depth is initially less apparent, and inflammation is not as readily observed until it is rather progressed. This factor leads to a general underestimate of overall burn severity and risk in the elderly.

Other age-related factors contribute to burns. General disability is increased among the elderly. Their frailty, inability to maintain posture, and poor memory increase the possible involvement of the elderly with burn agents. A large number of burns are sustained in falls against hot surfaces or while spilling hot liquids. Many elderly no longer possess the coordination to handle matches, cigarettes, or hot appliances safely. The elderly often suffer from impaired sensory perception including decreased visual, auditory, and olfactory acuity, which impedes their detection of flames and smoke. An increase in physical impairments makes many elderly unable to respond in order to remove themselves from danger before it is too late. There is often an inability to react when clothes catch fire. The configuration of the controls on the stove may be confusing for older persons, or the gas jet may be turned on and forgotten until later when a match is lit nearby.

Besides general physical and mental disability, there are social factors that affect burn incidence. These factors are less frequently discussed in the literature reviewed. As previously mentioned, the social isolation faced by many elderly persons affects the amount of supportive resources they have at their disposal. This problem not only affects burn incidence, but also relates to the expedience with which elderly burn patients receive care for their injuries, as well as the outcome of treatment and rehabilitation. Astonishing delays in seeking burn treatment sometimes occur among older people. Some patients delay treatment anywhere from 10 to 23 days after injury (Brodzka et al., 1985). Rossignol and associates (1985) indicate that approximately 26% of their elderly burn patients received initial medical care at least one day after their burn incident. Delays in treatment often result in complications caused by infection and other consequences that often prolong disability or hasten death. These kinds of delays may be more frequent among elderly people who live alone.

Environmental factors play a large role in burn incidence. The elderly may be unable to maintain the safety of their home environments or to urge others (i.e., landlords and legislators) to maintain the safety of rental and government-funded housing. The lack of heat and electricity in some living quarters leads some elderly to go to great lengths to provide warmth, however unsafe and inefficient their methods may be.

Preventive Strategies

Eyeglasses, hearing aids, smoke detectors, sprinkler systems, controlled hot water temperature, safe furnaces, adequate electricity, and home maintenance programs can prevent many burn injuries in the elderly.

The relationship between burn incidence and many nonbehavioral factors indicates several areas for intervention. Biologically we cannot change the elderly. Elderly persons could be more avidly counseled by family, physicians, nurses, and general society to obtain proper eyeglasses and hearing aids, and to install smoke alarms to increase the length of time in which to respond to the threat of being burned. Improvement of living conditions would have a great impact on general injury prevention among the elderly. Widespread installation of antiscald devices or mixing valves, particularly on bathtub faucets where the majority of such accidents occur, would decrease the risk of hot water scalds among both children and adults (Anti-

Scald Devices, 1977). Regulation of hot water heaters, especially in mul-
tiunit dwellings where a large proportion of hot water scalds occur, would
not only decrease scald burn risk but add up to major energy savings as
well (Baptiste and Feck, 1980). Installation of safe furnaces to prevent unsafe heating practices and sufficient electricity to prevent use of candles as a
light source could decrease burn incidence. Legislation could be proposed
requiring smoke alarms and sprinkler systems in rental properties. Schmeer
and colleagues (1986) describe an effective house fire burn prevention program of distributing smoke alarms in areas of substandard housing that was
founded by a hospital-based support group of recovered burn patients.
Their efforts serve as a model for other similar communities. Additional improvements might be brought on through community organization of elders
in sites where large numbers of elders congregate, such as senior centers,
senior high-rise apartment buildings, or local churches. Informal and formal
home maintenance and community renewal projects designed specifically for
aid to the elderly are currently active in many localities. More of these programs are needed for elderly people who are not able to perform home
maintenance activities on their own. Increased reimbursement for home
health care and visiting nurses would help to insure some basic health maintenance of the infirm elderly, decrease length of hospital stay and postburn
institutionalization, and assist with rehabilitation of the burned elder. More
extensive programs and governmental reimbursement for homemaking services are needed, since most elderly suffer burn injury while performing basic self-care or household activities. Design of clothing, particularly sleep-
wear such as nightgowns and robes, made of flame-retardant material with
close-fitting sleeves, would have an effect on the major problem of clothing
ignition for many elderly individuals.

Based on information from the Health Promotion and Disease Prevention Supplement to the National Health Interview Survey, the elderly are
relatively knowledgeable about home injury prevention, but, like persons of
other age groups, their behavior does not correspond to their knowledge or
attitudes concerning burn and fire prevention (National Center for Health
Statistics, 1986). Slightly over half of the homes inhabited by elderly persons have any working smoke detectors. Only about one-third of the elderly
know their home's water temperature. Compared to other age groups, a
smaller proportion of the elderly population live in homes where someone
has tested the hot water temperature with a thermometer. A larger proportion of elderly, however, do not know the temperature at which water will
cause injuries. Families of elderly persons can play a large part in equipping
the hot water heaters of homes in which elderly persons live with antiscald
devices or by presetting hot water heaters at 120 degrees, selecting safe
cookware and dishware, and providing increased supervision for persons
who are only marginally functional. Health education outreach programs
can assist not only in the prevention of burns, but also in shortening delays
in seeking medical attention for burn injury.

More work must be done in the area of treatment and rehabilitation of
elderly burn patients. Little is known of the postburn psychosocial needs of

older persons. Equal attention to the medical and psychological needs of elderly persons compared to that paid to needs of younger burn patients is needed and will require a change in perspective toward the elderly in general as more valued contributing members of society. By examining these needs, we seek not only to maintain the elderly person's independence and prevent costly institutionalization, but also to maintain the productivity, self-satisfaction, and quality of life of the elderly burn patient.

Motor Vehicle Injuries: Driver, Occupant, and Pedestrian

Motor vehicles are the most frequent cause of unintentional fatal injury for ages 1 to 74. Above age 75, falls replace motor vehicles as the most frequent cause. Motor vehicle injury accounts for roughly 30% of all injury deaths in persons over age 65 (National Safety Council, 1985b). The following section will discuss motor vehicle injuries that occur to both occupants and drivers of automobiles, riders of pedal cycles (bicycles, mopeds) and motorcycles, and pedestrians.

Morbidity and Mortality

Elderly persons are at a higher risk of adverse outcome from motor vehicle trauma than younger persons. Persons age 75 and older were hospitalized as a result of motor accidents at least twice as often as those of any other group and seven times more often than children less than one year old, the group with the lowest case-admission ratio. The likelihood of adverse outcome from both motor-vehicle-related and non-transport-related accidents was significantly higher for the elderly than for any other age group. In particular, female pedestrians aged 55 to 64 had the highest case-admission ratio of any age–sex–road-use category. Among injured passenger car occupants, males aged 15 to 19 and both sexes of elderly aged 75 and over had the highest case-admission ratios for this category. High case-admission ratios for injuries involving pedal cycles were not a significant problem among older persons (Barancik and Kramer, 1985; Barancik et al., 1986).

Fatalities involving motor vehicle injury in elderly persons are also of significant concern. Among males, pedestrian fatality ratios increase steadily from age 35, peaking in the 75+ age group. This fatality ratio was the highest of all age or road-use categories, three times higher than that for females of the same age, and twice as high as the peak female ratio at 55–64 years of age.

The increasing likelihood that an older driver will be involved in a fatal crash may be due to a decreasing ability to survive injury. Baker and Spitz (1970a) observed that older drivers were less likely to have died immediately following a crash than were younger drivers. Older drivers who died a month or more following the crash had less serious injuries than younger persons who survived.

Automobiles

There are 15.2 million licensed drivers age 65 and over in the United States, accounting for 9.6% of all licensed drivers. The proportion of older drivers continues to rise despite tightened licensing restrictions (Hogue, 1980). The 65-and-older portion of the driving population has been cited as the segment displaying the most rapid growth (Planek and Fowler, 1971). Drivers age 65–74 have the lowest rates of all accident involvement (13 per 100 drivers licensed in each age group); the highest rate is for drivers aged 20–24, 34 for every 100 licensed drivers (National Safety Council, 1985a).

Although the motor vehicle accident rate per driver is lower among the elderly, the accident rate per mile driven equals that for young persons.

However, when the rate of accident involvement is calculated using number of miles driven as the denominator, as opposed to number of licensed drivers, the rates for older drivers approach or equal those of the 20–24 year age group. Older males tend to drive more than older females, and for both sexes drivers 65 years and older travel fewer miles annually than do drivers under age 65 (Waller, 1967; Planek and Fowler, 1971). Consequently, the elderly have fewer crashes per driver, but more crashes per mile driven. In addition, drivers 65 years of age and over drive substantially less during rush hour, in darkness, and in the winter. However, they do not differ from the young in types of roads driven.

In 1984, 6,300 persons age 65 and older died from injuries involving motor vehicles, either as drivers, occupants, or pedestrians, comprising 7% of such victims (National Safety Council, 1985a). Persons ages 55–64 suffer 6.9% of all automobile occupant fatalities and represent 5.9% of all occupants involved in fatal crashes. Persons aged 64 years and older comprise 11.3% of all automobile occupant fatalities, yet still represent only 7.4% of all occupants involved in fatal crashes.

Characteristics of Crashes Involving Older Drivers

Day of Week and Time of Day. Fatal crashes among motor vehicle occupants (or drivers) over age 55 reach their peak occurrence on Fridays. The peak for the over-65 age group is slightly higher than that of 55–64-year-olds. The same general pattern is evident for time of day of crash, the peak period for which is noon–4 P.M. for both the 55–64 age group and for those 65 and over. One minor deviation, however, is that the crash incidence among the older group appears to be higher in the earlier hours and lower in the later hours than that of the younger age group (National Highway Traffic Safety Administration, 1985). Baker and Spitz (1970a) also support the pattern of a decreasing proportion of nighttime crashes with increasing age, both in drivers who had been drinking prior to the crash and in those who had not.

Circumstances. The findings of the Duke Adaptation Study are similar to those reported for older drivers in other studies (Palmore, 1974). Only 12% of crashes took place in the rain and none in snow. Of the crashes that occurred, 82% took place in the driver's home county and 7% in the adjacent one. Residential or business sections were the scene of 79% of crashes among older drivers.

The percentage of fatal crashes involving more than one vehicle decreases with age (Baker and Spitz, 1970a). In the Duke Adaptation Study, all but two of the 56 crashes among older drivers involved two or more vehicles.

Baker and Spitz (1970a) blindly and systematically assigned responsibility for crash to drivers involved in their series of fatal crashes and determined that the percentage of drivers not at fault in each age group increases with age until age 60, then drops off. The percentage of drivers at fault in an age group depends partly on the percentage of crashes involving more than one vehicle.

Alcohol Involvement. Of fatally injured drivers, drivers over 60 years of age are least likely to have been drinking prior to a crash. Drivers killed at night (6 P.M. to 6 A.M.), however, are three times more likely to have been drinking during the daytime hours (Baker and Spitz, 1970a).

Palmore (1974) found that only two of 56 older drivers involved in a motor vehicle crash were under the influence of alcohol with ability impaired.

Predominant Errors. The Duke Adaptation Study reports that the predominant driver errors recorded for crashes involving older drivers were disregard for stop signs or failure to yield the right of way. Only one driver was cited for excessive speed as a contribution to the crash.

Problems of Aging Drivers

Planek and Fowler (1971) surveyed a population of older drivers in order to elicit their concerns regarding their driving behavior. The following list summarizes driving difficulties as perceived by older drivers:

Yielding the right of way

Turning

Changing lanes

Keeping up with traffic

Own slow speed

Inattention

Failure to read traffic signs

Running red lights and stop signs

The latter three items were considered to result in a significant number of violations among older drivers, despite the fact that older drivers frequently use good driving judgment. Additional observed driving infractions include a very high frequency of failure to yield, failure to signal, and improper turning. The largest proportion of violations appear to be problems of moving from one traffic lane to another, an action which requires a rapid series of judgments and actions. Such violations may be the result of slowed perception or of the way reception and processing of information are affected by age.

Medical Conditions and the Older Driver

One of the more significant debates involving older drivers concerns the role of medical conditions in automobile crashes. The threat of sudden death at the wheel has led to the restriction of driving privileges among many older people, particularly those with heart disease. Despite much discussion the question remains to what extent medical conditions contribute and whether they contribute causally to motor vehicle crash incidence. An analysis of data from the Duke Adaptation Study found no association between road crashes and vision, hearing, cardiovascular disease, musculoskeletal impairment, general functional status, life change, or coping resources (Hogue, 1974).

Baker and Spitz (1970b) reviewed a number of studies that explored the relationship between highway safety and driver medical conditions, the majority of which failed to demonstrate that collisions actually result from driver impairment. In their own study, no pedestrians and no drivers of other cars died in collisions as a result of another driver's death at the wheel. They suggest that sudden death at the wheel is not likely to account for a substantial number of motor vehicle injury deaths, and that costly examinations and screening for medical conditions prior to license renewal may not be justified.

The notion of retesting older drivers is based on the premise that certain limitations and deficiencies are progressively more likely to affect drivers as they age, such as memory, vision, alertness, and general health. Thus many states have a policy regarding license renewal for older drivers that involves both vision and general medical examinations and, less often, knowledge and road tests. However, the relationship of health characteristics to actual driving performance or risk of collision is unclear. Numerous authors conclude that the presently available data do not support a positive safety effect of the current license renewal process (Christensen et al., 1976; Kelsey and Janke, 1983; Kelsey et al., 1985).

Pedestrians

Slightly fewer than 8% of all pedestrian deaths occur in persons 65 years of age and over. Injured pedestrians have the highest overall risk of adverse outcome. Both the case-admission and case-fatality ratios increase progressively with age (Barancik et al., 1986).

Data from the nationwide Fatal Accident Reporting System reveal the following concerning pedestrian death rates (National Highway Traffic Safety Administration, 1985):

Age (years)	Death Rate per 100,000 Population
<14	2.0
14–64	2.6
64+	5.1
All	2.8

Among fatally injured pedestrians aged 14–64, 74% are male and 26% female. Over age 64, 56% of fatally injured pedestrians are male and 44% female (National Highway Traffic Safety Administration, 1985).

Increased age was associated with fatal pedestrian accident involvement both in the absence of measurable prior alcohol consumption and in the presence of low concentrations of alcohol.

The National Safety Council (1985a) reports that 77.7% of pedestrian deaths and injuries occur while crossing or entering the intersection, 5.6% while walking in the roadway, and 2.1% while standing in the roadway.

Motorized Cyclists

Although most injuries among motorized cyclists occur in young adult males, there is a progressively worsening injury outcome with rising age. Adverse outcome is more common for older cyclists injured on the roadway. In a comparison of motorcycle and moped injuries in a Swedish population, where there is a long history of moped use (Matzsch and Karlsson, 1986), 21.3% of mopedists injured were 60 years of age or older (mean age, 30.1 years; range, 9–87 years), and these accounted for 56% of fatalities observed. The most frequent circumstance in which moped injuries occurred was collision with a car; among injured motorcyclists (mean age, 20.7 years; range, 6–66 years; of whom less than ten were under age 35), the most frequent case involved overturning or running off the road. The mean age of fatalities among mopedists was significantly higher than that of motorcycle fatalities. Among fatally injured mopedists the highest number of fatalities occurred to those over 60 years of age. Fatally injured mopedists died as a result of less severe injuries (lower Injury Severity Score values) than did motorcyclists of the same fate. Because the moped fatality group contained a large number of elderly persons, this higher fatality rate is thought to be a result of the increased vulnerability of older persons to injury.

In the United States in 1985, persons between the ages of 45 and 64 accounted for 8.1% of pedal cyclist fatalities. Those over 64 years of age comprised 5.5% of pedal cyclist crash fatalities, the majority of which were nonintersection fatalities on the roadway (National Highway Traffic Safety Administration, 1985).

Preventive Strategies

Motor vehicle accidents of the elderly could be reduced by vehicle design that includes airbags, adaptive mirrors, shatterproof glass, modified headrests, and brighter taillights and headlights in better locations.

Strategies for prevention of injuries to motor vehicle drivers and occupants, pedestrians, and cyclists run the gamut of approaches. Vehicle design may utilize a passive approach to passenger protection through the manufacture and retrofitting of automobiles with airbags, adaptive mirrors for the elder who is visually limited, and shatterproof windshields. Additional options, such as modified head restraints for the elder whose posture is not fully upright and headlights and taillights that afford proper visibility through increased illumination and better placement, would do much to increase the amount of protection offered to the older driver.

Engineers need to reexamine roadways and explore new design options to maximize the safety of all motorists, keeping in mind that the population will be an older one. Illumination on highways should be increased and be of a reduced glare variety. Pavement striping should be more vivid; signs should be larger and their message made more clear so as to lessen confusion of the older driver; the time allowed for passage through an amber signal light should be lengthened to allow for the slower reaction time of the older motorist.

The notion of driver reeducation needs to be examined more closely. Currently several organizations conduct defensive driving courses aimed at the older adult. Such programs need to deal directly with the problems of the older adult as empirically evaluated, and should include the provision of information on safety features to consider when buying an automobile and on modifications to increase visibility, such as convex mirrors. Screening of older drivers and restricted licensing should not be accepted as a panacea for problems on the roadway. With the increase in the number of elderly drivers and a commensurate decrease in the number of younger individuals to provide transportation for the elderly, we must either find ways to maintain the driving skills and assure the safety of the older population or increase the accessibility of mass transportation and social services such as Meals on Wheels, shoppers' programs, and physician housecall services.

SECTION TWO

Strategies for Care

James Eastham, Jr., and Judy Bobb

Initial Assessment

Initial assessment of the trauma victim is designed to identify injuries which are potentially life threatening and to initiate therapy before the full extent of the injury is determined. Knowledge of the mechanism of injury provides information that is a helpful indication of the possible severity of an injury. For example, injury sustained in a high-speed motor vehicle collision raises a higher index of suspicion for multiple-system injury than does a stabbing injury.

The initial assessment needs to be rapid but comprehensive. It must be organized in such a fashion as to determine *all* injuries that are potentially life threatening. A useful approach is to examine the patient from head to toe, noting all abrasions, lacerations, wounds, deformities, and loss of function.

Stabilization

Once all injuries are noted, initial stabilization and treatment of the patient proceeds in order of priority. The airway is inspected and adequacy of respiration determined. If necessary, an artificial airway is placed and ventilatory support is established. Obvious external hemorrhage is controlled and intravenous access is established.

Brief neurologic examination should include response to commands, movement of extremities, and pupillary signs. The cervical spine should be stabilized as rapidly as possible. Neurological examination may be hindered by the presence of visual or hearing disorders, or by the excessive sensory stimulation that is associated with most emergency departments. Testing the ability of the individual to obey verbal commands should be preceded by gaining the attention of the patient and by verifying that the patient can hear and understand the instructions. Care should be exercised that speaking is done in view of the patient and that the language is kept simple. Remember that aging may produce changes in the eyes, such as cataracts, that may cloud the pupillary examination.

More thorough examination of these priority systems, as well as of the abdomen, pelvis, and extremities, can be performed as the patient is stabilized.

Initial Treatment

The stress associated with injury trauma creates added ventilatory demands that the elderly are less able to manage. Early endotracheal intubation and mechanical ventilatory support may be required.

Experience has shown the need for thorough assessment of respiratory status following trauma. Many persons are capable of sustaining ventilatory efforts despite profound degrees of hypoxemia. It is not always readily apparent that the individual requires mechanical ventilation for purposes of optimal oxygenation. Arterial blood gases will help to demonstrate this need. Because the elderly appear less able to respond to the additional ventilatory demands imposed by the stress of trauma, consideration should be given to early endotracheal intubation and mechanical ventilatory support. However, it should also be recognized that, once intubated, the older person will likely require a prolonged period of artificial ventilatory support. The hazards associated with mechanical ventilation must also be weighed against the increased possibility of pneumonia, a frequent cause of death in the hospitalized elderly. Allen and Schwab (1985) have suggested that elderly persons with single-system chest trauma can often be managed successfully without resorting to artificial means. This is less likely to be true if the patient has sustained injury to more than one body system. Should the patient require endotracheal intubation, it should be carried out under as ideal circumstances as possible to offer minimal risk to the patient. Until the cervical spine has been proven intact by X ray no manipulation of the spine will be possible.

Hemorrhagic shock is presumed in the victim of blunt trauma until proven otherwise. Therefore, to stabilize the cardiovascular system it is nec-

Close monitoring of intravenous therapy is necessary to avoid hypovolemia, as well as circulatory overload.

essary to have intravenous access sufficient to administer large quantities of fluid and blood, if indicated. Large-caliber intravenous lines should be placed in multiple locations. Cardiac rhythm should be monitored continuously, and a retention urinary catheter placed for monitoring of urinary output.

Statistics indicate that approximately one person in five over age 65 years has some cardiovascular disease. Caution needs to be exercised before assuming that the elderly trauma victim has significant impairment in this system. Failure to replace lost intravascular volume rapidly and adequately may subject the patient to an unwarranted period of hypovolemia and increase the risk of complications from shock. Conversely, it is not advisable to overload the capacity of the older cardiovascular system. Intensive monitoring of the response of the patient to fluid loading is possible with early placement of catheters for monitoring pulmonary artery wedge pressures.

Cardiac rhythm disturbances should also be approached with caution in the elderly. Following trauma, the most frequent causes of rhythm disturbances are hypoxemia and electrolyte disturbances. These causes should be thoroughly investigated and ruled out before assuming any arrhythmia is from preexisting heart disease.

Diminished gag and cough reflexes increase the older individual's vulnerability to aspiration. Gastric intubation should be initiated early, particularly when impairment in level of consciousness is present.

Additional Examination

Ideally, rehabilitation needs of the injured person are identified during the initial assessment.

Unless the patient requires emergency surgery for an injury identified during the initial assessment, the examination should continue with thorough assessment of all body systems and review of past history. During this phase formulation of rehabilitation plans is begun, for many needs can be anticipated based upon the nature and extent of injury. Additional points to remember during assessment relate to anticipating normal aging changes.

Changes in the conformation of the chest and function of the lungs may yield findings that are different from those found in the young. Aging lowers the number of functional alveoli, a process called senile emphysema. This should be differentiated from the disease emphysema. In the former, breath sounds may be lowered in intensity as lung volumes decrease, but arterial blood gases do not reflect chronic hypoventilation. Arterial oxygen tension, however, can be expected to fall gradually with age. Individuals with the disease emphysema show signs of marked decrease in arterial oxygen tension along with chronic hypoventilation. Loss of respiratory muscle mass is common in the elderly, along with diminished gag reflexes and a weaker cough.

Cardiovascular assessment includes heart sounds, cardiac rhythm, and examination of the peripheral vasculature. Heart sounds may be more audible in those persons with diminished fat and muscle mass over the chest. The presence of a cardiac murmur may be detected. Functional systolic murmurs are estimated to occur in approximately 50% of those over 65 years of age. Arrhythmias may be found in those patients with prior cardiac disease. Each arrhythmia should be assessed for its impact on cardiac output and treated accordingly.

The peripheral vasculature should be examined for presence and equality of pulses and for peripheral edema. Peripheral vascular disease needs to be distinguished from acute changes associated with injury. Pulses that are difficult to palpate should be assessed using a Doppler ultrasound device. Determination of the past history may provide additional information, should any abnormality be detected. Peripheral edema resulting from injury is usually unilateral, whereas that of cardiac origin is most often bilateral. Again, past history may prove helpful in differentiating acute from chronic edema.

In addition to the neurological examination, the patient should be examined for sensory and motor function. Sensation to light touch is frequently diminished. Perception of pain may be diminished or may be different from what is expected in the young. Gross as well as fine motor function should be examined, keeping in mind that joint disease may limit range of motion. Abdominal and ankle reflexes are often unobtainable in the elderly, and the knee reflex can be limited by arthritis. However, plantar, biceps, and triceps are usually present and equal.

Neurological examination should also focus on the mental health status of the patient. Depression and a sense of worthlessness may be present. Look for life stress events in the immediate past history of the patient. These events, such as loss of a spouse or retirement, increase the stress the patient experiences and predispose him or her to accidents.

Musculoskeletal assessment should include muscle mass and tone, range of motion, and presence of deformities. The skin should be thoroughly examined for scars and lesions, both acute and chronic. Look for ecchymoses in dependent areas indicating recent bleeding into the soft tissues. Examine the nail beds for clubbing. Overall assessment of the cleanliness and care of the skin may give clues to the self-concept of the individual.

Look to the skin also for clues to other chronic disease that may affect the patient's response to injury. Skin lesions may indicate neoplasm or diabetes, which are more common with advancing years.

Assess the abdomen for masses and organ enlargement. Abdominal tone is frequently reduced, and abdominal reflexes may be absent. Bowel sounds are of limited value acutely, since they are frequently absent.

History

If the patient is judged an adequate historian, a brief review of his or her past experience is indicated. History should include past illnesses and hospitalizations, allergies, and medications. Items of particular interest in the elderly are presence of chronic disease and medication use.

It is estimated that a majority of those over age 65 years have at least one chronic disease. The medical diagnosis alone may not be of much value. It is important to determine what impairment in daily living the chronic disease imposes. Related to limitations, it is helpful to determine how active the individual is. It has been suggested that the person who lives an active life and is not restricted to the home environment is better able to tolerate the stresses of injury.

Medication history should include the number and type of prescribed medications the patient takes and whether he or she deviates from the prescribing information. In addition, it should be determined if the patient uses over-the-counter medications. This information can be elicited with questions such as, What do you take for headache? How many? How often? Lack of compliance with prescribing information or interaction of medications may have contributed to the accident or may affect the patient's response to injury. The patient's personal physician and frequency of visits should be determined. Inquire whether the patient sees more than one physician, for what reason, and how frequently. If possible, have a family member bring prescribed medications to the hospital for examination.

Definitive Treatment

The specific treatment selected for an elderly patient will be based upon the injuries sustained, the medical history, and an estimate of the patient's response to treatment. Some decisions will need to take age into account for rehabilitation purposes, although most treatment is independent of age. For example, a decision to amputate an extremity may be influenced by age if mobilization can be expected to occur sooner with amputation than with external fixation and if prolonged bed rest is likely to increase the risk of complications.

As mentioned earlier, artificial support of the airway and ventilation are indicated early in the patient with multiple-system injury, even if no primary injury to the chest or lung is present. Traumatic injury places exceptional demands on ventilatory effort even in the young. The elderly person is more likely to experience respiratory embarrassment, is more susceptible to aspiration, and is less able to sustain the needed respiratory effort. Therefore, consideration must be given to early intubation and mechanical ventilation. The decision to institute artificial support must also be done with the consideration that, once instituted, support must be expected to continue for a longer period of time than for the young. This decision carries an additional risk of respiratory infection or other complications of mechanical ventilation.

Whether mechanical ventilation is instituted or not, the elderly person requires close attention to tracheobronchial toilet. Within the limitations of the original injury and the treatment selected, chest physical therapy and postural drainage, aseptic suctioning of secretions, and frequent turning are essential to reduce the risk of pneumonia. The patient must be well hydrated, and airway gases must be humidified to facilitate removal of secretions. Artificial airways must be secured to prevent soft-tissue irritation. Plans should be made for mobilization, even before mechanical ventilation is discontinued.

Cardiovascular support is frequently indicated. Once fluid volume has been restored, attention should be paid to the adequacy of perfusion. This can be assessed through peripheral pulses and urinary output as well as by direct measurements of cardiac output. Assessment of filling pressures and afterload are helpful in providing adequate cardiac output without overloading the cardiovascular system. Inotropic support is often indicated acutely until the patient has sufficiently recovered his or her own ability to maintain perfusion.

Lowered resistance to infection and altered presentation of symptoms demand that nurses closely observe for signs of infection.

Injury lowers immune competence even in the young. Protection from infection must be balanced against the need for invasive monitoring or treatment. Judgment as well as benefit-risk assessment is required to determine when the patient can safely be discontinued from invasive therapy, but invasive devices should be removed as quickly as possible. The patient must be closely monitored for signs of developing infection. Remember that the elderly may not manifest infection as clearly or as rapidly as the younger person.

Adequate nutritional support fosters repair and healing of injuries. The caloric demands of multiple trauma can be extremely large. Accordingly, nutritional support should be instituted early in the postinjury phase. The intravenous route will be selected initially, but it should be followed by enteral feedings as soon as bowel function returns. Each individual should be monitored closely for tolerance of feedings. The elderly may exhibit lower tolerance for glucose loads; therefore, blood sugar monitoring is indicated. Usually blood sugar can be controlled through adjustments in feedings and by the addition of regular insulin.

Attention to the mental health of the patient is essential once the patient has been treated initially. The stress of injury followed by the stress of hospitalization favors depression and a lowered sense of self-worth. Nursing plays a unique role in this area of patient care.

Communication is important to the recovering injury victim. Mechanisms to communicate should be based on the individual's unique capabilities.

Of primary importance is a means of communication with the patient. Communication strategy should be based on assessment of the visual, auditory, and educational capabilities of the patient. It is essential that the individual's comprehension be continually determined regardless of the method chosen for communication. Paper and pencil may be ideal for communicating with the person who has an artificial airway in place, but if the patient cannot see adequately no communication is possible. The method chosen should be consistent so the patient is exposed to fewer new stimuli. When possible, familiar objects can be introduced into the environment and family or friends allowed to visit. The patient may need frequent orientation to time and place if windows, clocks, and the like are not available. The nurse should remember that touch can be an excellent form of communication whatever the status of the patient.

As the patient regains independence, it is helpful to allow him or her as much control over the environment as possible. Placing and keeping objects in the same place help reduce disorientation. Scheduling activities, such as ambulation, at the same time each day provides the patient with a sense of security.

An important component to successful recovery of the elderly is early mobilization. Getting the elderly patient out of bed may be time consuming and difficult to accomplish, but it offers the best cost-benefit ratio of all therapies. No other single therapy has the same multisystem effect. Mobilization improves respiratory and cardiovascular function, promotes a positive mental outlook, improves orientation, encourages joint motion, spares the skin additional pressure and abrasion, stimulates appetite and gastrointestinal function, facilitates rehabilitation, and fosters healing of all body systems.

> Early mobility can promote physical and mental function and prevent a host of complications.

Summary

Ideally the increase in the elderly population together with knowledge of injury-prevention techniques should stimulate social changes and reduce the incidence and severity of injury in this segment of the population. The reality, however, is that these changes will be slow in coming. For the present, society in general and health care providers in particular must adapt to the reality of increasing numbers of elderly trauma victims.

Present and past experience need to be combined with research efforts to determine the optimal methods for treatment of the older individual when injury occurs. Modifications of treatment protocols are needed that can reduce the impact of injury, shorten the recovery time, and return the individual to society.

REFERENCES

Allen JE, Schwab CW: Blunt chest trauma in the elderly. Am Surg 51:697–700, 1985.

Anous MM, Heimbach DM: Causes of death and predictors in burned patients more than 60 years of age. J Trauma 26:135–139, 1986.

Anti-scald devices are saving money for contractors. Contractor, June 15: 73, 1977.

Ashley MJ, Gryfe C, Amies A: A longitudinal study of falls in an elderly population. II. Some circumstances of falling. Age and Ageing 6:211, 1977.

Baker SP: Determinants of injury and opportunities for intervention. Am J Epidemiol 101:98–102, 1975.

Baker S, Dietz PE: The epidemiology and prevention of injuries. In Zuidema GD, Rutherford RB, Ballinger WF II (eds): The Management of Trauma. Philadelphia, WB Saunders, 1979.

Baker SP, Harvey AH: Fall injuries in the elderly. Clin Geriatr Med 1: 501–508, 1985.

Baker SP, Karpf RS, O'Neill B: The Injury Fact Book. Lexington, MA, Lexington Books, 1984.

Baker SP, Spitz WU: Age-effects and autopsy evidence of disease in fatally injured drivers. JAMA 214:1079–1088, 1970a.

Baker SP, Spitz WU: An evaluation of the hazard created by natural death at the wheel. NEJM 283:405–409, 1970b.

Baptiste MS, Feck G: Preventing tap water burns. Am J Public Health 70:727–729, 1980.

Barancik JI, Chatterjee BF, Greene-Cradden YC, Michenzi EM, Kramer CF, Thode HC Jr, Fife D: Motor vehicle trauma in Northeastern Ohio. I. Incidence and outcome by age, sex, and road-use category. Am J Epidemiol 123:846–861, 1986.

Barancik JI, Kramer CF: Northeastern Ohio trauma study: Overview and issues. Public Health Reports 100:563–565, 1985.

Beverley EV: Reducing fire and burn hazards among the elderly. Geriatrics 31:106–110, 1976.

Birky MM, Halpin BM, Caplan YH, Fisher RS, McAllister RM, Dixon AM: Fire fatality study. Fire and Materials 4:211–217, 1979.

Birnbaum H: Costs of Catastrophic Illness. Lexington, MA, Lexington Books, 1978.

Brody EM, Kleban MH, Moss MS, et al.: Predictors of falls among institutionalized women with Alzheimer's disease. J Am Geriatr Soc 32:877, 1984.

Brody JA, Brock DB, Williams TF: Trends in the health of the aging population. Annu Rev Public Health 8:211–234, 1987.

Brodzka EA, Thornhill HL, Howard S: Burns: Causes and risk factors. Arch Phys Med Rehab 66:746–752, 1985.

Campbell AJ, Reinken J, Allan BC, Martinez GS: Falls in old age: A study of frequency and related clinical factors. Age Aging 10:264–270, 1981.

Christensen P, Glad H, Pederson T: The Safety Value of Driver License Renewals: An Analysis of Research Results. Oslo, Norway, Institute of Transportation Economics, 1976.

Clark ANG: Factors in fracture of the female femur. Gerontol Clin 10:257–258, 1986.

Cobey JC, Cobey JH, Conant L, et al.: Indicators of recovery from fractures of the hip. Clin Orthoped 117:258–262, 1976.

Cummings S, Kelsey J, Nevitt M, O'Dowd K: Epidemiology of osteoporosis and osteoporotic fractures. Epidemiol Rev 1:178–208, 1985.

Czaja SJ, Hammond K, Drury CC: Accidents and aging: A final report. Prepared by the Buffalo Organization for Social and Technical Innovation, Inc., for the Administration on Aging, Washington, DC, NTIS, PB84-158849, December 1982.

Dahl E: Mortality and life expectancy after hip fractures. Acta Orthoped Scand 51:163–170, 1980.

Deitch EA, Clothier J: Burns in the elderly: An early surgical approach. J Trauma 23:891–894, 1983.

Droller H: Falls among elderly people living at home. Geriatrics 10:239–244, 1955.

Exton–Smith AN: Functional consequences of aging: Clinical manifestations. In Care of the Elderly: Meeting the Challenge of Dependency. London, Academic Press, 1977.

Feck G, Baptiste MS: The epidemiology of burn injury in New York. Public Health Reports 94:312–318, 1979.

Feller I, Crane K: National Burn Information Exchange. Surg Clin North Am 50:1425–1536, 1970.

Feller I, Tholen D, Cornell RG: Improvements in burn care, 1965–1979. JAMA 244:2074–2078, 1980.

Granek E, Baker SP, Abbey H, Robinson E, Myers AH, Samkoff JS, Klein LE: Medications and diagnoses in relation to falls in a long-term care facility. J Am Geriatr Soc 35:503–511, 1987.

Gryfe CI, Amies A, Ashley MJ: A longitudinal study of falls in an elderly population: I. Incidence and morbidity. Age Aging 6, 1977.

Haddon W, Baker SP: Injury control. In Clark D, MacMahon B (eds): Preventive and Community Medicine. Boston, Little, Brown, 1981.

Hajek S, Peskova H: Fatal thermic accidents in old people. Acta Chirurgiae Plasticae 16:164–170, 1974.

Halpin BM, Radford ER, Fisher R, Caplan Y: A fire fatality study. Fire J 69:11–13, 98–99, 1975.

Hogue CC: Coping resources, stress and health change in middle age. Unpublished dissertation. University of North Carolina, Chapel Hill, 1974.

Hogue CC: Epidemiology of Aging. Proceedings of the 2nd White House Conference on the Epidemiology of Aging, March 28–29, 1977. USDHHS, Public Health Service, NIH, July 1980.

Hornbrook MC: Prevention of falls in the elderly: Study of accidental falls in the elderly. Progress Summary Presented at The National Institute on Aging, April 1, 1987.

Housinger T, Saffle J, Ward S, Warder G: Conservative approach to the elderly patients with burns. Am J Surg 148:817, 1984.

Iskrant AP, Joliet PV: Accident and Homicide. Cambridge, MA, Harvard University Press, 1968.

Janken JK, Reynolds BA, Sweich K: Patient falls in the acute care setting: Identifying risk factors. Nurs Res 35:215–218, 1986.

Jensen JS: Determining factors for the mortality following hip fractures. Injury 15:411–414, 1984.

Jensen JS, Bagger J: Long-term social prognosis after hip fractures. Acta Orthoped Scand 53:97–101, 1982.

Jensen JS, Tondevold E, Sorensen PH: Social rehabilitation following hip fractures. Acta Orthoped Scand 50:777–785, 1979.

Kelsey SL, Janke ML: Driver license renewal by mail in California. J Safety Res 14:65–82, 1983.

Kelsey SL, Janke M, Peck RC, Ratz M: License extension for clean-record drivers: A 4-year followup. J Safety Res 16:149–167, 1985.

Linn BS: Age differences in the severity and outcome of burns. J Am Geriatr Soc 28:118–123, 1980.

Lucht U: A prospective study of accidental falls and resulting injuries in the home among elderly people. Acta Socio-Medica Scandinavica 2:105–120, 1971.

MacArthur JD, Moore FD: Epidemiology of burns: The burn-prone patient. JAMA 231:259–263, 1975.

Maisels DO, Ghosh J: Predisposing causes of burns in adults. The Practitioner 231:767–773, 1968.

Matzsch T, Karlsson B: Moped and motorcycle accidents—Similarities and discrepancies. J Trauma 26:538–543, 1986.

Mierley MC, Baker SP: Fatal house fires in an urban population. JAMA 249:1466–1468, 1983.

Miller CW: Survival and ambulation following hip fracture. J Bone Joint Surg 60-A:930–933, 1978.

Moncrieff JA: The body's response to heat. In Artz CP, Moncrieff JA, Pruitt, BA Jr (eds): Burns: A Team Approach. Philadelphia, WB Saunders, 1979.

Morfitt JM: Falls in old people at home: Intrinsic versus environmental factors in causation. Public Health (London) 97:115–117, 1983.

Morgan VR, Mathison JH, Rice JC, Clemmer DI: Hospital falls: A persistent problem. Am J Public Health 75:775–777, 1985.

Moritz AR, Henriques FC Jr: The relative importance of time and surface temperature in the causation of cutaneous burns. Am J Pathol 23:695–720, 1947.

Mossey JM: Social and psychological factors related to falls among the elderly. Clin Geriatr Med 1:541–552, 1985.

Myers AH, Baker SP, Robinson EG, Abbey H, Timms E, Levenson S: Injurious falls among the institutionalized elderly. J Long Term Care Admin, October 1989.

National Center for Health Statistics. Vital and Health Statistics. Current Estimates from National Health Interview Survey, United States. Series 10, No. 139, Washington, DC, U.S. Government Printing Office, 1980a.

National Center for Health Statistics. Vital and Health Statistics. Inpatient utilization of short stay hospitals by diagnosis, United States. Series 13, No. 74, Washington, DC, U.S. Government Printing Office, 1980b.

National Center for Health Statistics, Feller BA: Americans needing help to function at home, 1979. Advance Data from Vital and Health Statistics, No. 92, DHHS Pub. No. (PHS) 83-1250. Hyattsville, MD, Public Health Service, September 1983a.

National Center for Health Statistics. Vital and Health Statistics. Utilization of Short-stay Hospitals, United States, 1981, Annual Summary. Series 13, No. 72. Hyattsville, MD, September 1983b.

National Center for Health Statistics, Collins JG: Persons injured and disability days due to injuries, United States, 1980–1981. Vital and Health Statistics. Series 10, No. 149. Hyattsville, MD, March 1985.

National Center for Health Statistics, Thornberry OT, Wilson RW, Golden PM: Health promotion data for the 1990 objectives, Estimates from the National Health Interview Survey of Health Promotion and Disease Prevention, United States, 1985. Advance Data from Vital and Health Statistics, No. 126, DHHS Pub. No. (PHS) 86-1250. Hyattsville, MD, Public Health Service, September 1986.

National Fire Data Center. Fire in the United States: Deaths, Injuries, Dollar Loss and Incidents at the National, State, and Local Levels. Washington, DC, U.S. Government Printing Office, 1978.

National Highway Traffic Safety Administration: FARS Report. Washington, DC, U.S. Department of Transportation, 1985.

National Safety Council: Accident Facts. Chicago, 1985a.

National Safety Council: Older Americans Accident Facts. Chicago, 1985b.

Palmore EB: Normal Aging II. Durham, NC, Duke Press, 1974.

Pawlson LG, Goodwin M, Keith K: Wheelchair use by ambulatory nursing home residents. J Am Geriatr Soc 34:860–864, 1986.

Perry BC: Falls among the elderly living in high rise apartments. J Family Pract 14(6):1069–1073, 1982.

Planek TW, Fowler RC: Traffic accident problems and exposure characteristics of the aging driver. J Gerontol 26:224–230, 1971.

Prudham D, Evans JG: Factors associated with falls in the elderly: A community study. Age Aging 10:141–146, 1981.

Rohde J, Myers A, Vlahov D: Clinical department as a risk factor for falls: Implications for prevention. Submitted for publication.

Rosen AM, Campbell RJ, Villanueva J, Morgan K: Factors affecting falling by older psychiatric inpatients. Psychosomatics 26 (February):117–123, 1985.

Rossignol AM, Locke JA, Boyle CM, Burke JF: Consumer products and hospitalized burn injuries among elderly Massachusetts residents. J Am Geriatr Soc 33:768–772, 1985.

Schmeer S, Stern N, Monafo WW: An effective burn prevention program initiated by a recovered burn patient group. J Burn Care Rehabil 7:535–536, 1986.

Sheldon JH: On the natural history of falls in old age. Brit Med J 2:1685–1690, 1960.

Slater H, Gaisford JC: Burns in older patients. J Am Geriatr Soc 29:74–76, 1981.

Smith C: Accidents and the elderly. Nursing Times, 1872–1874, 1976.

Sobel KG, McCart GM: Drug use and accidental falls in an intermediate care facility. Drug Intel Clin Pharm 17:539–540, 1983.

Stegman MR: Falls among elderly hypertensives—Are they iatrogenic? Gerontology 29:399, 1983.

Tinetti M: Discussion. Clin Geriatr Med 1:512, 1985.

Tinetti ME, Williams TF, Mayewski R: Fall risk index for elderly patients based on number of chronic disabilities. Am J Med 80:429–434, 1986.

Torbis JS, Reinsch S, Swanson JM, Byrd A, Scharf T: Visual perception dominance of fallers among community-dwelling adults. J Am Geriatr Soc 33(5):330–331, 1985.

Waller JA: Cardiovascular disease, aging, and traffic accidents. J Chron Dis 20:615–620, 1967.

Waller JA: Emergency care for fatalities from injury and illness in the non-highway setting. J Trauma 13:54, 1975.

Waller JA: Injury in the aged: Clinical and epidemiological implications. New York State J Med 77:2200–2208, November 1974.

Waller JA: Falls among the elderly: Human and environmental factors. Accident Analysis and Prevention 10:21–33, 1978.

Waller JA: Injury Control: A Guide to the Causes and Prevention of Trauma. Lexington, MA, Lexington Books, 1985a.

Waller JA: Unintentional injury among the medically impaired and elderly. Public Health Reports 100:577–579, 1985b.

Wieman HM, Obear ME: Falls and the use of physical restraints in a skilled nursing facility population. Presented at the meeting of the American Geriatrics Society, 1986.

Wild D, Nayak US, Isaacs B: How dangerous are falls in old people? Brit Med J 23:282, 1981.

BIBLIOGRAPHY   Anderson GC: Card tables as side rails. Geriatr Nurs 7(2): 103, 1986.

Bobb JK: Trauma in the elderly. J Gerontol Nurs 13(11): 28–31, 1987.

Cogliano JF: Justifying those environmental rounds. Contemporary Long Term Care 11(7): 80–81, 1988.

Godwin MP, Mohn SP: Easy transfer with the long board. Geriatr Nurs 8(6): 333, 1987.

Hernandez M, Miller J: How to reduce falls. Geriatr Nurs 7(2): 97–102, 1986.

Jonathan T: Providing security for residents of retirement communities. Contemporary Long Term Care 11(6): 94–95, 108, 1988.

Neuberger J: New for old . . . better design of clothing and furniture for elderly patients. Nurs Times 82(41): 22, 1986.

Parsons MT, Levy J: Nursing process in injury prevention. J Gerontol Nurs 13(7): 36–40, 1987.

Schwartz AR, Bosker G, Grigsby JW (eds): Geriatric Emergencies. Bowie, MD, Robert J. Brady Co., 1984.

Tynan C, Cardea JM: Community service home health hazard assessment. J Gerontol Nurs 13(10): 25–28, 1987.

Watkins R: The high cost of hip fractures in older adults. Contemporary Long Term Care 11(7): 78–79, 1988.

CHAPTER 8

Geriatric Rehabilitation

Melinda D. Fitting and Susan K. Brock

Chapter Objectives
At the completion of this chapter the reader will be able to:

1. Define rehabilitation.
2. List the types of disabilities that can benefit from rehabilitation.
3. Describe the components of assessing functional capacity, social support, psychological state, and environment.
4. Discuss the unique features of the elderly that affect rehabilitation.

We who are old know that age is more than a disability. It is an intense and varied experience, almost beyond our capacity at times, but something to be carried high. If it is a long defeat it is also a victory, meaningful for the initiates of time, if not for those who have come less far.

F. Scott-Maxwell, The Measure of My Days

Philosophy of Rehabilitation

What is rehabilitation? It is the practice of rehabilitating, or making capable of living again. The focus is upon *function* rather than cure. Rehabilitation specialists strive to teach a person how to function at his or her maximal level within the limits imposed by an injury or a physical or mental impairment. It is this maximization of potential through education, training, and the integration of a person's remaining abilities that is the hallmark of rehabilitation. It includes physical, social, psychological, and vocational aspects of a person's life. The person as a whole is assessed throughout the rehabilitation process in order to establish specific rehabilitative goals unique to each individual.

Can older people benefit from rehabilitation? Older people are able to utilize the skills of a rehabilitation team to the same degree as younger people. However, there are some specific characteristics of the older years that may need to be considered in the treatment plan. Treatment goals may differ at different stages of the life span, but goals should always be focused upon a return to premorbid functioning as much as possible. Age should *not* be the criterion that determines goals, because older people are not a homogeneous group. In fact, as people get older there is more heterogeneity than in the younger years. For example, it may be appropriate to set a goal of independent ambulation in the home with a 90-year-old widowed female after her hip fracture. She may be able to return to her home after a period of rehabilitation in a hospital or nursing home and continue with her premorbid activities. Another elderly woman may feel that a broken hip signifies the end of her life; she may begin making arrangements to move out of her home where she has lived for 40 years and to move in with her daughter. If a 40-year-old woman broke her hip, the rehabilitative goal would be the restoration of function to her premorbid status, but this would most likely include a return to work and family responsibilities. Goals differ for different people but should be based on the unique characteristics of each individual and not on age.

> The focus of rehabilitation is not cure but improvement of function to one's maximal potential.

Rehabilitation to one's maximal potential can and should take place after an acute injury such as a traumatic fall with a resultant hip fracture, and yet, even in acute injuries with the elderly, rehabilitation does not always occur (see Chapter 7). Acute medicine assumes that a disease can be diagnosed and cured, thus enabling the person to resume his or her premorbid functional level. Traumatic insults to the body such as head injury, spinal cord injury, fractures, or strokes may prohibit restoration of the person's premorbid functional level. Even in diseases with a progressive deterioration such as Alzheimer's disease, Parkinson's disease, or arthritis, the rehabilitation model can be applied to establish a new equilibrium that maximizes the functional level.

Disabilities and the Elderly

Chronic degenerative diseases are a fact of life for most elderly people. The risk of chronic illness increases with age, including arthritis, heart disease, hearing or visual impairments, diabetes, Alzheimer's disease, and orthopedic impairments. Four out of five older people report suffering from at least one chronic illness, and the elderly often have multiple medical problems. Arthritis, hypertension, auditory impairments, and heart disease are the most common diseases, accounting for almost 60% of all chronic conditions reported by the noninstitutionalized elderly population (Soldo and Manton, 1985). Institutionalized elderly as a group have high prevalence rates of circulatory diseases (Soldo and Manton, 1985) and cognitive impairments such as Alzheimer's disease (Rovner and Rabins, 1985).

The data on depression in the elderly are equivocal. While there is evidence to suggest that the rates of depression are as high as 40% in the disabled population (Blazer, 1982), the rates for depression in the general population appear to be highest in the middle years and to decline in the later years (Kramer et al., 1985). It is important to note that the suicide rate for elderly males is higher than any other group in the United States, and the prevalence of disability is a risk factor (Miller, 1979).

How do these chronic illnesses affect functional capacity? Data on per-

TABLE 8-1. Principles of Rehabilitative Nursing

1. Maintenance and restoration of function is important at all ages.
2. Goals for the elderly may be different from those for younger people. The individual patient needs to be included in establishing his or her treatment goals.
3. Age should not be a primary consideration, but the unique characteristics of each patient should be used to determine treatment goals.
4. The rehabilitation process is slower in older people than in younger people because of physiological changes associated with age, such as slowed reaction time, longer healing time, pain, less organ reserve, decreased kidney function, and increased susceptibility to infectious disease.
5. Care should focus on the patient in the context of his or her family.
6. Education for family and patients is a vital part of the rehabilitation process.

sonal care assistance suggest that there is an association between age, chronic illness, and functional capacity. Only 6.7% of persons in the age group 65–74 require personal assistance, in contrast to 15.7% for those aged 75–84, and the numbers increase dramatically to 44% for the 85-plus age group (Soldo and Manton, 1985).

The functionally disabled older woman is less likely to have a spouse available to provide care and will need to depend on family, friends, or formal caregiving systems, such as nursing homes, for assistance.

Of the approximately 2.8 million older people with functional disabilities, almost 70% are women. One immitigable fact of aging is the preponderance of widowed females. Undeniably, being an unmarried white female who is very old is a risk factor for nursing home placement. Why is this so? Women are more likely to become widows than men are to become widowers; however, women are less likely to remarry than widowed men. Thus women are left without help from a spouse as their functional status changes, and they become more reliant upon informal caregiving from family, friends, or community. Wives generally provide the majority of the support services for impaired husbands, in contrast to husbands who contribute relatively less assistance for their impaired wives (Soldo and Manton, 1985). When there is no spouse to provide care, the caregiving responsibilities are usually assumed by the adult daughters and daughters-in-law. Parent care has been conservatively estimated to affect more than 5 million people at any given time (Brody, 1985).

A Rehabilitation Assessment Model

Given the multiple interwoven factors that affect medical problems in the elderly, it is best to utilize a team approach. The skills of a nurse, a physician, occupational, speech, physical, and recreational therapists, a social worker, a psychologist, and a chaplain are all useful in designing and implementing a rehabilitation treatment plan. This chapter will address the global aspects of a rehabilitation model but will not delineate each profession's unique contribution. Determining what the problems are is the first step in an effective treatment strategy with physically or mentally impaired elderly. Each professional on the team helps to define the "problem list." An important caveat for all team members to remember throughout the evaluation and treatment process is, Illnesses or disabilities affect everyone in the family.

Functional Evaluation and Treatment

Functional assessment typically includes an evaluation of the individual's independence in the activities of daily life: bathing, dressing, toileting, transferring, feeding, and continence.

One of the cardinal features of rehabilitation is its emphasis upon function. Function has been operationally defined in a number of scales that typically focus on activities of daily living (ADL). These include bathing, dressing, toileting, transferring, feeding, and continence. The Katz Index of ADL (Katz et al., 1963) is an example of an objective assessment to determine the conditions under which a person can function independently without modifying the environment or having assistance from others (see Figure 8-1). The degree of home modification or personal care assistance required is indicated through application of the ADL scales.

Assessing instrumental activities of daily living has proved to be useful in working with the elderly. These include using the telephone, shopping, preparing food, housekeeping, doing laundry, using transportation, taking medications, or being able to do one's own finances. The impact of either physical or mental impairment on one's ability to function in one's home is implicit in the use of this type of measurement. Independence in daily activities is a continuum with a range of possibilities within each specific task.

Occupational and physical therapists contribute an understanding of the neuromuscular system in an individual. The recovery process is promoted through instruction in range of motion and strengthening exercises. The use of adaptive equipment may significantly increase a patient's level of function and compensate for the disability. Often therapists will work with a patient in a simulated home environment just prior to the time of discharge; many homebound treatment programs complete the rehabilitative process. Speech therapists evaluate the patient's language and communication skills. Treatment may range from the simple use of a letter board to complex reasoning and mathematical skills. Therapists may suggest specific aids to increase a patient's independence in communications skills once she or he is home. Recreational therapists encourage and teach the patient how to incorporate recreational pleasure into his or her life after an illness or onset of a disability.

Social Support Evaluation

An evaluation of a person's social support system is typically performed by the social worker or psychologist on the team. If there is a gerontological nurse practitioner she or he may be skilled in family evaluations and may collect this information. Pertinent information regarding the patient's relationship to spouse, children, siblings, or other relatives is essential to a patient's data base. Are there additional friends, co-workers, neighbors, or contacts through religious affiliations who will offer emotional, spiritual, or physical support throughout the convalescence? What is the attitude of the patient or family toward using ancillary services such as Senior Ride, Meals on Wheels, or senior centers? A person's willingness to accept a variety of social supports that are available will influence their utilization during and after the rehabilitative process.

The availability of social support systems and the older adult's willingness to use them can influence the rehabilitation process.

(*Text continues on page 152*)

Index of Independence in Activities of Daily Living

The Index of Independence in Activities of Daily Living is based on an evaluation of the functional independence or dependence of patients in bathing, dressing, going to the toilet, transferring, continence, and feeding. Specific definitions of functional independence and dependence appear below the index.

A   Independent in feeding, continence, transferring, going to toilet, dressing, and bathing.

B   Independent in all but one of these functions.

C   Independent in all but bathing and one additional function.

D   Independent in all but bathing, dressing, and one additional function.

E   Independent in all but bathing, dressing, going to toilet, and one additional function.

F   Independent in all but bathing, dressing, going to toilet, transferring, and one additional function.

G   Dependent in all six functions.

Other   Dependent in at least two functions, but not classifiable as C, D, E, or F.

Independence means without supervision, direction, or active personal assistance, except as specifically noted below. This is based on actual status and not on ability. A patient who refuses to perform a function is considered as not performing the function, even though he is deemed able.

Bathing (sponge, shower or tub)
Independent: assistance only in bathing a single part (as back or disabled extremity) or bathes self completely
Dependent: assistance in bathing more than one part of body; assistance in getting in or out of tub or does not bathe self

Dressing
Independent: gets clothes from closets and drawers; puts on clothes, outer garments, braces; manages fasteners; act of tying shoes is excluded
Dependent: does not dress self or remains partly undressed

Going to Toilet
Independent: gets to toilet; gets on and off toilet; arranges clothes, cleans organs of excretion (may manage own bedpan used at night only and may or may not be using mechanical supports)
Dependent: uses bedpan or commode or receives assistance in getting to and using toilet

Transfer
Independent: moves in and out of bed independently and moves in and out of chair independently (may or may not be using mechanical supports)
Dependent: assistance in moving in or out of bed and/or chair; does not perform one or more transfers

Continence
Independent: urination and defecation entirely self-controlled
Dependent: partial or total incontinence in urination or defecation; partial or total control by enemas, catheters, or regulated use of urinals and/or bedpans

Feeding
Independent: gets food from plate or its equivalent into mouth (precutting of meat and preparation of food, as buttering bread, are excluded from evaluation)
Dependent: assistance in act of feeding (see above); does not eat at all or parenteral feeding

FIGURE 8-1. The Katz Index of ADL. (Katz S, Ford AB, Moskowitz RW, Jackson BA, Jaffe MW: Studies of illness in the aged: The index of ADL: A standardized measure of biological and social function. JAMA 185:914, 1963. Copyright 1963, American Medical Association.)

Evaluation Form

Name _____ Date of Evaluation _____

For each area of functioning listed below, check description that applies. (The word *assistance* means supervision, direction of personal assistance.)

Bathing—either sponge bath, tub bath, or shower

☐	☐	☐
Receives no assistance (gets in and out of tub by self if tub is usual means of bathing)	Receives assistance in bathing only one part of body (such as back or a leg)	Receives assistance in bathing more than one part of body (or not bathed)

Dressing—gets clothes from closets and drawers—including underclothes, outer garments and using fasteners (including braces, if worn)

☐	☐	☐
Gets clothes and gets completely dressed without assistance	Gets clothes and gets dressed without assistance except for assistance in tying shoes	Receives assistance in getting clothes or in getting dressed, or stays partly or completely undressed

Toileting—going to the "toilet room" for bowel and urine elimination; cleaning self after elimination and arranging clothes

☐	☐	☐
Goes to "toilet room," cleans self, and arranges clothes without assistance (may use object for support such as cane, walker, or wheelchair and may manage night bedpan or commode, emptying same in morning)	Receives assistance in going to "toilet room" or in cleansing self or in arranging clothes after elimination or in use of night bedpan or commode	Doesn't go to room termed "toilet" for the elimination process

Transfer

☐	☐	☐
Moves in and out of bed as well as in and out of chair without assistance (may be using object for support such as cane or walker)	Moves in or out of bed or chair with assistance	Doesn't get out of bed

Continence

☐	☐	☐
Controls urination and bowel movement completely by self	Has occasional "accidents"	Supervision helps keep urine or bowel control; catheter is used or is incontinent

Feeding

☐	☐	☐
Feeds self without assistance	Feeds self except for getting assistance in cutting meat or buttering bread	Receives assistance in feeding or is fed partly or completely by using tubes or intravenous fluids

FIGURE 8-1. *(Continued)*

There may be a real reduction in the social system because of the death or disability of a spouse, or loss of siblings or friends through death, disability, or geographical relocation. The elderly person may be experiencing a new sense of dependence upon children, and this change may be a difficult transition for all involved.

Psychological Evaluation and Treatment

One of the biggest dilemmas in rehabilitation is motivation and how to encourage and support patients in the pursuit of their goals. While professionals may evaluate a person and set goals based upon their evaluation of the physical data, there is also the psychological component to rehabilitation. Older people should be included in the process of making decisions about their treatment plan unless they are incompetent to make decisions (see Chapter 10). When people are not included in making decisions that affect their health, they are less likely to feel committed to the treatment goals and may be noncompliant or passively resistant.

Psychological evaluation consists of a mental status examination in which a patient's appearance, speech, cognition, mood, affect, judgment, and memory are briefly tested. A complete history may be taken that would include data on the family, marital relationship, prior medical and psychological problems, and prior stresses or problems in the patient's life. Further, an assessment is made of the patient's coping style, the strengths and weaknesses of the patient's support system, and his or her current living situation. Depending upon the nature of the illness, further cognitive or personality tests may be administered over the course of the treatment period.

The person's perception of his or her disability can affect motivation to participate in the rehabilitation plan.

An understanding of the patient's perception of the illness or disability is vital because people can and do perceive illnesses or disabilities in a variety of ways. The meaning of a disability to one individual may not be the same as it is to another, and it is this meaning that can affect their motivation and goals of recovery. For example, to some people a broken hip may mean that they are getting older; they feel angry and sad and perceive that the nursing home is not for rehabilitation and convalescence but the last stop before death. To another person who is the same age and has the same physical problem, a broken hip may mean that she or he will have to be more dependent upon the spouse and may feel guilty about this dependence; therefore, that person is determined to become physically independent as soon as possible. Because expectations affect outcomes, a patient's expectations of the rehabilitation process need to be understood by the team.

Environmental Assessment

How does the environment affect a specific patient? Patients who display excessively dependent behaviors in the hospital (often misinterpreted to represent low motivation) frequently respond with surprising independence once placed in their own homes. Functional activities such as getting to the toilet, dressing, sitting in a favorite living room chair, or preparing food assume immediate importance in the context of a patient's personal environment.

Foremost when preparing for any home placement is an awareness of safety features:

- Are there throw rugs that would hinder ambulation?
- Does the bathroom need grab bars, tub stool, or toilet arm rails installed?
- Does the bed height need altering and should bed rails be installed?
- Are the chairs high enough from the ground so the patient can get up easily or independently?
- Are there lights at all stairways?
- Is the kitchen set up for easy access, and is adaptive equipment indicated?
- Is a telephone available, especially at night?
- Does the home require any additional architectural modifications for accessibility or safety?

Note: See Chapter 7 for an in-depth discussion of the issues and methods of preventing injury among the impaired elderly.

Evaluating the patient and the family in the home setting can provide valuable practical information useful in planning for aftercare. Nurses may want to participate in home assessment with the therapists. Environments can be modified to accommodate the patient and thereby increase his or her independence. For example, a stroke victim may need his or her kitchen rearranged so that everything is a certain height and one-handed utensils are available. Grab bars, a tub stool, and toilet rails may be installed in the bathroom. (Examples of adaptive aids can be found in Chapter 22.) Alzheimer's victims may benefit from having their stoves turned off permanently because of their forgetfulness in turning them off after use, and meals could be delivered by Meals on Wheels.

It is important to assess the manner in which the family works together to solve problems. This kind of assessment will help the team to understand whether the family would benefit from more counseling and discussion of how the illness or disability is affecting all of them. There may be a further need to educate the family and the patient about the illness or disability and the practical aspects of living within the limits imposed by the patient's changed physical status.

Unique Characteristics of the Elderly

Research and clinical experience suggest that it is not death that is feared by older people, but rather prolonged illness or dependency upon one's children or spouse for caregiving (Lieberman and Tobin, 1983). The event of going to a nursing home, even though it may be for convalescence after surgery, often is interpreted by older people as the final relocation, and they are usually fearful that they will never return home. Personality types that are vulnerable to "narcissistic wounds" or normal physiological changes with age (i.e., wrinkles, arthritic joints) may have a more difficult adjustment to an illness or disability in their later years because of their negative interpretation of the event.

Older people as a group have less prestige in American society. Prestige is tied to productivity in Western societies, and retirement implies a decrease in productivity in the work setting. Feelings of powerlessness may be accentuated in older people by the social milieu. There may be feelings of loss associated with the illness or disability. Abandonment fears may surface during an illness because patients may fear being left by their loved ones; these fears are particularly activated by hospitalization and nursing home placement. It is important to recognize these fears because they can greatly interfere with the treatment plan if not worked through.

Another characteristic of older people is the physiological fact of slowed response time, slowed healing time, and decreased energy. There is less organ reserve and more susceptibility to infectious diseases. Medications are not absorbed or excreted as quickly because of decreased kidney function. All of these contribute to an increase in length of time that the rehabilitation process takes.

Older people may underreport their symptoms to their physicians and not want to "bother the doctor." Some people are fearful of appearing to be perceived as complainers, and when this fear is coupled with a belief that older people are supposed to have physical problems because of age, underreporting or omission of important clinical information may occur. Health professionals have to make sure in their interviews with older people that they ask questions that elicit the information they are seeking.

Resources are also finite in the elderly population. While today's elderly are in a better financial position than previous generations, there are still subgroups that are at the poverty level. Older women are still the poorest group; many have suffered loss of income after the death of a spouse. There is a great fear of becoming dependent upon their children financially and of requiring assistance from the government. The expense of health care in office visits, copayments for hospitalization, or prescription drugs can be prohibitive, and older people will struggle to pay their bills because being financially responsible has been highly valued in the older population. The expense of nursing home placement (approximately $20,000–30,000 per year) is frightening to older people, and the current system of "spend down" to qualify for Medicaid also depletes a family's resources. Most families have not planned ahead for catastrophic illness and are devastated financially by it (Hunt, 1987). The current maze of options (i.e., HMOs, PPOs, catastrophic illness insurance, Medigap insurance) in health care is baffling to older people, and there is rarely an easily accessible resource to provide comprehensive information.

Changes in Health Care

The impact of the diagnostic related groups (DRGs) on rehabilitation is apparent in the changing patterns of health care delivery. Today people are discharged from hospitals earlier and sent to nursing homes, health units in life-care communities, their own homes, or their children's homes for conva-

Careful discharge planning is essential to sustaining and continuing the rehabilitation gains achieved.

lescence and rehabilitation. Are these facilities prepared to provide a complete rehabilitation program? Are the home health agencies prepared to provide rehabilitation services for the elderly? There has been a dearth of qualified health professionals, including nurse specialists, in the long-term care field. There will be a need for nurses who have specialized in geriatric care in order to meet the changing health care needs of the elderly (Davis et al., 1985).

What is the impact on the family that is thrust into providing full-time caregiving for an ill family member? Two facts are clear: (1) Caregiving takes time, and (2) caregivers are usually women. Research suggests that caregiving responsibilities are assumed first by spouses if they are available, and secondarily by daughters or daughters-in-law (Ory, 1985; Fitting et al., 1986). Sons may provide financial help but become caregivers only if there is no available female sibling, and then the actual care may be provided by the daughter-in-law (Horowitz, 1985). The research on parent care data suggests that women reduce their work hours from full- to part-time or in many instances leave a job because of the caregiving needs of their elderly parents or parents-in-law (Brody, 1985). With the entrance of women into the professions, and with a decline in birth rate, there is speculation that there will be fewer available informal or family caregivers in the future to provide care for the elderly. The estimate is that "80% of the elderly with functional limitations rely, in whole or in part, on informal caregiving" (Soldo and Manton, 1985, 237). There will undoubtedly be a growing need for public or family caregiving assistance, as well as the services provided by the home health industry.

One positive change has been the introduction of the teaching nursing home. This will bring many health professionals into the nursing home setting on rotations as a learning experience and may begin to change the attitudes of health professionals when they are in training (Schneider et al., 1985). The ageist attitudes that exist in society have existed in health professionals as well, and there has been a real paucity of professionals interested in or educated in geriatric care. Hopefully, the teaching nursing home will help foster a rehabilitative approach to the long-term care system.

REFERENCES

Blazer D: Depression in Late Life. St. Louis, CV Mosby, 1982.

Brody E: Women in the middle and family help to older people. The Gerontologist 21:471–480, 1985.

Davis AR, Small NR, Andersen LM: The role of the gerontological nurse in the care of the elderly. In Health Care for an Aging Population (special issue), Socio-economic Planning Sciences, ed. ED Pelegrino, JT Howell, 19:279–288, 1985.

Fitting MD, Rabins PV, Lucas MJ, Eastham J: Caregivers for dementia patients: A comparison of husbands and wives. The Gerontologist 26:248–252, 1986.

Horowitz A: Sons and daughters as caregivers to older parents: Differences in role performance and consequences. The Gerontologist 25:612–617, 1985.

Hunt M: A common sense guide to health insurance. New York Times Magazine, May 10, 46–53, 108, 1987.

Katz S, Ford AB, Moskowitz RW, Jackson BA, Jaffe MW: Studies of illness in the aged: The index of ADL: A standardized measure of biological and psychosocial function. JAMA 185:94ff, 1963.

Kramer M, German PS, Anthony JC, von Korff M, Skinner E: Patterns of mental disorders among the elderly residents of eastern Baltimore. J Am Geriatr Soc 33: 236–245, 1985.

Lieberman MA, Tobin SS: The Experience of Old Age. New York, Basic Books, 1983.

Miller M: Suicide after Sixty: The Final Alternative. New York, Springer, 1979.

Ory MG: The burden of care: A family perspective. Generations 10:14–18, 1985.

Rovner B, Rabins PV: Mental illness among nursing home residents. Hosp Comm Psych 36:119–120, 128, 1985.

Schneider EL, Wendland CJ, Zimmer AW, List N, Ory M: The Teaching Nursing Home: A New Approach to Geriatric Research, Education, and Clinical Care. New York, Raven Press, 1985.

Soldo BJ, Manton KG: Demographic challenges for socioeconomic planning. In Health Care for an Aging Population (special issue), Socio-economic Planning Sciences, ed. ED Pellegrino, JT Howell, 19:227–247, 1985.

BIBLIOGRAPHY

Belk J: Federal policy and disabled people. Caring 6(8): 6–9, 52–54, 1987.

Miller ET: Evaluating Orthopedic Disability: A Commonsense Approach, 2nd ed. New York, Medical Economics Books, 1987.

Neuberger J: New for old . . . better design of clothing and furniture for elderly patients. Nurs Times 82(41): 22, 1986.

Orr AL: The elderly visually impaired: What every health care provider should know. Caring 6(8): 55–58, 1987.

Penn ND: Toilet aids. Brit Med J 296(6626): 918–919, 1988.

Reffer J: Data systems set to measure rehabilitation effectiveness. Hospitals 61(1): 51–52, 1987.

Slimmer LW, Lopez M, LeSage J, Ellor JR: Perceptions of learned helplessness. J Gerontol Nurs 13(5): 33–37, 1987.

Staebler R: Community: A home and family for the disabled. Caring 6(8): 47–51, 1987.

Sullivan M: Atrophy and exercise. J Gerontol Nurs 13(7): 26–31, 1987.

Wong RA: Geriatric emphasis in physical therapy: A historical survey. Phys Therapy 68(3): 360–363, 1988.

CHAPTER 9

Legal Aspects of Gerontological Nursing

Sheryl A. Feutz

Chapter Objectives
At the completion of this chapter the reader will be able to:

1. List the sources of laws.
2. Describe liability risks for the gerontological nurse and methods to assure a legally safe practice.
3. Discuss the purposes and correct uses of the medical record.
4. Describe issues relevant to informed consent, living wills, competency, use of restraints, intentional torts, and false imprisonment.
5. Identify ways to minimize the risks associated with administrative responsibilities.

As a result of increased consumer involvement in health care and a new recognition of medical ethics, societal attitudes have swung from reverence toward health care providers to the current jaundiced view of the entire health care industry. The increased specialization, mechanization, and sophistication of health care have also caused substantial depersonalization of health care. Consequently, medical malpractice litigation has been increasing.

In contrast to the resultant depersonalization of health care, consumers actually anticipate high-quality, personalized care, as advertised by the media. This expectation is frequently unrealistic in today's health care system. Technology, specialization, and fractionalization have altered health care and its delivery.

The trend among consumers is to seek compensation for perceived misfortune through legal action. The belief exists that an unexpected or undesirable result reflects negligence, for which compensation should be made. Thus institutions and health care providers that were once blindly trusted are now scrutinized. As a result of this critical analysis, errors that inevitably arise from human endeavors are revealed, providing a foundation for lawsuits.

Similarly, nursing liability has increased dramatically over the past decade, thus affecting how nurses practice. A new emphasis is directed toward actions that may prevent or limit liability. Gerontological nurses must learn to adjust their practices accordingly and to practice defensively without becoming defensive.

Because the elderly have numerous and complicated illnesses, gerontological nurses have a significant exposure to liability. Both the magnitude of this population and the potential complications of their illnesses continue to grow, creating a corresponding rise in liability exposure.

This chapter is designed to educate the gerontological nurse about basic legal principles and to discuss those principles in various situations common to gerontological nurses.

> The multiplicity of older adults' problems and their increased vulnerability increase the legal risks for the gerontological nurse.

The Legal World of Nursing

Sophocles once said, "The happiest life consists in ignorance, before you learn to grieve and to rejoice." From this evolved the adage "Ignorance is bliss." However, in the legal world, ignorance is not a defense and only leads to legal liability. Decreasing ignorance prevents liability and lawsuits.

The legal system in the United States is based on laws—rules of human conduct. Laws are created to manage complex human interactions and to protect society. As society progresses, laws are changed to reflect new societal values and norms.

There are four sources of laws:

- Statutes
- Regulations
- Court decisions
- Attorney general opinions

All are equally effective and binding on all citizens, and any violation may subject the individual to civil or criminal liability.

Statutes are laws enacted by state legislatures or the United States Congress. States have wide discretion in enacting statutes; however, they may not violate or conflict with any federal statutes. Through statutes, state and federal regulatory agencies are given their powers to function.

A state nurse practice act is an example of a series of statutes designed to regulate nursing. Every state nurse practice act differs; each one is periodically revised to reflect the changes in how nurses may practice in that state. Through the nurse practice act, a state's board of nursing is given authority to function as a regulatory agency of nursing. The board's authority typically extends to licensing nursing schools, granting or revoking nursing licenses, and defining the practice of nursing.

A second source of laws is regulations. Regulations are enacted by state and federal regulatory agencies to implement statutes and enable the agencies to achieve their purposes. Regulations define the methods to achieve the goals and objectives of statutes.

Court decisions are a third source of laws. Separate court systems exist on the state and the federal level. Both systems contain two types of courts: trial courts and appellate courts.

Trial courts decide issues of fact and apply the law of the state or the United States. Lawsuits are first filed and heard in a trial court.

Appellate courts, the second type, are called upon to decide difficult legal issues and to interpret statutes and regulations. Appellate courts consist of the courts of appeals and supreme courts. Like trial courts, these exist both on the state and the federal levels.

A state supreme court is the highest authority within a state, and its rulings are binding on all other courts in its state. The United States Supreme Court is the highest authority in the country. Its decisions are binding on all other courts throughout the United States, both trial courts and appellate courts.

The fourth source of laws is attorney general opinions. The attorney general is the chief attorney for the government of the state or the United States. Opinions rendered by the attorney general are treated equally with statutes, regulations, and court decisions. An attorney general may be asked to render an opinion about an issue, such as whether or not an activity is illegal, prior to the filing of a lawsuit.

Laws in the form of statutes, regulations, court decisions, and attorney general opinions govern how nursing is practiced. They establish the legal requirements for which nurses will be held accountable. This accountability has expanded significantly over the past 20 years and is the cornerstone of modern nursing.

As the autonomy of nurses continues to increase, the accountability also increases. Consequently, the autonomy now granted to nurses also imposes increased potential liability upon nurses. A key legal principle is that every individual is responsible for his or her own actions. The level of accountability is directly related to the ability of the individual to make educated judgments and to exercise appropriate actions. Nurses are now recognized as being capable of performing patient assessments, formulating judgments, implementing decisions, and evaluating the effectiveness of intervention, and in fact they are expected to do these things. For these expected capabilities, nurses are held accountable.

When nurses assume managerial and administrative roles, they are not only responsible for their own actions, but also accountable for tasks that they delegate to others.

In addition to the individual liability of the nurse who performs or fails to perform a nursing action, other individuals may also have responsibility for how a nursing action was carried out. Nurses who are in administrative or management positions are held accountable for those duties delegated by them. A typical example is staff assignments. The nurse administrator or manager is accountable for the appropriate delegation of duties to the staff. A nurse may not be assigned to a patient unless competent to provide the required care or unless adequately supervised.

This is an important and frequently misunderstood concept. Merely supervising or managing nurses, or even other personnel whether or not they are licensed, will not automatically impose liability upon the nurse administrator or manager when negligence is committed. Accountability for the acts of another individual is limited to responsible delegation of duties or sufficient supervision.

In addition, nurse administrators or managers routinely have administrative duties and responsibilities for which they are personally accountable. These may include staff evaluations, physical facilities on their nursing units, safety of patients and staff, and maintenance of equipment.

The health care institution has its own responsibilities relative to patient care for which it will be held accountable if negligence to the patient occurs. Two ways exist in which an institution may be held responsible for negligent patient care.

Under the doctrine of *respondeat superior* the employer is liable for all acts of employees that fall within the scope of employment. This liability reinforces the importance of proper hiring and supervision of personnel, as well as the need to provide adequate resources for staff to complete their jobs.

First, under the doctrine of *respondeat superior,* an employer is automatically liable for all acts of its employees that occur within the scope of employment. This responsibility imposed by law is also referred to as vicarious liability. No independent negligence on the part of the institution is required to subject the institution to vicarious liability. Public policy supports this automatic imposition of liability because it encourages employers to take adequate measures to hire and maintain employees who are competent and capable of carrying out their assigned duties.

In addition to vicarious liability, a health care institution may also be subjected to other allegations of negligence because of the accountability of its administrators and managers for the operation of the institution. The institution is responsible for such patient care activities as providing the necessary equipment for staff to provide nursing care that meets the requisite standard of care, maintaining the equipment, and providing in-service training on use of the equipment. Furnishing adequate and competent nursing staff is another institutional responsibility. The institution must provide policies and procedures for delivery of nursing care, and provide the necessary opportunities to keep them updated and revised as necessary.

The conduct of the individual nurse, the nurse administrator or manager, and the health care institution is measured against that level of conduct which has been established as the minimum standard of care required for that individual or institution. Most states recognize that minimum standards of care are national standards. *Standard of care* is defined as that level of skill and learning ordinarily used under the same or similar circumstances by a member of the same profession or similar institution. In determining the applicable standard of care, the court looks to standards that have been promulgated by national organizations, such as nursing standards established by the American Nurses' Association or other specialty nursing organizations, and hospital standards established by the Joint Commission for the Accreditation of Hospitals and American Osteopathic Association. In addition, courts will look to any standards that have been established internally, such as institutional policies and procedures.

Standards of care are quite flexible because they must accommodate the rapidly shifting fields of medicine and nursing. The standard of care for which an individual or institution is held accountable is the standard in existence at the time of the event, *not* the standard that was in effect when the individual practitioner was in school or when the institution was established. Thus it is important to keep pace with changes in health care so that knowledge, skills, competency, and equipment can continually be updated.

To impose legal liability on a nurse or institution requires proof of four elements: duty, negligence, proximate cause, and damage. All elements must be proven; only three of four is insufficient to impose liability. The burden is on the plaintiff, the individual filing the lawsuit, to present evidence to the court of all four elements.

In order for legal liability to exist there must be (1) duty: a relationship which obligates that care be provided; (2) negligence: deviation from acceptable standards of care; (3) proximate cause: injury resulting from a specific action or inaction; and (4) damage: physical, emotional, or financial injury.

The first element is that of a *duty.* Duty is a legal obligation that arises when a relationship between a patient and a nurse is established. A relationship is created when a nurse is assigned to a specific patient, or when a nurse on duty in a health care institution becomes aware that a patient needs assistance.

Once the duty arises, the nurse is required to be accountable to that patient and therefore to comply with the applicable nursing standards of care. This duty is expansive; in addition to a nurse being accountable for personal actions, a nurse is also required to act affirmatively if it is observed that other health care providers are or the institution is failing to comply with an appropriate standard of care.

The second element of legal liability is *negligence.* Negligence arises when conduct falls below the standard of care, thereby breaching the duty owed to the patient. Professional conduct of a nurse below the standard of care is referred to as malpractice.

In most actions alleging nursing malpractice, an expert witness must testify that the nurse's conduct fell below the standard of care. This testimony must be from an individual with sufficient credentials and qualifications to make the testimony credible.

Causation or *proximate cause,* defined as that which, in a natural and continuous sequence, produces injury, is the third element necessary for liability. The injury to the patient must result directly from the negligence of the nurse. Nursing malpractice without injury to the patient cannot result in liability. Causation also is established by the testimony of an expert witness, either medical or nursing.

The fourth requirement for liability is *damage.* The patient must sustain damage as a direct result of the injury. Damages may include physical, financial, or emotional injuries. Compensation for damages is money awarded by the court for the injuries sustained by the patient.

In addition to compensation for injuries, punitive damages also may be awarded to punish grossly negligent or intentional conduct. Examples of acts for which punitive damages might be imposed include assault and battery, false imprisonment, defamation, purposely administering a lethal dose of medicine, or attempting to provide nursing care while under the influence of alcohol or drugs.

Knowing what is required to prove nursing malpractice and what actions are subject to liability is the first step in preventing a lawsuit. Remaining competent in performing nursing actions is the second step.

The remainder of the chapter focuses on common areas of nursing liability for gerontological nurses.

Documentation Principles and Common Pitfalls

A patient's medical record has acquired new meaning during the last 15 to 20 years. Initially, the medical record was created for the purpose of communicating among health care providers; with this comprehensive documentation, quality and continuity of care could be provided. Today the medical record serves additional important functions: to obtain third-party reimbursement and to provide legal documentation.

Yet the primary purpose of the medical record remains as a communication document created for the benefit of the patient. If that purpose is kept in focus, the other two functions will also be fulfilled.

Information in the medical record must be meaningful. It should describe definitive observations and acts of the nurse. It is inappropriate for a nurse to chart events not personally observed or performed unless indicating who related that information. Statements must be written with certainty, avoiding "appears," "seems," or "apparently." This is a change in how nurses were traditionally taught to chart to avoid accusations of practicing medicine. As previously discussed, charting is an example of a changed standard of care.

Information must be relevant to the specific patient, focusing on the problems and diagnoses identified by nurses and physicians. Data are recorded in terms of what is seen, heard, smelled, felt, and done relative to the specific patient.

A fundamental legal principle of medical record keeping that is continually reinforced to nurses is that if information is not charted, it was not done or observed. An expansion of this principle is that if reasons for actions are not documented, they were not considered. Thus it is imperative to document the thought processes behind nursing judgments and assessments that determine acts performed or not performed by nurses. This documentation is typically important when weighing the risks and benefits in restraining a patient, and showing why a decision is made against or for restraints.

A new purpose for the medical record is that of providing the basis for third-party reimbursement to the institution. Whether or not an institution is reimbursed the allocated amount, or perhaps more, for patient care is determined by information contained in the medical record. Reimbursement is not based solely on medical diagnoses and physician progress notes, but is in fact also based upon nursing care plans, nursing diagnoses, and nursing notes. The length of time in the institution for which reimbursement will be made on behalf of a patient may be extended because of documentation by nurses. Additional reimbursement is frequently made when complications develop or when more time is required for patient teaching and discharge planning.

A third purpose of the medical record is to provide a legal document reflecting patient care. Documentation is necessary to protect the health care institution and providers if a subsequent claim is made against them by the patient. A comprehensive and accurate medical record can be the best defense available to a defendant nurse, *or* it can become the best offensive weapon for the plaintiff. The medical record is used in court to reflect to the jury the medical and nursing care that were provided to the patient. As a result, documentation must be designed for legal purposes as well as for the above purposes.

Gerontological nurses must be aware of all information contained in a patient's medical record prior to initiating care. It is not sufficient to rely merely upon verbal reports; a nurse is expected to know all information contained in the medical record even if the information was also passed on verbally. However, this requirement does not void the nurse's responsibility to advise another health care provider orally of a significant change in a patient's condition requiring immediate attention, or gradual changes brought to the attention of the absent physician. In fact, failure to do so may precipitate nursing malpractice.

Knowledge of the information contained in the medical record also imposes a responsibility upon the nurse to document everything in a timely and accurate manner in the record. A health care provider may not be negligent for not knowing pertinent information that is not in the record; the negligence will be placed on the nurse who failed to chart it in a timely and accurate manner.

| Legally sound documentation is accurate, objective, timely, and legible.

Several criteria are important to observe when charting in a patient's medical record. The information should be documented objectively, avoiding opinion and characterization. While this rule sounds simple, in reality documentation errors of this kind are frequently committed by nurses. For example, a patient's medical record may read, "Patient fell out of bed and fractured hip." When questioning the nurse who wrote this finding, one discovers that the nurse did not observe the patient fall, but rather made that assumption or was told so by the patient. In reality, the nurse charted subjectively, adding opinion and characterization of the facts. An objective documentation would read, "Heard loud noise from patient's room; upon entering found patient on floor, lying on left hip. Patient stated: 'I needed to go to the bathroom and fell when I tried to get out of bed by myself.' " If such a medical record were entered as evidence in a court case, the defense counsel would have a difficult time trying to convince the jury that the patient had a spontaneous fracture rather than a fall that caused the injury.

The second criterion is that charting must be timely. Recognizing the limitations and realities of situations in which nurses deliver care, frequently it is not possible to chart at exactly the time when observations have been made or care has been delivered; however, the nurse has several options. For instance, the nurse can make notes on a piece of paper to be entered into the medical record when time is available. Another suggestion is better utilization of the care plan as a guide for documentation. Reviewing each problem and related plans will prompt the nurse to recall significant events that should be documented.

Charting should also be as time-specific as possible. If a nurse knows that a treatment was administered at 9:00 A.M., the chart should so state. When the exact time is uncertain, the nurse should chart the activity with a time range: "Visitors present for brief period between 4:00 and 5:00 P.M." Charting should be done in chronological order of events.

A third criterion of charting that has gained increased importance is the legibility and spelling accuracy of the chart content. With medical records routinely enlarged to allow the jury to read them during testimony, illegible handwriting or misspelled words create a negative impression in the minds of the jury. As professionals, nurses are expected to spell correctly, including the basic words of the English language along with medical terminology. Careless documentation implies carelessness in the nurse.

Along with legibility and correct spelling is the need to use only those abbreviations approved by the institution. Unapproved abbreviations negate the ability to communicate. If a health care provider cannot interpret an abbreviation and the result is negligence to the patient, the nurse who charted the unapproved abbreviation has deviated from the acceptable standard of practice and may be guilty of nursing malpractice.

The method for correcting errors in the medical record is critical. There is nothing improper about making a correction in the medical record; in fact, it is usually better to correct a mistake than to allow it to remain. A correction should never be made if the medical record has become the subject of a claim or lawsuit; if corrections are necessary, legal counsel should be consulted.

Corrections are made by drawing a single line through the mistaken entry. The original entry should not be obliterated, because doing so would create the perception that something previously charted should not now be read. A single line through the entry with the notation "mistaken entry" is sufficient. The nurse making the correction should sign and note the date and time. Where appropriate, the nurse should explain the mistake and chart the correct information. The corrected entry should also be dated, timed, and signed by the nurse.

Telephone calls made to health care providers that advise of a significant change in a patient's condition or circumstances where immediate attention is required must be recorded. The nurse must observe the patient and notify the physician as necessary; the physician's responsibility is then to respond to the nurse's request for assistance.

The exact time, or as close as possible to the exact time, at which the call was made should be documented. If the nurse charting the call did not personally place the call, that fact should be stated in the nursing notes, along with the name of the person who initiated the call. The chart should also reflect who was called and whether the conversation took place directly with the party or if a message was conveyed through another party.

The nurse should document when the telephone call was returned if the person was not immediately available, as well as by whom the call was returned. Any information communicated during the phone conversation should be reflected in the chart. Merely stating "Dr. Kildare advised of patient's condition" does not provide sufficient information to determine whether the physician was actually informed of the change in the patient's heart rate and coloring. Without documentation, it becomes a matter of the nurse's word against the physician's word.

The multiple functions of the medical record place a greater burden on all gerontological nurses. Mechanisms must be developed to document efficiently and comprehensively without allowing the amount of time spent in documenting to interfere with the delivery of patient care. Nursing care plans, written policies and procedures in the context of the documentation, and the development of patient-specific flow charts are mechanisms that can decrease the amount of time required for charting.

Issues in Patient Care

Informed Consent

An advocacy function of the gerontological nurse is to assure that the older adult's right of choice in health care treatment has been protected; this assurance is reflected in informed consent.

One of the most important patient rights is that of informed consent. A fundamental principle is that every individual has the right to choose whether or not to have health care treatment, select the kind of treatment, and decide who should render that treatment. The right of informed consent is guaranteed by the First Amendment of the Constitution, which provides that every person has the right of integrity of one's own body.

While the law is clear about the patient's right to informed consent, it is not so clear as to when explicit permission must be obtained. It is accepted that patients implicitly consent to routine procedures when they enter a health facility or seek treatment from a health care provider. Such routine procedures include performing physical examinations, taking blood pressures, administering medications and intravenous fluids, or other similar kinds of procedures that are minimally invasive or pose minimal risks.

A specific written informed consent is generally required for nonroutine procedures, especially when they are invasive or have potentially serious side effects or complications. The necessity for obtaining specific consent has been extended to the administration of certain drugs and is no longer limited to surgical procedures or treatments. If in doubt, it is always better to obtain specific written informed consent to prevent any possibility that an allegation of lack of informed consent will be raised (see Table 9-1).

Patients always have the option of accepting or rejecting any form of treatment or procedure, even where specific written informed consent is not required. Any time a patient refuses a medication, feeding, or even a bath, the implicit consent is revoked, and those treatments should not be carried out unless the patient reinstates the consent.

Any adult, as defined by state law, may give consent. The adult must not be suffering from any legal disability such as incompetency or insanity, as determined by a court. For an incompetent or insane adult, the legal guardian may give consent. Whether or not a family member has authority to consent for an incompetent or insane adult depends upon individual state law. While consent of a family member is frequently obtained, in many states the family member has no legal authority to give consent, and therefore any consent given would be invalid.

The process of informed consent is divided into two steps: (1) the giving of information to the patient so that an informed judgment may be made;

TABLE 9-1. Highlights of Informed Consent

- Informed consent is based on the individual's fundamental right to determine what is right for his or her own body.
- Consent is implied for routine procedures when a patient is admitted to a health care facility or seeks care or treatment from a health care professional. The patient maintains the right to refuse routine care or treatment.
- Informed consent is required for all nonroutine procedures.
- For patients to give informed consent they must be told a description of the treatment or procedure, possible hazards and complications, expected results, and reasonable alternatives.
- Persons witnessing the consent should have reasonable belief that the signature on the consent is the patient's, that the patient is competent, and that consent is being given voluntarily without coercion.
- The information reviewed with the patient in the process of obtaining consent should be documented in the patient's record.
- Usually, relatives or others can only grant consent for the patient if they have been appointed by the court to be legal guardians because the patient has been judged legally incompetent to grant consent.

and (2) the witnessing of the consent form. The two steps may be carried out by different individuals or jointly by one person. It is important to recognize the distinction between the two steps.

The first step of giving information to the patient is best accomplished by the person performing the procedure or treatment or prescribing the medication. That person is presumed to know what information the patient needs to make an informed decision. While this is usually a physician, legally a nurse may provide the information but will then be accountable for its completeness and accuracy.

There are five areas of information that must be provided to the patient to make informed consent possible. First, the patient must receive an explanation of the procedure or treatment to the extent of the patient's capability of understanding and interest. Before agreeing to a procedure or treatment, the patient must have a general idea of what it will entail.

The second area of information is knowledge of possible hazards indirectly related to the procedure or treatment but known to occur sometimes. Examples include an allergic reaction to a dye, anesthetic agent, or medication, or an embolism developing after surgery or prolonged bed rest.

Third, patients must be informed about possible complications. It is not expected that every known risk be told to a patient, but only those that have been well documented. Examples of potential complications are side effects of drugs, impotence after surgery, the development of keloids, or extravasation of a chemotherapy agent. The goal is for the patient to understand what can go wrong with the proposed procedure, treatment, or medication.

Patients must be informed of the expected results of the treatment. What is the purpose of the procedure, treatment, or medication? Is cure the goal? Is it an attempt to alleviate pain? And what is the chance of success? No nurse should ever guarantee that a procedure, treatment, or medication

The information provided to the individual in the process of obtaining informed consent should include an explanation of the procedure or treatment, associated risks, potential complications, expected outcome, and alternatives to the procedure or treatment.

will achieve its desired goal, because failure to achieve that guarantee can result in liability. Patients must be made to realize that health care is not an infallible or a perfect science. Realistic explanations are essential.

The final element to informed consent is providing reasonable alternatives. Whenever possible, the patient should be given a choice among several options and not be limited by the personal judgment of the nurse or physician. The available alternatives may involve value judgments based upon social, economic, and personal factors. The patient is to be allowed to select an alternative consistent with personal values.

The information given to the patient for purposes of informed consent must be specifically documented. The documentation must include what was discussed with the patient and whether anyone was present during the discussion, the providing of an opportunity for questions, what indication the patient gave of understanding the information, and whether the patient intends to give consent. This information can either be documented in the medical record, in the progress notes or nursing notes, or be included in the informed consent form that will be read and signed by the patient.

The second step in the process of informed consent is witnessing the consent form. Witnessing does not imply that the witness is responsible for giving information to the patient or has any knowledge of the information given. However, if while witnessing the consent form the patient asks questions that the witness answers, the witness thereby assumes part of the duty to provide the information for the informed consent and can be held partially accountable for the process of giving information.

The primary purpose of the witness is to ensure the competency of the person signing the form and the authenticity of the signature. The witness must have reasonable belief that the patient signing the form is the person reflected by the signature, and that the patient is competent to give consent at the time the form is signed. The patient must be given time to read the form prior to signing and an opportunity to ask any questions. The form may be read to a patient unable to read, and this fact has to be indicated on the form. Any changes made on the consent form are to be initialed by both the patient and the witness.

Another important aspect of witnessing the informed consent is ensuring that the patient is consenting freely, voluntarily, and without coercion. Frequently the nurse is in a position to know that the patient's decision regarding a procedure, treatment, or medication is altered because of statements made by other health care providers or family members. While a patient certainly is entitled to alter a decision, a signature should not be witnessed unless the nurse can testify in court that the patient's consent was given without coercion.

In emergency situations, actions may be taken without obtaining informed consent. Emergency is usually defined as the necessity to take action to prevent jeopardy to life, health, or limb; disfigurement; or impairment of faculties. The nature of the emergency must be documented in the medical record, along with the reasons informed consent could not be obtained.

The failure to obtain informed consent in other than emergency situations can lead to liabilities and lawsuits. There are three different allegations that may be made when informed consent is not obtained: malpractice, assault and battery, and breach of contract. A nurse or physician may commit malpractice for failing to obtain informed consent. Allegations of assault and battery may also be made because of attempted or actual physical contact with a patient without informed consent.

Proving lack of informed consent is a difficult burden for patients. The court must be convinced that consent would not have been given if all of the necessary information was known. In most states, whether or not consent would have been given is judged by what a reasonable person would have done. In addition, a successful procedure or treatment does not negate liability for lack of informed consent.

A third allegation is breach of contract. The informed consent form constitutes a contract between the patient and the named physican or other health care provider to perform a specific procedure or treatment. Violation of any of those elements constitutes a breach of contract. For example, if a physician other than the one named performs a procedure, the contract has been breached, and the patient may sue.

While actual damages may be minimal, patients may prove liability and be awarded compensation because their right of privacy and body integrity has been violated. In addition, patients may be entitled to punitive damages if there is proof of gross misconduct or willful disregard of their right to informed consent.

All competent individuals have the right to refuse to grant consent for a treatment or procedure, and this is a right the gerontological nurse should protect and respect.

Equally important with the right to give informed consent is the right to refuse consent. This is a right of every competent adult, even if death may result. No court will intervene to order a procedure or treatment for a competent adult. Court intervention may be sought where a patient is incompetent and without a legal guardian, or when the decisions of the legal guardian conflict with decisions that the health care providers deem to be in the patient's best interest.

Living Wills

Many states have legalized living wills, which allow a competent person to leave directives regarding the amount or kind of medical care and treatment that may be rendered once a diagnosis of a terminal or irreversible condition has been made. The living will becomes effective when the person becomes incompetent and is therefore unable to make decisions regarding medical treatment. Even in states that have not legislated living wills, such a document at least has the force of an oral directive that enables the court to know the patient's wishes.

It is the nurse's responsibility to know state law regarding living wills and the statutory provisions that are required to ensure their validity. Such information may include (1) a requirement for witnesses; (2) the prescribed form of the living will; (3) the required content; (4) the length of time the living will is effective; (5) how it may be revoked; (6) how it becomes effective; and (7) the extent to which the directives are binding on health care providers.

If there are no state statutory provisions for living wills, it is recommended that patients draft a document in compliance with the formalities required in the state for executing any other type of will. Alternatively, they may draft a document with the formalities required in other states that statutorily recognize the living will. Because a court often struggles to determine the wishes and views of a patient, a living will is convincing evidence of what the patient would have chosen if competent to make a decision. The living will is the legal statement of the patient's desires.

Once a health care provider becomes aware of the existence of a living will, the document should be placed in the medical record and its existence revealed to the other health care providers. Appropriate orders are to be written by the physician to reflect the intent of the living will. If there are any questions about the interpretation of the living will, clarify the terms with the patient, if still competent, or with a family member who might be able to explain what the patient intended.

Mental Competency

Gerontological nurses are frequently confronted with issues of a patient's mental competency. Each state has its own definitions and procedures for determining incompetency and appointing a responsible party for making decisions on behalf of the incompetent. Generally, incompetency is determined based upon whether an individual is mentally able to make rational decisions regarding person or property. The court will ask such questions as these:

Can the person make choices regarding life?

Are outcomes of choices reasonable?

Are choices based on rational reasons?

Is the person able to understand the implications of the choices?

Does the person actually understand the implications of the choices?

The nurse should recommend legal evaluation of a client who has a questionable level of mental competency. If the family is unwilling or unable to obtain such an evaluation, the facility's legal counsel, as well as state agencies, can be consulted.

A fundamental principle is that every person is presumed to be competent. Therefore, an individual is entitled to make decisions about health care until such time as the individual has been declared incompetent by a court of law.

Questions of competency may arise in several legal settings. Competency may be a factor in determining whether a patient will be civilly committed or placed involuntarily in a mental health institution or hospital. It may also arise when a patient must make informed decisions regarding health care. In both of these settings, the gerontological nurse has important functions (see Table 9-2).

The nurse may be in the best position to raise the issue of competency and to bring it to the attention of the appropriate persons to allow a legal

TABLE 9-2. Highlights of Competency

- All patients are presumed to be competent unless declared incompetent by a court of law.
- States vary on their definitions and procedures concerning incompetency.
- Nurses who suspect patients of being incompetent should raise this issue with the legal representative of the patient, facility, or state office on aging.
- Supporting documentation concerning patients' behaviors, speech, decision making, and physical and mental status are beneficial.
- Involuntary commitments or guardianships are reviewed periodically by the court to assess the continued need.

---

determination to be made. To support the nurse's perceptions of competency, nurses' notes and other documentation in the medical record will provide excellent support and evidence of the competency concerns. Documenting the patient's behaviors, speech, activities, physical and mental status, and prior decisions made by the patient may clearly reflect the patient's level of competency.

In conjunction with the documentation, the nurse may also be called upon to give testimony in a guardianship or commitment hearing. Commitment or appointment of a guardian is a protection for an elderly person who has been deemed incapable of living adequately and safely. But if the nurse has reason to believe that the patient is not in need of commitment or a guardian, the nurse's responsibility is to act as an advocate for the elderly individual. Gerontological nurses too frequently observe situations in which a family member does not agree with a decision made by the elderly individual and unjustly labels him or her incompetent.

Involuntary commitments and guardianships are reviewed periodically by the court to assess the continued necessity of the imposition upon the individual's freedom. Reviews may also be made at any time at the request of the patient. The nurse may be in a position to encourage and support a patient in requesting a review when a change has occurred in the patient's level of mental competency.

Restraints

One of the most basic human needs is that of control. An individual who loses control develops a sense of helplessness that can lead to complete lack of functioning. As a result, an individual will go to great lengths to maintain some control over any aspect of life. Especially in the elderly, who are fighting to maintain some control, the use of restraints has even greater significance. Therefore, restrictions on activities and orders for assistance will be ignored as an attempt to prove that the individual can still act independently and maintain personal control. Physicians and nurses may be talked out of restricting activity or freedom of movement by a very persuasive patient.

Restraints can cause a patient both physical and psychological harm. Deciding whether to use restraints and what type to use requires sound

TABLE 9-3. Highlights of the Use of Restraints

- Restraints should be used with caution and discretion. All patients have the right to independence and freedom of movement.
- The risks and benefits to the individual patient must be weighed in making the decision whether or not to restrain.
- Restraints require a physician's order.
- Agencies should have policies and procedures pertaining to the use of restraints, and documentation should reflect that these standards were adhered to in actual practice.
- When restraints are refused by the patient or legal guardian, this refusal should be documented in the patient's record with a signed statement by the patient or guardian indicating that the use of restraints was refused although the risks were explained. Unless an emergency situation exists, facilities have the right to discharge a patient who refuses restraints when the restraints are deemed essential to care.

nursing assessment and judgment. Restraints should not be indiscriminately applied without determining the effect on the individual patient. A policy that "all patients over 65 years of age must have all bed side rails elevated when sleeping" is not acceptable. Instead, an institution must identify specific criteria to be assessed when making a judgment regarding the use of restraints.

Historically, health care institutions, through their nursing employees, were not held legally responsible for the failure to restrain a patient without a specific order from a physician. It was the responsibility of the physician to make that determination.

That responsibility has been very emphatically transferred from the physician to the health care institution, which in turn places the ultimate responsibility upon nurses to exercise independent professional judgment. It is the standard of care for a nurse to make nursing diagnoses; assess the patient's age, medications, level of orientation, or other factors; determine the necessity for restraints; and decide what kind should be used. In fact, a physician's order to restrain or a physician's failure to order restraints will not automatically exonerate the nurse or the employer. Therefore, nurses must make independent determinations of the need for restraints, request the appropriate order, and apply adequate restraints (see Table 9-3).

The concern about reducing the incidence of falls and accidents that may occur with independent activity must not infringe upon the patient's civil liberties, freedom of movement, and independence. The patient should not be forced into a category based upon age or diagnosis, resulting in the application of restraints without a specific determination of the necessity for them.

The balancing of risks and benefits when restraining a patient requires the nurse to identify the pros and the cons for a particular individual and to arrive at a nursing judgment based upon those considerations. Because the nurse usually observes the patient more frequently than the physician, the nursing assessment and judgment should be given sufficient consideration when arriving at a decision regarding the use of restraints. Similarly, comments from family members may also be taken into consideration, since they may be in a better position to offer input into this decision. Yet it is also important for the nurse to remember that the ultimate decision must be that of the nurse and physician, and not the family member.

If a determination has been made to restrain a patient and the patient or legal guardian refuses to consent to restraints, the nurse must take one of several actions to prevent liability. In any situation where a patient or the legal guardian refuses to comply with recommended medical or nursing treatment, a release from liability should be signed by that individual. The release should state what activity is being refused, the implications and ramifications of failing to comply with the recommended treatment, and the personal acceptance of responsibility and liability by the patient or legal guardian.

Alternatively, where a patient or a legal guardian refuses to comply with recommended treatment, the patient may be immediately discharged from the institution unless doing so would create an emergency situation. Patients do not have a right to be hospitalized, especially when they fail to comply with the proposed medical or nursing regimens.

An increasing area of nursing liability is a nurse's failure to comply with institutional policies and procedures regarding restraints. First, it is important to know how restraints may be initiated, whether a physician's order is required, or whether a nurse may apply restraints initially, with a physician's order to follow. If there are identified criteria to be utilized in making a determination regarding the application of restraints, the nursing assessment of those criteria in the patient should be reflected in the medical record.

Policies and procedures typically specify how frequently restraints must be removed and what actions are to be carried out, such as range of motion, assessing circulation and skin condition, and the manner of securing restraints. If the stated policy and procedure are not practical or being complied with, the reason for the deviation for a particular patient must be documented. If a policy or procedure is not workable with most patients, it should be rewritten to be reasonable. Failure to comply with a policy and procedure regarding the frequency with which restraints are to be removed constitutes a deviation from the acceptable nursing standard of care and may lead to nursing malpractice.

Several important areas regarding restraints must be documented by the nurse, including the patient assessment and factors taken into consideration in making the determination to restrain or not restrain. Both nursing judgments are equally important and must be well documented. The decision to restrain a patient has the same potential liability as the decision not to. If no reasons for the judgment regarding the use of restraints are reflected in the medical record, the nurse is going to have a very difficult time several years later recalling and explaining to a jury why a certain decision was made.

The necessity for restraints is reviewed periodically and documented because it is well known that a patient's condition may change and alter the initial nursing judgment. This principle is also applicable to the choice of restraints, since most courts require the least restrictive form of restraints to be utilized that will serve the intended purpose.

It is perfectly acceptable to reference any written policies or procedures or nursing care plan in the context of the documentation to prevent rewriting the same activities multiple times during a shift. For example, charting "Restraint care per nursing care plan/policies and procedures" can be interpreted to mean that any activities identified in the nursing care plan or the institutional policies and procedures regarding the use of restraints were complied with by the nurse who so charted.

Intentional Torts

Torts are laws that deal with harm that may come to an individual through inadvertence or actual intent by another. Tort laws generally pertain to conduct recognized as socially undesirable. Nursing malpractice is an example of a tort.

Tort laws were developed as a means to compensate those injured by the wrongful conduct of another. They seek to restore status quo by placing the injured party in a position equivalent to that held before the tort was committed.

Intentional torts are defined as those torts where conduct is intended to bring about a result that invades the interest of another in a way not sanctioned by law. Intentional torts require the element of foreseeability; the result must have been predictable. There are several areas of intentional torts that may be alleged against nurses, either in conjunction with an allegation of nursing malpractice or as a separate allegation. These include assault and battery, defamation, invasion of privacy, and false imprisonment.

Assault and Battery

Assault and battery are actually two independent torts that may be alleged together or separately against a nurse. *Assault* is an unjustifiable attempt to touch another person or even the threat of doing so, while *battery* is the actual carrying out of the threatened physical contact. The element to be proven in claims for assault or battery is the absence of consent of the individual who was threatened. In health care, this absence of consent is referred to as lack of informed consent.

Allegations of assault and battery may be made where a procedure is performed by a nurse without the patient's consent. In addition, a patient has the right to specify who performs such treatment or procedure. Forcing medicine upon a patient constitutes assault and battery.

In one case, an elderly patient in a state hospital required help with eating. The defendant nurse fed the patient cubed potatoes. She held the patient's head back by grasping the patient's hair with one hand and feeding her with the other. During the feeding the nurse occasionally covered the

Threatening to harm another person physically can be considered assault; unconsented physical contact with another can be battery.

patient's mouth and nose with a towel. Another attendant held the patient's arms. The patient died from aspiration of stomach contents. The nurse was found guilty of assault and battery leading to involuntary manslaughter. She served one year in a county detention facility and was on probation for three years.

Defamation

Defamation of character occurs where a person discusses another individual in terms that diminish reputation. *Libel* is written defamation, and *slander* is oral defamation.

Injury to the reputation may occur by a showing of diminished esteem, respect, or good will. It may result from derogatory or adverse opinions that disgrace or ridicule the individual, causing shunning or avoidance.

Making a false statement about a patient or employee to a third party can be viewed as defamation of character. Nurses must assure that only accurate information is communicated to persons with a legal right to that information.

To constitute defamation, the communication must be made to a third party. It is irrelevant whether the communication is intentional or unintentional. Merely overhearing another conversation is sufficient to meet this requisite element. Consequently, conversations about patients in an elevator, in the hallway, or in the cafeteria may lead to allegations of defamation.

The allegation of defamation is personal to the person who has been injured. Thus, if the person dies, a relative may not bring a lawsuit based upon allegations of defamation unless the allegations also reflect upon that surviving individual.

Four criteria are required to prove defamation. First, the person must have deliberately made a particular statement. Second, the person making the statement must have understood that it referred to the injured party. Third, the person's intent in making the statement must have been to convey defamatory meaning. Fourth, the statement must be false. Truth is a defense in defamation actions.

To win a defamation action, the patient must be able to show actual financial injury to personal reputation or business. As previously discussed, the failure to sustain actual damages will prevent a finding of liability.

The exception is that many states have statutorily defined certain types of defamatory statements where specific financial injury is not required for a successful action. Such statements are referred to as "per se defamation." Examples include charges of contagious or venereal diseases, the imputation of a crime, fornication, adultery, or unchastity.

Invasion of Privacy

Individuals have a constitutional right to be left alone, and failure to respect that right may constitute invasion of privacy. There are four distinct areas of private interests:

1. Intrusion on an individual's physical and mental solitude and seclusion.
2. Public disclosure of private facts.
3. Publicity placing the individual in a false light in the public eye.

4. Appropriation of an individual's name or likeness for the benefit or advantage of another.

Allegations of invasion of privacy may be based upon the use of photographs of patients without express consent. Any disclosure of confidential information without appropriate consent could also constitute an invasion of privacy.

False Imprisonment

Keeping patients from leaving a facility against their will and using restraints improperly are examples of false imprisonment in a health care setting.

The improper use of restraints or forceful detention of a patient is false imprisonment, defined as an infringement upon an individual's freedom of movement. Allegations of false imprisonment may involve elderly or psychiatric patients who are being detained or restrained without sufficient justification. The important considerations for using restraints have previously been discussed in that section.

Nursing Administration

Errors in nursing administration are increasingly giving rise to nursing malpractice claims. With allegations of administrative errors there are typically multiple defendants as responsibility goes up the chain of command. Therefore, nurses in high administrative positions must recognize their responsibility, and ultimate liability, for the negligence of the staff they manage.

Ensuring Staff Competency

An area of increasing liability is that of failing to employ competent staff. The employment process must be well defined and followed. Applicants for employment should complete a comprehensive application for employment that includes information pertaining to education, prior employment, prior claims or lawsuits involving alleged nursing malpractice, current nursing, licensures, prior disciplinary actions or investigative proceedings conducted by the state board of nursing, and references. Information must be verified to the extent possible with contacts made to prior employers and references. The employment process is to be well documented in the employee's personnel file.

It is also becoming desirable to review periodically the credentials and qualifications of nurses. Competency at the time of employment does not ensure continued competency. Employee evaluations should be specific to the area in which the nurse is assigned and must adequately evaluate the nurse's performance and competency. Skills labs can be used to evaluate a nurse's level of performance and identify weaknesses. The more comprehensive the evaluation of an employee, the less likely the nursing management will be to find itself the subject of a lawsuit for unqualified staff.

Ensuring Appropriate Delivery of Care

Staffing of nurses is a perpetual problem in the nursing field. However, we are now seeing specific allegations of failure to have sufficient numbers of staff and lack of qualified staff as the subject of nursing malpractice lawsuits. With patient acuity levels defining staffing needs, plaintiffs have an easier time proving their allegations.

The types of quality-assurance and peer-review activities within an institution are also being questioned in lawsuits. Programs must be in place that effectively evaluate both patient care outcomes and nursing performances. They must demonstrate that problems are identified and corrective actions implemented to resolve those problems.

Finally, nurse administrators must recognize their responsibility for institutional policies, procedures, and standards of care. These are the guidelines with which nurses are expected to comply in order to meet the minimum standards of nursing care. The failure to have policies and procedures or standards of care that reflect the current minimum standards may lead to nursing malpractice. Policies, procedures, and standards of care must be reviewed periodically by nurses in the specialty areas to which the policies pertain. Nurse administrators also have a responsibility for evaluating compliance with the institution's policies and procedures and its standards of care.

There must also be verification that any institutional guidelines comply with national standards of care, such as those promulgated by the American Nurses' Association or other specialty nursing organizations. Nurses are expected to comply with the national minimum standards of nursing care and will be held accountable for providing that level of nursing care. If institutional policies, procedures, and standards fall below the minimum standards, the institution is subject to liability for failing to establish the appropriate standards for its staff.

Conclusion

By decreasing the mystique of the law and their personal ignorance of the law, gerontological nurses will decrease their exposure to liability. Nurses should identify available resources where legal information pertaining to the nurse's specific practice can be obtained, such as state nurses' associations, the American Nurses' Association, state boards of nursing, and other professional health and legal organizations. By working closely with attorneys in the employment setting, nurses will also aid in decreasing nursing liability by preventing potentially liable acts or omissions or minimizing the effects of negligence.

Instead of fighting the current litigious attitude of the public, nurses must accept it and plan for it. Adopting practices that minimize exposure to liability is as much a part of nursing as any other nursing actions.

BIBLIOGRAPHY   Bernzweig EP: Why you need your own malpractice policy. RN 48(3): 59–60, 1985.

Connaway N: Documenting patient care in the home: Legal issues for home health nurses. Home Healthcare Nurse 3(5): 6–8, 1985.

Fiesta J: The Law and Liability: A Guide for Nurses, 2nd ed. New York, Wiley, 1988.

Fox TC (ed): Long Term Care and the Law. Owings Mills, MD, Rynd Communications, 1986.

Henry KH: Nursing Administration and Law Manual. Rockville, MD, Aspen Systems, 1987.

Kapp MB, Bigot A: Geriatrics and the Law. New York, Springer, 1985.

Marks DT: Legal implications of increased autonomy. J Gerontol Nurs 13(3): 26–31, 1987.

Northrop CE: The ins and outs of informed consent. Nurs 85 15(1): 9, 21, 1985.

Shapiro R: Taking precautions. Nurs Times 81(9): 20–21, 1985.

Smith D, Weaver B: Guidelines for decision making. J Gerontol Nurs 13(3): 47–48, 1987.

CHAPTER 10

Ethical Issues

Melinda D. Fitting

Chapter Objectives
At the completion of this chapter the reader will be able to:

1. Define an ethical dilemma.
2. Discuss the ethical principles of fidelity, autonomy, beneficence, and justice and how these principles apply to nursing practice.
3. Identify the role of ethics committees in health care agencies.

Ethical dilemmas occur in all professions. The field of gerontological nursing is faced with many dilemmas that are ethical in nature. Nurses are frequently pulled in different directions with equally compelling moral ideals or principles. How should a nurse make a decision between two equally compelling choices? Ethical dilemmas arise when there is a conflict between choices and there is evidence that each choice has justifiable moral arguments and ethical principles that support it. A typical dilemma in geriatric nursing care arises between choices that involve beneficence and autonomy. Nurses have both a commitment to take care of a patient (beneficence) and a moral obligation to respect the patient's right to do what he or she thinks is best, that is, to act autonomously. Examples of ethical dilemmas in applied settings are whether or not to use physical and pharmacological restraints, how much information to provide ill patients, whether to institute or discontinue life-saving technology with terminal patients, how to allocate resources (nursing services) in a shift of limited time and resources, or how to decide upon a discharge plan when a patient, family, and staff differ on the aftercare plans.

Ethics may be divided into metaethics and normative ethics. Metaethics is more abstract and analyzes the meaning of ethical concepts such as "good," "virtuous," or "right." Normative ethics concerns itself with what is right or wrong, good or bad, or what our obligations are to others. Such ethical principles as fidelity, beneficence, autonomy, nonmaleficence, and veracity are the foundation of normative ethics. Applied ethics is a part of normative ethics and is what most of us are doing when we apply ethical principles or ethical codes of our professions to clinical situations. This chapter will demonstrate a method of integrating factual information with ethical principles and show how to weigh the different options in an ethical dilemma.

Professionalism carries with it a responsibility to the individuals or organizations served and to society at large. As professionals we are governed by legal and regulatory means, which are methods to protect the consumer from fraud, malpractice, exploitation, or injury. We are also bound by the ethical codes of our professions and by personal ethical integrity. Nurses must not only know the American Nurses' Association Code of Ethics, but they must also be aware of their personal ethical beliefs and standards (ANA Code of Ethics, 1985).

Ethical Principles

Fidelity

The principle of fidelity implies the need to be faithful to a duty, obligation, or trust. Truthfulness, or the duty of veracity, may be thought of as being derived from this principle (Beauchamp and Childress, 1983, 238). A nurse's initial relationship with a patient should be founded upon trust and a commitment from the nurse to provide care for the patient to the best of his or her abilities. Fidelity is always central to covenantal and contractual relationships and depends on trust between the persons involved, which in turn depends on the integrity and conscientiousness of the parties involved. Fidelity thus "entails a certain presence, a quality of 'being there' for someone—of making a patient, for example, feel the nurse is with her and for her" (Mitchell and Achtenberg, 1984, 18).

Respect and trust in the nurse-patient relationship results from the nurse demonstrating honesty and commitment to the patient in the delivery of services.

According to the Code for Nurses (Table 10-1), "The nurse provides services with respect for human dignity and the uniqueness of the client." This statement implies respect and trust between the nurse and patient that constitute a moral bond and carries with them an expectation that the nurse will be faithful to her or his relationship with the patient. It is this faithfulness and respect that allow the public to trust nurses in the role of service provider. Nurses are "to maintain the integrity of nursing" and "to implement and improve standards of nursing." It is in the context of relationships with our patients that we demonstrate these qualities and thus engender a belief in the integrity of the nursing profession.

Dilemmas arise for health professionals as they attempt to live up to this ideal of faithfulness. Care decisions in such applied settings as hospitals, nursing homes, and day care centers, as well as those of home health organizations, are often ambiguous for nurses. Ethical principles may conflict with one another as we attempt to be faithful to our patients' desires and choices as well as faithful to ourselves and to act in a responsible and competent manner as professionals (ANA Code, items 4 and 5). Dean Jost (1981) emphasized the point that decisions to place elders in nursing homes require a special consideration of the inherent trust in the patient-provider relationship. If we view our responsibilities to our patients first, with everything else secondary, then fidelity and faithfulness are prima facie binding. Therefore, health providers must act in accord with their duty of fidelity to

TABLE 10-1. American Nurses' Association Code for Nurses

1. The nurse provides services with respect for human dignity and the uniqueness of the client, unrestricted by considerations of social or economic status, personal attributes, or the nature of health problems.
2. The nurse safeguards the client's right to privacy by judiciously protecting information of a confidential nature.
3. The nurse acts to safeguard the client and the public when health care and safety are affected by the incompetent, unethical, or illegal practice of any person.
4. The nurse assumes responsibility and accountability for individual nursing judgments and actions.
5. The nurse maintains competence in nursing.
6. The nurse exercises informed judgment and uses individual competence and qualifications as criteria in seeking consultation, accepting responsibilities, and delegating nursing activities to others.
7. The nurse participates in activities that contribute to the ongoing development of the profession's body of knowledge.
8. The nurse participates in the profession's efforts to implement and improve standards of nursing.
9. The nurse participates in the profession's efforts to establish and maintain conditions of employment conducive to high quality nursing care.
10. The nurse participates in the profession's effort to protect the public from misinformation and misrepresentation and to maintain the integrity of nursing.
11. The nurse collaborates with members of the health professions and other citizens in promoting community and national efforts to meet the health needs of the public.

American Nurses' Association, Code for Nurses, 1985. Reprinted with the permission of ANA.

their relationship with their client, and this duty may only be overridden if there is a stronger moral obligation. Prima facie duties are duties that are always to be acted upon unless there is a conflict with another equally compelling duty. Fidelity, beneficence, autonomy, and justice may all be thought of as principles that are prima facie binding. We have a responsibility to reason morally through our commitments to these ethical principles and our professional codes and to justify specific decisions. Following this section on the ethical principles is an example of an ethical dilemma faced by a nurse as she or he cares for a terminally ill woman in pain.

Autonomy

The right of a person to make choices affecting his or her life is an essential component of autonomy. Immanuel Kant, an 18th-century German philosopher, proposed an ethical theory that was based upon respect for people's autonomy and a belief in rationality as an attribute of the human species. According to Kant, autonomy is linked with respect for another person, and in this sense the foundation of this principle is similar to fidelity. Kant argued that "persons should always treat each other as autonomous ends and never as the means to the ends of others" (Beauchamp and Childress, 1983, 60). In other words, people have unconditional worth and are to be treated as an end in themselves. Mutual respect between people implies that people are autonomous agents who are capable of making their own decisions.

Nurses should respect the patient's decisions concerning health care, even if those decisions are not consistent with the recommendations of the health care team.

This right to act autonomously is highly esteemed in Western societies; in the United States it is guaranteed by law to adults unless there is convincing evidence that this right should be overruled because of some form of incapacity. This principle is emphasized in the ANA Code (1): "The nurse provides services with respect for human dignity and the uniqueness of the individual, unrestricted by considerations of social or economic status, personal attributes, or the nature of health problems." Nurses are expected to respect the individual patient and to honor his or her choices about medical care. This principle can sometimes be difficult to follow because a patient may weight information about an illness in a way that is different from the nurse's and consequently may make a health decision that the nurse does not agree with. Unless the patient is incompetent, he or she has the right to make his or her own health care decisions.

Providing informed consent is an aspect of respecting patients' autonomy. Telling patients the truth and respecting their ability to participate in decisions regarding their care is an integral part of informed consent. The assumption is that health professionals and patients are partners in a collaborative effort to promote the patient's best interests. The President's Commission for the Study of Ethical Problems in Medicine and Biomedical and Behavioral Research argued that informed consent and collaboration between health care provider and client are essential to promote the client's best interests. They emphasized that "the risk of wrongly abrogating decision making for many patients seems generally more grievous than the pain of confronting some seriously ill patients with choices that they would rather not face" (1983a, 51). In other words, nurses and other health professionals have a responsibility to inform patients of their choices and to help them to understand these choices.

Marginal competence, or limited capacity to "think" rationally and therefore act rationally, can affect the degree of autonomy a patient is able to exercise. Marginal competence is also called diminished capacity or limited competence. A person is considered to be diminished in competence or limited in decision-making ability if he or she is dependent upon others (i.e., children) or incapable of making and acting upon rational deliberation (i.e., a psychotically ill person). The concept of marginal competence is particularly important for helping professionals working with the elderly because we are often expected to make judgments about elders' capabilities to make decisions rationally. Rarely is decisional incapacity absolute except in the case of infants. The concept of decision making is now thought of as a continuum with an emphasis upon specific tasks or decisions, for example, finances, self-care, medical decisions.

Ethical dilemmas can occur with marginally competent older patients because nurses must both protect them from harm that may result from their compromised mental capacity and respect their autonomy. Assessments of mental capacity are critical in health care because they "diminish two types of errors: mistakenly preventing persons who ought to be considered competent from directing the course of their own treatment, and failing to protect incapacitated persons from the harmful effects of their decisions"

(President's Commission, 1983a, 122). Patients may be incapacitated temporarily by a depressive illness, or be delirious from an interaction effect of medication, or be limited in decisional capacity because of organic changes as a result of illnesses like Alzheimer's disease, Parkinson's disease, or multi-infarct dementia. Assessment and evaluation are vital to understanding each patient, and the ANA Code stresses competency in both items 4 and 5. Consultation is a part of item 6, and nurses may find that consulting with psychologists or psychiatrists about the mental status of their patients is useful.

Beneficence

Beneficence is the principle of doing good for others. It means helping people by both preventing harm and actively intervening to benefit someone. Some moral philosophers distinguish between the act of doing good, or benefiting someone, and the act of preventing harm, which is the principle of nonmaleficence. Beneficence is a central tenet in nursing and other health professions. Health professions are commonly called "helping professions" because we are expected to have a commitment and a moral obligation to do good because of our professional choice. People seek the expertise of physicians, nurses, psychologists, and other health professionals when they are ill or vulnerable in some way. It is due to this service provision and specialized education that we "incur a particularly powerful duty to help those in need" (Caplan, 1985).

Nurses must carefully balance their obligation to help people and prevent harm against the patient's right to make choices and take actions independently.

If beneficence includes preventing harm, it implies that certain people need protection from harm. This need is implied in item 3 of the ANA Code, "The nurse acts to safeguard the client," and in item 10, "The nurse participates in the profession's effort to protect the public from misinformation and misrepresentation." Groups of people who might need protection are children and developmentally disabled or mentally impaired adults. Paternalism is a subset of beneficence invoked to protect someone from harm. A nurse who acts paternalistically is assuming that he or she knows best and must invoke his or her authority to prevent the patient from harm. Paternalism is used to justify involuntary commitments to psychiatric hospitals to prevent suicidal or homicidal harm.

When is it justified to use paternalistic interventions? This is a key question with persons who are marginally competent. It is important to examine our motives for invoking the principle of beneficence as a justification for paternalistic actions that override a person's desire for autonomy. It has been argued that

it takes a heavy burden of justification to intervene in such cases, especially when intervention limits free choices and actions by competent persons. According to this position, paternalism can be justified only if (1) the harms prevented from occurring or the benefit provided to the person outweighs the loss of independence or the sense of invasion suffered by the interference, (2) the person's condition seriously limits his or her ability to choose autonomously, and (3) it is universally justified under relevantly similar circumstances always to treat persons this way. (Beauchamp and Childress, 1983, 172)

Justice

The ethical principle of justice describes the moral obligation to treat other people fairly and as equals. The ANA Code (item 1) refers to this when it states, "The nurse provides services with respect for human dignity and the uniqueness of the client, *unrestricted* by considerations of social or economic status." Justice also implies that people are to get that which is due to them. The distribution of goods and services should be related to what people justly deserve. Ethical dilemmas arise because the world is not ideal and there are inequities and injustices. Nurses encounter ethical dilemmas in their work environments with the allocation of resources and nursing time to patients.

Whether or not one's access to health care is a right or an ethical obligation on the part of society is a controversial subject. The President's Commission, in their report entitled *Securing Access to Health Care,* stated:

Furthermore, while some people have some ability—through choice of life-style and through preventive measures—to influence their health status, many health problems are beyond their control and are therefore undeserved. Besides the burden of genetics, environment, and chance, individuals become ill because of things they do or fail to do—but it is often difficult for an individual to choose to do otherwise or even to know with enough specificity and confidence what he or she ought to do to remain healthy. Finally, the incidence and severity of ill health is distributed very unevenly among people. Basic needs for housing and food are predictable, but even the most hardworking and prudent person may suddenly be faced with overwhelming needs for health care. Together, these considerations lend weight to the belief that health care is different from most other goods and services. In a society concerned not only with fairness and equality of opportunity but also with the redemptive powers of science, there is a felt obligation to ensure that some level of health services is available to all. (1983b, 12)

Nurses' ability to provide service in an unrestricted manner can be challenged by limited resources and the rationing of health care.

Even if society agreed that some type of access to health care was an ethical obligation, we would still be faced with how much is enough and what constitutes adequate health care. These are questions that American society as a whole is grappling with at the macro level, and we will be faced with continued changes in health care delivery in our society as we struggle to parcel out finite amounts of money for defense, health care, housing, education, and other competing interests.

CASE EXAMPLE

Ethical dilemmas arise in clinical settings because there are competing claims made by each ethical principle and we are not always sure how to make the most ethical choice as we weigh all the alternatives. Let us evaluate a case and discuss a method of reasoning through ethical dilemmas:

Virginia was a black older woman, age 63, who was diagnosed with cervical cancer at age 60 and refused treatment at that time. She was ultimately hospitalized in a terminal state. She was in constant pain and was given Dilaudid every hour for pain. She was no longer cognitively alert to ask for the pain medication and her body could no longer adequately process the quantity of pain medication. She was expected to die from the toxic effects of the medicine. (Anderson, 1978, 57–63)

The nurses working with Virginia wanted to act beneficently toward Virginia and help her manage her pain and yet they wanted her to be actively involved in the decision about how much pain medication to take, since this medicine had a potentially life-threatening impact. There was also the possibility that nurses might have differing opinions among themselves as well as with the treating physician. The ANA Code specifically states that nurses are to act in a competent manner and be accountable for their own actions. Even if the pain medication is ordered by a physician, nurses have an ethical obligation to their profession and to their patients to evaluate the patient and recommend a treatment plan. If a nurse has questions about a plan, it is his or her responsibility to voice these questions and be in agreement professionally and morally with the plan that is being implemented with a patient. The "Interpretive Statements" section of the ANA Code for Nurses states:

If ethically opposed to interventions in a particular case because of the procedures to be used, the nurse is justified in refusing to participate. Such refusal should be made known in advance and in time for other appropriate arrangements to be made for the client's nursing care. If the nurse becomes involved in such a case and the client's life is in jeopardy, the nurse is obliged to provide for the client's safety, to avoid abandonment, and to withdraw only when assured that alternative sources of nursing care are available. (3–4)

Facts in a case are extremely important because they help define the medical issues in that case. We use facts in conjunction with the ethical principles as we reason through the moral dilemma. What is Virginia's diagnosis, current condition, and prognosis? She is in the last stages of cancer and in great pain. There is no hope of recovery, and the medical staff agrees on this fact. Medical interventions had been tried after she was diagnosed with the cancer three years before, but she voluntarily refused any surgical interventions, and the cancer had spread. She is being given antibiotics, re-

spiratory treatments, medications, and intravenous feedings but is not to be coded if her heart stops (Anderson, 1978, 59). She has asked for pain medication and been given it on a regular schedule.

Virginia's autonomy must be respected; therefore, the staff must adequately inform her of all of her choices. One obligation of the nurses and the physicians caring for Virginia is to discuss the use of pain medication with her when she is alert and competent to participate in decisions surrounding her care. Does she know the side effects of the medicine and what will happen if she continues to take more and more of it? Have the alternatives been discussed with her, together with their risks and benefits? In other words, has she been fully informed of her treatment plan and understood the risks and benefits as well as the alternatives? Has she had time to process the information provided her and discuss with the staff her questions or her thoughts and fears about her choices?

Pain relief is controversial in this case because on the one hand it can be seen as an act of beneficence with the care of the patient and the amelioration of pain as the primary goal, and on the other hand it can be viewed as causing harm because the end result is a compromise of respiratory function that will hasten her death.

In such situations, should maintenance of adequate respiratory status take precedence over pain relief? Relief of pain and maintenance of compromised function are both goals of medicine. It can be plausibly argued that in the situation of the dying patient, the goal of maintenance of compromised function is itself related to the goal of prolonging life. (Jonsen et al., 1982)

It is this goal of prolonging life that also must be evaluated. The ANA Code states in the "Interpretive Statements" that "the nurse may provide interventions to relieve symptoms in the dying patient even when the interventions entail substantial risks of hastening death" (4).

Personal ethical beliefs influence how the nurse will identify and manage ethical dilemmas in the workplace.

We need to be aware of our own ethical beliefs because they influence how we choose to understand the medical choices in our work. Work experience may broaden one's knowledge and teach nurses about the ambiguity of medical and moral decisions, but it may not change the decisions made because these are tied to one's ethical and moral beliefs about life. The nurses who did not want to give pain medicine to Virginia when she was not alert did not feel comfortable ethically with a treatment plan which they saw would hasten her death. If she had been alert and asked for the pain medicine they would have been more comfortable because then it would have been an autonomous choice by Virginia. Weighing the benefits of pain medicine versus the risks and the burden of the choice is important. If Virginia chooses to be sedated even though it hastens her death, and a nurse feels ethically obligated to refuse to administer the pain medication, it is incumbent upon the nurse to inform her or his supervisor in the institution of this decision. Other arrangements for the care of the patient can then be made.

Euthanasia

The treatment of Virginia is an example of the complexities inherent in treating terminally ill patients. Arguments can be made in favor of aggressively treating her pain and consequently hastening her death. This choice can be justified because medical staff have a responsibility to ameliorate pain. However, the other side of the argument says that we have a responsibility to prolong life and to actively attempt to maintain life. Is hastening death euthanasia? Is euthanasia ever justified?

There are two main categories of euthanasia, passive and active. In this case the decision not to code Virginia may be conceptualized as voluntary passive euthanasia. Passive euthanasia is considered voluntary when a competent patient gives informed consent to a particular treatment or nontreatment. In this case the use of antibiotics, respiratory treatments, medications, and intravenous feedings were still to be used if necessary, and if these were discontinued it would be a situation of involuntary passive euthanasia. Decisions about withholding treatment must be made very carefully and only after taking into consideration the ethical issues involved in each decision.

Active euthanasia, on the other hand, occurs when a health professional actively intervenes to hasten a death. In this case, if a nurse knowingly administered a lethal dose of medicine to Virginia she or he would be actively causing death. This has been termed "mercy killing." One of the strongest arguments against this type of euthanasia is the "slippery slope" or "wedge" argument (Beauchamp and Childress, 1983). This argument suggests that if killing is allowed, even for those in pain or with terminal illness, it may set the stage for "undesirable" people to be killed and for society to justify the murders. Elderly people who are sick and no longer productive may be seen as a drain on society, and it is foreseeable that mercy killings could be justified by some people. The importance of human life is an essential tenet of American society and the first principle in the ANA Code for Nurses. Even though we feel compassion for our patients and want to prevent them from harm and decrease their pain, the slippery slope argument is an important one against active euthanasia.

Even in situations that are not a matter of life and death, it is crucial that we weigh out the benefits and the risks of our treatment plans. An example would be the use of physical restraints in a nursing home or on an inpatient hospital unit. Are the restraints for the benefit of the staff or the patient? Beneficence should not be used as a ruse to override autonomy, nor should it be used as a justification for an action that benefits the medical staff or family but is not in the best interests of the patient.

Advance Directives

Dilemmas may also arise when a patient plans for the future by signing a living will or writing an advance directive. One of the difficulties with living wills has been the fact that no one can foresee every potential problem, and thus wills are only guidelines for future action. The benefit of advance planning is that it is a means by which persons can express their autonomous wishes in case they become cognitively impaired in the future and become unable to express their choices. An important point is that "living wills work only for treatment refusal; they do not serve as directives for those who want all possible treatments applied. For that, a durable power of attorney is needed" (Mishkin, 1985, 30). Durable powers of attorney are flexible in that they do not lock a patient into a specific decision. Rather, the designated agent who is given the durable power of attorney is allowed to make a decision based upon the specific circumstances of the patient at any given time. The designated agent may be anyone chosen by the patient (Mishkin, 1985). This procedure allows competent persons to choose agents who will act in their best interests and make health care decisions for them should they become incapacitated.

Gaining an understanding of the patient's and family's views on resuscitation, the use of life-sustaining technology, and similar issues can aid in the management of ethical dilemmas that may arise during caregiving.

Nurses often have more contact with the families and the patient and may be more in touch with their emotional responses than the physician (Younger, 1987). Nurses are an important link between the health care team and the patient and family and are in a position to help the family think about the pros and cons of the health care alternatives at different stages of an illness. Therefore, in order to provide the best clinical care for patients it is vital that nurses understand their ethical beliefs so that these do not influence or hinder the patient's or family's decisions.

Ethics Committees

Ethics committees are forming in many hospitals and in nursing departments. Nurses have an ethical responsibility to themselves and to their patients not only to think about the ethics of their decisions, but also to use appropriate channels in their institutions to examine ethical dilemmas in their practice. Often ethics committees begin with an educational focus to build a common foundation for the various members. After this phase the committee may begin to discuss actual clinical dilemmas in the institution and help clinicians think through the ethical issues in a case. It is essential that professionals know the policies of an institution and the mechanism within the institution to use when there are differences between clinicians on care decisions. Sometimes it may be the role of the nurse to point out the lack of a specific policy and the need for the staff and institution to decide on a policy for clinical decision making. An example is the do-not-resuscitate order and the institution's guidelines for this order. What is important to remember in making clinical decisions is that "if the decision is founded on accurate and complete information, acceptance of consequences, and advance planning" (Bernal and Hoover, 1987), then a nurse should be able to justify her or his decision as an ethical one in the service of the patient. As long as nurses can ethically justify their actions using the principles of beneficence, autonomy, fidelity, and justice, the integrity of the nursing profession will continue to be maintained, and nurses will continue to feel proud of their profession.

REFERENCES

Anderson P: Nurse. New York, Berkley Books, 1978.

Beauchamp TL, Childress JF: Principles of biomedical ethics, 2nd ed. New York, Oxford University Press, 1983.

Bernal EW, Hoover PS: The nurse's appeal to conscience. Hastings Center Report, 17, 25–26, 1987.

Caplan A: Our brother's keepers. Hastings Center Report, 15, 46–47, 1985.

Jonsen AR, Siegler M, Winslade WJ: Clinical ethics. New York, Macmillan, 1982.

Jost T: The problem of consent for placement, care and treatment of the incompetent nursing home resident. St. Louis University Law Journal 26:63–103, 1981.

Mishkin B: Advance decision-making for health care: Living wills and durable powers of attorney. In Taking charge of the end of your life: Proceedings of a forum on living wills and other advance directives. Washington DC, American Bar Association and Older Women's League, 1985.

Mitchell C, Achtenberg B: Code gray study guide. Boston, Fanlight Productions, 1984.

President's Commission for the Study of Ethical Problems in Medicine and Biomedical and Behavioral Research. Deciding to forego life-sustaining treatment. Washington, DC, US Government Printing Office, 1983a.

President's Commission for the Study of Ethical Problems in Medicine and Biomedical and Behavioral Research. Securing access to health care, vol. 1: Report. Washington, DC, US Government Printing Office, 1983b.

Younger SJ: Do-Not-Resuscitate orders: No longer secret, but still a problem. Hastings Center Report, 17, 24–33, 1987.

BIBLIOGRAPHY

Cody M: Withholding treatment: Is it ethical? J Gerontol Nurs 12(9): 24–26, 1986.

Edwards BJ: Establishing a bioethics committee. J Nurs Admin 18(3): 30–33, 1988.

Flech LM: Decisions of justice and health care. J Gerontol Nurs 13(3): 40–46, 1987.

Floyd J: Research and informed consent: The dilemma of the cognitively impaired client. J Psychosoc Nurs Ment Health Serv 26(3): 13–14, 17, 21, 1988.

Last JM: The ethics of paternalism in public health. Can J Public Health 78(1): 3–5, 1987.

Meier RH: Recent developments in rehabilitation giving rise to important new (and old) ethical issues and concerns. Am J Phys Med Rehab 67(1): 7–11, 1988.

Muyskens JL: Acting alone. Am J Nurs 87(9): 1141–1142, 1146, 1987.

Phillips LR: Respect basic human rights. J Gerontol Nurs 13(3): 36–39, 1987.

Ramsey P: The patient as person. New Haven, Yale University Press, 1970.

Urden LD: Building a case for decision making. J Nurs Admin 16(11): 6, 1986.

Veatch RM, Fry ST: Case Studies in Nursing Ethics. Philadelphia, JB Lippincott, 1987.

CHAPTER 11

Quality Assurance

Charlotte Eliopoulos

Chapter Objectives

At the completion of this chapter the reader will be able to:

1. Outline the components of a comprehensive quality assurance program.
2. Describe the significance of philosophy, mission, standards, policies, and procedures to the quality assurance program.
3. State the differences among structure, process, and outcome audits, and give examples of them.
4. List sources of data that can give indications of the quality of services provided.
5. Describe mechanisms for ongoing monitoring of quality.

Professional nursing practice in any specialty is built upon a solid foundation of standards. These standards guide actions and form a structure against which those actions can be evaluated. Although standards and monitoring mechanisms are important to any professional practice setting, they are particularly significant to gerontological nursing practice for the following reasons:

- The body of gerontological nursing knowledge is relatively new and continually growing.
- Advanced age alters certain norms and responses to therapy.
- The margin of safety is smaller in elderly individuals.
- A large proportion of direct services in many geriatric care settings are delivered by nonprofessionals.
- Geriatric services are in the midst of change as a result of cost-containment efforts.

Consequently, quality assurance must be more than a paper compliance activity to fulfill regulatory requirements: It must be superimposed on all nursing functions.

The QA Program

Quality assurance (QA) is a complicated concept that defies a single definition. For operational purposes QA can be considered a program that defines standards of practice, systematically evaluates how those standards are being met, and corrects problems discovered in the evaluation process.

189

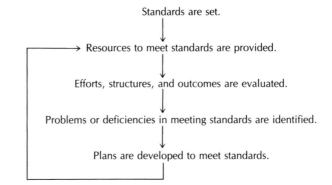

FIGURE 11-1. Flow Chart for QA Program.

The goal of a QA program is to provide a safe, effective, and appropriate level of service to consumers.

The desired level of service is determined by several value systems. The society we live in has values regarding the rights of human beings to health care. The nursing profession has values that are articulated by the American Nurses' Association and the National League for Nursing that describe the role of nurses and their responsibility to consumers of nursing services. Individual health care agencies have a set of values that determine how they treat consumers of their services. Also, individual nurses have personal value systems that guide them in their nurse-patient relationships. These value systems join to create the assumptions underlying service delivery.

A well-thought-out QA program translates an agency's value system into operational form. Components of the QA program include

- A definition of desired expectations for practice, that is, standards.
- Mechanisms for evaluating the extent to which standards are being met.
- Planned actions to correct problems in meeting standards.
- Although the assurance of a high quality of service should be the responsibility of all employees, designating a QA coordinator or QA committee to monitor the program can prevent problems from escaping attention (see Figure 11-1). In a human service organization, such as a health care agency, there are many changing variables, including staff turnover, different patient populations served, new reimbursement mechanisms, and expanding technology. These changes affect the manner in which standards are met; thus one can never rest on previous accomplishments.

> The quality assurance program includes a description of standards that should be met, mechanisms to evaluate the extent to which those standards are being met, and measures to correct deficits.

QA Foundations

A variety of factors have an impact on the quality of nursing services, such as the quality and quantity of staff, personnel and management practices, the quality and quantity of material resources, and organizational structures (e.g., policies, procedures). These factors are guided by the *philosophy* and *mission* of the employing agency. Although these statements may be viewed

Mission statements describe the purpose for which the organization exists, and the philosophy presents the beliefs that guide staff in meeting the organization's mission.

as abstract and irrelevant, they set the tone for the concrete operational activities that exist. A lack of understanding of organizational mission and philosophy can cause frustration and conflict between the agency and its employees, ultimately affecting direct care services. For example, the following demonstrate three different mission statements for long-term care facilities:

Facility A. The purpose of this facility is to provide professional and supportive services to those dependent and frail older persons who desire and have the resources for a luxury life-style in a private retirement community.

Facility B. The purpose of this facility is to provide a care environment for Jewish aged who wish to maintain their unique religious and cultural practices.

Facility C. The purpose of this facility is to care for the sick aged who, because of inability to pay or complexity of care requirements, are unable to obtain care in any other setting.

Imagine the conflicts that could result if a nurse employed in Facility A believed persons from all socioeconomic groups should have access to the facility, or the staff in Facility B wanted to decorate for and celebrate Christmas, or the director in Facility C felt that an affluent patient population ought to be recruited. The mission describes "what the agency is in business to do." It can aid staff in gaining a realistic understanding of the organization's purpose. An example of a philosophy follows, stating the beliefs that guide an organization in fulfilling its mission:

Our agency believes:

- Clients and their families should participate fully in the care-planning process.
- Career mobility should be afforded to all employees.
- Accountability for cost containment should be shared at the level closest to the service delivery.
- The neighboring community should participate in the planning and evaluation of services.

The nursing department's philosophy must be compatible with that of the overall organization.

Standards are the accepted and desired levels of performance that reflect the philosophy and values of the department. In addition to the general standards of professional practice, there are standards specific to gerontological nursing practice, developed by the American Nurses' Association. These standards (Figure 11-2) basically state that:

- Data are collected about the health status of older people and used to form nursing diagnoses.
- Actions are prioritized and focus on meeting goals derived from nursing diagnoses.
- The older person and significant others participate in the development and revision of the care plan, delivery of care, and evaluation of efforts.

Standard I. Organization of Gerontological Nursing Services
All gerontological nursing services are planned, organized, and directed by a nurse executive. The nurse executive has baccalaureate or master's preparation and has experience in gerontological nursing and administration of long-term care services or acute care services for older clients.

Standard II. Theory
The nurse participates in the generation and testing of theory as a basis for clinical decisions. The nurse uses theoretical concepts to guide the effective practice of gerontological nursing.

Standard III. Data Collection
The health status of the older person is regularly assessed in a comprehensive, accurate, and systematic manner. The information obtained during the health assessment is accessible to and shared with appropriate members of the interdisciplinary health care team, including the older person and the family.

Standard IV. Nursing Diagnosis
The nurse uses health assessment data to determine nursing diagnoses.

Standard V. Planning and Continuity of Care
The nurse develops the plan of care in conjunction with the older person and appropriate others. Mutual goals, priorities, nursing approaches, and measures in the care plan address the therapeutic, preventive, restorative, and rehabilitative needs of the older person. The care plan helps the older adult attain and maintain the highest level of health, well-being, and quality of life achievable, as well as a peaceful death. The plan of care facilitates continuity of care over time as the client moves to various care settings, and is revised as necessary.

Standard VI. Intervention
The nurse, guided by the plan of care, intervenes to provide care to restore the older person's functional capabilities and to prevent complications and excess disability. Nursing interventions are derived from nursing diagnoses and are based on gerontological nursing theory.

Standard VII. Evaluation
The nurse continually evaluates the client's and family's responses to interventions in order to determine progress toward goal attainment and to revise the data base, nursing diagnoses, and plan of care.

Standard VIII. Interdisciplinary Collaboration
The nurse collaborates with other members of the health care team in the various settings in which care is given to the older person. The team meets regularly to evaluate the effectiveness of the care plan for the client and family and to adjust the plan of care to accommodate changing needs.

Standard IX. Research
The nurse participates in research designed to generate an organized body of gerontological nursing knowledge, disseminates research findings, and uses them in practice.

Standard X. Ethics
The nurse uses the code for nurses established by the American Nurses' Association as a guide for ethical decision making in practice.

Standard XI. Professional Development
The nurse assumes responsibility for professional development and contributes to the professional growth of interdisciplinary team members. The nurse participates in peer review and other means of evaluation to assure the quality of nursing practice.

FIGURE 11-2. Standards of Gerontological Nursing Practice. (American Nurses' Association: Standards and Scope of Gerontological Nursing Practice. Kansas City, MO, ANA, pp 3–18, 1987. Reprinted with the permission of ANA.)

As can be noted, a knowledge of the unique characteristics of the elderly population is essential in achieving these standards. Within various practice settings there are standards specific to the service. Regulations, for instance, developed on the local, state, and federal level, are the *minimal* standards an agency or provider must meet to maintain licensure. These often are the standards with which nurses are most familiar. Beyond the minimum standards, agencies voluntarily can adopt higher performance standards by achieving accreditation from the Joint Commission on Accreditation of Hospitals (JCAH).

> Regulations define only minimal standards of care. The professional nurse should aspire to the highest standards attainable.

Every organization may have its unique method for implementing standards into practice, and it is in this area that policies and procedures emerge. Policies and procedures have a complementary relationship to each other: *Policies* give the principles that guide actions, and *procedures* give the desired steps in implementing actions, as shown by the following example:

Standard. Comprehensive data are systematically collected on the health status of the older adult.

Policy. All newly admitted clients will have a physical, mental, and social assessment performed within 48 hours of admission.

Procedure.

- A member of the nursing staff is to complete Section I of Assessment Form 000 within the first hour of admission.
- A registered nurse is to complete Sections II and III and develop a list of nursing diagnoses within the next 48 hours.
- The charge nurse will place the form in the portion of the client's chart labeled "Admission Information."
- The unit secretary will schedule the admission conference with the interdisciplinary team, the client, and the client's family within one week after admission.

Policies and procedures need to be compatible with the legal scope of responsibility of the organization or the provider. Policies and procedures stating that a long-term care facility can perform heart transplants, a home health aide can dispense prescription drugs, a day care program can refuse admission to nonwhite persons, or a hospital can retain a person against his will for nonpayment of a bill are invalid because they either exceed the authority of the provider or violate civil law. Policies and procedures should be reviewed regularly to assure their continued validity and incorporation of new concepts.

An important standard that promotes quality service is that care must be rendered by qualified staff. To facilitate this standard, realistic job descriptions must exist before staff are recruited and hired. Qualifications, lines of responsibility, and specific job functions are detailed on the job description. Using the job description as a guide in the hiring process can prevent misunderstanding and promote the likelihood of the employee matching the job. For example, a home health aide may have only bathed and fed patients in her previous job, and she may believe that similar expectations exist when she applies for a vacancy in another agency. Once the aide learns that the new agency expects aides to shop for groceries, prepare meals, perform light housekeeping, and take vital signs, she may not be interested in the position. It may also be learned that the aide is unable to take vital signs, although she has worked in home health for 15 years. Every item on the job description should be reviewed with job applicants and their competency in fulfilling each responsibility evaluated. Upon employment, new staff should participate in a comprehensive orientation in which their knowledge, skills, and attitudes can be evaluated further. As their job responsibilities change or new practices are implemented, in-service education accompanied by an evaluation of related competencies is essential.

Evaluating Quality

Once standards have been established, clinical and managerial practices need to be monitored regularly as part of a QA effort. A formal mechanism for evaluating how closely actual practice has followed standards is the audit. There are different types of criteria by which practice can be audited:

Structure. Who did what, when, and where? A structure audit would include the type and qualifications of staff, equipment, fiscal resources, and physical plant. For example, did each unit stay within its allocated budget? Was a licensed nurse on the unit every shift? Were all telephone orders signed by the physician within 48 hours?

Process. How was it done? The activities or procedures conducted are evaluated by process audits. For example, was the patient toileted every two hours during the day? Were families counseled as patients' conditions changed? Did all depressed patients have companionship during meals?

Outcome. Were desired results obtained? The end product is examined during an outcome audit. For example, did the patients who participated in the bladder retraining program have decreased episodes of incontinence? Has sick time usage declined since the employee clinic was established? Was there less of a decline in functional capacity among widows who received grief counseling?

Time frame is another consideration in the audit process. Data can be reviewed in three ways:

Retrospectively. After something has been done, for example, looking at absenteeism for the past year or determining how many incontinent patients developed decubiti over the past month.

Concurrently. As an activity is being performed, for example, noting the amount of time it takes for a call light to be answered, or accompanying a nurse on a home visit and observing whether she changes the dressing according to the written procedure.

Prospectively. Identifying future cases or situations for study, for example, identifying and evaluating over the next six months all patients who display new signs of confusion, or reviewing the causative or contributing factors for the next 20 employee injuries. Thus audits will be based on the criteria being evaluated for a specific time frame, such as a retrospective structure audit or a concurrent process audit.

Other mechanisms can be used as indicators of quality:

Incident or accident records

Infection rate

Decubitus rate

Sick time use pattern

Employee injuries

Compliments and complaints

Admissions, transfers, and discharges

Length of stay

Supply usage

Health department survey findings

Data pertaining to these indicators often are readily available and can offer tremendous insights if analyzed:

- The agency's purchasing agent may be concerned because the supply costs are exceeding the budgeted amount. Rather than freeze future expenditures or ignore the purchasing agent's comments, it could prove useful to evaluate the nature of the supply use. It may be discovered that the agency has begun using disposables, or the patient population has become a sicker one with more treatment needs, or that a new adult diaper is of lower quality than the former one and staff are compensating by doubling their applications.
- Decubitus rates may appear to be stable over a six-month period for the nursing home; however, evaluation may reveal that although the overall number has been constant, the incidence of new decubiti on one of the units has been progressively increasing to the extent that this single unit is responsible for 90% of all the facility's decubiti. Investigation could reveal that the quality of care on the unit has been declining, or staffing patterns are inadequate, or this unit's patient population is more frail than that of other units and is at greater risk of skin breakdown.
- The number of complaints from private physicians to the home health agency has increased, and referrals to the agency are beginning to decline. In exploring the nature of the complaints it is found that they stem from the frustration of physicians' secretaries in being placed on extended hold when they call in a referral. The agency may need to examine whether the telephone intake process is too cumbersome, the number of incoming calls has exceeded the ability of one clerk to manage, or the clerk lacks an understanding of telephone courtesy.

Questionnaires, suggestion boxes, focus groups, consumer councils, and open-door policies are effective means to promote consumer feedback.

All feedback, regardless of how minor or insignificant it seems, should be analyzed.

An often overlooked method for promoting and evaluating quality is involving the consumer. Older adults increasingly are demanding a strong voice in service delivery, and as advocates for aging persons, gerontological nurses should promote this active participation of the consumer. Consumer involvement and feedback can be achieved by a variety of activities, as discussed in the following paragraphs.

Questionnaires. During involvement with the service, clients can be asked to evaluate the responsiveness and receptiveness of staff, environment, meals, and quality of services delivered. Multiple-choice or short-answer questionnaires can be used, or patient advocates or volunteers can ask the questions. Clients should be assured that their criticisms are welcomed feedback to assist in the improvement of service and will not result in uncomfortable repercussions. Evaluations can also be requested after a client's discharge from service. Coding the questionnaires may be helpful in identifying problems specific to one unit or work group.

Resident and Family Councils. Regular meetings with consumers can demonstrate an agency's interest, help clients understand changes or problems, and correct problems in early stages. Cochairing of these councils by a consumer and a member of the professional staff can be useful. Follow-up is essential to maintain credibility; negative feelings can be created when consumers have uncovered a bona fide problem and nothing is done.

Town Meetings, Focus Groups. Consumers and potential consumers of the service can be invited to share their perceptions, problems, and recommendations. These sessions can take the form of a "reunion" of all patients discharged from the cardiac unit a month earlier in which their experience with the unit is evaluated, a wine and cheese party for family members of home health clients in which additional ways that the agency can be of service are discussed, or an open forum for the community to share perceptions of the nursing home.

Suggestion Box. A highly visible suggestion box can provide an opportunity for problems and recommendations to surface from persons who may not otherwise share their thoughts. Posting a summary of the suggestions and the agency's reaction near the box as a means of follow-up may demonstrate the agency's interest and concern.

Open-door Policy. Staff and clients need to feel that they have access to the people who are able to act on problems and suggestions. This goal can be achieved in several ways: The agency may state that administration will welcome unscheduled appointments between 1:00 and 2:00 P.M. on Mondays and Wednesdays; supervisors may visit new admissions and inform them that they can call the supervisor with problems at any time; or nursing administrators may emphasize to staff that they encourage clients and staff to share concerns with them. Also, spending time talking to clients and staff during regular rounds can afford the opportunity for feedback.

Follow-up. A basic but important means to obtain consumer evaluations is to call or visit clients during and after their service contact. For example, a supervisor can sit in a dayroom with a client and ask how his or her hospital stay could be improved; a member of the administrative team could call the family a week after their relative's admission to the nursing home and ask how they are finding the facility; or the secretary from the home health agency can call a client recently discharged from the agency to ask how the client is doing and what the client thought of the agency's service.

Consumers often see different facets of the service and can offer insights that could be missed through formal evaluation mechanisms. In addition, consumers are more apt to feel positive about an agency that recognizes it is not perfect and thinks enough about its clients to use their input in improving services.

Any dynamic service will have considerable data to monitor and areas to improve. It is easy for some data to "fall through the cracks," be forgotten, or chronically be given a low priority. A *quality assurance log* can aid in follow-through. Figure 11-3 shows an example of this log. When issues are centrally located in easily retrievable form, they can be more easily tracked; also, certain patterns can be more easily detected.

Problem	Date Identified	Corrective Action	Respon- sibility	Date Due	Resolu- tion

FIGURE 11-3. Quality Assurance Log.

Hospitals that have historically displayed little interest and expertise in geriatric care will be serving growing numbers of elderly and developing new programs to capture this "market." Home health agencies will be helping increasing numbers of family caregivers (often sick and old themselves) to gain skill in meeting the complex care needs of their relatives. Nursing homes will be challenged with providing expert services to a more medically complicated population, as well as one with more psychiatric impairments. Day care and other community programs will be maintaining more frail, old individuals in their own homes for longer periods of time. Will hospitalizations result in new sets of problems for older clients? Will the quality and quantity of nursing home staff be sufficient to meet the more complicated care needs of their changing population? Will community-based care create a new set of risks to older clients and their families? These and hundreds of other questions must be asked. It is certain that the dramatic changes within the health care system will continue and will affect services to older adults. Gerontological nurses, now more than ever, must monitor the quality of care the elderly receive, within their own practice settings and throughout the health care system.

BIBLIOGRAPHY

Brower HH: Determinants of quality nursing care. J Gerontol Nurs 14(2): 7, 41, 1988.

Dailey-Murray M: The New Long Term Care Survey Process: A Facility Guide. Owings Mills, MD, National Health Publishers, 1988.

Eliopoulos C: A Guide to the Nursing of the Aging. Baltimore, Williams and Wilkens, 1987.

Evashwick CJ, Weiss LJ: Managing the Continuum of Care. Rockville, MD, Aspen, 1987.

Herbelin K: Components of a quality assessment and assurance program. Contemporary Long Term Care 11(5): 70–72, 1988.

Hoch CC: Assessing delivery of nursing care. J Gerontol Nurs 13(1): 10–17, 1987.

Patterson CH, Kranz D, Brandt B: A Guide to JCAH Nursing Service Standards. Chicago, Joint Commission on Accreditation of Hospitals, 1986.

Roberts KL, LeSage J, Ellor JR: Quality monitoring in nursing homes. J Gerontol Nurs 13(10): 34–40, 1987.

Thomas B, Price M: Drug reviews. J Gerontol Nurs 13(4): 17–21, 1987.

Tucker SM, Canabbio MM, Paquette EV, et al.: Patient Care Standards: Nursing Process, Diagnosis, and Outcome, 4th ed. St. Louis, CV Mosby, 1988.

CHAPTER 12

Promoting Positive Attitudes toward the Aged

Charlotte Eliopoulos

Chapter Objectives

At the completion of this chapter the reader will be able to:

1. Describe the factors that influence people's attitudes about the elderly.
2. Outline strategies that can be used to identify people's attitudes about the elderly.
3. List activities that can improve the understanding of the older population.

Attitudes toward the elderly can be influenced by education about, exposure to, and experience with older persons that individuals have throughout their lives.

Attitudes encompass the way we act, think, and feel. They are deeply embedded, influenced by family upbringing, religion, experiences, education, and other factors. In American society distinct attitudes about old age exist that imply that old age is undesirable. Terms such as "old fogy," "senile," "old bag," "dirty old man," and "over the hill" cast a negative light on the old of our society. The pace of life, clothing styles, and media portrayals of "average" people focus on youth. Billions of dollars are spent on cosmetics and plastic surgeries that hide the manifestations of aging. "New and improved" are preferred to "old and stable." Rather than being valued for their wisdom and experience, the elderly are often viewed as useless burdens who remind society of the reality of aging. These attitudes permeate all of society and influence behaviors, including those of health care personnel.

Each individual has a unique set of attitudes toward old people based on a multitude of factors. For example, attitudes can be influenced by the fact that individuals

Were not exposed to older persons as they were growing up.

Have recollections of older people who were frightening or unkind.

Bear resentment over sacrifices that had to be made for older relatives.

Have been exposed to myths, such as that old people are senile, incontinent, asexual, useless.

Hold feelings of unresolved guilt or anger from their relationships with significant persons in their lives who were old.

In addition, personal ethics can influence attitudes toward the old. Some people may believe that all individuals should be treated equally regardless of age and that the elderly deserve the same resources, care, and respect as the young. Other people may believe that the old have lived their lives and should not drain the resources that could benefit the young. Differences can exist in attitudes toward children's responsibility for their old parents, life-sustaining measures for the elderly, and other issues.

Because health care workers are a diverse group, nurses can expect to see a wide range of attitudes toward the elderly in health care settings. They may see some staff who make a special effort to comfort older patients, while others find older patients unwelcome burdens. Some staff may be embarrassed to admit to friends that they work with older patients or question the competencies of persons who do work in geriatric settings. Job applicants may seek employment in geriatric settings because they perceive the work to be easy and the patients "too senile" to make demands, or because of their lack of success with other jobs.

It is unrealistic to think that the deeply ingrained attitudes people hold about the elderly can be easily or quickly changed. However, it is important to be knowledgeable about the attitudes that people possess, particularly if those people are in caregiving roles with older adults, and to promote positive attitudes through knowledge, experiential training, and clarification of expectations.

Identifying Attitudes

One of the first measures in helping people improve their attitudes toward the elderly is to aid them in bringing their attitudes to the surface. A variety of individual and group activities that can be used with lay and professional persons to assist in this process are discussed in the following paragraphs.

Open Discussion. In a comfortable environment with a trusted group leader, people may be willing to share their perceptions and feelings about the elderly. This process can be facilitated by presenting dilemmas to which the group can react, on such topics as the appropriateness of life-sustaining measures, use of funds for senior services versus hiring more schoolteachers, or children's obligations to their parents. A nominal group approach can be used, where the use of a round-robin style gives each person an opportunity to contribute a thought or feeling until all comments have been shared or a predetermined number of contributions has been reached. The list is then discussed. This method allows participation by all persons and can offer a wide range of possibilities for discussion.

Role Playing. Many familiar situations can be simulated through role playing. For example, for a staff group, an Alzheimer's patient undresses herself for the fifth time during the shift. For a family group, an older parent makes them feel guilty for not visiting more frequently. Or the presentation of a script describing a situation can provide a forum through which feelings can surface and positive attitudes be demonstrated.

Television Characters. Many of today's popular television programs contain interesting older characters. Sensitivity to stereotypes and attributes of the aged can be gained through discussions of the profiles portrayed by older television characters.

Elder Tree. People can be asked to trace their memories of the older persons they have known as far back as possible. This personal exercise can stimulate interest and help to develop a personal understanding of why certain attitudes are held. This can be a useful exercise in the work setting during orientation to gain insight into employees' personal experiences with the elderly that could influence their behavior toward older patients.

Crystal Ball. Another personal exercise entails having individuals "look into a crystal ball" and imagine what their lives will be like when they are age 70. For some persons, this may be the first time that they've given any serious thought to the significance of relationships, leisure activities, and income in retirement.

Distinguishing Myths from Realities

Although there has been a significant proliferation of knowledge about aging and the older population, many people, including health care workers, continue to possess misinformation in this area. Community groups and health care workers can benefit from educational programs on the following topics:

Demographics of the aging population

Normal aging process

Losses experienced with aging

Safe medication use

Recognition of illness and complications

Mental health and illness

Hazards and risks

Patients' rights

Health insurance benefits

Even persons who possess this core knowledge can benefit from updates. In this constantly evolving specialty one can never feel confident that there is nothing new to learn.

Trading Places

Experiential educational sessions offer an interesting means of enhancing understanding of what it is like to be old, frail, sick, or dependent. Techniques that can be used include simulation games and other techniques.

Simulation Games. Group members can be paired, with one being the older person and the other the caregiver. The "older persons" are given deficits experienced by many elderly by placing earplugs or cotton in their ears, padding or gloving their hands, having them wear eyeglasses that have been smeared with petroleum jelly or blindfolding them, placing a mouthpiece (available at sporting goods shops) in their mouths, and restraining them to a wheelchair or bed. The "caregiver" then performs activities such as feeding cold oatmeal or vegetables, asking the "older person" to identify various objects placed in the hand, leaving him or her alone for a block of time and asking for an estimate of how long the time seemed, and whispering instructions. This experience tends to give a new understanding of the behaviors displayed by the elderly. Conducting this exercise during orientation or as an in-service exercise with staff can be useful in gaining insight into the sensitivity that caregivers do or do not display toward the elderly.

Handicap for a Day. Another simulation technique is to give participants handicaps (e.g., blindfolds, braces, wheelchairs, restricted use of an arm) and have them attempt to negotiate through a mall, a business district, a health care facility, or their normal environment. Obstacles never before realized surface and provide new awareness to participants.

Elder Panels. No one else knows what it is like to be old as the old themselves know it. Much can be gained by asking the elderly to participate in a discussion group or on a panel in which their perspective, feedback, and suggestions can be heard.

Defining Expectations

Attitudes are deeply ingrained and may not be alterable; however, caregivers should be informed and held accountable for behaviors that are consistent with positive treatment of the elderly.

Not all persons understand what is meant by a good attitude or acceptable behavior in working with older adults. They may lack skills, not be highly motivated, or have problematic personal lives. Some people may come from backgrounds in which family members are curt, insensitive, and even abusive to each other. They may have seen elderly persons treated disrespectfully and inappropriately in work settings or within their own families. These are among the reasons why it is essential to be clear and specific about the desired attitudes toward the elderly. Staff need to be told that the lack of dignity, respect, and courtesy in their interactions with older persons will not be tolerated. Family caregivers need to be informed that the older person has a right to privacy and decision-making ability over affairs that affect his or her life. Behaviors inconsistent with a positive attitude, such as talking about the older person as though he were not present or treating the elder in a childlike manner, should be tactfully corrected.

Demonstrating Positive Attitudes

As advocates for aging persons, gerontological nurses must be role models for positive attitudes toward the elderly. Staff, family caregivers, and others can be greatly influenced by the manner in which the gerontological nurse communicates with older adults, respects their privacy, demonstrates interest in their activities, responds to their needs, and intervenes in their behalf. The nurse's leadership role in gerontological care would be incomplete without the demonstration and promotion of positive attitudes toward aging and aged persons.

BIBLIOGRAPHY

Brown M: Nursing assistants behavior toward the institutionalized elderly. QRB 14(1): 15–17, 1988.

Finley NJ: Motivators and inhibitors of attitudes of filial obligation toward aging parents. The Gerontologist 28(1): 73–78, 1988.

McMahon MA: The value of intergenerational relationships. J Gerontol Nurs 13(4): 24–29, 1987.

Pergrin JV: Are we sensitive enough? J Gerontol Nurs 13(4): 11, 1987.

Phillips LR: Respect basic human rights. J Gerontol Nurs 13(3): 36–39, 1987.

Shimamoto Y, Rose CL: Identifying interest in gerontology. J Gerontol Nurs 13(2): 8–13, 1987.

Snape J: Nurses' attitudes to care of the elderly. J Advanced Nurs 11(5): 569–572, 1986.

Specht J: Nurse aides: The word is respect. J Gerontol Nurs 13(11): 5, 1987.

CHAPTER 13

Effective Communication with the Elderly

Kay Seiler

Chapter Objectives
At the completion of the chapter the reader will be able to:

1. Describe the communication process and factors that can interfere with effective communication.
2. List the causes and manifestations of hearing, visual, and language deficits.
3. State specific measures to assist persons who have hearing, visual, or language deficits.
4. Discuss methods to communicate with confused persons.
5. Identify resources to assist in promoting effective communication with aging persons.

Regardless of the setting in which it occurs, one can rarely mention the word "communication" without evoking comments about problems with the process. "Communications here are poor." "Mrs. Jones only hears what she wants to hear." "My supervisor never communicates with us." "She misunderstood what I said; she never listens."

Just as myths exist about aging, so, too, there are numerous misconceptions prevalent about communication. Many people, for example, hold these views:

- A good definition of communication is sending information from one person to another.
- A written message is more likely to be clear than a verbal one.
- Simple, concise words will assure understanding.
- A large vocabulary makes communication more effective.
- If the other person does not understand the message, he or she will usually acknowledge it.
- People are all basically the same and therefore communicate in a similar fashion.
- When a communication is misunderstood, it is the fault of the receiver (in essence, the other person).

Communication has been defined in numerous ways—sometimes as simply as the sending of verbal and written messages. *Webster's Concise Dictionary* (1984) states that to communicate means "to exchange ideas through speech, writing, or signal." Indeed, communication is a complex process, dynamic in nature—that is, constantly changing. Who of us cannot recognize how word meanings and usage change over the years. For example, many older persons have never used the word "gross" to mean anything other than twelve dozen. Yet in more recent times, the slang expression "gross" implies something repulsive. Is the bewildered look on the face of the senior, then, any surprise when words are used differently from what they recollect?

In another example, an older woman had gone to great lengths and sacrifice to purchase a very much desired birthday gift for her granddaughter. The present elicited a most enthusiastic, "Wow, that's really bad!" from the teenager. The grandmother's face showed shock, hurt, and disappointment; and it took a great deal of persuasion to convince her that the word "bad" in that context really meant very good, or "swell." It behooves us as professionals to be aware of the changing use of words and to recognize nonverbal clues that indicate that our messages may not be received as we may have intended.

Key words in Webster's definition are *exchange* and *ideas*. The sending of messages alone does not make for effective communication. Ideas and information must be exchanged; that is, the receiver must understand the message. Kron (1972) describes the communication process as a perpetual triangle (Figure 13-1). Without feedback, or receiver's response, the sender cannot be sure that the message has been interpreted as intended; and the process, therefore, has not been completed.

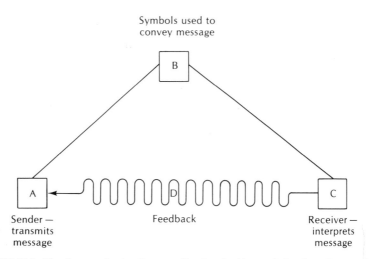

FIGURE 13-1. The Communication Process. (Reprinted with permission from Kron T: Communication in Nursing, 2nd ed. Philadelphia, WB Saunders, 1972, 28.)

The Communication Process

Numerous factors affect the communication process. Each person has his or her own background, value systems, education, experiences, beliefs, biases, and emotions, which influence the message. The prudent nurse will recognize that these factors on the part of both the sender and receiver are constantly overlapping. As a result, there can be six sides to every message:

- What speaker means to say (intended message).
- What speaker actually says.
- What receiver hears (the words).
- What receiver thinks he hears (words screened through his experiences and emotions).
- What receiver says in reply (his words).
- What speaker thinks listener said in reply (message screened through his experiences and emotions). (Harris, 1987. Reprinted by permission.)

Further, there can be numerous obstacles to the communication process, some of which include

Cultural and ethnic differences	Stereotyping
Age	"Loaded" words
Sex	Language barriers
Physical impairments	Stating inferences as facts
Prejudice, bias	Distractions, noise
Lack of mutual trust	Failure to listen

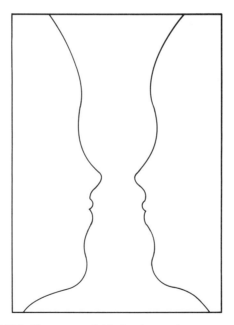

FIGURE 13-2. The content of this drawing can be perceived differently by various viewers.

FIGURE 13-3. "My Wife and My Mother-in-Law."

Perception also plays an important role in the exchange of ideas. For example, in Figure 13-2 one might see a vase or a chair leg. Yet, others may see two profiles. What do you see?

Or, consider the illustration "My Wife and My Mother-in-Law," created by cartoonist W. E. Hill and published in *Puck,* November 6, 1915 (Figure 13-3).

Communication is a vital part of life in all its aspects—family and inter-personal relationships, work environment, and social situations. For the older person, especially after retirement, it plays an even more important role than during years of employment, because with increased leisure time comes a greater need for socialization and interaction with other human beings.

People communicate in a variety of ways. Generally, we tend to think that writing, speaking, and graphics are the only methods of exchanging information and ideas. Yet the unconscious use of body language, or nonverbal communication, plays a major role in the process by setting the emotional climate in which the message is received. Consider, for example, how the following could facilitate understanding or have an adverse effect on it:

Silence	Touch
Action	Listening
Lack of action	Tone of voice
Facial expressions	Laughing, crying
Gestures	Smiling
Closeness	Symbols
Eye contact (or lack of it)	Emotions

Because one uses the entire body in communicating, the nurse must be alert to this nonverbal component when speaking with older persons. He or she must not only become skillful at recognizing the underlying meanings of messages, but also make sure that his or her nonverbal language reinforces the message content.

Effective communication is everyone's responsibility. Contrary to popular belief, misinterpreted messages are not the fault of the sender; nor can the receiver be blamed. All parties in the process bear an equal burden to assure that ideas and information are truly exchanged. One cannot assume that others know what is meant.

Listening

Perhaps the most important element of the communication process is listening. Just hearing the message does not assure that one has really listened. Hearing is a passive process that occurs automatically in response to sounds (unless one has a physical handicap). Listening, on the other hand, is an active process, requiring conscious concentration on what is being said.

A number of factors or habits can interfere with effective listening. Of prime significance is a phenomenon known as gap time. A person, on the average, can talk at the rate of 125–150 words per minute; yet the brain is capable of hearing and assimilating 350–450 or more words per minute. Therefore, the mind has time to wander away from the topic at hand. As a result, the listener often engages in daydreaming or responds to distractions. Other listening faults include

- Pretending to listen.
- Interrupting the speaker in midsentence.
- Completing speaker's sentences before he has a chance to.
- Being distracted by speaker's appearance or voice.
- Planning a retaliation while speaker is still talking about a subject with which the receiver disagrees.

The self-quiz in Figure 13-4 will help you determine your listening ability. A good listener will respond "no" to all the questions. Probably none of us will score 100% on this test, if we are totally honest. Since the questions are designed to point out the major listening faults, try to determine which is your greatest problem; then actively work to correct it. Once you have mastered that one, proceed to the next; and so on. Dedicating time and energy to correcting the faults will undoubtedly improve your listening skills.

To listen effectively, one must first stop talking. One can practice listening by making oneself concentrate on a specific sound for five minutes at a time. For example, listen to the chatter of a toddler or the singing of a bird. Learn to use the gap time to advantage—to determine what is being said between the lines.

A filmstrip, "How to Listen More Effectively," describes a key to listening that enables one to achieve a "meeting of the minds." Note that the initial letters spell the word "ears":

Are You a Good Listener?

	Yes	No
1. Do you frequently find yourself thinking about something completely different when someone is talking?	____	____
2. Do you doodle, shuffle papers, knit, or look at the clock or out the window?	____	____
3. Do you argue silently with each person while he is talking?	____	____
4. Do you listen only for facts or ideas that seem to fit in with what you believe?	____	____
5. Do you feel that most people have little that is important or interesting to talk about?	____	____
6. Do you listen passively, without any change in facial expression?	____	____
7. Do you frequently interrupt others in the middle of a sentence or an idea?	____	____
8. Do you try to complete another person's sentence when he seems to be at a loss for words?	____	____
9. Do you criticize a speaker's looks, voice, and manner of speaking?	____	____
10. Do you frequently have to ask a speaker to repeat something because you have forgotten what he said?	____	____

FIGURE 13-4. A Self-quiz for Listening. (Reprinted with permission from Kron T: Communication in Nursing, 2nd ed. Philadelphia, WB Saunders, 1972, 153.)

Earnestly—one listens earnestly when serious about wanting to listen; shows interest in what is being said.

Actively—when one accepts the task of understanding the message by giving total attention.

Receptively—listening with awareness that one's own emotions affect interpretation of the message.

Sensitively—listening with awareness that speaker's emotions affect the message. (Harris, 1987. Adapted by permission.)

Given the complexities of the communication process, it seems incredible that effective exchange of ideas ever occurs. In order to achieve the basic purpose of communicating (i.e., the maintenance of harmonious interpersonal relationships), one needs to focus on the other person(s) involved in the process.

Sensory Deficits and Communication

Sensory deficits can seriously affect an individual's ability to communicate and, consequently, his quality of life. The results can be frustrating and frightening, creating difficulty in social interaction and interpersonal relationships. In the elderly, these problems can lead to withdrawal or isolation.

Early detection of impairment is important in obtaining proper treatment in a timely manner. Whatever the impairment, the nurse should call upon resources to assist in the management of persons with sensory deprivation. The audiologist, speech-language pathologist, or low-vision specialist can provide advice concerning assistive devices and techniques to manage deficits and help the person maintain independence.

Visual Deficit

Persons who are "legally blind" are rarely totally without sight. To many, the term "blind" is offensive; the preferred expressions are "visually impaired" or having "low vision."

Low vision is defined as "reduced visual acuity and/or abnormal visual fields resulting from a disorder in the visual system" (Lighthouse National Center for Vision and Aging, 1987, 29).

One is considered legally blind if he or she meets the following criteria:

- Central visual acuity (ability to perceive detail or objects in the direct line of sight) is 20/200 or less. This means that the person can see no more at 20 feet than someone with normal vision can see at 200 feet.
- Visual field is 20° or less. This indicates difficulty with peripheral vision, which enables one to distinguish motion, size, and color of objects to the side while looking straight ahead. (Lighthouse National Center for Vision and Aging, 1987, 29)

The most common age-related diseases that cause visual impairment are outlined in Table 13-1.

The nurse can often be instrumental in early recognition of significant visual impairment. Signs that warrant investigation include

- Bumping into objects or furniture.
- Unnecessary fumbling.
- Holding reading material close to one's face.
- Peering at signs, such as names or numbers on doors.
- Hesitancy or uncertainty in movement.
- Inability to recognize people.
- Sudden hazy or blurred vision.
- Frequent changes of glasses that do not improve vision.
- Withdrawal from former activities, often making excuses for nonparticipation.

There are a number of things one can do to help the visually impaired:

- Address by name; identify yourself when you enter the presence of the visually impaired.
- Be natural; treat the person like anyone else.
- If the visually impaired enters the place where you are, make your presence known.
- When leaving the room, let the person know that you are going.
- Describe things—clothing, surroundings, activities, objects.
- Leave furniture, articles, doors, and windows as you find them, unless otherwise requested.

TABLE 13-1. Age-Related Diseases Affecting Vision

Disease	Symptoms	Treatment/Management	Comments
Cataract (clouding of lens)	Blurred vision without pain. Sensitive to glare. Sun and fluorescent lights may increase haze. Colors appear faded. Frequent changes of glasses that do not help.	Surgery to remove lens (interocular lens implant becoming more common). Glasses or contact lens postoperatively.	Special sunwear often helpful.
Diabetic retinopathy (complication of diabetes in which blood vessels leak fluid or blood)	Details distorted, blurred, or absent. May see cobweb-like strands. Colors may be affected.	Surgery or laser photocoagulation to seal blood vessels.	Hypertensives also at high risk.
Macular degeneration (deterioration of cells in macula—area of sharpest vision)	Central vision is blurred or lost. Peripheral vision not affected. Straight lines ahead appear wavy. Print blurred. Difficulty with fine detail.	Laser or surgery sometimes to halt progress (does not restore loss). No effective treatment. Low-vision optical and nonoptical aids may help.	Family history may predispose.
Glaucoma (deterioration of optic nerve by pressure due to increased fluid)	Decreased or lost side vision. Inability to adjust to dark room. Blurred, foggy vision, especially on waking. Difficulty in moving around—bumping into objects outside field of vision. Sensitivity to glare. Sees poorly in dim illumination.	Eye drops or diuretics. Surgery in some cases. Decrease pressure by assisting drainage or reducing inflow of fluid.	If untreated, may lead to total blindness. High risk—eye injury, family history, diabetes, long-term steroid therapy.
Open-angle (chronic)			Develops slowly over time because of improper drainage of fluid.
Acute angle-closure	Above symptoms, plus severe pain, nausea and vomiting, and rainbow halos around lights.		Acute onset due to obstruction; if not treated immediately, can cause blindness in 1–2 days.

- Ask if you can be of assistance.
- Learn proper sighted-guide technique.

A sighted guide is especially helpful when the individual is among a group of people or in unfamiliar surroundings. Safety is of prime concern, and the visually impaired must have utmost confidence in the guide. The following suggestions are adapted from the Canadian National Institute for the Blind (1987):

- Approach the individual, identify self, and ask if assistance is desired.
- Touch back of hand of the visually impaired person (signaling him to take guide's arm). He will take your arm just above the elbow, thumb outside and four fingers inside. This positions him one-half step behind the guide and allows him to feel the guide's movements.
- Hold arm in relaxed vertical position except to signal passage through a doorway, narrow area, etc. In this case, the guide moves his arm backward and diagonally across his back.
- Advise him when approaching a door: "The door is to the left and opens away from (or toward) us."
- Approach stairs and curbs squarely, not at an angle; alert the individual. Allow person being guided to be on side with railing.
- Come to a full stop before maneuvering stairs; step up or down, one step ahead of person being guided; stop at end of stairs.
- Approach chairs from the front; guide individual so that his knees touch edge of chair; inform him of the type of chair (arm, straight, rocker, etc.). He will brush the seat with his hand to determine if there is anything on it.

The nurse should be familiar with low-vision programs in the community and initiate referrals. Highly trained specialists are available to help the impaired person to maximize residual vision and to maintain independence. Performing activities of daily living, money handling, food shopping and preparation, and safe travel are among the many skills that can be taught. (See chapter appendix for list of available resources.)

The ophthalmologist and low-vision specialists determine which, if any, optical devices may be of benefit. Among these are

- Magnifiers (stand and hand held).
- Telescopic lenses (which attach to glasses).
- Special lenses and sunwear to reduce glare.
- Television reading machines that greatly magnify print.

Nonoptical aids include

- Large print books and magazines (*Reader's Digest*, etc.).
- Proper illumination.
- Radio reading programs.
- Talking books.
- Marking of electrical appliances, such as stoves, ovens, thermostats.

Hearing Impairment

Hearing loss can cause social isolation and increase the possibility of depression. This impairment is frequently overlooked; indeed, in some cases, it is denied by the older individual. Because responses to conversations are sometimes inappropriate, the person with hearing loss may be viewed as confused.

Hearing impairment is defined as any degree of loss of loudness or pitch of sound. Causes include

- Injury
- Noise exposure
- Medications (as streptomycin, erythromycin, some diuretics, large doses of aspirin)
- Disease (infection; CVA; diseases that disrupt blood flow)
- Heredity
- Obstruction (cerumen, foreign body)

"Hearing loss may be more *common* as we get older, but it is *not normal*" (Laufer, 1984, 6). If hearing loss is suspected, the individual should promptly be referred to an otolaryngologist to determine the extent and cause of the problem. The physician will probably request an audiogram, which measures how loud a sound must be at different frequencies to be heard. Results are plotted on a graph that indicates hearing capabilities in each ear.

During audiometric testing, intensity (loudness) and pitch (frequency per second) are measured.

Both intensity and pitch are measured during audiometric testing. Intensity (loudness) is measured in decibels (db). A whisper measures 30 db, average conversation 50–60 db, a jet plane 90–110 db, and loud rock music 115 db. Pitch is measured in hertz (Hz), or cycles per second. Deep male voices, bass drums, and vowel sounds are low pitched, about 500 Hz. Doorbells, soprano voices, and consonants are high pitched, approximately 3,000 Hz.

From the audiological examination, the physician and audiologist can determine the type and extent of loss. Some telltale signs of hearing loss include

- Inappropriate responses to questions.
- Frequent failure to answer doorbell or telephone.
- Irrelevant comments during conversation.
- Difficulty in following directions.
- Inattentiveness to others.
- Frequent requests to repeat what was said.
- Turning one ear toward speaker.
- Suspiciousness (resulting from hearing only fragments of conversation).
- Changes in voice quality.
- Social withdrawal.
- Tendency to monopolize conversation (probably an attempt to control).

Hearing loss may be conductive (resulting from conditions that block sound transmission), sensorineural (inner ear or nerve damage), or central (as a consequence of brain damage) (see Table 13-2). Most hearing impairment in older persons is due to presbycusis, a sensorineural deficit which causes sounds to be distorted and limits the ability to hear high-pitched sounds. Consonants may be misinterpreted; for example, "wise" may sound like "wide."

TABLE 13-2. Types of Hearing Loss

Type	Causes	Characteristics	Comments
Conductive (dysfunction in outer or middle ear; normal inner ear)	Impacted wax. Foreign body. Perforated or scarred membrane.	Sound does not reach inner ear; therefore interferes with transmission of sound. Person often speaks softly.	Usually not permanent; can be remedied by removal of obstruction or surgery.
Sensorineural (pathology in inner ear or along nerve pathway to brain)	Excessive noise. Ototoxic drugs. Ménière's disease. Tumor. Decreased blood supply.	Interferes with ability to discriminate sound. Sounds distorted, especially consonants *m, n, f, s, d, b, p, k*.	Permanent deficit.
Presbycusis (hearing loss that accompanies aging)	Aging process.	Sounds muffled and distorted; loss greater for high-pitched sounds. Good hearing at low frequencies.	Permanent; worsens with age.
Central hearing loss (damage to part of brain that interprets sound)	Injury. Disease process.	Sounds not interpreted when transmitted to brain.	Permanent.

Most hearing deficits, including nerve damage, can be helped with hearing aids, which amplify sounds but do not make speech clearer. (One must be aware that all sounds are increased, including background noises.) These mechanical devices should be maintained properly. Check the ear mold for cracks or rough edges. Avoid moisture or contact with hair spray. Clean ear mold with warm, soapy water, using a pipe cleaner or tipped applicator; rinse, dry thoroughly.

Communicating with the hearing impaired is difficult. Here are some tips to remember:

- Get the person's attention; address him or her by name when initiating a conversation.
- Speak in a normal tone of voice or with *slightly* increased volume; loud talking or shouting worsens the difficulty.
- Articulate clearly, but avoid elaborate mouthing of words.
- Talk at a moderate rate.
- Be patient.
- Use nonverbal communication to complement verbal messages.
- Face the person to whom you are speaking; be sure lighting is adequate so that your expressions can be seen; make eye contact.
- Avoid covering your mouth when speaking; some hearing impaired read lips.
- Avoid speaking from behind the person or from another room.
- Avoid chewing or smoking while speaking.
- Observe the face of the listener; reword the message if it is not understood.
- Decrease background noises, such as television sets.

- Do not assume that the hearing impaired are unable or do not want to talk.

There are a number of mechanical devices that can benefit the hearing impaired:

- Visual flasher signals for doorbells or telephones.
- Audioloop systems in some public buildings (which use electromagnetic fields to generate signals that can be picked up by hearing aids).
- Television caption device (decoding machine that allows one to read subtitles on the screen).
- Television, radio, and telephone amplifying devices.

The resources listed in the chapter appendix can supply additional means of help.

Speech Impairment

Aphasia is the "loss, or reduction in, ability to process language as a result of brain injury" (Ryan, 1982, 3). This deficit may affect comprehension, production of speech, or all language usage, depending upon the location and degree of damage to the brain (see Table 13-3).

Every person with this type of sensory disorder deserves an evaluation by a speech-language pathologist. Severe isolation that can result makes professional consultation imperative. The nurse may have to take the initiative by convincing the physician to request such an assessment and by following recommendations of the speech pathologist.

TABLE 13-3. Speech Disorders

Type	Causes	Characteristics
Expressive aphasia (Broca's area)	Damage to anterior brain, frontal lobe.	Can understand incoming message; difficulty in speech or writing.
Receptive aphasia (Wernicke's area)	Temporal lobe damage (toward back of brain).	Can speak, although it may sound strange; difficulty in understanding incoming message.
Transcortical aphasia (global)	More extensive damage involving both Broca's and Wernicke's areas of left hemisphere.	Extensive; may only be able to utter overlearned or automatic speech (swearing, counting, repeating days of week, etc.).
Dysarthria (disorder that interferes with pronunciation)	Damage to nerve cells that control muscles associated with speech.	Understands messages. Difficulty coordinating muscles associated with speech production. Speech may sound slurred or "thick."

```
A  B  C  D  E  F  G  H  I  J  K  L                          YES

M  N  O  P  Q  R  S  T  U  V  W  X  Y  Z                    NO


I        NEED     PAIN      WIFE

YOU      WANT     DRINK     SON

WE       HAVE     FOOD      DAUGHTER

         AM       TIRED     NURSE

FEEL              HUNGRY    MINISTER

                  THIRSTY   DOCTOR
```

FIGURE 13-5. Communication Board for Speech-Impaired Persons.

One technique that can be useful for many aphasic persons is a communication board. Key words, letters, and numbers are indicated by pointing. The board can be adapted to the needs and capabilities of the user. A sample is shown in Figure 13-5. Or, for the individual who is unable to read or who has visual difficulty, the nurse might be creative in devising a simple graphic board, utilizing symbols that are applicable, such as shown in Figure 13-6.

The speech-impaired person who can write should be supplied with pencil and paper or a melamine board and magic marker. Flash cards are also useful tools for enhancing communication.

Guidelines for dealing with the communicatively impaired include the following:

- Treat the individual as an adult; assure that he or she is treated with dignity and compassion.
- Talk to the individual as if he or she understands.
- See that recommendations made by the speech pathologist are carried out consistently.
- Back off if the person appears tired or frustrated.
- Provide psychological support; praise any progress.
- Talk in a quiet, relaxed manner.
- Reinforce verbal communication with nonverbal; for example, when offering fluids, pick up glass.
- Write or print key words.
- Use touch therapeutically.
- Recognize that "no" sometimes means "yes" in speech impaired; try to determine response in context of situation at hand.
- Use normal tone of voice; speech impairment does not automatically mean the person is hard of hearing.

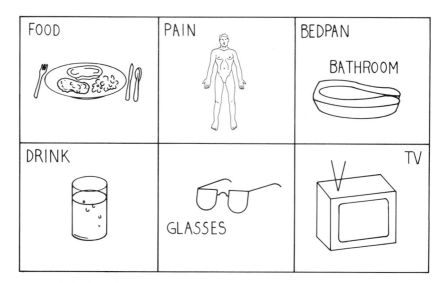

FIGURE 13-6. A graphic communication board can be used when the individual has limited visual ability or education.

- Use short, simple sentences, accompanied by gestures to help clarify meaning.
- Involve individual in therapeutic recreational activities.
- Allow adequate time for person to respond; be patient.
- Pronounce words clearly; face individual.
- Take time to assess strengths and capabilities and encourage individual to use them.
- Be aware of message you are communicating nonverbally.
- Suggest that family members who cannot visit make short tape-recorded messages that can be played for the impaired individual.
- Encourage to try to sing familiar songs (sometimes the person can sing, even though he or she cannot speak).
- Include individual in decision making.
- Find some way to communicate, even if the person can only blink eyes or squeeze one's hand; seek the advice of the speech-language pathologist to recommend techniques that might help.
- Do not respond to swearing or scold; divert attention to another topic.

The following list provides tips for communicating with the elderly:

1. Avoid stereotyping and labeling. These are probably the greatest barriers when working with older persons. The myth still exists that all older people will eventually become senile. The facts are that senility or confusion is a symptom of a disease process or some adverse psychosocial condition. Also, it should not be assumed that all older people are hearing impaired.
2. Avoid jargon. As professionals, we become so accustomed to our own terminology that it is easy to forget that it is a "foreign language" to

the lay person. For example, do we instruct an older person that he is on "NPO" after midnight for test preparation, and then scold him when he takes a drink of water? We cannot assume that he will ask the meaning.

3. Try to elicit feedback when you are communicating. Observation of the receiver's actions and nonverbal communications, as well as asking pertinent questions, can help determine if the message was received as intended.

4. Be aware of your own nonverbal communication. To say "Good morning" and then slam down a basin on the bedside stand probably will communicate, "I've got to watch out for her—she's in a bad mood today!"

5. Be aware of "loaded" words (words that elicit strong negative feelings), such as "idiot," "deaf," "drunk," "unfair." Each of us responds vigorously to certain expressions. Know yours; and learn to defuse them.

6. Be aware of the fact that, over time, meanings of words change. Observe for clues that indicate the receiver is not understanding the word in the way in which you are using it.

7. Assess the individual for sensory deficits; if present, adjust communication techniques to help compensate for them.

8. Be aware of terminology related to sensory limitations. Use the words "low vision" rather than "blind," and "hearing impaired" instead of "deaf."

9. Recognize that the meaning of a word is often determined by how it is combined with other words, or where the emphasis is placed, for example:

    Only the aide told me to take a bath.
    The *only* aide told me to take a bath.
    The aid *only* told me to take a bath.
    I *run* every morning.
    I have a *run* in my hose.
    I want to *run* for president of my club.

10. Learn to use touch in a therapeutic way. As children, many of us were scolded and told "Don't touch"; so touch becomes uncomfortable for some people. A hand lightly touching an arm or shoulder, or a hug, can convey caring and tenderness. Yet a touch from a passerby to a patient sitting in a hallway may be received with great distaste. It is important to determine how the older person feels about being touched and then to act accordingly.

11. Develop listening skills. Look for what's not said—underlying concerns, issues, value systems. Focus attention on the other person's feelings.

Cognitive Impairment

Intellectual loss results from many sources. The professional should make every effort to assess the individual carefully, report to the physician, and advocate a thorough evaluation, since most cases of memory loss and confusion are treatable. It is essential that the nurse be able to differentiate between acute, sudden-onset, reversible conditions (delirium) and those that are chronic, progressive, and irreversible (dementia).

Along with disorientation and memory loss, confusion may also be manifested by impaired concentration, comprehension, short attention span, misinterpretation of environmental clues, mood swings, poor compliance, and difficulty in learning new things. Any or all of these components can occur in varying degrees.

All behavior has meaning. It is incumbent upon the professional to make every effort to determine what is behind the behavior. Confusion can result from numerous causes, and the nurse must be familiar with those conditions that can precipitate reversible confusion and with appropriate interventions.

Diagnostic labels of irreversible processes, such as Alzheimer's disease, must be avoided until the myriad of other possibilities is ruled out. Depression and drug intoxication/reaction are two of the most common causes of confusion that mimic senile dementia. Both are treatable and reversible. It is a great disservice to the individual to be labeled with the diagnosis of an irreversible condition and not to receive the treatment that could correct the problem.

Some other factors that may precipitate confusion in the elderly are the following:

- Metabolic disorders (hypoglycemia, hyperglycemia, hypothyroidism)
- Cardiovascular problems (congestive failure, myocardial infarction)
- Cerebral disturbances (trauma, tumor, stroke, infectious process)
- Infection (most commonly, urinary tract, pneumonia)
- Anemia (particularly pernicious anemia)
- Hypothermia
- Hypoxia (as from COPD)
- Electrolyte imbalance
- Dehydration
- Malnutrition
- Sensory deficits
- Changes in location (relocation trauma can be quite significant in some persons)
- Changes in activity and ability to perform activities of daily living
- Pain (especially that associated with fecal impaction, urinary retention)

Whatever the origin of the confusion, one must be careful to avoid both diagnostic and behavioral labels. The nurse can play a key role in preventing such labeling by making careful, ongoing assessments and by working closely with the physician to see that a thorough evaluation occurs. By serving as a role model, the professional can make other disciplines and non-professional staff aware that stereotyping and labeling behavior are inappropriate in the care of the cognitively impaired older person.

The confused person must be treated as a unique individual, and the caregiver must make every effort to support his or her dignity and self-esteem.

Communicating with persons suffering from intellectual loss is difficult, at best. Following are some helpful hints:

- Treat each person as an adult, even if the individual may be exhibiting childlike behavior.
- Use a normal tone of voice.
- Stand close, but not too close.
- Talk to the person directly.
- Gain attention, address by name, gain eye contact, touch arm or shoulder lightly.
- Avoid talking about the person in his or her presence or within hearing distance.
- Use gestures to reinforce verbal communication.
- Use short, simple sentences.
- Avoid lengthy directions; give one step at a time (cognitively impaired person cannot process complex communcations).
- Avoid asking complex questions or those that require choices. (Example: Instead of "Would you like the chicken, beef, or fish?" mention one choice at a time.)
- Expect repetitious conversation or questions (person will have forgotten he or she asked); avoid showing irritation.
- Watch for nonverbal cues to help clarify what person is trying to say.
- Be aware of your nonverbal communication; make it coincide with your words.
- Do not expect accurate answers from a severely impaired person, or that your directions will be followed precisely.
- Talk about sensory things (weather, flowers, smells, etc.); reinforce when possible. (Example: When discussing the snow that is falling, bring in a snowball so the person can see and touch it.)
- Talk about familiar things; encourage reminiscence (which can stimulate long-term memory).
- Reduce noise and maintain calm environment. (Cognitively impaired will quickly pick up on a hurried, tense atmosphere.)
- Recognize that such a person frequently experiences confabulation (little "fibs" or "white lies"); this is probably due to misperception of stimuli or facts or may be the person's attempt to make sense of what is happening.
- Touch to improve interaction, gain attention, show you care, and reduce feelings of isolation. Hugs are therapeutic. However, recognize that some people do not like being touched—they will usually withdraw or tell you not to do that.
- Explain what is happening and what you are doing. Assume that the impaired person understands. Use a calm, reassuring voice.
- Avoid precipitating a catastrophic reaction by pushing too hard; if one occurs, avoid scolding. (It may increase, rather than stop, the undesired behavior.)
- Do not react to swearing; distract by changing the subject.

- Play soft music to establish a calming effect; music therapy is now being recognized as a major contribution in the management of confused persons.
- *Listen.*
- Learn what works with a given individual, and share that information with other caregivers.

Summary

Whether interacting with the healthy elderly or those with some type of impairment, it is crucial that the nurse develop and constantly improve skills in all forms of communication. Of primary concern is the need to support dignity and respect, and to help the older person maintain (or regain) self-esteem.

Working with older persons is a real privilege and is very rewarding. Effective communication is often quite a challenge, but adds to the rewards of our own lives and enriches them.

Appendix: Resources

Visual Impairment

American Foundation for the Blind
15 West 16th Street
New York, NY 10011
(212) 620–2000
    Nonprofit organization—provides information; sells aids and appliances; catalog of products.

American Bank Stationary
7501 Pulaski Highway
Baltimore, MD 21237
(301) 866–1900
    Provides checks in large print and braille.

Bible Alliance
P.O. Box 1549
Bradenton, FL 33506
(813) 748–3031
    Provides cassettes of Bible messages or the Bible, free of charge. Certification from physician or vision professional required.

The Lighthouse
New York Association for the Blind
111 East 59th Street
New York, NY 10022
(212) 355–2200
    Provides information and some products.

National Library Service for
Blind and Physically Handicapped
The Library of Congress
Washington, DC 20542
(202) 287–5100
> Large-print, braille books; recorded media. Talking books, cassette players (headphones, amplifiers, and pillow phones available to use with talking books). Requires certification from physician or vision professional. These services may be available at a state level, also.

National Society to Prevent Blindness
500 East Remington Road
Schaumburg, IL 60173
1–800–221–3004
> Provides educational materials and assistance to professionals. (Call for affiliated society.)

The New York Times Large Print Weekly
P.O. Box 2570
Boulder, CO 80302
1–800–631–2500

Reader's Digest Large Type Edition
P.O. Box 241
Mount Morris, IL 61054

American Academy of Ophthalmology
655 Beach Street
P.O. Box 7424
San Francisco, CA 94120
(415) 921–4700
> Provides public education materials. Initiated National Eye Care Project (NECP), which provides eye care to persons who do not have an ophthalmologist and are unable to pay. NECP Hotline 1–800–222–EYES.

Local Gas and Electric Companies
> Can provide adaptation to oven, thermostat to help visually impaired.

Lions Clubs
> Visual (and hearing) screening.
> Collect used eyeglasses for recycling.
> Sometimes provide visual aids and devices.

Hearing Impairment

Alexander Graham Bell Association for the Deaf, Inc.
3417 Volta Place, NW
Washington, DC 20007

American Academy of Otolaryngology
Head and Neck Surgery, Inc.
1101 Vermont Avenue, NW, Suite 302
Washington, DC 20005
(202) 289–4607

National Association of the Deaf
814 Thayer Avenue
Silver Spring, MD 20910
(301) 587–1788 (Voice/TTY)
> Nonprofit membership—advocate for deaf and hearing impaired. Brochures, catalog, referral lists of service providers.

National Information Center on Deafness
Gallaudet College, Kendall Green
800 Florida Avenue, NE
Washington, DC 20002
(202) 651–5109 (Voice/TTY)
> Clearinghouse for information.

Speech Impairment

American Speech-Language-Hearing Association
10801 Rockville Pike
Rockville, MD 20852
(301) 897–5700

Alzheimer's Disease

Alzheimer's Association
(Formerly Alzheimer's Disease and Related Disorders Association)
300 North Michigan Avenue
Chicago, IL 60601

General

Local Area Office on Aging

Local commission or department of low vision and/or blindness

Local Social Security association

National Council on Aging
600 Maryland Avenue, SW
Washington, DC 20024
(202) 479–1200

American Association of Retired Persons (AARP)
1909 K Street, NW
Washington, DC 20049
(202) 728–4300

REFERENCES

Canadian National Institute for the Blind: Step-by-Step: Guiding the Blind Person. Winnipeg, Manitoba, Canadian National Institute for the Blind, 1987.

Harris F: How to Listen More Effectively. (Filmstrip HR–200–3). Burbank, CA, Harris-Tuchman Productions, Inc., 1987.

Kron T: Communication in Nursing, 2nd ed. Philadelphia, WB Saunders, 1972.

Laufer B: Have You Heard? Hearing Loss and Aging. Washington, DC, American Association of Retired Persons, 1984.

Lighthouse National Center for Vision and Aging: A Better View of You. Washington, DC, Administration on Aging, DHHS, 1987.

Ryan WJ: The Nurse and the Communicatively Impaired Adult. New York, Springer, 1982.

Webster's Concise Dictionary. New York, Modern Publishing, 1984.

BIBLIOGRAPHY

Aasen N: Interventions to facilitate personal control. J Gerontol Nurs 13(6): 20–28, 1987.

Burnside IM (ed): Working with the Elderly: Group Processes and Techniques, 2nd ed. North Scituate, MA, Duxbury Press, 1984.

Doty L: Communication and Assertion Skills for Older Persons. Cambridge, MA, Hemisphere, 1987.

Hollinger L: Communicating with the elderly. J Gerontol Nurs 12(3): 8–13, 1986.

Rempusheski VF, Phillips LR: Elders versus caregivers: Games they play. Geriatr Nurs 9(1): 30–34, 1988.

Shadden BB: Communication, Behavior and Aging: A Sourcebook for Clinicians. Baltimore, Williams & Wilkins, 1988.

Steffl BM: Communication with the elderly. In Steffl BM (ed): Handbook of Gerontological Nursing, 67–72. New York, Van Nostrand Reinhold, 1984.

PART TWO

Gerontological Nursing in the Community Setting

The vast majority of older adults function in the community satisfactorily and independently. They meet the demands of daily living, fulfill responsibilities, maintain meaningful roles, and engage in activities that are to their liking and choice. This is the normal way of life for most adults and one that is expected and desirable.

Slower responses, reduced activity tolerance, and other outcomes of aging can affect independent function. An independent and normal life-style can be further threatened by one's own illness or that of a loved one. Impairments in the ability to maintain health and home can increase the risk of institutionalization.

A wide range of community resources must exist to enable persons with various levels of function to remain maximally independent in their homes and avoid threats to their health and social well-being. Related services could include education, support groups, screening programs, caregiver assistance, housing modifications, and direct care on an intermittent basis. This part will describe the important roles nursing plays in the prevention and management of biopsychosocial problems that influence independent living. The activities of nurses in maximizing self-care capacity are reflected in chapters discussing the nursing role in senior multipurpose centers, and continuing care and retirement communities. The way in which nurses minimize self-care limitations is demonstrated in chapters that review the support and educational needs of family caregivers, and the environmental modifications that promote independent living for disabled and frail individuals. Chapters on the topics of home health, hospice, and geriatric day care highlight nursing activities that provide direct interventions without threatening individuals' maximum participation in and responsibility for their care.

Increasing numbers of persons of advanced age who possess complex health problems will reside in the community and want assistance in maintaining an independent life-style as long as possible. The economics of health care will futher intensify the interest in community-based services that place major care responsibilities on individuals and their caregivers. Nursing will be challenged to coordinate the vast array of available services, be creative in caregiving techniques, and stimulate the development of new services that promote the health and well-being of community-based elderly and their caregivers.

CHAPTER 14

Home Health Care

Barbara Santamaria

Chapter Objectives
At the completion of this chapter the reader will be able to:

1. Describe factors that contribute to the growing use of home health services by the elderly.
2. Outline the steps clients typically follow in accessing home health services.
3. Discuss the nurse's role in home health care.

The care of the ill elderly at home is not a new concept. For as far back as many people can remember, caring for older relatives at home has been an accepted part of family life. There are several factors that caused home care to be a normal family pattern rather than a rarity:

Characteristics of health services. Community-based services were scarce. Hospitals were the focal point of care, and few people utilized hospital services except for surgery and emergency care. Prior to the middle of this century, long-term institutional care was not widespread, and where it did exist, conditions left much to be desired. Thus it was viewed as an option of last resort.

Location of services. Until World War II, the population of the United States was largely rural. Most hospitals and other health care services were located in urban areas and were not readily accessible and available to most persons.

Cost. The absence of health insurance caused people to have to pay for services directly (or accept charitable care); thus families without resources had little option but to provide care on their own.

Proximity of families. In the past, there was a greater geographic proximity of family members; intergenerational service exchange was easier.

Women in the labor force. Most women were not employed outside the home and were available to assist in the care of family members.

The population shift to urban from rural areas began during World War II, and it continues to the present time. With urban growth came greater employment in factories than in agriculture. The ideas of rugged individualism faded, and communal ideas emerged, such as unionism. Of the many areas of concern to unions was hospital insurance for the ill and in-

TABLE 14-1. Medicare-Certified Participating Home Health Agencies, Selected Years 1966–1983

Year	Official Agency[a]		VNA		Proprietary		Combined Government and Voluntary		Private Nonprofit		Hospital Based		Other[b]		Total
	No.	%	No.	%	No.	%	No.	%	No.	%	No.	%	No.	%	
1966	579	45	506	40	—	—	83	7	—	—	81	6	26	2	1,275
1971	1,311	57	559	24	50	2	67	3	66	3	232	10	—	—	2,285
1975	1,228	55	525	23	47	2	46	2	109	5	287	13	—	—	2,242
1978	1,212	47	491	19	129	5	45	2	359	14	293	11	69	3	2,598
1980	1,253	41	506	17	230	8	59	2	520	17	401	13	83	3	3,052
1982	1,232	37	519	16	452	14	55	2	583	18	452	14	31	1	3,324
1983	1,230	29	494	12	997	24	58	1	674	16	579	14	187	4	4,219

[a]Agency administered by a state, county, or other unit of government.
[b]Includes skilled-nursing-facility-based programs, rehabilitation-based programs, and others.
Source: Reprinted with permission from Spiegel AD: Home Health Care. Owings Mills, MD, Rynd Communications, National Health Publishing, 1983, 561–562.

jured. Hospitalization insurance soon became a major part of most collective bargaining packages.

As care of American workers improved, concern was raised for the health care of the unemployed, poor, and aged, giving rise to the birth of Medicare and Medicaid in 1965. Most health services were directed to hospital-based curative care or long-term institutional care. Although home health care has been available under Medicare since its inception, this form of care was slow to grow. Americans tolerated the institutional or hospital-based care for decades, and only recently has there been significant interest in shifting care to the home setting. In addition to the desire for community-based care, the recent increase in home health care has been promoted by the reality that hospital-based and institutional care has become prohibitively expensive. In response to this increased interest in home health care, the number of home health agencies has grown remarkably: Medicare-certified home health agencies increased by 64% from 1972 to 1981 and 17% from 1981 to 1983 (Table 14-1).

> The desire of persons to be cared for in their own homes and the rising costs of hospital and institutional care have contributed to the dramatic growth in home health agencies.

Many health care professionals have heard the charges that patients are now discharged from hospitals "quicker and sicker" as a result of diagnostic related groups (DRGs). Each of the 470 DRGs carries a fixed rate of reimbursement based on the cost of treating the average patient. If the hospital can treat the patient for less, the hospital keeps the profit; if the patient's care exceeds the payment, the hospital must absorb the difference. Financially, the DRG system seems to be working, evidenced by the reduction in average lengths of hospital stays for Medicare patients (7.5 days in 1985 compared to 9.5 days in 1983) and a control in the increase in hospital costs to 5% annually. The effect on patients has been less salutary; anecdotal accounts indicate that many patients have been discharged prematurely. Home health agencies are affected by this earlier discharge pattern in that home care has become more complex and intense than in the past.

The Elderly and Home Health

Many of the demographic changes in the aging population (see Chapter 1) have had an impact on the utilization of home health services:

- Not only are greater numbers of persons achieving age 65, but they are surviving to later years once they reach that segment of life. In the seventh decade and beyond, the prevalence of disease, disability, and dependency increases; thus assistance with health care is required to a greater extent.
- The reality that women have a longer life expectancy than men often means that older women do not have a spouse to fill a caregiver role. Most of these women live alone; thus the likelihood of having a family caregiver in the same household is small. These women and their family members may seek formal home health care as a means of addressing care needs that the family is unable to meet.
- Older persons, whether living alone or with a spouse, prefer independence and wish to avoid being a burden to their children or other family members. Obtaining services through a home health agency affords these individuals the ability to have their care needs met while preserving self-concept and family roles.

Limited reimbursement options for care also have influenced the elderly's utilization of home health services. Limited options exist through private insurance companies for the reimbursement of long-term care in institutional settings. Medicare is selective and limited in its reimbursement of nursing home care, and financial resources of the older adult must be "spent down" to a meager level before Medical Assistance becomes a possible option for payment of institutional services. Older adults needing assistance often find nursing home care a costly option that can exhaust their financial resources. Third-party payment of home health care may be easier to obtain than reimbursement for institutional care; if paid for privately, home health care may be more affordable (as well as preferable) for older individuals.

The aforementioned needs, preferences, and financial realities of care support the growing significance of home health care in the continuum of geriatric care services. The elderly will continue to require home health services in growing frequency and intensity. Whether they provide home health services directly or make referrals from another service setting, nurses need to become knowledgeable about home health care so that they can assist the elderly in obtaining quality services.

Accessing the System

Many older adults enter the home health system for continued care following an acute hospital stay. Hospitalization, however, is not a requisite. Persons may have an exacerbation of an illness or a change in caregiver status that warrants assistance through home health care.

Although Medicaid will reimburse for personal care in the home, Medicare reimburses only for prescribed, skilled care of a patient who is homebound and unable to obtain services at another site.

Requests for service can come from the patient, physician, family, or any other concerned person; however, in order to meet the criteria for home health care under Medicare the following conditions must be met:

- The patient must be homebound.
- There must be a need for skilled intermittent care.
- The care must be ordered by a physician.

Medical Assistance (Medicaid) reimbursement for home health care is available if the individual in need of home care meets his or her state's income and asset criteria (see Table 14-2). Unlike Medicare, Medicaid reimburses for personal care in the home. Some private health insurers also pay for home health care. Of course, persons without third-party reimbursement can contract and pay privately for home health care.

Preliminary screening is done on the intake call. The intake person (usually a nurse) will ask questions about the patient's care needs, including the following:

Is the problem new?

Has there been a recent hospitalization?

Is the patient homebound?

Is the physician aware of the problem?

What other agencies are providing services?

Are there special dietary needs?

Do any mobility problems exist?

What medications are being taken?

Is there a caregiver in the home? Who?

What services are being requested?

This information supplements the general demographic data collected. If the call provides ample information to determine that home health care is appropriate, the physician will be called for orders. If there is uncertainty about the patient's need for service, the agency may make a home visit to evaluate the situation and assist the physician in determining whether the patient meets insurer's guidelines.

The evaluation of the care plan's effectiveness should consider the impact of caregiving on the entire family unit. A plan is inappropriate if it achieves the patient's care goals at the expense of the physical, emotional, or socioeconomic health of other family members.

Although physiotherapists and speech therapists can serve as case managers for home health patients, nurses most often fill this role. The case manager initiates the service, coordinates with other caregivers, and delivers or monitors the care.

Astute assessment of patients and their environments is essential on the first home visit. This assessment will enable patients' unique physical, psychological, and social needs to be identified so that an individualized care plan can be developed (Figure 14-1). Environmental factors are evaluated, such as cleanliness, kitchen facilities, relationship of bathrooms to patient bedroom, stairs, obstacles to fulfillment of activities of daily living, and safety hazards. Of prime importance is the family assessment, not only in

(*Text continues on page 234*)

TABLE 14-2. Sources of Reimbursement for Home Health Care

Source	Eligibility	Requirements	Coverage	Limitations (Not Covered)
Medicare, Title XVIII of the Social Security Act	1. Over 65, payment into Social Security or Railroad Retirement System. 2. Disabled at least 24 months. 3. End-stage renal disease. 4. Spouse of 1, 2, and 3.	1. Homebound. 2. Need of skilled care on intermittent basis. 3. Treatment plan by a physician.	1. Skilled nursing. 2. Physical therapy. 3. Speech therapy. If one of the above is needed, coverage may also be provided for the following: Home health aide. Occupational therapy. Medical social work. Medical supplies and equipment.	1. Custodial care. 2. Homemaker chore services.
Medicaid, Title XIX of the Social Security Act	1. Persons meeting categorical and income requirements.	1. Need of medically necessary care on an intermittent basis. 2. Treatment plan by a physician.	*Federal Mandates:* 1. Nursing care. 2. Home health aide. 3. Medical supplies and equipment. *State Option:* 1. Physical therapy. 2. Occupational therapy. 3. Speech therapy.	1. Medical social work services.
Older American Act, 1. Titles III and VII	1. Persons over 60, with special emphasis to those with low income.		1. Senior centers. 2. Home-delivered meals. 3. Transportation. 4. Home repair. 5. Information and referral.	
Social Services Act, Title XX of the Social Security Act	1. Primarily based on need; criteria vary from state to state.		1. Homemaker chore service workers.	
Private insurance	1. Paid-up policy with home health benefits.	1. Usually in lieu of hospitalization.	1. Varies greatly.	1. Depends on policy.
Veterans' Administration	1. Service-connected disability.	1. Prior hospitalization at a VA facility.	1. Same as Medicare.	1. Available for service-connected disability with occasional coverage for veterans with no other funding source.

Source: Stuart-Siddall S: Home Health Care Nursing. Reprinted with the permission of Aspen Publishers, Inc., Rockville, MD, © 1986, 28.

Patient No. _____

Patient History and Initial Assessment

Code: + = Problem present   Ø = No problem present

Name: _____ Age: _____ Date: _____

Address: _____ Tel: # _____

Information Obtained from Patient: _____

Family Member: _____ Other: _____

Diagnoses: _____

History of Present Illness (include onset dates, operations, patient reactions, reason for home care): _____

_____

_____

_____

Allergies: _____

Social and Environmental History

Marital Status: _____ Religion: _____

Family Members in Home: _____

Name & Tel. # of Primary Caregiver: _____

Name & Tel. # of Person to Contact in case of emergency: _____

Are there steps in Patient's Residence? Yes: _____ No: _____ Number: _____

Environmental Problems: None _____ Inadequate _____ Space _____

Utilities _____ Safety _____ Pests _____ Other Environmental Problems: _____

_____

Is this Patient known to other Community Agencies? If so, please list: _____

_____

Vital Signs

Temp.   0 ____   R ____   AX ____   RESP ____   BP R _____   L _____

Height _____   Sitting: _____

Pulse AP _____   R _____   Weight _____   Standing: _____

Recent Weight Loss/Gain: Yes ____ No ____ Lying: _____

Review of Systems

Vision: No Problem ____ Glasses ____ Last Checked ____ Blurring ____

Diplopia ____ Inflammation ____ Cataracts ____ Glaucoma ____ Pain ____

Contact Lenses ____

RN Observation/Physical Findings: _____

Hearing: No Problem ____ Limited ____ Aid ____ Pain ____

Tinnitus ____ Discharge ____

RN Observation/Physical Findings: _____

Speech: No Problem ____ Can Understand ____ Can Express ____

Language Barrier ____

Interpreter's Name and Telephone Number: _____

RN Observation/Physical Findings: _____

Skin: No Problem ____ Dryness ____ Color ____ Turgor ____

Nails: ____ Toes: ____

(condition)

Rashes _____ Location _____ Fingers: _____

_____ Lesions/Wounds _____ Location _____

FIGURE 14-1. Patient History and Initial Assessment Tool. (Reprinted with permission, HomeCall, Inc., Frederick, MD)

RN Observation/Physical Findings: _____

Respiratory: No Problem ____ DOE ____ Pain ____ Cough ____
   Sputum ____ Sinusitis ____ Tobacco ____ Expistaxis ____ Cold Freq. ____
   D.A.R. ____ Orthopnea ____
   Pillows: 1 ____ 2 ____ 3 ____ Tracheotomy Old ____ New ____ Rales _____
   Rhonchi ____ IPPB ____ 02 ____ Vaporizer ____ Respirator ____ Other _____
RN Observation/Physical Findings: _____
Cardiovascular: No Problem ____ Edema (location) ____ Numbness _____
   Syncope ____ Dizziness ____ Cyanosis ____ Anemia ____ Bruising ____ Pain ____
   Palpitations ____ P.N.D. ____ Angina ____ Abnormal Heart Sounds _____
   _____ Pedal Pulse _____
RN Observation/Physical Findings: _____
G.I.: No Problem ____ Chewing Problems ____ Dysphagia ____ Dentures ____
   Full ____ Partial ____ Mouth: Needs Care ____ Healthy ____ Lesions ____
RN Observation/Physical Findings: _____
   Polydypsia ____ Polyphagia ____ Pain ____ Emesis ____ Hematemesis _____
   Nausea ____
   B.M.'s: No Problem ____ Loose ____ Constipated ____ Melena _____
      Ostomy ____
   Appliances Used: _____ Hemorrhoids _____ Incontinence _____
   Abdomen: Soft ____ Tender ____ Distended ____ Bruits ____ B.S. ____
RN Observation/Physical Findings: _____
G.U.: No Problem ____ Dysuria ____ Frequency ____ Hesitancy _____
   Urgency ____ Hematuria ____ Polyuria ____ Nocturia ____ Control ____
   Pain ____ Ileostomy ____
   Appliances Used: _____ Ureterostomy _____ Appliances Used ____
   Catheter: Past ____ Present ____ Size ____ Type ____ Reason ____ Date ____
RN Observation/Physical Findings: _____
Musculoskeletal: No Problem ____ Deformities ____ Pain ____ Stiffness ____
   Contractures ____ Arthritis ____ Exercises ____ Done by _____
   Amputation _____ Prostheses: _____
RN Observation/Physical Findings: _____
Neurological: No Problem ____ Seizures ____ Paralysis ____ Paresthesia ____
   Weakness ____ Balance Problem ____ Gait Problem ____
   Decreased Sensation ____ Dominant Hand ____ Pain ____
RN Observation/Physical Findings: _____
   Present Mental Status: Alert ____ Confused ____ Forgetful ____ Orientation _____
   Present Behavior: Cooperative ____ Anxious ____ Depressed ____ Isolated _____
   Distrustful ____ Lethargic ____ Talkative ____ Withdrawn ____
RN Observation/Physical Findings: _____
Nutritional: Intake Route: Oral ____ Naso-Gastric Tube ____ Parenteral ____
   Intake: Adequate _____ Excessive: _____
   Dietary or Vitamin/Mineral Supplement Used: No ____ Yes (specify) _____
   Special Diet (specify) _____ Appetite (describe) _____
   Compliance ____ Copy of diet in Home: No ____ Yes ____
   Instruction Needed _____
   Person preparing food _____
RN Observation/Physical Findings: _____
ADL: No Problem ____ Needs Assistance with: Ambulation ____ Transfer ____
   Hygiene ____ Bathing ____ Bed Bath ____ Shower ____ Tub Bath ____
   Dressing __ Feeding __ Meal Prep. __ Shopping __ Housework __ Laundry __
   Sleep: Hours __ Naps __ Aids __ Insomnia __ Due to: _____
   Other Caregivers Assisting: _____ How Often _____
   Homebound: Yes ____ No ____
RN Observation/Physical Findings: _____

Continued

FIGURE 14-1.   *(Continued)*

Hobbies/Interests: Reading ____   T.V. ____   Games ____   Cards ____   Handwork ____
          Other _____   Limitation Imposed by Illness: _____
          Comments: _____
Supplies/Equipment Needed: _____
_____

Assessment of Patient's Level of Understanding of Disease Process and Required Care:
(Include learning abilities, present habits, etc.)
_____
_____
_____

Additional information concerning this patient which should be known to other staff
members _____
_____
_____
_____
_____

Skilled needs to be included in Nursing Care Plan _____
_____

Need assessed for other disciplines   P.T.   ____
                                                             O.T.   ____
                                                             S.T.   ____
                                                             MSW   ____
                                                             HHA   ____

Illustrate Skin Lesions, Bruises, Amputations, etc.

_____
                                                        RN Signature

FIGURE 14-1.   *(Continued)*

terms of the family resources present, but also the family dynamics, health status and caregiving capabilities of family members, and impact of the home health process on the total family unit. Goals and care plans must be specific and realistic, developed with the maximum active participation of patients and their family members. Care plans must be evaluated regularly and revised as necessary. Consideration must be given to the effectiveness of the care plan for the total family unit: The patient's home care should not pose a threat to the health and well-being of his or her caregivers.

The home health agency usually has some type of agreement form that patients or guardians sign to give consent for services to be provided. This form also may include permission for the agency to release pertinent medical information to other providers and stipulations as to the payment and duration of services. Patients may receive a copy of the "Patient's Bill of Rights" (Figure 14-2) to keep in their homes.

Services

The needs of the patient will determine the services required. Some individuals may need assistance in stabilizing and improving their function, as with the person who requires special therapies in order to regain independence following a stroke. Others may need short-term guidance and instruction as they adapt to a disability or disease, such as the new diabetic who must learn to self-administer insulin. There are also persons who will need ongoing direct care, as in the case of a patient who needs dressing changes to a sacral decubitus. Based on the diversity of service needs that patients may present, home care agencies may use several types of personnel:

Nurses. Nursing is the backbone of home health services. Assessment, planning of services, and evaluation of the effectiveness and appropriateness of care usually fall within the responsibility of the nurse. In addition, nurses perform a variety of functions, including education, counseling, medication administration, treatments, and checking on the function of equipment.

Physical therapists. This professional will provide education, guidance, or direct care to improve the patient's mobility, transfer techniques, balance, ambulation, and use of assistive devices.

Occupational therapists. OT's stimulate the patient's mind, as well as dexterity, strength, and coordination. They provide significant assistance in enabling the patient to become more self-sufficient and identifying assistive devices that can promote independence.

Speech therapists. Patients with a variety of speech disorders can benefit from therapists. Services may range from helping the stroke victim with comprehension and expression, to teaching swallowing methods that will reduce anxiety and dysphagia in the patient with a medically or surgically induced speech problem.

Medical social workers. Since emotional or social problems can slow the patient's recovery and interfere with care activities, the assistance of social workers can be significant. Social workers may provide counseling to patients and family members, and link patients with resources.

Home health aides. Aides are used primarily to provide personal care to patients. They follow through on the recommendations of professional staff (e.g., exercising the patient, encouraging independent function, changing simple dressings) and communicate the patient's status to the team. The reg-

Patient's Bill of Rights

I. THE HOME HEALTH *PATIENT*, THE PATIENT'S FAMILY AND/OR AUTHORIZED REPRESENTATIVE HAVE THE *RIGHT* TO EXPECT:
   A. Safe and efficient care that is sufficient to improve or maintain the patient's maximum possible state of health or comfort in the individual's own home, including at a minimum:
      1. Professional assessment and reassessment at appropriate intervals.
      2. A broad spectrum of home health services to assure a continuum of care which is delivered in an efficient convenient manner to all clients regardless of race, color, religion, sex, age, handicap, national origin, or source of payment.
      3. Assistance in obtaining services of other community resources as needed.
      4. To be treated with courtesy, respect, sensitivity, and concern at all times.
      5. The assurance that all services are provided by supervised personnel, qualified for their jobs through education and experience.
      6. Each patient receiving home health services from HomeCall shall, at all times, know the name of the individual staff person responsible for the treatment plan in effect and the manner in which the patient (or legal guardian) or family may contact the responsible staff in charge.
   B. That upon request, a written statement of services shall be made available. Such statement shall include the frequency, unit, and current charges for such services.
   C. The home care plan shall be developed cooperatively by the physician and HomeCall staff with appropriate participation of the patient and in consultation with the family (or legal guardian).
   D. That an itemized bill for services shall be made available upon request of the patient. Such bill for services shall include the date of service and unit charge; those services charged to third party payors and the amount of such charges shall also be provided to the patient.
   E. HomeCall's policy regarding uncompensated care states that no patient receiving care shall have this care interrupted because of non-payment. In such cases HomeCall will continue to provide medically necessary care up to a maximum of 30 days or until a new source of funds becomes available and/or arrangements are made for the transfer of care with the family or legal guardian.
   F. Medical records shall be kept confidential and accurate in all matters that relate to the care delivered. However, patients or their legal guardian shall have the right to receive a summary report of care at any time upon written request.
   G. A patient receiving home health services from HomeCall shall receive instruction and training about the illness or disability for which care is being provided; know their responsibilities in the overall treatment plan and be appraised on a continuing basis of likely outcome.
   H. Any patient receiving home health services from HomeCall has the right to refuse any portion of planned treatment without relinquishing other portions of the treatment plan, except where medical contra-indications to partial treatment exist.

II. POLICIES REGARDING COMPLAINT MADE BY PATIENTS, FAMILY OR AUTHORIZED REPRESENTATIVE
   A. The Administrator shall be responsible for the investigation of all complaints made by a patient, family member, or legal guardian. Address:
      HomeCall of Frederick
      54 East Patrick Street
      Frederick, MD 21701
   B. The investigation of all complaints will begin within 48 hours from the time it is received by the Administrator, and a decision will be forwarded to the complainant within two weeks.
   C. A summary report of all complaints and their resolution shall be made to the Professional Advisory Group at their regular quarterly meeting by the Administrator or designated staff.

FIGURE 14-2. Sample Patient's Bill of Rights. (Reprinted with permission, HomeCall, Inc., Frederick, MD)

D. On an annual basis, a summary report will be made available to the State Regulatory Agency and upon request, to appropriate department personnel.

E. The summary report shall be available for public inspection upon request.

F. Appropriate designated staff shall participate in the investigation and resolution of complaints by providing all necessary records, reports and findings to the Administrator. When it is deemed necessary or upon request, designated staff shall assist in the preparation of a written complaint by the patient.

G. No disruption of services shall result from the filing of a complaint.

H. Complete files shall be maintained on the source, category, and disposition of all complaints.

I. The patient or patient's family or representative has the right to contact directly the State Regulatory Agency:

STATE DEPARTMENT OF HEALTH AND MENTAL HYGIENE
Division of Licensing and Certification
201 West Preston Street
Baltimore, Maryland 21201
Telephone: (301) 383-2517

FIGURE 14-2. (Continued)

istered nurse case manager develops a care plan (Figure 14-3) for the aide to follow and assures that the aide understands the unique needs and care of the patient; a supervisory visit is performed periodically to monitor the aide's activities.

The frequency of home visits is determined by the patient's condition. Initially, particularly with a patient newly discharged from an acute hospitalization, visits may be daily; the frequency of visits will likely decline as the patient's condition improves. Discharge from home health service may be judged appropriate when the patient can perform the activities of daily living and fulfill special care needs independently or with the assistance of family caregivers. At times, patients are transferred to other care settings, thus discontinuing the need for home health services.

For the Medicare patient, the physician signs a plan of care for a 60-day certification period; if care is needed beyond that time the nurse may send a plan of treatment to the physician for recertification for another 60 days. The home health agency usually will assist patients in obtaining resources if their care needs no longer qualify for Medicare reimbursement.

Regulation

The federal government has standards, expressed through regulations, that specify the responsibilities of home health agencies that participate in the Medicare and Medicaid programs. The Health Care Financing Administration supervises the various state administrations and fiscal intermediaries (private insurers) that are responsible for the provision or purchase of health services through Medicaid and Medicare. Each state has a licensing division that monitors and conducts annual audits on licensed home health agencies to ensure that federal and state standards are being met.

Homemaker Home Health Aide Care Plan

Dates _____

Client: _____ HomeCall Number: _____
Others Helping: _____
Doctor: _____ Tel: _____
Major Goals of Aide Service: _____
HomeCall Nurse Signature: _____

Personal Care

A. Bath _____

B. Hair _____

C. Oral Hygiene _____

D. Shave _____

E. TPR _____

F. Toileting _____

G. Help Dress _____

H. Help Walk _____

I. Transfers _____

J. Exercise _____

K. Use Appliances

L. Observe Medications _____

M. Observe Conditions _____

N. Feed _____

O. Range of Motion _____

P. Observations _____

Homemaking and Supportive Assistance for Patients Only

A. Meal Planning/Prep. _____

B. Encourage to Eat/Drink _____

C. Light Marketing _____

D. Encourage Indep. _____

E. Encourage Activity _____

F. Limit Activity _____

G. Make Bed/Change Linen _____

H. Light Housekeeping (areas) _____

I. Light Laundry _____

J. Teaching _____

K. Other _____

Emergency Telephone Numbers:
Ambulance _____
HomeCall Office _____
Family _____
Neighbor _____

FIGURE 14-3. Care Plan Developed by Nurse for Use by Home Health Aide. (Reprinted with permission, HomeCall, Inc., Frederick, MD)

```
┌─────────────────────────────────────────────────────────────────┐
│                        Private Pay Services                       │
│                                                                   │
│  Homemaking Services for Family          Other Services           │
│  A. Regular Housekeeping (areas) _____   _____  │
│  _____    _____  │
│                                            _____  │
│  B. Laundry _____    _____  │
│  _____    _____  │
│  C. Marketing _____    _____  │
│  _____    _____  │
│  D. Mending _____                            │
│  _____                           │
│  E. Companionship _____                            │
│  _____                           │
│  F. Observations _____                            │
│  _____                           │
│  _____                           │
│  _____                           │
│                                                                   │
│  Supportive Assistance                                            │
│  A. Accompany Doctor/Outing _____                            │
│  _____                           │
│  B. Transportation _____                            │
│  _____                           │
│  C. Socialization Activities _____                         │
│  _____                           │
└─────────────────────────────────────────────────────────────────┘
```

FIGURE 14-3. (Continued)

The Nurse's Role

The demands placed upon home health nurses require that they possess a wide range of knowledge and technical skills.

Home health care requires skilled nurses who are highly creative, caring, and competent. A wide range of clinical, family, and environmental problems are faced in home health nursing; therefore, nurses must be able to make accurate assessments, plan actions, provide interventions, and evaluate outcomes. Unlike nurses in hospital settings, home health nurses do not have professionals and resources readily accessible when they are in the home and must function in a highly independent manner. Home health nurses must be extremely skilled generalists, competent in techniques ranging from Hickman catheter care, to establishing a safe environment for the mentally impaired person, to educating patients in safe drug use. Nurses must possess sufficient comprehensive knowledge to identify nonnursing needs that require referral to other professionals. Not to be forgotten is the creativity demanded of home health nurses as they must improvise and adapt care to meet patients' unique circumstances.

The family plays an important role in home care. Family members frequently follow through on professional staff's plans and perform many direct care activities. They are the ones who monitor intravenous feedings and ventilators, change dressings, administer medications, feed, bathe, reposition, exercise, and supervise patients a majority of the time when agency staff is not present. The intensity and length of caregiving responsibility can be quite significant for families. It is important for nurses to assess family dynamics (roles, responsibilities, communication, problem-solving skills, coping abilities) to determine the ability and willingness of family members to offer assistance to the patient. Often, home health nurses find that support, education, and assistance to the entire family unit are essential to achieving goals for the individual patient.

Communication is the key to continuity and quality care. Regular communication with the patient's primary physician is important to keep the physician aware of progress and the need for adjustments to the plan of care. Communication with other professionals and agencies involved with the patient is beneficial in assuring consistency of goals and approaches, and avoiding duplication of services. Of course, communication with the patient and family occurs with each visit as progress and problems are shared.

The complexities of care and independence of practice support the need for highly skilled, well-educated nurses to be employed in home health. For this reason, many agencies seek nurses with baccalaureate education who have had preparation in community health nursing. Home health nurses without community health nursing education (and even those possessing it) increasingly are recognizing the necessity for more specialized skills and seeking continuing education to improve or maintain their competencies. With the ever-growing diversity and complexity of caseloads, home health nurses must be committed to maintaining competency through continuing education. The flexibility to grow with their changing caseloads and motivation to be self-directed in delivering high-quality services are core attributes of home health nurses.

The Future

What does the future hold for home health? The current trend of early hospital discharge will lead to greater utilization of home health care services. More persons will be surviving to advanced years in which the need for care assistance heightens; more of these persons will desire that care assistance be in their home settings. The increased inclusion of home health benefits in various health coverage plans will likely affect utilization, not to mention the cost benefit of providing care in community settings. All of these factors support the belief that home health care will continue to grow at a rapid rate. By providing leadership in this arena, home health nurses can promote safe, high-quality, and cost-effective care in the setting of choice for most patients—their own homes.

Appendix: Home Health Care Organizations

American Affiliated Visiting Nurse Associations
21 Maryland Plaza
Suite 300
St. Louis, MO 63108

American Federation of Home Health Agencies
429 N. Street, SW
Suite S-605
Washington, DC 20024

Home Health Services and Staffing Association
815 Connecticut Avenue, NW
Suite 206
Washington, DC 20006

National Association for Home Care
519 C Street, NE
Stanton Park
Washington, DC 20002

National HomeCaring Council
235 Park Avenue South
New York, NY 10003

National League for Nursing Council of Community
Health Services
10 Columbus Circle
New York, NY 10019

BIBLIOGRAPHY

Blazer D: Home health care; House calls revisited. Am J Public Health 78(3): 238–239, 1988.

Braun K, Rose C: Geriatric patient outcomes and costs in three settings: Nursing home, foster family, and own home. J Am Geriatr Soc 35:387–397, 1987.

Campion EW: The merits of geriatric consultation. JAMA 257(17): 2336–2337, 1987.

Cushing MR: Perils of home care. Am J Nurs 88(4): 441–442, 1988.

Hall GR: Care of the patient with Alzheimer's disease living at home. Nurs Clin N Am 23(1): 31–46, 1988.

Harris MD: Home Health Administration. Owings Mills, MD, National Health Publishing, 1988.

Haskell DJ: Home with a new heart. Am J Nurs 87(6): 813–816, 1987.

Jaffe MS, Skidmore-Roth L: Home Health Nursing Care Plans. St. Louis, CV Mosby, 1988.

Keating SB, Kelman GB: Home Health Care: Concepts and Practice. Philadelphia, JB Lippincott, 1988.

Omdahl DJ: Changes in Medicare home care forms. Am J Nurs 88(4): 487–489, 1988.

Omdahl DJ: Home care charting do's and don't's. Am J Nurs 88(2): 203–204, 1988.

Omdahl DJ: Preventing home care denials. Am J Nurs 87(8): 1031–1033, 1987.

Spiegel AD: Home Health Care, 2nd ed. Owings Mills, MD, National Health Publishing, 1988.

Tynan C, Cardea JM: Community service home health hazard assessment. J Gerontol Nurs 13(10): 25–28, 1987.

CHAPTER 15

Family Caregiving: Education and Support

Beverly A. Baldwin and Georgia Stevens

Chapter Objectives
At the completion of this chapter the reader will be able to:

1. Describe the recent trends in family caregiving.
2. Identify the causes and manifestations of caregiver stress.
3. Discuss the ways in which nurses can assist family caregivers.

Recent years have brought about a significant change in the caregiving role in families that have older members who need assistance. In the past, family members offered support and family ties to their elderly relatives. Today, longer life expectancies and advances in the management of health problems result in families providing more intense, complex care to their elderly members for a considerably longer period of time than ever before. It is estimated that at least 5 million adults in the United States are providing direct care to an elderly relative at any given time, with another 4 to 5 million assuming some type of responsibility for an elder relative (Brody, 1985).

The fact that family members are committed to the care of aging spouses or parents is significant today, given the prevailing myth in American society that family members do not care for the elderly as they did in years past. Eighty-five percent of the elderly (persons over the age of 65 years) reside in homes with spouses, other family, or friends, or live alone. Another 10% reside on a temporary basis in a hospital or other type of health care facility. Only 5% of persons over the age of 65 reside in nursing homes or similar long-term-care institutions. Shanas (1979) notes that more than twice as many frail and ill elderly are cared for by spouses or children than live in facilities such as nursing homes. Observers of home health care point out that families of today provide more than 80% of the home care required by older adults (Friedman, 1986; Horowitz, 1985; "Who's Taking Care?" 1985; Springer and Brubaker, 1984).

Female spouses (wives) represent the largest group of family caregivers of the elderly, constituting approximately 50%. Adult daughters represent 40% of all family caregivers, with the remaining 10% composed of sons,

> The reality that more people are surviving to later years than ever before with a host of health problems has increased the amount and intensity of family caregiving.

siblings, and other extended family members. Approximately 5 million (18%) of all elders live with an adult child ("Who's Taking Care?" 1985).

Family caregiving can carry with it numerous stresses, accumulated strain, and, for some, a sense of burden. As the dependency (both physical and psychological) of an aging adult increases, conflicts may arise, placing stress on various individuals and the family system as a whole. Unresolved family issues or conflicts may be heightened by the physical, emotional, and, often, financial strain of caregiving. With 54% of today's women in the work force, the added responsibility of giving care to a parent can create tremendous pressures for the adult daughter and her spouse and children. Adult children often report feeling reluctant or resentful in assuming a "parenting role" in the care of their own parent. Increasing dependency of frail or ill older adults raises many concerns related to role reversal between parent and adult child. This role reversal situation may become especially difficult for middle-aged women who care for an adult parent in addition to their own spouse, children, and sometimes grandchildren. Four-generation families are more common in society today than ever before in American history.

The role of families in the care and support of the elderly will continue to gain the attention of health care providers, given the impact on both individual caregivers and families as a whole of long-term care of the chronically ill and dependent. The purpose of this chapter is to examine how the responsibilities and concerns of families may be taken into account by health care providers through both formal and informal education and health teaching, as well as in psychological support and referral to appropriate resources for managing the care of the elderly.

Issues and Concerns of Family Caregivers

Caregiver Stress

Stress, strain, burden, and burnout are words that are used to reflect the negative impact of family caregiving. A number of studies have documented the fact that caregiving places added burdens and increases stress for the caregivers of frail elders (Brody, 1981; Cantor, 1983; Johnson and Catalano, 1983; Zarit et al., 1980). Family caregiving does in fact have a number of positive features both for the frail elder and for those providing care, including reaffirmation of close parent-child ties, the perception of being needed, and an opportunity to repay parents for their caregiving in early developmental years. However, the level of stress and strain seems to be related to the nature of the caregiving role and the interrelationships of the people involved. It is these factors that contribute to the pervasiveness and sometimes frustrating nature of family caregiving. The issues and concerns of family caregivers are related to (1) the work required in caring for a frail relative; (2) the previous and current caregiver relationships; (3) the impact on other family members; (4) resulting changes in the caregiver's life-style; and (5) concerns of the caregivers about their own well-being.

Caring for a family member can strengthen relationships, provide an opportunity to reciprocate for care the older adult has provided, and give the caregiver a sense of purpose and satisfaction.

Caring for a Frail Relative

Caregiving is a relatively undefined role for which few people are prepared. For many individuals, the thought of assuming a caregiving role is not seriously considered until a crisis occurs, such as an acute illness or injury of the elder. During crises, decisions frequently are made in haste. A family member may commit to a caregiving role without evaluating the realities of the responsibilities or acquiring the preparation that could aid in caregiving. Springer and Brubaker (1984) note that unlike other roles or jobs that people may undertake, the caregiving role is one that lacks clarity. Caregivers may lack the knowledge and skills demanded of the caregiving role and feel a certain degree of anxiety and uncertainty. This anxiety and uncertainty can heighten as caregiving responsibilities increase.

Physical and mental dysfunction of the elder results in symptoms that require both physical and emotional care. Symptoms may appear as functional and cognitive deficits, deficits in social functioning, or disruptive behavior (Deimling and Bass, 1986). The different types of deficits require different types and levels of care on the part of a relative. Functional disability can diminish the elder's ability to carry out activities of daily living. The caregiving required thus relates to the family member doing or assisting with tasks that the elder can no longer manage alone. Decline in intellectual abilities requires that the caregiver provide structure and guidance for an elder who may be experiencing forgetfulness and confusion. Caregiver concerns about social functioning relate to an elder's relationships or level of isolation and withdrawal, as well as variation in mood. Disruptive behavior on the part of the elder, such as wandering, combativeness, and acting out, require that the caregiver try to anticipate and minimize the behaviors as well as the resulting disruption. Thus, depending on the kind of impairment and symptoms that an elder experiences, care requirements differ from tasks relating to activities of daily living, dealing with mental decline, enhancing social functioning, and decreasing the disruptiveness of behavior. There are a number of new books and other publications for family caregivers, listed in the chapter appendix, that identify pragmatic ways to deal with these various components of elder care.

In addition to providing care for an elder displaying various symptoms, the very chronic nature of the elder's decline presents another set of concerns for family caregivers. Thus, as an elder continues to show signs of decline, the responsibilities of the caregivers are increased. These responsibilities may well involve responsibility 24 hours a day, 365 days a year (Browne and Onzuka-Anderson, 1985). The level of responsibility for a caregiver of a family member with Alzheimer's disease was aptly noted by Mace and Rabins (1981) in their book *The 36-Hour Day*. The constancy of the demands for care is further compounded by the chronicity of the demands. That is, there is "no end in sight" for the caregiver. What a caregiver sees ahead, in fact, is increasing demands over time. The chronic nature of caregiving responsibilities requires respite or other forms of relief that may or may not be available to the caregiver. Unfortunately for most

Caregivers may feel overwhelmed as their relative's condition declines and needs grow. Some form of respite can assist the caregiver in managing the increased demands and preserving his or her own health.

family caregivers, respite is not available on a consistent basis. This form of relief from caregiving responsibilities may range from a few hours a day to several days, weeks, or months.

In addition to the "how-tos" of providing specific care and continuing this care daily and over time, the caregiver is also faced with her or his own response to the decline of a family member. The elder's losses in function often awaken feelings in the caregiver of anxiety, grief, depression, and anger, as well as guilt. Caregivers not only have to deal with the losses in terms of providing care, but also in their own reactions to these losses. The psychological implications for the caregiver may be profound and persistent long after the caregiving role is relinquished.

Elder and Caregiver Relationship

The current caregiving relationship is very much influenced by the emotional and relationship patterns of the past. The influence of past family history has been widely recognized (Browne and Onzuka-Anderson, 1985; Zarit et al., 1985). Patterns of relating to each other, as well as unresolved issues from the past, may interfere with the current relationship. For instance, a caregiver daughter may harbor feelings that her brother was treated with favoritism by the mother, and upon assuming caregiving responsibilities for her mother, the daughter may resent that she, rather than the "favorite child," should carry this burden. Likewise, the adult child may have difficulty giving instructions and care to a parent who had been domineering. The relationship between the elder and caregiver also reflects changes in dependency patterns in the relationship. Although the elder and caregiver may have had a reciprocal relationship in the past, the relationship changes as the elder becomes increasingly dependent. The shift in dependency in the relationship often results in uncomfortable feelings, as well as the child's unrealistic expectations regarding the parent's capabilities. If these conflicts in the relationship are not resolved, the caregiver may assume reponsibilities that the elder can fulfill independently or have difficulty setting limits (Mace and Rabins, 1981; Vandivort, 1985). Flexibility on the part of the caregiver is essential if realignment of the parent-child relationship is to occur with a minimum of disruption to both the elder and the caregiver.

The Rest of the Family

The relationship between the caregiver and the elder does not occur in a vacuum, but rather within the larger context of the extended family. A primary issue for caregivers is the competing demands presented by the elder, usually a spouse, as well as the caregiver's children (Brody, 1981; Deimling and Bass, 1986; Johnson, 1983; Springer and Brubaker, 1984). Caregivers frequently report feeling overwhelmed or fatigued from trying to meet their responsibilities in other relationships, while at the same time caring for their elderly relative. For adult children of frail elders, these competing demands have been termed "middle-age squeeze." One factor that may enhance the caregiver's ability to deal with these competing demands is the level of support provided by the rest of the family, whether that support is providing actual care for the elder or in recognizing the many demands that caregiving places on individual and family members. Support from other family members may not be forthcoming, and caregivers may perceive that they are alone in carrying the burden of care. This lack of support may leave the caregiver feeling alienated from the rest of the family, creating other problems such as the caregiver experiencing feelings of resentment toward other family members.

Family conflict may arise from both the competing demands of caregiving and the lack of support by other family members (Zarit et al., 1985). Family conflicts appear to be inevitable, although the level of conflict differs from family to family. Family conflict, then, is another potential source of distress for family caregivers that increases their feelings of pressure and overresponsibility toward their elder.

> The changes in the caregiver's social life, privacy, and living space can result in conflict within the caregiver's nuclear family. Friction between spouses, problem behaviors of children, and tremendous stress may develop.

Some family conflict results from the changes in family routine and life-style that result from caregiving (Cantor, 1983; Deimling and Bass, 1986; Springer and Brubaker, 1984; Vandivort, 1985). Some of the changes that are experienced by the family include changes in amount of space, privacy, ability to entertain, and leisure time once the elder is moved into the home. Most family caregivers report that the introduction of a frail, dependent elder into the home dramatically alters the way in which the family grows emotionally. For example, young or adolescent children may regress to earlier levels of developmental maturity, especially if demands are made on their time or leisure activity. The spousal relationship for a caregiver may become strained, particularly if the elder's needs take priority over needs of the caregiver's spouse.

Restrictions in Life-style

The changes in family routine and life-style may increase family conflict as caregivers experience restrictions (Browne and Onzuka-Anderson, 1985; Cantor, 1983; Deimling and Bass, 1986; Springer and Brubaker, 1984). At times the restrictions are perceived by the caregiver as overwhelming because they occur in so many spheres of life. For caregivers who work outside the home, the demands of caregiving can, in fact, interfere in their ability to carry out their jobs to their satisfaction. Thus the work or their caregiving responsibilities may suffer. Some caregivers report a fear of having to give up employment in order to provide the care for the family members (Kleeman et al., 1987).

Caregivers also report changes in their ability to enjoy leisure time, participate in recreation, and enjoy social relationships. Very often they will fulfill their responsibilities to their elder, other family members, and their work and sacrifice time for leisure and social pursuits. This may increase the caregivers' feelings of isolation and burden as they do not see themselves able to pursue activities for fun and enjoyment.

Inherent in the restrictions on work, leisure, and socializing are loss of time for self and others, loss of freedom, and loss of privacy. Caregivers must actively find time for themselves in order to decrease their feelings of being trapped. In addition to the personal and social restrictions, caregivers may also face financial problems as resources are depleted in caring for the elder. As noted by Browne and Onzuka-Anderson (1985) the current reimbursement system favors institutional over home care and thus increases the financial burden placed on the caregiver.

Concerns of Caregivers about Their Own Well-being

In a current study of caregiver stress being conducted by this author and others at the University of Maryland (Kleeman et al., 1987), caregivers who were daughters and daughters-in-law were asked to describe their major concerns regarding their own well-being. These concerns include not having enough time for self, concerns about their own health, not having enough time for other family members, concerns about their marriages, not having enough time for fun and friends, lack of privacy, interference with work, chronic stress and tension, fatigue and lower level of energy, lack of freedom, and increasing impatience and temper.

Attending to the well-being of the caregivers is of prime importance if these caregivers are to be able to continue to provide care for an elderly family member as well as to prevent the onset of chronic stress, physical strain, and physical and emotional illness in the caregivers themselves. If these well-being concerns go unattended or ignored, the negative outcomes will have an impact not only upon the caregivers, but also on the rest of their family and the elder who requires care.

Stress management and coping strategies are needed for caregivers to be able to provide care for a frail relative, maintain a relationship with the elder, maintain relationships with the rest of the family, decrease restrictions, and increase their own sense of well-being. If stress is identified and handled throughout the caregiving experience, the likelihood of a negative impact on the physical and emotional health of the caregiver diminishes.

Needs of Family Caregivers for Education and Support

In spite of the number, complexity, and sometimes overwhelming problems that family caregivers may face on a day-to-day basis, they continue to provide the majority of care for the elderly. If family members are to continue to provide care, benefiting the elder without extending the caregivers beyond their limits, then the need for caregiving education and support must be addressed. A number of educational and support programs have been developed (Clark and Rakowski, 1983; Crossman et al., 1981; Hartford and Parsons, 1982; Zarit et al., 1985). While more information is needed on the implementation of these programs, long-term effects, and characteristics of caregivers likely to benefit, there is evidence to substantiate the need for both education and social and emotional support by family caregivers if they are to sustain care to elderly family members.

Needs for Education

There are a number of ways in which the educational needs of caregivers may be met. One approach involves presentation of content on areas such as normal versus pathological aging, family systems, family caregiving, and stress and stress management. While family members' need for such information may vary according to their stage of caregiving as well as the degree of responsibility, such information provides caregivers with the means to carry out their caregiving role, maintain supportive relationships with elders and other family members, and enhance their own well-being. Sucn information must be pragmatic and help caregivers to deal with immediate concerns, as well as assisting them in planning for the future. Caregivers also need information on health care resources, social and community services, finances, and respite care.

Educational programs may be undertaken in a variety of ways, including caregiver groups, family support meetings, books, pamphlets, and information disseminated by the popular press. Caregiving needs and issues are being increasingly recognized by the media. This type of education serves several needs. First, the needs of present caregivers may be addressed through such avenues. In addition, society at large is made aware of the realities of family caregiving. This public awareness has the potential for preparing future caregivers as well as increasing the community's responsiveness to the needs of current caregivers.

Another source of educational support is the health care system. While adult day-care programs (few in number but growing rapidly, with approximately 1,200 in the United States) have been especially responsive to the educational needs of family caregivers of frail elders, other health care programs, including acute care, home care and long-term care settings, can assist family caregivers through formal and informal educational programs.

Social and religious communities are another potential source of educational support for caregivers. These sources may, in fact, be more accessible to caregivers and thus have potential for greater impact.

Formats for educational programs for family caregivers may range from formal, didactic teaching settings to more informal group structures. Reinforcement of learning, especially stress and stress management, should be included in any type of formal educational program; caregivers must be given the opportunity to practice what they have learned about their own stressors and ways in which they may inhibit or modify the negative effects over time. Reassurance and support of learning is necessary for a change in behavior and in attitude regarding caregiving.

Social and Emotional Support

Education may assist family caregivers to cope more effectively with many issues and concerns; however, social and emotional support are also needed. Such support, whether offered in individual counseling, family meetings, and caregiver groups, or informally through friends and family, can assist family caregivers in a number of ways. When support is offered, family members learn that they are not alone. Another aspect of social support involves the sharing of experiences as a form of socialization. When caregivers come together in groups or talk to others and listen to others about caregiving concerns, then some of their needs for social involvement are met.

Caregivers consistently report the need to talk about their caregiving experiences and the impact that these experiences are having on their lives. However, many caregivers express reluctance to burden other family members and friends with their concerns. When they do come together with other caregivers and share their experiences, they express relief. This relief comes in part from being able to talk to someone who understands. It is interesting to note that many informal support systems focus primarily on the elder rather than the needs of the caregiver. Such inattention to caregiver needs further increases their sense of isolation and burden. In addition to decreasing a caregiver's sense of isolation, talking about the caregiving experience provides a way to ventilate some of the negative emotions and support positive emotional well-being.

> Caregivers may need the assistance and support of friends, family members, and professionals to recognize that there are limits to their caregiving responsibility.

Social and emotional support can also provide family caregivers with an opportunity to step back from the caregiving experience and identify possible negative patterns of relating that could be changed. Because this is the first step in problem solving, it offers caregivers the perspective that some of their needs can be addressed and met.

Social and emotional support can also help caregivers to recognize that there are limits to their responsibility to their elder. As discussed earlier, dependency in the elder may result in overresponsibility in the caregiver. Very often caregivers do not perceive that there are limits to their responsibility and thus may become overwhelmed by the limitless nature of their role. Friends, family members, professionals, and other caregivers can offer support to assist the caregiver to set some reasonable limits and thus decrease the restrictions that they experience in their day-to-day life.

An important and underdeveloped source of social and emotional support for caregivers is respite care. Their responsibilities continue 24 hours a day, 365 days a year, and may extend for years given the long-term nature of many of the chronic impairments in old age. It is not possible to continue in this cycle without relief. Such relief can be offered in a number of ways, such as respite care provided by nursing homes, adult day care, group homes, or cooperative ventures between caregivers in order to offer each other time out from the daily responsibilities. Families must be encouraged to use respite whenever possible, since relief from ongoing care has been demonstrated to provide positive long-term effects for the caregiver.

Increasing the availability of education and social and emotional support for family caregivers offers a number of benefits. First, caregivers may be able to offer a high quality of care for a longer period of time. Second, their relationships with the elder, other family members, and friends may become less strained and thus enhance the potentially supportive nature of these relationships. Third, education and support offer caregivers ways to deal creatively with the restrictions that they experience in their everyday life. Finally, support and education offer caregivers the chance to enhance and maintain their own social and emotional well-being.

Teaching Stress Management

Numerous aspects of the caregiving role have been identified as stressful. Increased responsibility for another adult may arouse self-doubt and concern over one's competency. Self-confidence of the caregiver may be threatened, especially with an older adult who has multiple physical and emotional needs, including degenerative illnesses. The burden of decision making and long-term planning for housing and health care imposes stresses on the caregiver, especially when his or her own abilities and stability in these areas are uncertain. Long-term consistent caregiving can disrupt and even alter completely the life-style of the caregiver. Moving the elder into the caregiver's home, for example, may unearth historical conflicts over control, dominance over one's environment, and unexpected housing arrangements. Teenagers may have to give up their room for a grandparent. Socialization and social activities, such as participation in clubs and organizations, attending the theater, and eating out in restaurants, have to be curtailed or altered to meet the needs of the frail elder member. Plans for retirement and postretirement activities of the caregiver, whether spouse or adult child, could be drastically curtailed or even terminated.

The psychosocial stresses of caregiving vary with the individual circumstances of the caregiver and his or her resources. Many family caregivers feel isolated from other family members, friends, or co-workers. No one "seems to understand" the situation unless in the caregiving role. Isolation from normal activities breeds psychological isolation and, often, loneliness. Caregivers may feel alienated from others, particularly if the situation calls for constant vigilance and supervision of the elder family member. Guilt plays a major role in the impact of caregiving on individuals and on families. Caregivers feel guilty over wrong or inappropriate actions, thoughts, and feelings. Guilt is the driving force for many, who, given previous history and relationship with the elder, finds this aspect of caregiving the most burdensome. Love-hate relationships often develop between caregiver and elder, particularly when the elder becomes more dependent on the caregiver.

> Gastrointestinal disturbances, headaches, sleep disorders, chronic upper respiratory infections, fatigue, irritability, mood swings, and depression are common symptoms reported by caregivers that demonstrate the psychobiological consequences of caregiving.

The psychobiological consequences of caregiving represent symptoms that may occur for the first time or exacerbate those in which the caregiver is most vulnerable. Commonly reported symptoms include gastrointestinal disturbances, headaches, sleep disruptions including insomnia, mood swings and depression, irritability, chronic upper respiratory infections, and general fatigue. The degree and variability of these symptoms depend, to a great extent, on the recognition by the caregiver of the stress inherent in the caregiver role. Most family caregivers, when queried, do not make the association between the stress as part of caregiving and their psychosocial and psychobiological symptoms.

Several strategies for recognizing and managing stress in caregiving can be learned and reinforced, in both the formal and informal learning settings and in support group situations described earlier. The following paragraphs describe techniques and suggestions that could be used in family education and support groups.

It is important for caregivers to identify the stressors in their life generally and those accompanying the caregiver role and responsibilities. Methods for self-evaluation of stress would include such techniques as making a stress list (i.e., listing the events, situations, and responsibilities that create or increase stress in one's life) and developing a mood inventory (i.e., listing activities each hour over a two-day period and noting one's mood or reaction at that time—mood changes, swings, and triggers will be identifiable).

Learning and practicing stress-management techniques provide the caregiver with skills to deal with the strains and frustrations of caregiving on a daily basis. Simple relaxation techniques, such as diaphragmatic breathing, cognitive restructuring, and mental imagery can be learned in a variety of formats, whether in formal educational settings or in support groups. Commercially produced books, audio and videotapes, and classes are offered in community colleges, community centers, YMCA, YWCA, and church groups. Stress management techniques, along with regular physical exercise, have been demonstrated to work effectively in reducing stress for a wide range of problems and situations (Matteson and Ivancevich, 1982).

Caregivers must learn, often through experience, to set realistic goals for themselves and for the elders under their care. Many times dramatic changes in behavior are expected of the elder with progressive memory loss, when, in fact, those global changes will not be realized. Short-term measurable goals must be identified, such as observing the frail elder assisting with activities of daily living when possible, even if this is not realistic all the time. Reversal of chronic, insidious behavior, particularly when brain damage is involved, will not be observed. The caregiver must develop a plan for what can be expected of the elder regarding his or her own care and how factors, such as fatigue, illness, or medications, can alter this behavior. Caregivers frequently express frustration over responses or behavior of the elder that they find problematic—they continue to look for changes in these responses or behavior even though the likelihood of such change may be slim.

Caregivers must learn the value of taking care of themselves and rewarding themselves for their caregiving efforts.

Family caregivers, especially those providing the primary, ongoing, consistent care, must learn to "be good to themselves." Guilt prevents many caregivers from reinforcing the positive aspects of their own behavior and giving themselves credit for a "job well done." Self-punishment and self-doubt reinforce each other and, from a mental health perspective, place the caregiver in a vulnerable position for the long-term consequences of stress. Positive attitudes can be learned and practiced. Longitudinal studies of adults indicate that those who have a positive outlook on life, acknowledge their victories and achievements, and reinforce accomplishment of goals have a more stable outlook on life in old age. Of course, caregivers cannot dismiss or overlook the negative aspects of their circumstances, but the way in which individuals view themselves and their behavior over time is important to emotional and mental health and to longevity (Frankfather et al., 1981). Utilizing respite when available is one way in which caregivers can help themselves to break the chain of frustration that may accompany daily caregiving. Relief from the caregiving role gives a fresh perspective and a new outlook, and stimulates the individual to utilize leisure, socialization, or cognitive potentials.

Caregivers often receive unsolicited advice and counsel from friends and other family members. Some suggestions may be helpful and allow validation or verification of the caregiver's assessment of the situation or decision making. However, according to many caregivers in the current study cited earlier, more often than not the advice is more stressful, more frustrating than helpful (Kleeman et al., 1987). Caregivers must therefore learn to screen this type of "assistance" from others and realize that, in many cases, family and friends have good intentions, but, unless they are actively participating in the caregiving experience, their perception of the situation may be biased or limited. Particularly when one or two caregivers provide the primary care and are responsible for the decision making, a great deal of input from others may be more confusing than clarifying.

The history of previous relationships between caregiver and elder plays an important part in the current caregiving situation. It is imperative that caregivers realize and accept that this history cannot be erased and that the effects continue to influence the current situation. Two positive reactions to the history of previous relationships, particularly if they are negative or fraught with conflict, are to work on resolution with the elder if this is possible and appropriate, and to concentrate on "letting go" of the burden of old hurts, conflicts, and resentments. Caregivers who have positive, loving relationships with the elder find their own life enriched by the caregiving experience, even though the stresses and daily strains are just as intense as they are for others who do not have the benefit of this type of relationship. Sometimes, professional individual counseling or psychotherapy is needed for resolution and "working through" the relationship to occur, and caregivers should seek this type of assistance if at all possible. The verification offered in support groups plays a similar role for many caregivers in that the relationship between the caregiver and the elder is often a focus of these types of groups. It becomes much easier for families to resolve these dilemmas if they perceive they are not alone or unique in the feelings they experience.

Developing and reinforcing a sense of humor is imperative to maintaining a positive perspective over the long term. Laughing at the small ironies of life and the ridiculous situations that may occur provides both an emotional and cognitive outlet for stress. Norman Cousins (1979), in a program of rejuvenation focused on humor, successfully demonstrated the benefits, both physiologically and psychologically, of using laughter to dispel hopelessness and break the cycle of despair. Humor may be enjoyed in a variety of ways: movies, cartoons, stories, anecdotes, and jokes. The deliberate use of humor on a daily basis is effective in promoting stress-reducing breathing, relaxation, lifting the mood, and giving a general feeling of contentment

Humor is therapeutic in relieving stress, improving mood, and coping with caregiving burdens.

and well-being. To learn to laugh at oneself requires practice and an ability to see yourself objectively, with the same potential and limitations as those around you.

One consequence of caregiving for many family members is isolation from usual activities, from friends and family. It becomes increasingly important throughout a long-term caregiving relationship to stay in touch with the "usual" of one's life-style, to maintain friendships, family ties, and church, social, and community affiliations. It has been well demonstrated that isolation from others breeds stress and that caregivers often report feeling isolated and, for some, alienated from the life they knew before the caregiving responsibilities began. Keeping ties and social activities intact helps caregivers to "get out of themselves" and reinforces the reality of their situation. It provides a balance between the life of a caregiver and that of an adult, spouse, employee, parent, and so on. To sever ties in an initial caregiving situation may elicit consequences later on, when the caregiver is in need of friends, family, and social activities—reinforcers of a positive life-style, with emotional and psychological benefits.

The activities of the family caregiver may become circumscribed; that is, they may "take on a life of their own." This possibility is particularly evident as the elder becomes more frail and dependent for both physical and emotional care. It becomes essential for the caregiver to place events of daily life in context, that is, not to overreact to any isolated incident or event and to strive to view the positive aspects of a situation. Diffuse anxiety may result when behaviors of the elder are evaluated from the perspective of being all-encompassing. Wandering or pacing behavior of the elder may be viewed as the "last straw" for some caregivers concerned over safety of the elder. Incontinence or other physical problems present a focal point of attention for others. Confusion, disorientation, and other problems with memory represent a third area of overreaction. Placing these and other behaviors in the context of the total situation may be more beneficial to the caregiver in identifying the nature of the problem, possible causes, and alternatives to deal with the situation on both a short-term and long-term basis.

Medication use, misuse, and drug reactions may be expected to represent a major concern for family caregivers. Keeping a chart of the type and amount of medication, dates, and times of administration provides a routine and schedule for evaluating this area of caregiving. If problems arise, the caregiver then has information that can be evaluated and communicated to the appropriate health care professional (physician, home health care nurse, adult day-care worker, etc.) for further investigation. This example has implications for assisting the caregiver in the short term to identify problems and in the long term to evaluate the elder's response to the medications. Understanding the reason for and effects of drugs on the elderly is important for the caregiver to provide helpful assistance in this area.

Caregiving may be a lonely experience for many, but when resources are available, they should be utilized to the fullest extent possible. Earlier in this chapter the benefits of respite from caregiving were addressed. The importance of accepting help and assistance from others, either family, friends,

The assistance and
support of friends,
family, and
professionals can
reduce the isolation
and burdens of
caregiving.

or professionals, cannot be overemphasized. To take on the burden alone is to increase the long-term effects of stress. Martyrdom breeds stress, resentment, and, for some, hostility regarding the caregiving situation. Caregivers must learn to actively seek help with problems or concerns encountered in their role with the elder. Allowing others to participate in the caregiving situation is one form of positive regard for oneself as well as providing an outlet for emotional and physical strain in giving care on a daily basis.

Taking one day at a time is a motto many caregivers report as sustaining them through the difficult times or situations. Worry, along with guilt, may have profound effects, both emotionally and physically. Anticipating what "might happen" or "what if" increases the anxiety and stress of the present situation and often results in "reading" into events more than there actually is. In addition, this type of thinking process and resultant behavior keeps the caregiver from focusing on problem solving in the present, the here and now. The majority of the time the most dreaded and negative consequences of an event do not materialize. Worrying about it can "gear up" the body to anticipate fight or flight, a common reaction to stress. If the stressor does not come about, the body has been forced into false readiness. The consequences can be detrimental to one's health over a long period of time. Fatigue is a common complaint of many caregivers, and the fatigue of the actual caregiving responsibilities and tasks may be exacerbated by worry over what may occur. The need to set limits becomes paramount if the caregiver is to maintain her or his own health and well-being over time.

Conclusion

The role of the family in the care of the elderly is now and will continue to be important. The fact that families are more involved in elder care than ever before and demonstrate both commitment to and interest in older family members illuminates the significance of caregiving in the family context. For many families, the caregiving experience is a positive, rewarding, and fulfilling one. Nursing intervention can facilitate good health for older persons and their caregivers, and contribute to meaningful family relationships during this process.

Appendix: Publications for Family Caregivers

Browne C, Onzuka-Anderson R (eds): Our Aging Parents—A Practical Guide to Eldercare. Honolulu, University of Hawaii Press, 1985.

Covell M: The Home Alternative to Hospitals and Nursing Homes. New York, Holt, Rinehart, and Winston, 1983.

Friedman J: Home Health Care: A Complete Guide for Patients and Their Families. New York, Norton, 1986.

Heston LL, White JA: Dementia: A Practical Guide to Alzheimer's Disease and Related Illnesses. New York, WH Freeman, 1983.

Horne J: Caregiving—Helping an Aging Loved One. Washington, DC, American Association of Retired Persons, 1985.

Mace N, Rabins P: The 36-Hour Day. Baltimore, Johns Hopkins University Press, 1981.

Parent Care: Resources to Assist Family Caregivers (newsletter). Gerontology Center, 316 Strong Hall, University of Kansas, Lawrence, KS 66045.

Powell L, Courtice K: Alzheimer's Disease—A Guide for Families. Reading, MA, Addison-Wesley, 1983.

Seuss Dr: You're Only Old Once! New York, Random House, 1986.

Silverstone B, Hyman HK: You and Your Aging Parent: The Modern Family's Guide to Emotional, Physical and Financial Problems. New York, Pantheon Books, 1982.

Springer D, Brubaker T: Family Caregivers and Dependent Elderly—Minimizing Stress and Maximizing Independence. Beverly Hills, CA, Sage Publications, 1984.

Zarit S, Orr N, Zarit J: The Hidden Victims of Alzheimer's Disease—Families under Stress. New York, New York University Press, 1985.

REFERENCES

Brody E: "Women in the middle" and family help to older people. The Gerontologist 21:471–480, 1981.

Brody E: Parent care as a normative family stress: The Donald P. Kent Memorial Lecture. The Gerontologist 25:19–29, 1985.

Browne C, Onzuka-Anderson R (eds): Our Aging Parents—A Practical Guide to Eldercare. Honolulu, University of Hawaii Press, 1985.

Cantor MH: Strain among caregivers: A study of experience in the United States. The Gerontologist 23(6): 597–604, 1983.

Clark NM, Rakowski W: Family caregivers of older adults: Improving helpers' skills. The Gerontologist 23(6): 637–642, 1983.

Cousins N: Anatomy of an Illness. New York, WW Norton, 1979.

Crossman L, London D, Barry C: Older women caring for disabled spouses: A model for supportive services. The Gerontologist 21:464–470, 1981.

Deimling G, Bass D: Symptoms of mental impairment among elderly adults and their effects on family caregivers. J Gerontol 41(6): 778–784, 1986.

Frankfather DL, Smith MJ, Caro FG: Family Care of the Elderly. Lexington, MA, Lexington Books, 1981.

Friedman J: Home Health Care: A Complete Guide for Patients and Their Families. New York, Norton, 1986.

Hartford ME, Parsons K: Groups with relatives of dependent older adults. The Gerontologist 22(3): 394–398, 1982.

Horowitz A: Sons and daughters as caregivers to older parents: Differences in role performance and consequences. The Gerontologist 25:612–617, 1985.

Johnson C: Dyadic family relations and social support. The Gerontologist 23:377–383, 1983.

Johnson CL, Catalano DJ: A longitudinal study of family supports to impaired elderly. The Gerontologist 23(6): 612–618, 1983.

Kleeman K, Baldwin B, Stevens G: Data from series I of "Stress and Mental Health: Caregivers of Day Care Elders." Unpublished report. Baltimore, University of Maryland, 1987.

Mace N, Rabins P: The 36-Hour Day. Baltimore, Johns Hopkins University Press, 1981.

Matteson MT, Ivancevich JM: Managing Job Stress and Health. New York, Free Press, 1982.

Shanas E: The family as a social support system in old age. The Gerontologist 19: 169–174, 1979.

Springer D, Brubaker T: Family Caregivers and Dependent Elderly—Minimizing Stress and Maximizing Independence. Beverly Hills, CA, Sage Publications, 1984.

Vandivort R: The family's role in eldercare. In Browne C, Onzuka-Anderson R (eds): Our Aging Parents—A Practical Guide to Eldercare, 30–38. Honolulu, University of Hawaii Press, 1985.

Who's taking care of our parents? Newsweek, 60–70, May 6, 1985.

Zarit S, Orr N, Zarit J: The Hidden Victims of Alzheimer's Disease—Families under Stress. New York, New York University Press, 1985.

Zarit S, Reever K, Bach-Peterson J: Relatives of the impaired elderly: Correlates of feelings of burden. The Gerontologist 20:649–655, 1980.

BIBLIOGRAPHY

Given CW: Sources of stress among families caring for relatives with Alzheimer's disease. Nurs Clin N Am 23(1): 69–82, 1988.

Hall GR: Care of the patient with Alzheimer's disease living at home. Nurs Clin N Am 23(1): 31–46, 1988.

Lipkin LV, Faude KJ: Dementia—educating the caregiver. J Gerontol Nurs 13(11): 23–27, 1987.

Rempusheski VF, Phillips LR: Elders versus caregivers: Games they play. Geriatr Nurs 9(1): 30–34, 1988.

Sommers T, Shields L: Women Take Care: The Consequences of Caregiving in Today's Society. Gainesville, FL, Triad, 1987.

Stetz KM: Caregiving demands during advanced cancer: The spouse's needs. Cancer Nurs 10(5): 260–268, 1987.

CHAPTER 16

The Geriatric Nurse Practitioner in a Multipurpose Senior Center

Sharon Kern

Chapter Objectives
At the completion of this chapter the reader will be able to:

1. Describe the services provided in a multipurpose senior center, including preventive and health promotion services, immunizations, education, screening, assessment, day care, and emergency services.
2. Discuss the clinical and managerial roles of the nurse in the multipurpose setting.

A unique and rewarding practice site was opened to nurses with the development of senior centers. The development of senior centers in the United States began in the early 1940s, with the initial purpose of providing social and recreational activities. Since that time many centers have become *multipurpose* ones and offer a variety of services to the older population, including recreation, education, social work, retirement counseling, music therapy, nutrition, case management, information and referral, buddy systems, and telephone check-in, as well as health screening, education, and primary care services. In the senior center setting, the opportunity exists for nurses to promote health and improve the functional capacity of older adults. Also, senior centers can serve a significant function in enabling older adults to remain maximally independent in the community.

For many years the focus of senior centers was on the well elderly. However, as an increasing number of disabled and ill elderly have remained in the community rather than institutional settings, senior centers have expanded services. It is believed that senior centers will continue to evolve in their provision of services to the old and frail elderly who have cognitive or physical impairment (Bechill, 1986).

Through the multifaceted services of a senior center an elderly person can be maintained in his or her home with improvement or restoration of functional capacities, or prevention of further deterioration. Nursing is instrumental in assisting the older person to achieve maximum function.

As senior centers evolve, so will the nursing role. This chapter will examine some of the services that can be provided in the senior center and various nursing roles and functions in this setting.

Preventive and Health Promotion Services

For many years little thought was given to the development of preventive health services for the elderly. There was a belief among elderly and many health care providers that in old age it was too late to screen for diseases. New knowledge in the field of geriatrics has increased our understanding of the interaction of disease and aging, and new treatment of disease can decrease morbidity and mortality and improve the quality of life.

Mass Screening Programs

Mass screening programs for hypertension, cancer, glaucoma, hearing deficits, and podiatry problems can be a cost-effective means of identifying serious diseases in an early stage.

Screening programs are essential to preventive health services. These programs are aimed at detection of disease in the early stages, often prior to symptomatology, so that treatment can be instituted to prevent the progression of the disease, sequelae, and disability (McCally, 1985).

It is useful to ask certain questions when developing a screening program:

- What problems does one want to identify?
- Can sufficient positive cases be detected to justify the cost and effort?
- Does the problem being screened for have a serious effect on morbidity, mortality, and quality of life?
- Are age-related norms being used to differentiate normal from pathological?
- Are appropriate equipment and tools being used?
- Are resources available to correct or improve positive findings?

Health fairs offer the opportunity to conduct many screening programs in one site. These can be conducted at the senior center or at other community sites. Some of the screenings could include

- Hypertension
- Fecal occult blood
- Hearing deficits
- Glaucoma
- Dental problems
- Foot problems

Hypertension screening programs are among the most popular and fruitful.

Mass preventive programs are attractive because of their relatively low cost and ability to reach large populations. Many community service organizations can offer assistance in providing personnel, equipment, or literature. For example, American Cancer Society chapters can supply hemocult cards and perform evaluations and follow-up for fecal occult blood. Nursing students also can participate in health fairs and offer invaluable assistance while having a meaningful field experience (Lewis and Glover, 1987).

Immunizations

Influenza in the elderly is associated with high hospitalization and death rates. Since the elderly are at high risk for developing influenza, immunization is advocated. The Centers for Disease Control (CDC) have recommended annual influenza vaccine for all persons over the age of 65, and to persons of any age who have chronic diseases that increase their risk of influenza. (Inactivated influenza virus vaccines have been the major method of influenza prevention used.) Influenza vaccination programs that could be offered at nominal or no cost to senior center participants could ultimately decrease the influenza rate significantly.

The literature is reporting that tetanus is a concern for the elderly (Lindberg, 1987; Albert, 1987). It is believed that tetanus mortality rates rise with age because tetanus vaccination is not kept current. The recommendation is that tetanus and diphtheria vaccinations be renewed every ten years. Specific inquiry as to the status of these immunizations should be included during routine assessments.

Pneumococcal vaccination is recommended by the CDC for all persons over the age of 65. This vaccination is relatively inexpensive, has a very low reaction rate, and offers protection with a single administration.

Hearing Evaluations

Problems with hearing are most commonly associated with the process of aging. Hearing impairments are second to arthritis as the most prevalent chronic condition affecting the physical health of senior adults (Maurer and Rupp, 1979). Auditory deficits can lead to a significant amount of functional impairment. Screening for the presence of these impairments and the extent to which they affect function can be done quickly and at a very low cost.

All hearing evaluation services should include an otoscopic examination, Weber test, Rinne test, and if possible, screening audiometry. The Rinne and Weber tests provide useful information about the older client's auditory health and hearing sensitivity. The Weber test reveals information about ears with unequal hearing sensitivity, and the Rinne test compares air conduction to bone conduction. Comparison of the examiner's perception of bone conduction with the client's is known as the Schawabach test. Tuning forks are the tools used in the administration of the Rinne, Weber, and Schawabach examinations.

Screening audiometry, either using an audioscope or a portable audiometer, completes the auditory screen. The audioscope is a relatively new instrument that is low in cost, portable, and ideal for screening purposes (Campbell, 1986).

Hardened cerumen frequently contributes to hearing deficits in the older population. Nurses can easily detect the presence of cerumen impaction through otoscopic examination. If excessive ear wax is seen blocking the canal, it should be removed. Ear wax removal clinics may prove to be a very popular and useful service in the senior center.

As part of the hearing evaluation the nurse should instruct older clients about the realities of hearing and aging, and the principles of ear care, such as the need to avoid using cotton-tipped applicators and hairpins to clean ears. Referrals can be made for more refined hearing evaluation or assistive devices if problems are detected.

Other Approaches to Health Promotion

There are other methods of health promotion in the elderly. Seminars on such issues as Alzheimer's disease, nutrition, home safety, diabetes, hypertension, physical fitness, cancer, osteoporosis, stress management, and safe medication use can be conducted or coordinated by the nurse.

Cameron (1986) states that programs aimed at risk reduction and changing health behaviors should include some method of assessing the senior's life-style behaviors. In this way the senior becomes cognizant that certain behaviors are not conducive to health. Cameron (1986) further describes the use of a written care plan, jointly promulgated and signed by the senior and the nurse, as a contract to develop behaviors that will promote wellness.

The multipurpose senior center is an ideal site for nurse-managed wellness programs.

Another concept that can be implemented in the senior center is the wellness center (Johnson et al., 1986). This health promotion program incorporates a team of nurses from various specialties to provide a range of services to older clients, including home visits and group programs on various health issues. There has been favorable client response to nurse-developed and -managed wellness centers (Johnson et al., 1986).

Education

Education of other center staff promotes esprit de corps and enables staff to understand the nurse's role and use nursing services fully. The nurse can be recognized as an expert on gerontological health issues and consulted as necessary. As the word spreads, the nurse will serve an active role providing educational programs within the center and to community groups.

Another format for disseminating information on health issues is the center's newsletter or other publications. The nurse can request space, and perhaps write a regular column, for health education articles. Topics such as hyperthermia, hypothermia, and influenza can be presented at the beginning of the seasons during which the risk that these illnesses will occur is highest.

The senior center is an ideal site for nursing students at all preparatory levels to learn about community-based elderly, as well as the way in which nurses can have an impact on the health status of the community-based elderly population. Many of the students' myths can be dispelled as they are exposed to well elderly and seniors who are highly functional despite chronic disease. The center's nurse can serve as an important role model, demonstrating nursing's potential in this unique setting.

Geriatric Care Services

Individual Assessment

Geriatric assessment programs are multifaceted. They include more intensive and comprehensive multidisciplinary evaluations than could be performed during mass screening programs. The purpose of the geriatric assessment process is to identify the presence of problems and their extent, and to develop a plan of care that will improve the function of the client. Many caregiver issues and problems also surface during an assessment session.

The literature supports the premise that assessment programs can identify problems and facilitate early intervention for the frail elderly that can result in multiple benefits. Positive outcomes include increased functional status, improved cognition, reduction of medication use, prolonged survival, and decreased nursing home use (Rubenstein, 1987).

A variety of the senior center's staff participate in the multidisciplinary assessment, and additional professionals may be utilized as the client is referred for follow-up evaluation and care. Initially, however, the nurse is often the person with whom the client or family has the first contact. It is at this time that the nurse begins to advocate and coordinate services for the client, as problems or needs are presented. Nursing assessment and problem identification also begin on the initial contact. During the telephone intake interview, the nurse gathers data related to health state, medications, activities of daily living (ADL) and instrumental activities of daily living (IADL) abilities, and reason for seeking the assessment. Based on the information gathered during the telephone interview, the nurse is able to ascertain the priority level of the situation.

The nursing assessment is a significant component of the geriatric assessment process. A major focus of the nurse's examination will be on the client's functional status, that is, eating, bathing, dressing, toileting, mobility, transfer, and cognition. Asking about and observing performance of ADL functions is essential. Further insight into functional status is derived from evaluation of three-position blood pressures, gait analysis, vision and hearing status, weight, energy level, and the impact of disease.

Cardiac and chest assessments, including evaluation for peripheral edema and jugular venous distension, are included under energy assessment. Elimination can be evaluated through pattern of bowel and bladder elimination, percussion of bladder size, and checking for rectal sphincter tone and pelvic floor relaxation. For an accurate assessment of cognitive status it is necessary to palpate and auscultate carotid arteries and perform an evaluation of mental function. There are many mental status evaluation tools available for the nurse to utilize, such as the Mini-Mental State Examination (MMSE), Mental Status Questionnaire (MSQ), and Short Portable

Mental Status Questionnaire (SPMSQ). Kane and Kane (1981) provide a critique of the various tools available to aid the nurse in selecting the ones most appropriate for a specific agency.

It is important for the nurse to analyze the tools used in the assessment program. Applegate (1987) has identified several issues that must be considered in the use of assessment instruments, such as the cultural, economic, social, and educational biases that may exist. Other factors to consider in instrument selection are required administration time and whether the tool is a self-rating instrument or requires a trained examiner. Many frail or impaired elderly persons are unable to complete a self-report instrument independently; others who assist them may inject their own observations and biases. Some tools are too lengthy to complete during the time available. Ideally, assessment tools will be selected that are realistic for use in the site and offer reliable, valid data.

The goal of the nursing assessment is not just to identify deficits, but to determine the client's strengths and resources that can be used to restore and maintain function and independence. Assessment is thus essential to planning services appropriately.

Day Care

Adult day-care programs represent a unique service in community-based long-term care, particularly within the multipurpose center. These programs allow older individuals who have limited mental or physical function to reside in the community while receiving health care and supervision.

Senior centers can offer either a social or medical model of adult day care. Social day care offers services that address the needs of socialization, nutrition, and leisure; health care is not a focus. A variety of health services such as assessment, management of illness, and physical, occupational, and speech therapies are included in the medical model. Nurses can play a role in either model that the center adopts. Carliner (1985) has identified the following responsibilities of a day-care nurse, and these are applicable to the multipurpose-center-based practice:

Health education

Dispensing medications

Assisting in hygiene practices

Monitoring vital signs

Screening for disease processes

Assisting with ADLs

Observing client behavior

Implementing rehabilitative nursing practices

Creating, implementing, and evaluating the treatment plan

A broader discussion of day care can be found in Chapter 18.

Emergency Care

The senior center nurse also must be responsible for triage of emergencies that occur within the center. Falls, seizures, syncope, dizziness, acute confusion, behavior changes, and suicide attempts are examples of problems that demand prompt evaluation and referral. Keen assessment skills are necessary to make rapid determinations of service needs.

The nurse should assure that the center has specific policies and procedures related to the management of emergencies and that all personnel are familiar with this information. It is imperative that the nurse maintain annual CPR certification; it is useful for the nurse to arrange for other center staff to obtain certification also.

Expanded Practice

The senior center is an ideal site for the nurse-practitioner role to be implemented. The frequent need for comprehensive assessments, clinical decision making, and monitoring of chronic diseases supports the usefulness of this role in the center. The presence of a nurse practitioner can also be a cost-effective means of providing health services to older adults in the community setting.

Management

In addition to the clinical component, there are nursing management opportunities for the senior center nurse. The nurse can coordinate the scheduling and delivery of various services, plan staff development activities, monitor student affiliations, and negotiate new services.

The management process frequently can be conceptualized as a modification of the nursing process model. Marquis and Huston (1987) identify the steps of the management process as

Planning

Organizing

Staffing

Directing

Controlling

The nurse manager plans program services and budget, as well as educational programs for clients and staff. The nurse can be involved in selecting, assigning, scheduling, and evaluating staff. Monitoring the quality, utilization, and effectiveness of services can be a responsibility of the nurse. The senior center offers opportunities for various levels of management experience for the nurse ranging from supervising other nursing personnel to directing one of the center's programs.

The options for nursing practice in the multipurpose senior center are innumerable. In the various functions that they can perform in this site, nurses are challenged in their use of knowledge, creativity, and skill. In this new setting for nursing practice, nurses can demonstrate the impact nursing can have on the well-being and health of community-based elderly.

Note: Many of the roles described are based on the author's experience at the Waxter Center for Senior Citizens in Baltimore, Maryland.

REFERENCES

Albert M: Health screening to promote health for the elderly. Nurse Prac 12(5): 42–56, 1987.

Applegate, WB: Use of assessment instruments in clinical settings. J Am Geriatr Soc 35(1): 45–50, 1987.

Bechill WD: Senior centers: Past, present and future. Paper presented to class in senior center administration, School of Social Work and Community Planning, University of Maryland, Baltimore, spring 1986.

Campbell SD: The audioscope: A valuable hearing assessment tool. J Gerontol Nurs 12(12): 28–31, 1986.

Carliner D: Adult Day Care: An Introduction. Baltimore, MD, Meridian Healthcare, 1985.

Cameron PW: Reducing risks for seniors (a nurse's role). J Gerontol Nurs 12(9): 4–8, 1986.

Johnson E, Igan J, Utley Q, Hawkins J: Wellness center. J Gerontol Nurs 12:22–27, 1986.

Kane RA, Kane RL: Assessing the Elderly. Lexington, MA, Lexington Books, 1981.

Lewis JA, Glover L: Joint efforts between education and the community. J Gerontol Nurs 13(1): 23–26, 1987.

Lindberg SC: Adult preventive health screening, 1987 update. Nurse Prac 12(5): 19–41, 1987.

Marquis BL, Huston CJ: Management Decision Making for Nurses. Philadelphia, JB Lippincott, 1987.

Maurer J, Rupp R: Hearing and Aging: Tactics for Intervention. New York, Grune and Stratton, 1979.

McCally M: Epidemiology of illness. In Cassel C, Walsh J: (eds): Geriatric Medicine, vol. 2: Fundamentals of Geriatric Care. New York, Springer, p. 49, 1985.

Rubenstein LZ: Geriatric assessment: An overview of its impact. Clin Geriatr Med 3(1): 1–15, 1987.

BIBLIOGRAPHY

Bowers AC, Thompson JM, Miller M: Clinical Manual of Health Assessment, 3rd ed. St. Louis, CV Mosby, 1988.

Butler FR: Minority wellness promotion: A behavioral self-management approach. J Gerontol Nurs 13(8): 23–28, 1987.

Clark CC: Wellness Nursing: Concepts, Theory, Research, and Practice. New York, Springer, 1986.

Evashwick CJ, Weiss LJ: Managing the Continuum of Care. Rockville, MD, Aspen Publishers, 1987.

Howe C: Helping the aged. Nurs Times 83(5): 40–42, 1987.

Lanning NM: The rainbow to wellness . . . health maintenance clinic for seniors' apartment complex. Can Nurs 82(11): 22–26, 1986.

Mackus ML, Millette JM: Supporting community elderly. J Gerontol Nurs 13(12): 26–29, 1987.

Neville K: Promoting health for seniors. Geriatr Nurs 9(1): 42–43, 1988.

Stanhope M, Lancaster J: Community Health Nursing: Process and Practice for Promoting Health, 2nd ed. St Louis, CV Mosby, 1986.

Taylor C, Gallagher LL: Structured learning guides in gerontology, Part 2. Geriatr Nurs 9(2): 104–109, 1988.

CHAPTER 17

Continuing Care Retirement Living: The Nurse's Role

Kay Seiler

Chapter Objectives
At the completion of this chapter the reader will be able to:

1. Describe the various types of continuing care retirement communities.
2. Discuss the nurse's role in continuing care communities.
3. List some of the health problems that may be identified in residents and related nursing interventions.

One of the more exciting trends in retirement living is the continuing care concept, offering an increasing number of choices for the older individual, as well as affording untold challenges to the nurse. Professionals in this setting must possess great sensitivity and knowledge about older people, be creative, and exhibit a specialized set of skills and talents, as in the areas of advocacy, education, counseling, and health promotion. Moreover, the nurse must, on a daily basis, function in this setting without all the usual supports immediately available in the hospital. For the nurse who wishes to apply principles and techniques in creative ways, enjoys making independent judgments and decisions, and respects the individuality of each older person, nursing in a retirement community can be truly satisfying and rewarding.

Continuing care can be defined as

furnishing shelter and either medical and nursing or other
health-related benefits to an individual 60 years or older . . .
for the life of the individual, or for a period in excess of one
year, under a written agreement that requires a transfer of
assets or an entrance fee notwithstanding periodic charges.
(Annotated Code of Maryland, 1985)

The terms "continuing care" and "life care" are used differently (sometimes interchangeably) in various parts of the United States. The variety of choices in continuing care runs the gamut from a single room in a traditional retirement community through opulent independent living accommodations in a full-service life-care community. Principally, the differences are found in the contractual arrangements, the extent of the amenities provided, and the elegance of the facility itself.

Though there are a number of other types of retirement housing, such as market-rate rental and domiciliary care, this chapter will deal with those types of retirement housing that are covered by the definition cited: the traditional retirement community, life care, and the continuing care retirement community.

Traditional Retirement Communities

The traditional retirement community has existed for decades and has provided well for the needs of retirees. Often conversion, or transfer, of assets is the financial arrangement leading to admission to such a facility. In other words, the retiree disposes of personal property and turns over the proceeds to the community in exchange for a guaranteed place to live and health care for life.

In the traditional retirement community, individuals transfer their assets or pay a per diem fee in return for the provision of all necessities. Ambulatory and long-term health care services are minimal.

In recent years, there has been an emerging trend toward offering an admission arrangement different from that of transferring assets, namely, paying a per diem rate. This choice is dependent upon the individual's possessing adequate resources, the extent of which is computed in accordance with actuarial tables. For instance, one may need to have $100,000 in assets to utilize this plan.

Those who have converted assets at the time of admission pay no additional "out-of-pocket" fees. However, earnings, such as Social Security income, revert to the community and are placed into an account for the individual. All necessities, such as clothing, are purchased from these monies; the retiree receives a small monthly stipend. Should the account fall below the actual cost of maintenance, the retiree is still guaranteed a place to live and whatever health care is needed.

Predominantly, traditional retirement communities have been owned and operated by religious groups. Others are managed by fraternal organizations or operated as nonprofit organizations.

This housing option allows for freedom from worry and for independence as long as the individual's health permits. The retiree usually has a private room and may bring those items of personal furniture that can be accommodated in the available space. All meals and services are provided, including extensive social and recreational activities.

Most retirement communities provide on-site long-term care. The resident may take advantage of this service for short periods of time, based on health needs. For example, he or she may enter the health center following hospitalization for a hip fracture. If medical condition so dictates, he or she can be transferred permanently.

Independence is highly encouraged in this type of community; nevertheless, it is somewhat restrictive. Choices and decision-making opportunities are more limited than in other continuing care facilities. Still, this choice offers a very comfortable life-style and is particularly appealing to individuals of moderate income who opt for the companionship of peers in a congregate facility and freedom from managing a household.

FIGURE 17-1. Pickersgill, a Nondenominational, Nonprofit, Traditional Retirement Community Located in Towson, Maryland

Life Care

Life care, along with other types of continuing care living, facilitates the pursuit of an active life-style, independence, and an active role in decision making. Usually, these facilities are luxurious and provide a diversity of services, most of which are included in the monthly fee. (The inclusion of the major services, including health care, is known as bundling.)

The residents enter into a contractual agreement with the owner or operator for a

> pre-determined sum of money—usually known as an endowment fee, admissions fee, or entrance fee—that allows them to have the assurance (usually not an absolute guarantee) that they will have a place to live and be taken care of for life—whether in an apartment, cottage . . . or health facility. (Worley, 1982, p. 30)

In addition, residents pay a monthly service charge, based upon the type and size of living accommodation selected. The contractual agreement, signed before the resident moves in, outlines services covered, as well as those excluded.

For about two decades after life-care communities originated in the 1950s, the facilities virtually guaranteed no increase, or very minimal increases, in the monthly service (or maintenance) charges. (Since that time,

FIGURE 17-2. Fairhaven, a Life-care Community in Sykesville, Maryland, Sponsored by Episcopal Ministries to the Aging, Inc.

the fixed-rate guarantee has been eliminated in most communities.) Double-digit inflation in the 1970s and longevity of residents beyond actuarial predictions drove many organizations into bankruptcy. Consequently, many retirees who had expended most of their life savings found themselves in precarious circumstances.

Some states have enacted legislation to safeguard residents from such catastrophe. The law in Maryland, for example, requires that such communities obtain a certificate of registration from the State Office on Aging, and they must be relicensed annually. Pursuant to application for the original certificate, a feasibility study must be submitted. Prior to construction, a specified percentage of living units must be under contract to prospective residents. Stringent guidelines are included regarding disclosure of financial information, the escrow of funds to assure that monies will be available for the eventual health care needs of the residents, contractual agreements, and the like. Persons considering this living option would be well advised to find out if such regulatory safeguards prevail in the state in which they choose to live.

Independent living accommodation choices are varied and numerous. Apartment options range from studio to two-bedroom, usually in mid-rise or garden-apartment buildings. Sometimes residents can choose cottages of one or two bedrooms. These are usually quite spacious and well designed, enabling retirees to furnish their homes very much like their former residences.

Sometimes, three meals are provided, with appropriate deductions from monthly fees if the individual chooses to take only one or two daily. Other communities include one per day, with the option to purchase additional meals. Under either plan, guests may dine with the residents, who are invoiced for this service. Mandatory meal provisions are included to assure that residents receive at least one adequately balanced meal daily to afford

FIGURE 17-3. Roland Park Place, a High-rise Life-care Community in Baltimore

socialization and allow staff to observe the resident in an unobtrusive manner.

Under the true life-care contract, health care is prepaid. Residents are generally required to subscribe to Part B Medicare and some type of Medigap insurance policy.* Often the community employs a physician available on site; in this case, costs of the physician's service and recommended consultants are usually covered under the contract. Of course, the resident may elect to receive the care of another physician, but will be expected to pay those fees. Whether care is required in the hospital, as an outpatient, or in the nursing center of the community, all costs not covered by third-party payers are borne by the facility.

---

*Part B Medicare, an optional medical insurance, can be purchased for a monthly premium and will cover a portion of physician and surgeon charges and other selected services. Medigap policies offer additional coverage to supplement Medicare policies.

Continuing Care Retirement Communities

New forms of continuing care are being developed offering a menu of services that older adults can select for specific fees.

While all the facilities mentioned thus far fall into the category of continuing care retirement communities, there is a type of community that lies somewhere between the two previously discussed. Independent living accommodations, congregate dining, services, and activities are all available; but prepaid health insurance is usually excluded. Entrance fees are required, as with traditional life-care communities, but because services are "unbundled," monthly service charges are usually lower. The services not included are available at an additional cost.

Prepaid health care is usually excluded in this type of community; however, most facilities provide some form of primary care through a health center. Residents are given priority for care in the health center, and pay for it at the prevailing rate. If permanent nursing home placement is required, the resident relinquishes his or her independent living unit and no longer pays the monthly service fee.

Similarities and Differences

Table 17-1 summarizes usual provisions in the various types of facilities. Basically, all types of communities provide living accommodations (ranging from semiprivate room to a cottage), housekeeping, linen service, heat, water, electricity, and at least one meal daily. Twenty-four-hour security and emergency call systems are present. Social and recreational activities are available, and other services may be provided on the premises, such as beauty and barber shops, banking, postal services, and convenience stores.

All types of communities require some monthly fee. Life-care and continuing care communities require an entrance fee; traditional retirement communities may or may not require an entrance fee.

Although basic health monitoring and ambulatory care are provided in each type of community, continuing care communities usually require additional payment for nursing home care, whereas the traditional and life-care communities include that service as a prepaid benefit.

In each of the communities, maximum activity, independence, and decision making are promoted. The level of resident involvement is limited only by each individual's interests and energies. (See Table 17-2 for a summary of the advantages and disadvantages of these communities.)

Making a Difference: The Nurse's Role

In any type of continuing care community, the nurse plays a key role and does, indeed, make a difference. The professional's understanding of the normal aging process, expertise in assessment, use of independent judgments, and decision-making ability are constantly challenged. Specific nurs-

TABLE 17-1. Differences among Retirement Communities

	Traditional Retirement Community	Life Care	Continuing Care Community
Financial arrangements[a]	Transfer or conversion of assets; or per diem rate, based on predetermined minimum asset level.	Entrance fees ranging from $30,000 to $125,000, based on type of unit selected, plus monthly service fee ranging from $550 to $2,200.	Entrance fees ranging from $30,000 to $125,000, based on type of unit selected, plus monthly service fee ranging from $250 to $700.
Living accommodations	Single or semiprivate room.	Studio, one-bedroom, or two-bedroom apartments; one- or two-bedroom-den cottages.	Studio, one-bedroom, or two-bedroom apartments; one-bedroom cottages through two-bedroom cottages with den.
Services:	All inclusive.	Bundled.[b]	Unbundled.
Meals	Three a day; snacks available.	Number per day depends on contract; usually three a day with reduced service fee if fewer meals are taken.	Usually one a day; additional at extra cost.
Light housekeeping	All housekeeping done by facility.	Usually once a week.	Usually once a week.
Laundry	Personal laundry and flat linens done by facility.	Flat linens provided and laundered weekly.	Flat linens provided and laundered weekly.
Utilities	All included except telephone; pay phone available.	All included except long-distance phone calls.	All included (telephone may be excluded in some contracts).
Nursing home	Short-term or permanent transfer based on medical condition.	On site; prepaid.	Usually on site; priority for admission; pay current rate.
Health monitoring	Scheduled doctor visits; education.	Ambulatory care; education.	Ambulatory care; education.

[a]Costs vary throughout the United States.
[b]Includes major services, including prepaid health care.

ing functions in this setting include advocacy, support, guidance, identifying and monitoring health problems, promoting self-care and independence, and conducting health education and wellness programs.

Advocacy

The nurse needs to balance the resident's right to personal choice against that which professionals believe to be in the resident's best interest.

Acting as ombudsman for the resident, the nurse needs to assist the caregiving team in striking a balance between presuming "we know what's best" and the right of the resident to exercise personal freedom and judgment. The nurse must work in tandem with other team members.

Problem solving requires careful analysis of the facts before any options for resolution are weighed. The nurse is in a key position to present data that will assist the team in their involvement with the resident. For example, the nurse may be aware of psychosocial problems in the resident's life, may have observed certain functional limitations in the resident's daily activities in the community, or may have learned through other residents that the resident has shown inappropriate behaviors.

Another way in which the nurse fulfills the ombudsman function is by serving as a role model, upholding residents' rights. (Each facility will have

TABLE 17-2. Advantages and Disadvantages of Life-Care Community Living

Advantages	Disadvantages
Healthful life-style; continuity of care; long-term care is provided or accessible; on-site location facilitates visitation by spouse.	Large "up-front" fees deplete investments and estate.
	Prepaid nursing home care, if included in fees, may never be used.
Independent living and continuation of former life-style.	There is no guarantee of solvency of the facility.
Protective environment; 24-hour security.	Some regimentation and loss of privacy in group living.
Management is usually professional.	
Numerous social and recreational opportunities; chance to make new friends and develop meaningful relationships.	
Provides needed support during crisis.	
Freedom from responsibility of maintaining residence.	
Meal preparation and shopping become choices, rather than requirements.	
Services and conveniences are used exclusively by residents of the community.	

Adapted from Worley HW: Retirement Living Alternatives USA. Clemson, SC, Columbia House, 1982, 30.

an established set of rights and responsibilities.) For example, privacy is frequently violated in this setting. Careless and thoughtless comments by other residents or staff members can lead to labeling ("She is senile"; "He is a dirty old man"; "She is an old crank"), with its negative connotations. All members of the team need to maintain confidentiality of information. Furthermore, to gain access to a person's independent living quarters, except in extreme situations, staff should be required to obtain the resident's permission. It will be necessary for the nurse to reinforce these principles to staff and residents.

Support and Guidance

Support should be provided in a manner that does not threaten the independence of the resident.

The nurse will take a leadership role in providing support and guidance to the resident. Often it will be necessary to remain "on the fringes"—to be supportive, yet noninterfering, avoiding overinvolvement in the resident's normal affairs. However, those who live independently may need assistance from time to time. When problems or crises arise, all the staff must be able to listen and provide guidance, offering options and helping the resident to make his or her own decisions.

Many supports are inherent in the continuing care facility. For instance, short-term home health nursing may be indicated for the independently living resident after an illness or injury, and may obviate the need to spend time in the health center of the facility. If the retirement community does not provide this service, it may be obtained through an outside agency. Similarly, in-home meal service, either through the facility or a community program, can help the resident remain independent. For the frailer resident, an emergency telephone answering service can supplement the call system built into independent living units. A special device attached to the telephone and a transmitter that can be carried on the person provide security for the older person by assuring that assistance will be quickly forthcoming.

Identifying and Monitoring Health Problems

The reality that nurses in continuing care communities function in a highly independent role without on-site physician support causes them to carry great responsibility for the prompt identification and referral of residents' problems.

During the admission assessment the nurse obtains data about physical and psychosocial status and functional capacity that will form the baseline for future reference and comparison. Accurate assessment will require the nurse to be familiar with the normal aging process and manifestations of pathology. Every encounter with the resident, be it passing in a hallway or having a casual conversation during an activity, can be used as an opportunity to evaluate changes in status and identify problems. Since physicians may not be in daily attendance at the community, the nurse bears greater responsibility for assessment and interpretation of findings. New findings or changes that the nurse identifies and promptly reports to the physician can save residents serious illness or complications.

Confusion. Probably the greatest need for accurate assessment lies in the area of confusion. The knowledgeable professional will investigate all the components of confusion, evidenced not only by changes in orientation, but also memory, concentration, comprehension, mood, compliance, attention, and interpretation of environmental stimuli. Distinguishing between delirium and dementia is crucial, inasmuch as the acute condition is treatable and reversible. Failure to recognize what is actually going on can lead to labeling and, consequently, mismanagement.

Confusion, especially of sudden onset, requires careful assessment. Here are some questions to consider:

Is confusion related to altered metabolism in the body or interaction between medications?

Has nutritional status been compromised?

Is the resident suffering from dehydration, with resultant fluid and electrolyte imbalance?

Are physical factors contributing to a state of hypoxia?

Are there changes in the resident's patterns of activity, communication, and socialization?

Is there any type of infection present?

Have sensory changes occurred (overload or deficits)?

Does the resident give a history of changes in elimination patterns?

Is the individual depressed?

Is there evidence of increasing immobility?

Is either hypo- or hyperthermia a possibility?

It is important to find out whether the confusion has occurred suddenly or in a gradual, progressive manner. Can it be related to a specific event that triggered the symptoms? Or, has it evolved in a "stair-step" fashion, which may indicate multi-infarct dementia? This condition may be amenable to measures that could reduce the frequency or severity of subsequent cerebral insult. In addition, the discerning nurse will be cognizant of a possible acute delirium superimposed upon a chronic dementia. The severely impaired resident may be unable to verbalize the presence of pain or other symptoms; therefore, the caregiver needs to be sensitive to hidden health problems.

Nurses can also intervene to minimize or eliminate externally caused confusion. The following example demonstrates this principle:

CASE OF MRS. D.

An 86-year-old woman was admitted to a general hospital from a traditional retirement community with a diagnosis of congestive heart failure. She normally wore glasses and a hearing aid. Prior to this episode, Mrs. D. was active, alert, and in full possession of her cognitive faculties. Although she had a long history of intermittent incontinence due to a cystocele, she was able to manage it adequately, and it did not interfere with her activities or socialization.

On admission to an intensive care unit her "valuables" were returned to the retirement community, including her watch, glasses, dentures, and hearing aid. After several days in the hospital, she was described as "very confused" and was physically restrained.

Clearly, failure of the staff to recognize the patient's relocation trauma, sensory overload attributable to this extremely stressful environment, and the sensory deprivation resulting from the loss of her assistive devices all contributed to her confusional state. Recognition of these factors, with appropriate interventions, would undoubtedly have kept confusion to a minimum. Explanation of procedures and environmental happenings, reassurance, use of eyeglasses and hearing aids, and placement of familiar objects within view are just some measures that could prove helpful.

Depression. Depression is a significant problem in older adults in which there is a loss of interest or pleasure in usual activities. Primary, or endogenous, depression is caused by factors internal to the individual. It can occur with or without stressful events. The person may become psychotic or may exhibit sleep and digestive problems and bodily dysfunctions, such as arrhythmias. Delusions and hallucinations may occur; thoughts are disoriented and confused. This type of depression generally responds well to antidepressant drugs.

Secondary, or exogenous depression, is externally caused, usually as a reaction to a crisis or event in the person's environment. This type is often short-lived, lasting two to three months on the average. Symptoms are generally less severe; there are fewer bodily dysfunctions. This type does not always respond to drug therapy. Interpersonal therapy and psychotherapy are more likely to be beneficial.

Regardless of the type, depression in older persons is more likely to lead to suicide than in the young. Furthermore, older people are more apt to complete the act.

In this setting, depression can be easily overlooked. The nurse can identify signs and symptoms that could indicate this serious disorder. Symptoms include emotional, cognitive, and physical components. Blazer (1982, 27) enumerates the following elements of depression in late life:

Decreased life satisfaction; loss of interest

Rumination over problems

Pseudodementia

Somatic complaints

Weight loss

Loss of motivation, low self-esteem, self-criticism

Blazer also lists these additional factors that heighten the risk of suicide:

Social isolation

Sense of emptiness

Pessimism about the future

Cognitive dysfunction

Poor physical health

Recent bereavement

Sleep difficulties, severe insomnia

Agitation

In the older population, white males are at greatest risk of suicide. They are often described as loners, with few close friends; visits by family or friends are infrequent; they do not actively pursue hobbies. Often they suffer from a serious physical illness and experience chronic sleeping problems. They are often unhappy or depressed.

Suicide is an erosion of one's ability to cope. It is a voluntary act; that is, the individual is consciously aware of what he or she is doing. Often the suicidal person provides clues of his or her intent. These signals may be verbal or behavioral, including the following:

Verbal:

"I'm going to kill myself."

"The family will be better off without me."

"You won't be seeing me around."

"I can't stand it much longer."

"I'm in the way all the time."

"Nobody needs me anymore."

"Life has lost all meaning for me."

Behavioral:

Previous serious attempt, especially within last three months.

Giving away valuable possessions.

Sudden inquiries about anatomical donations.

Poor adjustment to a recent loss.

Composing of a suicide note in advance.

Sudden, unexplained recovery from severe depression (may indicate "resolution" of problem by decision to commit suicide).

Depressed persons should be asked if they have considered suicide and given the opportunity to discuss their thoughts openly. These individuals may benefit from referral for psychiatric treatment and close supervision until their mood improves.

These clues, coupled with poor sleeping habits, loss of appetite, and other symptoms of depression, should be taken seriously. It is appropriate to ask if the individual feels so bad as to think about killing himself. Wenz (1986) points out the unlikelihood of "giving someone the idea." Rather, it may be a great relief to bring the question into the open and discuss it freely. Such discussion shows that you are taking the person seriously and responding to his or her potential for distress. If the individual has a plan and the means are available, that person is at very high risk.

The nurse will promptly report such findings to the physician. It is important to *listen* carefully to the resident; focus on his or her problems. Building trust and rapport is imperative. Allow the resident to talk about feelings. Be supportive. Know one's professional limitations, and ensure that appropriate psychiatric treatment is provided. If the nurse believes that the resident is in immediate danger, he or she should not be left alone until help arrives or the danger is past.

Sensory Deficits. Sensory deficits affect the individual's well-being, mental status, and quality of life. The nurse can assist in early detection of deficits and be instrumental in obtaining proper treatment in a timely manner.

Low vision results from age-related disease, such as macular degeneration, glaucoma, diabetic retinopathy, and cataracts. Impaired mobility, safety, reading and writing skills, and self-care capacity frequently accompany vision loss; these problems further compound concurrent losses associated with aging.

It is erroneous to assume that one who is "legally blind" is totally without sight. A goal, therefore, is to maximize residual vision. There are many things that can be done to make life more livable and maintain independence. For example, adjustments can be made to the stove; lighting can be adjusted to provide optimal benefit; safety devices may be installed in the living unit. The individual may be taught travel skills and techniques for performing activities of daily living, as well as leisure pastimes. It is important to investigate low-vision programs in the community and initiate referrals. In the absence of such services, information can be obtained from the American Foundation for the Blind (see sources of help listed in chapter appendix). The manual "Making Life More Livable" (Dickman, 1983), provides many helpful suggestions for improving independence.

Periodic eye examinations are vital for older adults. The nurse should reinforce this fact and, in addition, initiate prompt referral when significant visual impairment is suspected. Likewise, auditory screening can be useful in detecting the underlying cause of problems such as inappropriate responses, social isolation, and depression. (For more discussion on hearing loss see Chapter 13.)

Probably the most neglected area of sensory deficit is speech impairment. There is a risk that the speech-impaired individual may be "written off" and not afforded potentially helpful interventions. The nurse must take the lead and help the client, family members, and caregivers recognize that "a decision not to treat (speech disorders) does not suggest that nothing can be done" (Ryan, 1982, 17). Attempts to establish communication through any means should be encouraged and reinforced (Ryan, 1982, 20). The nurse in the continuing care facility should make every effort to see that residents are evaluated by a speech pathologist when problems are suspected, and that recommendations to enhance communication are consistently followed.

At times, a visit to the resident's living quarters can assist in identifying factors in the environment that can be having a negative effect on health. If the resident resides with someone else, interaction between household members can be observed, thus providing clues about what is actually going on with the resident. Inspection of the medicine cabinet might reveal duplicate medicines, outdated drugs, or other information that could alert the nurse to a potential hazard or possibility of adverse reaction.

Other disciplines might be enlisted to assist in specific monitoring functions. For example, the dining room staff should be trained to observe and report significant changes in eating habits. Many facilities have developed a system to record residents' food selection, either routinely or as needed; such a record is useful when there is a question about a person's nutritional status. Housekeeping staff might be asked to observe certain aspects of the surroundings, such as improperly stored food or presence of insects. During the weekly cleaning, for instance, the worker might note moldy or spoiled food in the refrigerator. This type of information might point out the need for assistance or supervision. In utilizing other disciplines to aid in monitoring, one must be careful to assure that shared information is treated as confidential and used only to benefit the resident.

The management team of retirement communities may hold periodic conferences to review those residents who are at risk of permanent placement in the health center. The nurse's reporting may make a significant difference in reaching proper decisions. Such meetings provide the opportunity to be sure that the entire team considers all viable options and reaches a consensus about what support systems might enable the resident to continue in independent living. Or the team may have to make the painful recommendation that the resident relinquish the independent living unit. In this situation, a caring, supportive attitude by all the team members will help the resident make this transition more easily.

Promotion of Self-care and Independence

Without a conscious awareness of their life-sustaining significance, all individuals routinely perform tasks that maintain life, health, and well-being. When these self-care requirements are not maintained, well-being is jeopardized; illness, or even death, could result.

Orem outlines the self-care requirements as the need for air, water, and food; excretion; activity and rest; solitude and social interaction; avoidance of hazards; and normalcy (Orem, 1985). Each person has unique capabilities to fulfill these self-care demands, but not all will meet them equally well, for various reasons. Age, illness, injury, psychosocial conditions, or disability may cause the individual to need assistance or require him or her to develop compensatory actions. For example, a poststroke patient may compensate for limited mobility by learning to use a walker. The nurse assesses deficits in meeting self-care needs and helps the individual increase capabilities and minimize limitations, in addition to performing specific actions for the resident.

Orem suggests that the nurse may assist in the following ways:

- Acting or doing for
- Guiding
- Supporting
- Providing environment that enables individual to meet needs
- Teaching

Using a different assessment tool, one might evaluate the resident's capabilities for performing activities of daily living (ADL) or instrumental activities of daily living (IADL). The nurse will determine which of these tasks the resident can perform independently and in which he or she is partially or totally dependent.

ADL	IADL
Walking	Shopping
Eating	Meal preparation
Bathing	Transportation
Dressing	Money management
Toileting	Telephone use
Transferring	Housekeeping
	Laundry

Whichever measure of performance one uses, the nurse is responsible for promoting independence wherever possible and for working with other team members to assure that all disciplines are striving for the same goals. Should the resident require hospitalization, the nurse shares information about his or her capabilities with the hospital staff, either through a transfer form or by telephone.

Constant encouragement may be needed to motivate the resident. Sometimes after an episode of illness, the resident may have become quite comfortable with some degree of dependency. The nurse may have to coax, or on occasion, even prod the individual to make maximal use of his or her abilities.

Assistance provided should be the least amount needed to achieve the task at hand. For example, if the cognitively impaired resident can use a fork or even a spoon to feed himself, he should be allowed to do so—not be spoonfed by staff. If instructing the Alzheimer patient how to bathe himself gets the job done, one should not give him a complete bed bath. It is difficult to sit back and watch someone perform simple acts in a clumsy fashion, but it is certainly more beneficial to his dignity and self-esteem.

Independence in decision making is just as important as in performing daily living activities. The resident who lives in the health center is at greater risk of losing this precious right than is the one who resides in the housing units. The staff can, at least, allow him or her to choose what clothes to wear—even if they do not match. The nurse can recommend policies that would allow flexibility in scheduling personal hygienic measures, such as allowing a resident to "sleep in" and not be awakened at the usual hour.

The nurse can encourage staff to examine policies and do what is possible to allow more freedom to the resident and to reduce regimentation. An individual who has always stayed up to watch the 11 o'clock news, for instance, should be permitted to do so, as long as she does not disturb other residents. Policies should serve the best interests of the residents, not the convenience of the staff.

> The essence of nursing in a continuing care community is the promotion of independence and self-care.

Health Education and Wellness

Traditionally, education has always been a function of the nurse; in this setting it takes on new meanings. In retirement communities, there are constant teaching opportunities, whether one-on-one or in groups. A great deal of incidental teaching occurs during routine interaction with each resident. The astute nurse will be alert to learning needs and will seize the "teachable moment."

Health education and wellness programs go hand-in-hand. The nurse can determine which topics need to be taught, based on health needs of the residents within the community. Programs on arthritis, hypertension, managing heart disease, diabetes, and osteoporosis are examples of disease-specific subjects that may be presented in group seminars. Or, discussions of safety and accident prevention, early detection of illness, dangers of excessive heat or cold, or other more general matters may be offered.

The nurse may do some, or all, of the teaching, utilizing available resources. Community colleges are an excellent source and are usually very eager to assist with such educational programs. These local educational institutions have well-trained instructors. Exercise classes, for example, can be geared to the various functional levels of the residents. Nutritional experts are available to instruct in proper dietary habits as a means to promote health. Use of such resources as these can contribute much toward a total program of wellness.

Nurses can organize and direct health screening programs, either on site or in conjunction with community agencies, allowing residents to participate in their health care without feeling that they are "sick." Taking part in such an activity enhances the resident's sense of control.

An important aspect of learning for the continuing care resident is preparation for hospitalization. While we, as nurses, take hospital procedures for granted, they are foreign, and often frightening, to the resident. Making him or her aware of what to expect will do much to alleviate anxiety and, perhaps, prevent complications or confusion while hospitalized. Similarly, one should educate residents about long-term care in order to ease the transition to the health center, should that become necessary. It can be useful for the nurse to be available to residents who may have received preoperative or test instructions from physicians' offices, hospital outpatient departments, and so on. The resident may have been overloaded with so many directives that bewilderment may result. The nurse can help clarify questions that may arise and reinforce what has been taught.

In this day of early hospital discharges and mandatory same-day surgery, the nurse can supplement teaching given to the resident by staff in other care settings. When indicated, these supplemental activities should include communicating with the doctor, hospital nurse, therapist, or other health professional about instructions that are not clear. The nurse might check with the resident who is returning to the retirement community to see whether help is needed.

Older adults can and will reduce risks if given adequate information, time to absorb it, and appropriate follow-up. The professional has a great responsibility to observe and interpret clues about potential learning needs and to see that appropriate intervention occurs.

Above all, the nurse must continually emphasize that the resident is responsible for his or her own health and encourage wellness practices.

As educator, the nurse must also assume responsibility for teaching personnel about matters relating to the health and psychosocial well-being of the resident. These personnel would include staff members in service departments other than nursing. First and foremost, misconceptions about the aging process, stereotyping, and negative attitudes need to be addressed. The professional is more likely to be able to bring about changes in these areas by becoming knowledgeable about techniques of adult learning. Community colleges and other providers of continuing education offer courses that can teach such skills.

Nursing Opportunities

Various opportunities exist for the nurse working in the continuing care community. In the outpatient department, if one exists, the nurse has a chance to observe residents over long periods of time, get to know them as unique individuals, promote wellness, provide health education, and intervene when physical or psychosocial problems arise. This position, sometimes filled by a nurse practitioner, also provides opportunity for the nurse to act as a case manager—to determine the resident's needs for services and to link with the appropriate services at the proper time. Knowing when to wean the resident from dependence on various services and providing support during this process are of equal importance.

In the health center of the facility, the nurse performs a leadership role in coordinating all aspects of care for the benefit of the resident. Multidisciplinary care planning guided by the nurse, advocacy, and role modeling are some of the means of accomplishing this purpose.

For one who has leadership skills and interests, the opportunity exists to assume managerial positions within the department of nursing. Or, beyond that, the nurse might pursue additional education to meet licensing requirements for nursing home administration.

As continuing care communities become more sophisticated and responsive to residents' needs, a greater depth of understanding of the characteristics of older people will be essential. One's nursing background, augmented by special training, might well lead to an emerging role for the nurse in housing management.

Appendix: Sources of Help

For assistance or further information the nurse should contact the following:

American Association of Homes for the Aging
1050 17th Street, NW, Suite 770
Washington, DC 20036
Publication: *Provider News*

American Health Care Association
1200 15th Street, NW
Washington, DC 20005

National Association for Senior Living Industries
125 Cathedral Street
Annapolis, MD 21401

American Speech-Language-Hearing Association
10801 Rockville Pike
Rockville, MD 20852

American Foundation for the Blind
15 West 16th Street
New York, NY 10011

Alexander Graham Bell Association for the Deaf
3417 Volta Place, NW
Washington, DC 20007

State and local Offices on Aging

REFERENCES

Annotated Code of Maryland, Article 70B, S7, 1985.

Blazer DG II: Depression in Late Life. St. Louis, CV Mosby, 1982.

Dickman I: Making Life More Livable. New York, American Foundation for the Blind, 1983.

Orem D: Nursing: Concepts of Practice. 3rd ed. New York, McGraw-Hill, 1985.

Ryan WJ: The Nurse and the Communicatively Impaired Adult. New York, Springer, 1982.

Wenz F: Geriatric suicide: Assessment and prevention. Unpublished paper presented at Pennsylvania State University Continuing Education Program, Harrisburg, PA, December 5, 1986.

Worley HW: Retirement Living Alternatives USA. Clemson, SC, Columbia House, 1982.

BIBLIOGRAPHY

Barbaro E, Noyes L: A wellness program for a life-care community. The Gerontologist 24(6): 568–571, 1984.

Evashwick CJ, Weiss LJ: Managing the Continuum of Care. Rockville, MD, Aspen Publishers, 1987.

Hendrickson MC: Assisted living: An emerging focus in an expanding market. Contemporary Long Term Care 11(7): 20–22, 1988.

Lanning NM: The rainbow to wellness . . . health maintenance clinic for seniors' apartment complex. Can Nurs 82(11): 22–26, 1986.

Lawhorn C: Transportation as an amenity in CCRC's. Contemporary Long Term Care 11(7): 24–26, 1988.

Seip DE: How is your retirement project doing? Contemporary Long Term Care 11(8): 24–25, 1988.

Thomas M: Retirement housing industry burgeoning. Contemporary Long Term Care 11(7): 27–35, 74, 1988.

CHAPTER 18

The Role of the Nurse in Adult Day Care

Kay Mehlferber

Chapter Objectives
At the completion of this chapter the reader will be able to:

1. Define adult day care.
2. Discuss the development of adult day care.
3. List the typical services of an adult day-care program.
4. Differentiate among the various types of day-care programs.
5. Describe the nurse's role in adult day care.

Nursing in an adult day-care setting is an exciting and challenging employment opportunity. More than merely a means of providing health care services in a community setting, nursing in an adult day-care program offers experiences in administration, grantsmanship, advocacy, counseling, direct care, mediation, problem solving, assessment and evaluation, fund raising, community networking, and education of clients, their families, and staff. Before describing the nursing role in adult day care, it will be useful to review this unique service.

Characteristics of Adult Day Care

The National Institute on Adult Day Care (NIAD) Steering Committee (1984, 20) defines adult day care as a community-based group program designed to meet the needs of functionally impaired adults through an individual plan of care. The program is structured and comprehensive, providing a variety of health, social, and related support services in a protective setting during a portion of the day (i.e., not on a 24-hour basis). Individuals attend on a planned basis, during specified hours. Adult day care helps families and other caregivers to continue caring for an impaired person at home by providing respite and supplemental care.

Development

Adult day-care programs were started in the 1920s in Moscow because of the shortage of inpatient facilities for psychiatric patients. Great Britain a decade later developed psychiatric day hospitals. The first geriatric center was developed in 1952 in the Oxford Day Care Hospital in England. Many of the early day-care programs grew from the need of the elderly for occupational therapy and recreationally and therapeutically oriented services, such as arts and crafts, games, and exercise. Initial day-care programs in England, in addition to offering occupational therapy, provided physical therapy and medical and social services. (In England, there is often little difference between day care and day hospitals in terms of services provided; the major differences lie in funding sources.)

Adult day care originated as a psychiatric treatment program. In the 1960s the focus of services shifted to chronic health care and an alternative to nursing home placement.

The adult day-care movement came later and more slowly in the United States. As in the Soviet Union and England, there was a need to reduce inpatient psychiatric hospital care by preventing institutionalization or deinstitutionalizing; thus the early day-care programs were psychiatric in focus. The Menninger Clinic in 1947 and the Yale Psychiatric Clinic in 1949 were early examples of adult day care under the psychiatric day hospital model.

As the movement toward alternatives to nursing home care and community-based care grew in the 1960s, day-care centers shifted from a psychiatric to a general health focus. The Handmaker Jewish Geriatric Center in Tucson, Arizona, and the Neshaminy Manor Day Care Program in Doylestown, Pennsylvania, emerged in 1967, soon to be followed by other programs.

In 1971, Dr. Lionel Z. Cousin, who introduced the day-care concept in Oxford and later developed an adult day-care program at Cherry State Hospital in North Carolina, testified to the Senate Subcommittee on Long Term Care on the viability of adult day care in the long-term care continuum. Dr. Cousin's testimony was influential in the authorization of funds (through Public Law 92–603, Section 222) for demonstration projects in which selected facilities could be reimbursed for adult day care through special waivers to Medicare. Since that time the number of day-care programs has steadily grown: By 1977 nearly 300 programs existed; in 1980 more than 600 programs were identified; and in 1985 the National Institute on Adult Day Care identified more than 1,000 programs.

In the late 1970s state day-care associations emerged to promote the growth and quality of services of adult day-care programs. Today there are 35 state associations that share common interests and goals through their affiliation with NIAD, a constituent of the National Council on the Aging, Inc. NIAD has been successful in developing and publishing national standards for adult day care, as well as promoting federal legislation to expand reimbursement of adult day-care services.

Services

Adult day-care programs provide individual and group services for adults with physical, emotional, or mental impairments. These innovative programs organize and mesh traditional health, social, and other therapeutic services to reduce the participant's isolation and loneliness, foster socialization and peer interaction, and promote a maximum level of health and

The goal of adult day care is not only to provide comprehensive services to the participant, but also to afford respite to family caregivers.

functional independence. Adult day care provides a holistic approach to individuals within their environments, recognizing their uniqueness in relation to the many factors affecting coping ability.

Building upon the supportive environment offered within a group setting, adult day-care programs work toward the following goals:

- Maintenance of participants at their present level of functioning as long as possible.
- Prevention or delay of deterioration.
- Restoration and rehabilitation of participants to their highest level of function.
- Increasing awareness and utilization of other services along the continuum of care.
- Promotion of maximum level of independence.
- Facilitation of socialization and peer interaction.
- Provision of support and respite for family members and caregivers.

As the goals imply, adult day care benefits caregivers and families in addition to participants. Caregivers can learn new techniques of care management and be offered support. Caregivers may be able to maintain employment with the knowledge that their elder is being supervised and receiving necessary care. Relationships between the participant and family or caregivers can be enhanced as respite and time away from each other are afforded. The utilization of adult day-care services can make community-based care a viable and manageable alternative to institutionalization.

Types of Programs

Many models of adult day care are operating today. Some fall under the category of *restoration programs* in which the monitoring of health problems and the provision of prescribed therapies are provided. *Maintenance day-care programs,* which offer basic health supervision, personal care, and psychosocial activities, are another model. *Social programs* range from the provision of mere socialization opportunities to those that include mechanisms to link participants with formal health services. Existing programs are located in senior centers, nursing homes, churches, psychiatric hospitals, life-care communities, and private homes. The unique location and population served influence the program model followed. For instance, a church-based day-care program may be interested primarily in providing a warm meal and socialization opportunities for participants, while a hospital-based program may provide aggressive rehabilitation services for continuing care of discharged patients.

Most day-care programs are sponsored by not-for-profit private and public agencies. Proprietary day care is beginning to be developed by corporations and individuals; only time and experience will determine whether adult day care can become a successful profit-making business.

Eligibility

To qualify for adult day care, most applicants must meet criteria established within the individual program. In most programs, applicants receive a comprehensive evaluation of medical, functional, and psychosocial status by a multidisciplinary team. Based on results of the assessments, the team determines whether applicants are appropriate for the specific program and whether their needs can be met by it.

Funding of day care is provided through Medicare, Medicaid, Title III of the Older Americans Act, and a mix of local public and private sources. Upon application, participants can have their eligibility for reimbursement determined by designated staff. Of course, participants can pay privately for this service.

Cost

The different models and locations of adult day care cause a wide range of program costs. The national average cost in 1986, according to NIAD, was $21.00 to $25.00 a day.

Staffing of Programs

Staffing patterns in adult day-care programs are influenced by the needs of the participants and the organizational environment in which the program is located. In addition, state regulations for licensure will dictate certain staffing requirements. Staff positions listed as a guide by NIAD include the following:

Program director

Nurse

Social worker

Activities director

Program assistants/aides

Physical, occupational, speech, and recreational therapists

Secretary/bookkeeper

Drivers

Consultants: physicians, psychiatrists, dentists, nutritionists, podiatrists, business and financial management personnel, attorneys

The Nurse's Role

The role of the nurse in an adult day-care program is indeed multidimensional. In many programs the nurse serves as the director, in addition to the program nurse. In the administrative role of director, the nurse has responsibility for the daily operation of the program, including hiring and firing personnel, scheduling, planning and monitoring the budget, developing policies and procedures and making sure they are followed, evaluating the program's performance, and maintaining a linkage with various providers and professional and community groups. Management competency is essential to fulfilling this role.

The clinical role is a major responsibility of the adult day-care nurse. Astute assessment skills enable the nurse to identify health problems and judge the appropriateness of applicants for the program. The nurse can plan interventions that facilitate the participant's ability to meet program goals and assure that the actions of all staff are consistent with the plan of care. A variety of direct services may be provided by the nurse, such as medication administration, range of motion exercises, and dressing changes. Extremely important is the nurse's ongoing monitoring of participants' health status; timely identification of changes in status and communication of these changes to participants' physicians can significantly reduce complications and promote maximum independence. For example, the nurse may determine that a participant developed an unsteady gait after an antidepressant drug was initiated. When this feedback is offered to the physician, the medication may be changed, sparing the participant functional limitations and a potential fall.

The nurse frequently serves as counselor to participants and their families. Participants may need to use the nurse as an objective sounding board in discussing personal issues, such as concerns over an offspring's lifestyle. Participants may need advice, information, or referral for a wide range of problems, including how to write a will, where to obtain financial aid, and how to confront a relative with a complaint. Effective listening skills are demanded of the nurse, as well as the ability to recognize his or her own limitations and obtain the assistance of other professionals.

The role of educator is also filled by the nurse. Participants and their caregivers can be instructed in techniques to perform prescribed procedures, ways to recognize adverse medication reactions, and how to complete reimbursement forms. Health education programs can be taught to groups of participants as an ongoing program activity. Special education programs can be offered to caregivers or the community at large. Of course, the nurse will conduct formal in-service education classes for staff, in addition to capitalizing on opportunities for informal learning during daily care activities.

Advocacy is intrinsic to all actions of the adult day-care nurse. The participants, as elderly, vulnerable individuals, will need an advocate to assist them in obtaining the resources and care they need. The nurse will ensure that participants are treated with dignity and individuality, and that their maximum level of independence is fostered. Family caregivers may need the nurse to advocate on their behalf by aiding their efforts to negotiate with formal systems, and the nurse may also have to support them as they balance their personal needs against the participant's. In addition, the nurse will advocate the expansion and reimbursement of day-care services as an effective means of community-based care.

This discussion hardly exhausts the roles available to the adult day-care nurse. There are ample opportunities for nurses in this setting to have an impact on the quality of life of the elderly, promote family health, and mold a relatively new health care service. Very significant, also, is the opportunity for nurses to demonstrate the difference nursing can make in the provision of adult day-care services.

REFERENCE

NIAD Steering Committee: Standards for Adult Day Care. Washington, DC, National Council on the Aging/National Institute on Adult Day Care, 1984.

BIBLIOGRAPHY

Cherry DL: Adapting day care to the needs of adults with dementia. The Gerontologist 28(1): 116–120, 1988.

Korhumel EA: Creating an adult day care center. Geriatr Nurs 9(1): 35–37, 1988.

Masson V: How nursing happens in adult day care. Geriatr Nurs 7(1): 18–23, 1986.

Nolan MR: The future role of day hospitals for the elderly: The case for a nursing initiative. J Adv Nurs 12(6): 683–690, 1987.

O'Brien C (ed): Adult Day Care Centers: A Practical Guide. Monterey, CA, Wadsworth, 1982.

Padula H: Developing Adult Day Care. Washington, DC, National Council on Aging, 1983.

Szekais B: Adult day centers: Geriatric day health services in the community. J Family Prac 20(2): 157–161, 1985.

CHAPTER 19

Support Groups for Caregivers of Alzheimer's Disease Victims: The Nurse's Role

Mary Edwards

Chapter Objectives
At the completion of this chapter the reader will be able to:

1. Describe the characteristics and reactions of caregivers of Alzheimer's victims.
2. Discuss the three popular models for support groups.
3. Outline the major roles of the nurse who works with support groups.

Alzheimer's disease (AD) has been defined as an irreversible, progressive, fatal neurological disorder that causes decline in intellectual functions and in the ability to perform routine activities. The disease slowly erodes victims' ability to remember, solve problems, and control their emotions and their bodies, ending in the ultimate "loss of self" (Cohen and Eisdorfer, 1986). Although AD has struck some patients as young as 40, most of its victims are 65 and older. According to the Alzheimer's Disease and Related Disorders Association (ADRDA), AD affects 9% of the U.S. population over the age of 55 and 20% of persons over 85 years of age. Therefore, as the American population grays, society can expect AD to become what many scientists label as the "epidemic of the next century."

Wives and daughters carry the major responsibility for the care of Alzheimer's victims.

Alzheimer's disease is no respecter of sex, race, income, or beauty. Actress Rita Hayworth, actor Edmond O'Brien, author Ross MacDonald, and artist Norman Rockwell had their talents robbed by AD. The disease affects 2.5 million Americans. When the impact on the victim's family is taken into account, the total toll reaches approximately 10 million.

The AD victim dies a double death: first the mind, and then the body. During this death course the caregiver becomes entrapped in the continuing grief process, described by some as "the long goodbye" and the "ongoing funeral" (Kapust, 1982), which adds to the already difficult burden of caregiving. As dementia becomes more widespread, health care providers must meet not only the needs of the victim, but also the needs of the "hidden patient" (Fengler and Goodrich, 1979), the victim's caregiver.

Caregivers: Profile and Reactions

Although many men are caregivers, most caregivers for the elderly are women (Cantor, 1983; Soldo and Myllyluoma, 1983). The female caregiving group may include wives, daughters, or other related and unrelated people.

During the early stages of dementia, caregiving may consume the caregiver's free or recreational time (Cantor, 1983). Later as the disease progresses and the victim loses more control, the caregiving activities begin to interfere with the caregiver's homemaking, work, family, and personal care activities.

A major factor affecting the caregiver is the degree to which the caregiver is stressed by competing demands (Woods et al., 1985). Many of the caregiver's demands depend on his or her developmental stages. If the caregiver is middle-aged, her demands may come from her roles as homemaker, mother, wife, employee, and community volunteer. These caregivers are described as "the women in the middle" (Brody, 1981) and "the sandwich generation" (Teusink and Mahler, 1984). They are torn between the conflicting demands of their work, marriages, children, and responsibilities to care both for older relatives and for the younger generation (Woods et al., 1985). One middle-aged mother and caregiver whose father was a resident in a nursing home was surprised when her adolescent daughter asked her if she would be spending more time at home when grandfather died. Additional stresses of the increasing divorce rate and distant families add to the burdens of the middle-aged caregiver.

Spouses of AD victims are especially vulnerable to the demands of caregiving. Because of their age, they may be adjusting to age-related health changes. Thus, maintaining a healthy equilibrium may be a precarious process for the older spouse.

Male and female caregivers of different developmental stages and life experiences tend to pass through various phases of reaction as the disease consumes their family member. Woods and colleagues (1985) describe "six phases of reaction":

1. Initial recognition of the problem.
2. Clarification and emotional acceptance of the diagnosis, sometimes including extensive seeking of opinions and potential cures.
3. Establishment of appropriate expectations.
4. Grieving.
5. Problem solving and coping with respect to the AD victim's deteriorating behavior.
6. Decision making regarding appropriate care for the AD victim.

In Teusink and Mahler's (1984) article "Helping Families Cope with Alzheimer's Disease," five reactive phases similar to the grief process described by Kübler-Ross (1969) are discussed.

Phase 1: Denial

Although denial can be beneficial in providing time for the caregiver to organize thoughts, it can be problematic in terms of preventing the caregiver from making important decisions and plans.

Denial is the avoidance of disagreeable realities by ignoring or refusing to recognize them. It is probably the simplest and most used of all defense mechanisms (Stuart and Sundeen, 1983). When a person is first faced with a crisis, denial may be therapeutic in that it prevents total emotional collapse and allows the person time to reorganize his or her thoughts. However, denial soon becomes untherapeutic when it prevents the person from making realistic assessments and decisions.

The family and the caregiver may find it quite easy to deny AD in the early stages. Many times caregivers fail to accept the diagnosis when grossly disturbed behavior and deterioration in functioning occur. For example, even after two physicians told one wife that her husband, in all probability, was a victim of AD, the wife continued to take her husband to their country club's golf course each day to play a round of golf alone. The victim would usually become disoriented on the second tee and wander around the course until a country club member brought him to the clubhouse. The wife only stopped taking her husband to the course when the manager insisted that her practice was unsafe for her husband.

Caregivers who exhibit unhealthy denial can be helped through education, and at times through confrontation, to recognize the extent of the disability of the AD victim. Only after the resolution of their denial can the caregivers make realistic plans for the future and move toward an acceptance of their loved ones' illness.

Phase 2: Overinvolvement

As the disease progresses, the caregiver must take on more responsibilities for the victim. Friends and relatives usually reduce their visits, and the caregiving falls to one person.

There is a risk of promoting unnecessary dependency in the victim and emotional stress in the caregiver when the caregiver performs activities for the victim that the victim is able to do independently.

It is well documented that the AD victim should be encouraged to perform as many self-care activities as possible, as long as safety is not jeopardized. With overinvolvement, the caregiver assists to the extent of denying the victim even the simplest participation in his or her care, thereby sacrificing the caregiver's personal life and freedom in giving minute-to-minute care to the loved one. For example, when confronted with her husband's diagnosis of AD, a wife pledged that she would care for him at home until he died. She immediately took a martyr role and stopped attending all her usual club and church meetings, thus allocating all her time to her husband's needs, even self-care needs that could be sufficiently met by the victim at that time. Overinvolvement may be a product of loyalty, guilt, or an attempt to gain love that was denied the caregiver before the victim became ill. Eventually, though, when the overinvolvement becomes unbearable, anger, grief, and depression may become a problem for the caregiver.

The caregiver who is experiencing overinvolvement must be helped to see his or her behavior as a hindrance rather than a help in dealing with the victim's needs. One helpful approach may be to confront the relatives with the specific difficulties their overinvolvement is creating for the victim and the other members of the family. Another approach that has proven to be successful is having caregivers who have experienced the same care needs consult with the overinvolved person and offer personal experiences of how they worked through and accepted the reality that help was needed from others, and that it was all right to give time and energy to their personal needs.

Phase 3: Anger

Changes in the roles, responsibilities, and relationships that result from care of the Alzheimer's disease victim can cause anger in the caregiver. This anger often is displaced to members of the family or health care teams.

Anger, a feeling of resentment that occurs when an individual perceives a threat, may develop not only from the physical burden of caring for the AD victim, the embarrassment caused by the victim's behavioral problems, or family role reversal, but also from the feeling of having been abandoned by the still living, yet afunctional, loved one. Anger is often projected onto the victim, other family members, or health care providers. For instance, one expression of anger occurred when a daughter whose demented mother lived in a local nursing home constantly complained to the administrator that her mother was receiving poor nursing care. Investigation by the nursing home administration and director of nursing service did not support the daughter's accusations. Subsequently, the daughter took her mother home, only to readmit her several weeks later.

Rabins and colleagues (1982) interviewed 55 primary caregivers of AD victims. Feelings of anger and sadness were reported by 48 of the caregivers. Other problems the caregivers cited were family conflicts, loss of friends and hobbies, difficulty with role reversal, and worry that they would become unable to care for the AD victim.

The need to discharge tension is fundamental in alleviating anger. If unrelieved anger continues, the caregiver may develop somatic complaints or depression, or displace his or her feelings on others. Caregivers must confront their anger, relieve their tension, and accept that it is all right to be angry. One man who was caring for his ill wife at home frequently became angry when he thought about their interrupted plans for travel during their retirement years. When his anger began to build, he would ask his neighbors to stay with his wife while he walked around the block several times.

Talking with other caregivers who have experienced similar needs may be a way of accepting the idea that it is all right to be angry at how AD has victimized one's loved one as well as one's own life. Anger is a normal emotion and can be therapeutically alleviated.

Phase 4: Guilt

Stuart and Sundeen (1983) describe guilt as a destructive activity by which an individual terrorizes and punishes himself. A caregiver's feeling of guilt may stem from his or her feeling that he or she did not recognize the loved one's illness early enough and delayed bringing the victim to the doctor, or that he or she was not attentive enough to the loved one before the onset of the illness. Probably the strongest response is the caregiver's feeling of wanting the ill loved one to die (Teusink and Mahler, 1984). For example, after hospitalization for depression, a husband of an AD victim admitted that many times he traced the steps he would take in murdering his ill wife. The medical bills had absorbed their savings, and the man thought that if he killed his wife he could save their home. The guilt he experienced from having such thoughts and plans resulted in his hospitalization.

> Wanting the victim to die can be a response of the caregiver that produces tremendous guilt. Through support group discussions the caregiver may learn that many caregivers have had similar feelings.

Teusink and Mahler maintain that caregivers can only deal with guilt after discovering its cause and taking corrective steps to alleviate it. One step may be to educate the caregiver about the illness, thereby providing reassurance that the caregiver has not harmed the AD victim by his or her delay in seeking medical advice. Another step may be to talk with the other caregivers of AD victims to learn that one is not alone or bad because of one's feelings of anger or guilt. In some cases personal counseling may be needed to help caregivers recognize and work through their feelings for the AD victim.

Phase 5: Acceptance

Teusink and Mahler (1984) list four steps that must be accomplished before acceptance of the disease and its consequences occurs:

1. Understanding the disease process that is affecting their loved one.
2. Finding sufficient resources within themselves and the community to deal with the increased burden of care for the loved one.
3. Working through their responses of denial, overinvolvement, anger, and guilt.
4. Recognizing that their loved one is no longer the person they once knew.

By working through these four steps, the caregiver learns that acceptance is not a time of hopelessness, but rather a time of acknowledging the terminal condition of the loved one and of realizing his or her own personal capabilities in caring for the loved one.

Every caregiver undergoes different but similar reactions to the AD that is destroying a loved one and interfering with the caregiver's personal life. However, an understanding of these reactions and the involved emotions can prepare the nurse and other health care providers for their role in the service of support groups.

Support Groups

Support groups are only one component of a continuum of care needed for chronic deteriorating illnesses. As with other services, such as adult day care, home care, and institutional care, registered nurses can be instrumental in leadership, research, and many other roles.

There are two support group organizations that specialize in assisting AD caregivers. These organizations are the Alzheimer's Disease and Related Disorders Association, Inc. (ADRDA), and the Family Survival Project for Brain-Damaged Adults. (The services and address of the ADRDA are indicated in its newsletter, shown in Figure 19-1.) One of the major functions of both of these organizations is the sponsorship of support groups. Because of the national scope of the ADRDA, this organization will be used as the major support group reference.

Benefits

Middleton (1984) defined a caregiver's support group as a coming together of people with common problems in an effort to understand and cope with their problems through shared experiences, as well as to gain reassurance that each is not alone in his or her situation. Kapust and Weintraub (1984) assert that this kind of support is especially needed for AD caregivers, who often feel powerless under their loved ones' incurable and irreversible diagnosis of Alzheimer's disease. Lieberman (1985) states that self-help groups produce measurable positive changes using processes distinct from those commonly employed in psychotherapy. Many experts maintain that the best way to provide support and information to caregivers is through support groups.

In contrast to these studies, there is some literature suggesting that support groups may be harmful for some people. Steuer (1984) states: "While we know little about the positive effects of these groups, we know almost nothing about the negative effects of these groups." Steuer found some evidence to suggest that some group members were more depressed and anxious after participation in group meetings. This negative effect may be in response to the caregiver's defense mechanism of denial. Also, it is to be remembered that not all persons respond positively to group participation and may find assistance from other therapies, such as one-to-one counseling and meetings with family members and friends, more therapeutic. The possibility of the caregivers attending an untherapeutic meeting with poor leadership and group dynamics may also be a factor in some caregivers' criticism of this mode of therapy.

Support groups can be effective in reducing feelings of isolation and hopelessness, increasing caregiving information and skills, and initiating ongoing supportive networks.

Because of the rapid growth in support groups and the many positive testimonials by group members, it is safe to state that vast numbers of people find support groups to be beneficial. Between 1980 and 1986, ADRDA grew from seven to 149 chapters and more than 1,000 support groups nationwide (ADRDA, 1986).

In a study of nearly 300 caregiver support groups, Lidoff and Harris (1985) listed four major benefits reported by group participants. First, the caregiver's feelings of hopelessness and isolation were reduced in the nonjudgmental company of others experiencing similar situations. Second, the caregivers received information about the progression of AD, new research breakthroughs, and community resources. Third, interaction among caregivers helped develop skills in stress management, problem solving, and home

A.D.™ Alzheimer's Disease
and Related Disorders Association, Inc.
NEWSLETTER

VOL. 8 NO. 1 SPRING 1988   70 EAST LAKE STREET, CHICAGO, ILLINOIS 60601

New Book Puts Vital Resources in Caregivers' Hands

Tremendous strides have been made during the past decade to make resources available to those individuals involved in caring for victims of Alzheimer's Disease (AD). *Understanding Alzheimer's Disease* organizes these resources into a single easy-to-use handbook format for families and other caregivers.

"Before 1974 there was a tendency to write off people who showed signs of senility," says Robert N. Butler, M.D., chairman of the Department of Geriatrics and Adult Development, Mount Sinai Medical Center in New York City. "It has (since) become clear that much can be done to improve the lives of Alz-

heimer victims if patients and caregivers can maximize their coping abilities... This book can help," added Butler, who wrote the book's foreword.

Edited by Dr. Miriam Aronson, associate professor of neurology and psychiatry at Albert Einstein College of Medicine, New York, *Understanding Alzheimer's Disease* is the first book by ADRDA. Drawing on the expertise of 26 leading researchers, physicians, nurses, psychiatrists, lawyers and caregivers, the book clarifies many complex issues surrounding Alzheimer's.

Case studies, checklists, illustrations, questions, and explanations of medical

(Please turn to page 2)

Presidential Candidates Speak Out on Long-Term Care

Introduction by Edward F. Truschke, President, ADRDA

The 1988 presidential campaign presents a unique opportunity to bring an issue of major importance to the forefront of the campaign: long-term care. This year we can play an active role in making long-term care a central issue on the political agenda.

Our commitment to raising America's consciousness on long-term care is driven by the threat of physical, emotional and financial bankruptcy faced by the 2.5 million Alzheimer patients and their families. We have joined hundreds of other organizations such as American Association of Retired Persons in a

national campaign called "Long-Term Care '88."

To increase awareness, we have invited the thirteen candidates for President of the United States to make their position on long-term care known to the readers of this newsletter. Specifically, each candidate was asked to explain 1) what actions he would take as President to bring about a more responsive, appropriate and cost-effective system of health care for the chronically ill and 2) how that system would be financed.

(Please turn to page 6)

FIGURE 19-1. ADRDA *Newsletter*. (Reprinted with permission from Alzheimer's Disease and Related Disorders *Newsletter*.)

care techniques. Finally, group participation built a support network that extends beyond group meetings into enduring mutual help and friendships.

Models

There are several models of support groups. Three of the most popular— educational, mutual support, and a combined type—are described by Schmall (1984). *Educational models* are open groups in which information is presented by professional or lay caregivers. Information may pertain to ethical issues, coping skills, legal issues, and decision making. The disadvantage of the educational model is that it does not provide emotional support; however, the model can serve as an effective springboard for participants eventually attending mutual support groups (Schmall, 1984).

In *mutual support groups* information is shared, and coping strategies for the care of the AD victim are given and received. Miller (1981) contends that sharing and listening increase understanding of problems, which in turn helps caregivers to develop new patterns of behavior. Validation of the caregivers' feelings is important—it may lead to caregivers accepting their right to care for themselves.

The third model, a *combination of the educational and mutual support* groups, frequently devotes the first hour of a two-hour meeting to a formal educational presentation, and the second to sharing and support.

There is debate about whether a mutual support group should be open to anyone interested in attending or closed to everyone except designated members. The problems with an open meeting are that heterogeneous groups may be less enduring than homogeneous ones, and new members may have a greater need for basic information than people who have been group members for years and whose needs may be to investigate extended care available to the AD victim. Of course, the big disadvantage to the closed group is that a caregiver may be excluded from the support of an available group.

Some groups have used the technique of dividing the group by relationship to the victim after the opening social time and introductions. Usually this results in two sections: one for spouses and one for adult children. This forms a more homogeneous group for personal sharing.

Younger family members need assistance with their reactions to the victim. Support groups for children and grandchildren can facilitate adjustment to and acceptance of the victim's disease.

The newest extension of support groups is the support group for children and grandchildren of AD victims. Weaver (1982) states that the AD victim's illness cannot be treated as a problem outside of the family system, and whenever the family system is threatened by AD, the child or grandchild becomes a part of that threat and needs to be included in the adjustment process. Support groups for children assist in the adjustment process by providing a place where it is okay to feel anger, resentment, and jealousy. After validating these feelings, the child is likely to become more tolerant and accepting of his or her demented grandparent and more willing to assist parents in the caregiving role.

The structure of a support group for children is different from that of an adult group. The most important difference is that, if at all possible, the leader should be a professional instead of a parent. The program should also be activity oriented and flexible, and thus promote participation by the children. Active discussion concerning the children's feelings of disappointment can be encouraged by the use of such stimulators as pictures of grandparents, parents, and children. Introduction of the book *Grandpa Doesn't Know It's Me* (Guthrie, 1986) may be used to stimulate discussions on their feelings of having a grandparent who is no longer the same person they once knew. Weaver suggested posing several open-ended questions such as "I get angry when . . ." and "Most days I feel . . ." to provoke expressions of additional feelings by the children. Most important, the focus of the group should be on the children's concerns, problems, and needs, not on the person with the disease (Schmall, 1984).

In addition to the selection of the model, other factors involved in establishing a successful support group include affiliation, membership, logistics, and most important, facilitation. Affiliation with a credible organization legitimizes the support group as well as assists in attracting caregivers and community support. ADRDA and the Family Survival Project are both worthy organizations that provide sponsorship, current information on AD, access to national, state, and community resources, and support-group organization guides.

Membership

Membership in open support groups is unrestricted; however, consideration should be given to the presence of professionals and AD victims in a mutual support group. Professionals who support group goals and guidelines can be a great asset in furnishing information and assisting as group facilitators. Controversy arises when professionals, by their sheer number, dominate the group and intimidate sharing by some caregivers. If at all possible, permission from the group should be gained before interested professionals who are not regular members attend the meetings.

Most groups have discovered that it is best not to invite persons afflicted with AD to the group meeting. Although finding care for the AD victim who is homebound while the caregiver attends group meetings is a major problem, the presence of persons with the disease may greatly inhibit some caregivers from expressing their feelings. During group meetings, care services for the victim can be provided, including having a separate group for victims nearby, as well as respite care programs such as adult day-care and sitter services. These services have proven to be successful in freeing the caregiver to attend support group meetings.

Logistics

Probably the most important detail involved with the logistics of the support group is the establishment of support-group guidelines. It is important that the guidelines be concise and direct in addressing the principles of confidentiality and sharing.

Other logistics involve the scheduling and the location of the meetings. Members should decide when, where, and how often they wish to meet. A support group composed of spouses whose wives and husbands are residents of a local nursing home may choose to meet weekly in the nursing home; however, many support group's members feel they can commit themselves only to one meeting each month. The time of day is also important to older, retired caregivers who must restrict their night driving and to those who must work during the day.

Another major consideration in selecting a meeting place is the maintenance of autonomy for the group. Support groups may avoid any conflict of interest by meeting in such neutral sites as libraries and schools.

Leadership

Schmall (1984) contends that the most successful support groups have facilitators who have knowledge about AD and related dementing illnesses, family dynamics, and group process skills. Effective facilitators have the ability to separate their personal needs from the needs of the group and its members. They are committed to support groups, believing that strength lies within the group members, who are all important teachers, drawing on a reservoir of knowledge and experience in coping (Reever and Thomas, 1985). Without such a facilitator the group process may become untherapeutic, lack direction, and develop into "gripe sessions" (Zarit and Zarit, 1982; Schmall, 1984).

There has been much discussion by experts whether facilitators should be professionals or caregivers. Reever and Thomas (1985) discuss the benefits and drawbacks to each type of facilitator. Professional facilitators can refer caregivers to the support group, link the support group with community resources, and offer credible knowledge about new research for AD. On the other hand, professionals may tend to treat group members like "patients" and may not have the personal experience of day-by-day coping with a family member afflicted with AD or a related disorder. Caregiver facilitators can bring empathy and practical coping skills to fellow caregivers. Drawbacks to caregiver facilitators may be their lack of group dynamic skills, and probably more common, their lack of time to devote to the group. Former caregivers may be the best caregiver facilitators because they have both the experience and the available time and energy to devote to a group.

Some groups capitalize on the strength of both professional and caregiving leadership by having cofacilitators. This partnership is especially valuable in the event that a group member becomes upset and leaves the room. Then one leader can continue directing the group while the second leader sees to the needs of the agitated member.

Role of Nurses in Support Groups

Nurses with "their broad knowledge base in the biological, psychological and social sciences, their theoretical and clinical insight into pathophysiology, and their practical experience in delivering direct care," are qualified to assume a leadership role in chronic care (Eliopoulos, 1983, 75). What caregivers for AD victims provide certainly falls into the health category of chronic care. Faced with the prolonged ordeal of losing a loved one, caregivers need sustained, long-term, and comprehensive support services during all stages of this illness. Nurses can be instrumental in providing care to the victim and caregiver throughout the illness.

The nurse plays three major roles in giving support to caregivers:

- Assisting the caregivers to work through their emotional reactions.
- Initiating support groups.
- Performing systematic research.

The nurse can provide an important service by helping to initiate support groups in communities where the need exists. Area Agencies on Aging can provide assistance in this effort.

Nurses, with their interpersonal and therapeutic communication skills, are qualified to assist caregivers in working through the emotional upheaval brought about by this devastating illness. This catharsis may be accomplished through one-to-one counseling, family therapy, or support group interaction. The emotional support offered to caregivers by nurses can help them to mobilize resources and maintain emotional stability.

Nurses have the opportunity to be catalysts in the development of support groups for AD caregivers (Gwyther, 1982). The demand is present, and organizational support is available from Area Agencies on Aging (AAA). The AAA have launched a special initiative to develop AD support groups throughout the United States. Each local AAA has trained staff to assist in starting support groups. (Resources for support groups are listed in the chapter appendix.)

In addition to the role of initiator of group development, the nurse may be a group facilitator, consultant, and liaison between the group and health care professionals and agencies. Nurses also have opportunities to publish in chapter newsletters and resource books for caregivers and professionals.

The components and effects of support groups are fertile areas for nursing research.

Nurses are excellent candidates to conduct methodical research concerning the support for caregivers. Most of the information pertaining to support groups presents no measurement other than the writers' feelings and opinions (Hepburn and Wasow, 1986). Hepburn and Wasow propose that research attention be given to three areas:

- Specific effects of groups.
- Structural issues.
- The demonstration of alternatives to support groups.

The first area, specific effects of groups, examines benefits the caregiver receives from support groups. Is there development of new skills, acquisition of new knowledge, improvement in patient care, or measurable positive effects on the caregiver's well-being (Hepburn and Wasow, 1986)? The second area, structural issues, concerns the variables involved in a successful group. When are groups helpful and when are they harmful? Which organization format is most beneficial to which people? The third area, demonstration of alternatives to support groups, focuses on the absence of firm data concerning the most beneficial way family caregivers can be supported. Different forms of support, studied in controlled demonstration projects, would supply some of this information. Hepburn and Wasow suggest that two sets of independent variables be used in establishing demonstration projects. The first set would focus on groups addressing emotional needs, educational needs, legal concerns, and sexuality. The second set of variables consists of other direct supports, such as reimbursed respite care, and reimbursed prevention health care for the caregivers. Research in this area may have an effect on the present nonsupportive public policy toward caregivers. Nurses are unique professionals who have the knowledge and capability, through research, of drawing local and national attention to the needs of the "hidden patient" and supporting him or her throughout the "long goodbye."

The Mid-Missouri Example

The Mid-Missouri ADRDA Chapter, a successful open group, demonstrates the impact and potential of nursing involvement in AD support groups. Members include caregivers, family members, and interested professionals. New members get basic written and verbal information from group members. The group has been open, kind, and considerate to the needs of new members, demonstrating the therapeutics of helping others who are now experiencing the frustration and uncertainty that members of the group had earlier experienced. Frequently an informal buddy system develops between a newcomer and a member of long standing.

A typical meeting's agenda consists of an informal welcoming and socialization time. Information concerning new developments in AD research and legislation are reported at the beginning of each meeting. Following the sharing of general information, the group, depending on its size, may break into two sections. One section usually consists of spouses of AD victims, the other of adult children of AD victims.

For the remaining hour or so, individuals share their confidential concerns, frustrations, and needs with the group. It has been a rewarding experience seeing group members help each other through their understanding, caring, and sharing of practical suggestions for the care of the AD victim, as well as support for caregivers.

The Mid-Missouri Chapter support group has two monthly meetings, one during the day at a local nursing home and one at night at a city hospital. The nursing home and the hospital offer private meeting rooms to the support group. These two locations have proven to be popular and accessible. It has been important for the group to make known to the community that, although it is accepting the generosity of the nursing home and hospital, the group in no way endorses specific health care agencies. The support group also purposefully invites local professionals from these facilities to speak at educational meetings. The quarterly educational meetings, which are open to the community, have covered a wide range of topics, such as "Alzheimer's Disease: What Is It?", the value of diagnosis by autopsy, legal rights, ethical issues, and community resources. Because the educational meetings are kept separate, the focus of the regular monthly support meeting is not lost.

Another community service the group offers is a monthly newsletter that lists meeting dates, time, and location. Regular features appear on legal issues, research, and new publications. Special articles deal with disease, new programs, events, and helpful caregiving information. Community, state, and national resources are listed. Memorials are printed in the newsletter, as well as the names, telephone numbers, and relationship to AD victims to enable other group members to make contact. Publication costs are covered by member's voluntary membership fees, memorial gifts, and special fund-raising events. In addition to keeping group members informed, the newsletter has proven successful in reaching caregivers who cannot attend the group meeting.

With increasing expectations being placed on lay caregivers, it is important that their needs be recognized and their physical, emotional, and social well-being preserved and promoted. Nurses are ideally prepared to assess, diagnose, and intervene for AD victims and their caregivers. An important opportunity exists for nurses to demonstrate leadership in their advocacy and assistance to support groups. If a society is judged by the care it gives its elderly, undoubtedly American society also will be judged by the assistance it offers the caregiver.

Appendix: Audiovisual Resources

Compiled by David A. Lindeman (1984) and published in volume 1 of *Alzheimer's Disease Handbook* for Administration on Aging, Washington, DC.

Confronting Confusion
25 min., b&w, 1977
This documentary shows an elderly patient who has withdrawn into a "fantasy" and is unmotivated and confused. Leaders of an advanced reality orientation group help the patient to confront his fantasies, offering support for the person he is. Improvement is shown in a variety of ways.
Distributor: Electric Sunrise Films
P.O. Box 11122, Piedmont Station
Oakland, CA 94611
(415) 655–2356

Consumer Survival Kit (A Series)
30 min. each, color
Many of the half-hour programs in this award-winning series of 75 titles are pertinent to the field of aging. Particular consumer issues are examined from all vantage points; thoroughly researched information is presented in a manner that appeals to all ages and economic groups. Programs are interspersed with humorous dramatizations to make the learning easy and enjoyable. Of particular interest for gerontology are titles such as *Nursing Homes, Hearing, Prescription Drugs, Physical Fitness, Nutrition, Retirement Planning, Social Security, Wills and Estates, Over-the-Counter Drugs, Home Security Systems, Shoes, Mobile Homes,* and *Financial Institutions.*
Producer and Distributor: Maryland Center for Public Broadcasting
Owings Mills, MD 21117
(301) 356–6500

Dementia in the Middle and Later Years

A series of four half-hour films containing interviews with patients with dementing illness and their families. Produced by Dr. Carl Eisdorfer and Dr. Donna Cohen, Department of Psychiatry and Behavioral Sciences, School of Medicine, University of Washington, Seattle, Washington.

Distributor: Sandoz Pharmaceuticals
                 Film Department
                 East Hanover, NJ 07936
                 (201) 386–7500 and (415) 341–8816

The Disturbed Nursing Home Patient
24 min., color, 1977

Composed of a series of vignettes, this film is intended to assist in training nursing aides, attendants, and other nursing home personnel to deal with a wide variety of typical, difficult situations involving disturbed patients, most of them elderly. It is designed to show one vignette at a time in order to facilitate discussion among group members. The simplified diagnostic and treatment regimes depicted in the film are not presented as the definitive last word, but serve to introduce the patients and the topics, and lead to sharing of common diagnostic and management problems while promoting discussion about these topics. Study guide available.

Producer: Washington State Mental Health Division
              Film Library
              Olympia, WA 98504

Facing It
24.5 min., b&w, 1974

As a therapeutic approach to the patient with organic brain disorder, this film documents the actual experiences of staff and patients in one institution where a program of reality orientation has been in operation for two years. The viewer sees the elements of an organized therapeutic approach applied again and again in actual situations. Staff give their reactions and talk about the changes they have noticed in their patients.

Producer: Maimonides Hospital and Home for the Aged, with John Geeza
Distributor: TM
              Canada: Dr. G. Rosenberg, Maimonides Hospital
                        5795 Caldwell Avenue
                        Montreal H4W 1W3
                        (514) 488–2301

Glass Curtain, A Poem in Prose

This is a picture of a woman coping with the dimming mind of her mother, who suffers from Alzheimer's. Featuring actress Jennie Ventriss, the film is extremely personal and yet has universal appeal. The woman speaks to the audience as an intimate friend, reliving her relationship with her mother—the pain as well as the love.

Producer and Distributor: Doris Chase
                            222 West 23rd Street
                            No. 722
                            New York, NY 10011

Gramp—A Man Ages and Dies
60 min., b&w, 16 mm, 1976

A realistic and touching filmstrip based upon photographs of a beloved grandfather as he becomes mentally impaired and terminally ill. The narration by his grandson explains the man's illness, his decision to end his life, and the family's decision to maintain him at home rather than in a hospital or nursing home.

Distributor: Mass Media Ministries
2116 North Charles Street
Baltimore, MD 21218
(301) 727–3270

The Inner World of Aphasia
24 min., color, sound, 16 mm

Presents the emotional world of two victims of aphasia—people who have lost the power to use and understand speech because of a brain lesion or emotional disturbance.

Distributor: Edward Feil Productions
4614 Prospect Avenue
Cleveland, OH 44103
(216) 711–0655

Looking for Yesterday
29 min., color, sound, 16 mm

This film was made to document the inner world of the cognitively impaired aged. It explores the feelings of severely disoriented persons and demonstrates how fantasy can be an important therapeutic vehicle for their adjustment to institutionalized living.

Distributor: Edward Feil Productions
4614 Prospect Avenue
Cleveland, OH 44103
(216) 711–0655

Memaw

This documentary tells about an 88-year-old woman with Alzheimer's Disease. The film was made on the last days Memaw spent on her farm and marks the end of an era for her, for her daughter, and for the 200-year-old farm. This film highlights the problems faced by adult children of aging ill parents.

Producer and Distributor: David Carnochan
4571 River Road
Scottsville, NY 14546

Organic Brain Syndrome: Recognition, Diagnosis, Management
40 min., color, 1971 (also 8 mm)

The importance of early recognition and diagnosis of acute brain syndrome is emphasized. Simple and practical diagnostic tests are shown in a straightforward teaching manner. Two geriatric patients and one alcoholic patient are presented. Award winning.

Author: Leon Marder, M.D.
University of Southern California
School of Medicine
Los Angeles, CA 90007

Distributor: Sandoz Pharmaceuticals
Film Department
East Hanover, NJ 07936
(201) 386–7500 and (415) 341–8816

Peege

18 min., color, 1974

The central theme of the film is the breaking down of communication barriers to reach those isolated by age and failing mental capacities. A family visits the dying grandmother in a nursing home. She is blind and has lost some of her mental faculties. The visit is awkward, and when the family leaves, the young grandson stays with her for a few minutes. He tries to trigger some response by whispering into her ear, reminding her of the happy times they had had before. He touches her. His efforts succeed, and when he leaves she is alone again—but now with a feeling of worth, knowing that someone cares.

Producers: David Knapp and Leonard Berman

Distributors: Mid-America Resource and Training Center
                5218 Oak Street
                Kansas City, MO 64112
                (816) 444–1121

A Time for Caring: Understanding and Managing Disruptive Behavior in the Elderly Patient

25 min., color, sound, 16 mm or video, free rental, 1980

Together with the booklet *A Time for Caring* this film provides information on mental disorders commonly seen in elderly patients and suggests guidelines for dealing with the disruptive behavior that often results from those disorders. Dramatizes an elderly man admitted to a nursing home and staff management of behavior. Suggested for new nurse's aides or home care workers.

Available from: McNeil Pharmaceutical
                 McNeilab, Inc.
                 Spring House, PA 19477
                 (215) 628–5413

The Silent Epidemic: Alzheimer's Disease

25 min., color, sound, 16 mm or video, 1982

Shows two people married to sufferers of Alzheimer's, explores issues of out-of-home care and nursing home visitation. Useful in fostering professional and public awareness.

Producer: Granada Television International

Available for purchase or rent from: Filmmakers Library, Inc.
                                       133 East 58th Street
                                       Suite 703A
                                       New York, NY 10022
                                       (212) 355–6545

Additional Audiovisual Resources

Alzheimer's Disease: Coping With Confusion

Portrays several patients with Alzheimer's disease in various stages of the disease process. Stresses specific interventions nurses might use to deal with common problems of personal hygiene, nutrition, exercise, incontinence, wandering, communication, and agitation.

For rent or sale from the *American Journal of Nursing*.

Alzheimer's Disease: Discharge Planning
   Focuses on the nurse's role in preparing the family for the return home of the Alzheimer's patient. Gives practical hints about patient care and safety.
For rent or sale from the *American Journal of Nursing*.

REFERENCES

ADRDA: Alzheimer's Disease and Related Disorders Association, Inc., Newsletter. Chicago, winter 1986.

Brody EM: Women in the middle and family help to older people. The Gerontologist 21(5): 471–480, 1981.

Cantor M: Strain among caregivers: A study of experience in the U.S. The Gerontologist 23(6): 597–604, 1983.

Cohen D, Eisdorfer C: The Loss of Self. New York, Norton, 1986.

Eliopoulos C: Chronic care and the elderly: Impact on the client, the family and the nurse. In Wells T: Aging and Health Promotion. Rockville, MD, Aspen Systems, 75, 1983.

Fengler AP, Goodrich N: Wives of elderly disabled men: The hidden patient. The Gerontologist 19(2): 175–183, 1979.

Guthrie D: Grandpa Doesn't Know It's Me. New York, Human Sciences Press, 1986.

Gwyther LP: Caregiver self-help groups: Roles for professionals. Generations 7(1): 37–40, 1982.

Hepburn K, Wasow M: Support groups for family caregivers of dementia victims: Questions, directions, and future research. In Abramson NS, Quam JK, Wasow M (eds): The Elderly and Chronic Mental Illness. New Directions for Mental Health Services, No. 29. San Francisco, Jossey-Bass, 1986.

Kapust LR: Living with dementia: The on-going funeral. Social Work Health Care 7(4): 79–91, 1982.

Kapust LR, Weintraub S: Living with a family member suffering from Alzheimer's disease. In Roback HB (ed): Helping Patients and Their Families Cope with Medical Problems, 453–480. San Francisco: Jossey-Bass, 1984.

Kübler-Ross E: On Death and Dying. New York, Macmillan, 1969.

Lidoff L, Harris P: Idea Book on Caregiver Support Groups. Washington, DC, National Council on Aging, 1985.

Lieberman M: Self-help groups: An overview. Generations 12(1): 45–49, 1985.

Lindeman DA: Alzheimer's Disease Handbook, Vol. 1. Washington, DC, Administration on Aging, 1984.

Middleton L: Alzheimer's Family Support Groups—A Manual for Group Facilitators. Tampa, FL, USF Medical Center, Suncoast Gerontology Center, 1984.

Miller JR: Family support of the elderly. Family Community Health 3(4): 39–49, 1981.

Rabins PV, Mace NL, Lucas MJ: The impact of dementia on the family. JAMA 248(3): 333–335, 1982.

Reever KE, Thomas E: Training facilitators of self-help groups for caregivers to elders. Generations 12(1): 50–52, 1985.

Schmall VL: It doesn't just happen. Generations 9(2): 64–67, 1984.

Soldo BJ, Myllyluoma J: Caregivers who live with dependent elderly. The Gerontologist 23(6): 605–611, 1983.

Steuer J: Caring for the caregivers. Generations 9(2): 56–57, 1984.

Stuart GW, Sundeen SJ: The Principles and Practice of Psychiatric Nursing, 2nd ed. St. Louis, CV Mosby, 1983.

Teusink PJ, Mahler S: Helping families cope with Alzheimer's disease. Hosp Commun Psych 35(2): 152–156, 1984.

Weaver DH: Tapping strength: A support group for children and grandchildren of Alzheimer's victims. Generations 7(1): 45–46, 1982.

Woods AM, Niederehe G, Fruge E: Dementia: A family systems perspective. Generations 12(1): 50–52, 1985.

Zarit S, Zarit J: Families under stress: Interventions for caregivers of senile dementia patients. Psychotherapy: Theory, Research, and Practice 19(4): 461–471, 1982.

BIBLIOGRAPHY

Caserta MS, Lund DA, Wright SD, Redburn DE: Caregivers to dementia patients: The utilization of community services. The Gerontologist 27(2): 209–214, 1987.

Erde EL: On truth telling and the diagnosis of Alzheimer's disease. J Family Prac 26(4): 401–406, 1988.

Given CW, et al.: Sources of stress among families caring for relatives with Alzheimer's disease. Nurs Clin N Am 23(1): 69–82, 1988.

Halford S: Personal interview. Columbia, MO, 1986.

Hall GR: Care of the patient with Alzheimer's disease living at home. Nurs Clin N Am 23(1): 31–46, 1988.

Huff FJ, et al.: Risk of dementia in relatives of patients with Alzheimer's disease. Neurology 38(5): 786–790, 1988.

Jarvik L, Winograd C (eds): Alzheimer's Disease: The Long Haul. New York, Springer, 1987.

Lipkin LV, Faude KJ: Dementia—Educating the caregiver. J Gerontol Nurs 13(11): 23–27, 1987.

Mann LM: Community support for families caring for members with Alzheimer's disease. Home Healthcare Nurse 3(1): 8–10, 1985.

O'Connor K, Prothero J: The Alzheimer's Caregiver: Strategies for Support. Seattle, University of Washington Press, 1987.

Rossi T: Step by Step: How to Actively Ensure the Best Possible Care for Your Aging Relative. New York, Warner Books, 1987.

Scott JP, Roberto KA, Hutton JT: Families of Alzheimer's victims: Family support to the caregivers. J Am Geriatr Soc 34(5): 348–354, 1986.

Sommers T, Shields L: Women Take Care: The Consequences of Caregiving in Today's Society. Gainesville, FL, Triad, 1987.

Whall AA: Therapeutic use of self. J Gerontol Nurs 14(2): 38–39, 46–47, 1988.

CHAPTER 20

Hospice Care

Monica Koshuta

Chapter Objectives

At the completion of this chapter the reader will be able to:

1. Describe the stages of death.
2. Discuss the characteristics of hospice care.
3. Identify factors that must be considered in pain management of the terminally ill.
4. Describe ways in which the fulfillment of basic self-care needs may be modified in hospice care.
5. Discuss methods of providing psychological support to the terminally ill and their families.

By the time old age is achieved, one has experienced considerable living, learning, loving, and losses. Through these experiences, the awareness of terminality and death may be heightened or diminished. What we are in later life is a result of our formal and informal education, our culture, and our intellect. As one moves on the continuum of life from birth to old age, one encounters the ultimate loss of control that is the possible failure of one's health, leading eventually to death. Realizing this fact may provide some elderly with peace, while others may experience a state of uncertainty, fear, and ambivalence. Although most elderly people have had experience with death, it was the death of others.

The manner in which people face their own death will vary. The acknowledgement that life is limited by a disease is initially a tremendous shock, and the reality that one will be forced to deal with dying can be overwhelming and devastating. Past losses—the death of family members, parents, children, or siblings—all surface. The type of death that one has witnessed, sudden or prolonged, and the place of death all flood the conscious or unconscious mind, sometimes all too vividly. But this time it is different, and patients must realize the death that they are facing is their own. Response to a terminal diagnosis, with a limited prognosis, will depend on a number of issues, the most important of which are one's ability to adapt to a shortened life, the availability of adequate support systems, and, finally, acceptance of death.

During the 1960s the media brought death into the home through their coverage of the assassinations of President John F. Kennedy and Martin

Luther King, Jr. The media also addressed the subject of death by their coverage of the Vietnam war. During this same period, Elisabeth Kübler-Ross, a psychiatrist, began her work with the terminally ill, at the University of Chicago. She interviewed many terminally ill patients, and from these interviews she discovered similarities among many of the dying. She noted that they were frequently isolated and that the health care professionals were uncomfortable in situations where patients were attempting to deal with their lives after being informed that they had a terminal illness. She encouraged open communication among staff members, so that they could interact in an open and nonthreatening manner with their patients who were trying to come to grips with their abbreviated lives.

Stages of Death

In 1969, Elisabeth Kübler-Ross published *On Death and Dying,* which soon became a worldwide best-seller. This book served as the catalyst for addressing death and dying realistically and viewing death through the eyes of the dying. In her writings she describes stages through which the terminally ill pass (Kübler-Ross, 1969). She states that patients, when they are initially diagnosed and confronted with the terminal illness, respond with *denial* or disbelief; this is the first stage she describes. Denial is used throughout life as a coping mechanism, and it serves this same purpose when one must encounter the issue of a terminal diagnosis. It is the one mechanism that may allow enough time for one to come to grips with reality and then be able to move on to coping with a limited future.

> The stages of death identified by Kübler-Ross aid in understanding the behaviors of the terminally ill. However, not all dying persons will experience each stage or progress through the stages in a set sequence.

The second stage described by Kübler-Ross is *anger,* and it usually follows denial. Anger may be directed toward anyone and everyone, including the family, health care professionals, and God. The purpose of the anger is to vent the frustration caused by the loss of control and the disease process.

Bargaining may follow the venting of the anger. This stage usually involves bargaining with individuals who may have some impact on the patient. It is not infrequent that patients bargain with their God, the health care professionals, and their families. The bargaining is individualistic, and requests vary. One common request is for quality time; another is a pain-free and peaceful death. This period possibly gives patients an opportunity to mend past relationships with family as well as their God.

Loss and depression are not synonymous, but they are closely associated when one is coping with a terminal illness. During this stage of *depression,* not only the impending loss is addressed, but also past losses or life's perceived losses. Depression is expected and normal.

Acceptance is the final stage described by Kübler-Ross. It is the time when there is neither anger nor depression, but a time when the reality of death has been acknowledged, and it is an inevitable expectation.

These stages that Kübler-Ross has identified may or may not be experienced by terminal patients; consequently, staging patients can lead to misunderstanding. Kübler-Ross developed this framework to help understand the terminally ill. Her works should be viewed as a framework and not as a mandate to which all patients must respond similarly.

Quality of Life

The gerontological nurse should make sure that treatment options for the terminally ill enhance rather than diminish the quality of remaining life.

The stages described by Kübler-Ross may be encountered by individuals when they are diagnosed and curative treatment may still be an option. One of the most significant issues for the terminally ill elderly who have the option of curative treatment is the impact that the treatment will have on their quality of life. What is quality of life? For each individual it is what he or she perceives it to be; there is no universal definition. Yet, this issue frequently is a major concern of terminal patients. The decision to receive curative or palliative treatment is determined by the patient, family, and physician. This decision-making process is stressful, and health care professionals may be asked for advice at this time. Patients and families often seek advice from clergy, physicians, nurses, and social workers as they ponder the question of quality versus quantity of life.

Moral and ethical concerns are examined and reflected on by the patient, family, and health care professionals. Elderly patients may decide to forgo life-sustaining treatment if it may have an adverse impact on their quality of life. They may perceive some treatments that are intended to prolong life as extraordinary measures, which may be interpreted not as extension of life but as prolongation of death. These issues continue to surface and are not uncommon. Our social systems will have to contend with these concerns as the elderly population continues to grow in numbers.

Options that are presented to the terminally ill elderly should include all services that are available to them and should be presented in a detailed, understandable fashion. Decision making ultimately rests with the competent patient, but consultation with physicians, family members, and support systems should be encouraged. Once a decision has been reached, the elderly should be supported in their choice.

This chapter will address support through hospice care for terminally ill patients, for whom there is no curative treatment, or those who choose to forgo curative treatment and seek palliative care during their final stage of life.

Hospice Care

During the 1960s and 1970s the hospice movement emerged. This movement was concerned with care of the terminally ill and has had a profound effect on care for terminal patients of all ages. Some of the first hospices were founded in England, where Dr. Cicely Saunders established St. Christopher's Hospice in London. It was after the success of the hospice movement in England and the publication of Elisabeth Kübler-Ross's findings that birth was given to the hospice movement in the United States. The Connecticut Hospice was the first American hospice program.

Hospice care is an alternative health care service. Hospice is a concept; it is not a specific place of care but rather a philosophy of care and caring. Philosophically, hospice care views and supports life to its fullest until natural death occurs. The goal of hospice care is to promote a high quality of life until the occurrence of biological death. Hospice does nothing to shorten life, nor does it prolong dying. And although the hospice concept realistically deals with death, its focus is on the quality of living until death comes with dignity. Comfort, care, and caring are foremost in the caregiver's mind and actions. Hospice programs were established initially as home care programs. Currently most hospice programs have the capability of providing inpatient care for a limited time, but 80% of hospice care is still provided in the home setting.

The goal of hospice care is accomplished by including the patient, family, and significant others as the unit of care and encouraging and supporting their participation in decision making, care planning, and caregiving with the goal of a quality life until death. The patients are viewed holistically, considering their physiological, emotional, social, and spiritual needs. To accomplish hospice goals, a collaborative effort by members of an interdisciplinary team is essential. The team is medically directed, and in addition to the physician includes nurses, social workers, volunteers, pastoral counselors, therapists, nursing assistants, homemakers, and bereavement counselors. Patients and families are informed about all services and options that are available to them.

The team members involve the family in goal setting and work to achieve the goals that the patient and family have set. Each discipline assumes its respective responsibilities and collaborates with the other team members. It is not unusual for these responsibilities to blur from time to time. The cohesiveness of the team is dependent on open communication and consistency with the goals outlined by the patient and family in the plan of care. Communication, collaboration, and consistency in the team effort to meet the patient's and family's goals are imperative whether hospice services are provided in the patient's home or a hospice inpatient setting.

> Hospice is a philosophy, not merely a place of care and caring.

Pain Management

All hospice care is palliative or comfort care that focuses on effective symptom management. A variety of symptoms may be present and can be attributed to an increase in the advanced disease process. The one symptom present in the majority of patients is pain. Elderly patients experience pain as the disease process invades surrounding tissue. Assessment of pain is essential both initially and on an ongoing basis.

Pain has numerous elements that must be considered throughout the terminal stage. The first of these is the patient's perception of the pain itself. Patients are their own experts in describing their pain, as it is part of them. The manifestation of pain, the intensity, the location, the frequency, the du-

> Ethnic and cultural expectations of pain management and the patient's effectiveness in communicating symptoms must be considered in assessing pain. The lack of expression of the presence of pain may not reflect the actual absence of pain.

ration, and the type (dull, sharp, throbbing, etc.) must all be considered. Past experiences with pain, its treatment, and the patient's response are an integral part of the assessment process. The impact of ethnic and cultural responses to pain must be included. All this input is essential if adequate pain control is to be achieved. To allow the patient to remain in control, acknowledgement of the patient's pain or absence of pain is imperative if a therapeutic relationship is to be maintained. The evaluation of analgesia must be ongoing. It may be difficult to describe pain accurately during the initial meeting of the team members. In elderly patients the absence or denial of pain may be due to an inability to describe the sensation as pain. The importance of nonverbal signs of pain should not be overlooked, and these signs should be incorporated into the pain assessment.

The patient and family must be made aware that changes may be frequent in the intensity of the pain and that medications to control pain will be regulated to meet the goal of pain control. Pain is what the patient says it is whether that pain be physiological, psychological, spiritual, or a combination of all. Pain control that permits the patient to live comfortably until death is achievable in the majority of cases. The issues of tolerance and addiction may be of concern to the patient and the family when narcotics are prescribed. The nurse's responsibility includes sound knowledge about analgesic medications, including narcotic and nonnarcotic drugs, the expected responses, and the possible side effects. The nurse's responsibility related to pain control involves not only an objective and subjective pain assessment and evaluation, but also education of the patient and family about the use of analgesia on a regular schedule. The goal of pain management is to control pain, not to chase it, by administering the analgesia on a schedule that does not allow pain to occur but manages it by preventing it from occurring. Reassurance and support of the patient and family members by the hospice team are necessary throughout the course of the illness, especially when trying to achieve and maintain pain control. Team and family members must acknowledge that the pain belongs to the patient and that he or she should continue to have input in the control of it as long as possible.

> Approaches that reduce the terminally ill person's psychological and spiritual pain must be considered in the plan of care.

Efforts to achieve physiological pain control may be time consuming and trying, and may overshadow other pertinent patient and family needs. Team members need to be aware of this danger and prevent it from occurring.

Patients often experience pain that may be attributed to causes not directly associated with the disease process. Psychological, sociological, and spiritual issues may lead to pain that is of greater intensity than the physical pain. Emotional and spiritual support often aids patients in resolving conflicts that may be the cause of these types of pain. Psychological pain and fears associated with dying may intensify pain. Life review and reminiscence may help the patient in resolution of psychological pain. The retelling of life events provides another chance to encounter the pleasures of past years. If psychological distress is brought to the surface and viewed from a different perspective, the pain associated with it may then diminish.

The spiritual counselor may assist the patient if the patient so desires.

Religion is so individualistic and personal that only the patient knows the depth and breadth of his or her religious beliefs and convictions. Spiritual needs may surface, and the patient may use this time to focus on reconciliation, contrition, meaning in life, and resolution of inner conflicts. Dealing with spiritual issues may diminish the intensity of the spiritual pain. The hospice movement views patients from a holistic viewpoint and consequently recognizes the need for spiritual counseling and religion as an optional service that is available to all hospice patients and families who desire it.

Diversional and relaxation activities may be therapeutic and potentiate the effect of the analgesia. The patient may be coached in these techniques and encouraged to use them appropriately. The combination of pharmaceuticals, distraction, relaxation, and reminiscence or the use of these elements alone allows most patients to experience a pain-controlled terminal phase of their illness. The patient and family should be aware of the options that are available to achieve maximum pain control.

One of the most challenging and sometimes difficult tasks for health care professionals is to acknowledge pain in the elderly. It is discomfort with analgesia, particularly with the use of narcotics, that all too frequently leads to inadequate pain control in this specific population. Hospice nurses have a commitment to assist the patient in achieving maximum pain control, thus enhancing this final stage of living.

Nutritional Support

Nutrition and hydration are two important aspects of terminal care in the elderly. Assessment of the patient's ability to eat and drink should be ongoing. Appetite is generally affected by the disease process, the medication, and metabolic changes in the body. Family members should be informed that anorexia is not uncommon, and the basis for this condition should be explained. The patient's food likes and dislikes should be discussed with the family. The importance of small feedings that are high in protein should be stressed. The use of commercially prepared liquid supplements, egg nog, and ice cream may be used as a substitute for regular meals. The patient and family should be encouraged to continue with regular family mealtimes because these afford the patient an opportunity to participate in a loving social environment. Food has been and continues to be an important part of living, as it provides nourishment not only of the body but also for people's social needs. As death nears, the nurse should explain to the family that the nutritional need of the patient will decrease. One of the greatest fears of family members is that of patient starvation. The team must actively listen to these concerns and respond appropriately. As the patient's condition deteriorates, swallowing may be problematic; hydration options should be presented and discussed with family members so that desired interventions may be implemented. The nurse should be knowledgeable about the issues of hydration and nutrition in the dying so the family may be informed of the available options.

Elimination

Ongoing nursing assessment of the dying individual's ability to tolerate and ingest food, eliminate wastes, and maintain bowel and bladder continence is a crucial component of hospice nursing.

Elimination problems are not infrequent in the terminal patient. The decrease of liquids, food, and exercise and the use of analgesia have a direct effect on the bowel. Consequently, constipation and fecal impaction are common problems. Prevention of constipation in the dying person can be challenging for the family and professional team. The establishment of a bowel regimen and strict adherence to it are extremely important for the patient if maximum comfort levels are to be maintained. The nurse is responsible for educating the family relative to this.

Urinary problems of polyuria, retention, and incontinence may develop as the patient becomes debilitated with the progression of disease or infection. Periodic evaluation of the patient's ability to control bladder functions should be performed by the nurse. The family should be prepared to face the reality of incontinence or retention so that adequate planning for the necessary interventions may be done.

Rest and Sleep

The acknowledgement that life is in its final stage may cause apprehension and anxiety that interfere with sleep and rest for the patient. There may be a need to verbalize fears and concerns, and each member of the team must be an active listener. The release of anxiety through talking about the fear of death and the dying process is recognized as a therapeutic intervention. Death is a stranger that is not usually welcomed without reservations at any age. Although the elderly may be realistic about death, the need to talk about this phenomenon does not diminish. Dying persons are coming to grips with their mortality and trying to adapt to and accept this final stage of life, but it still provokes anxiety. The remainder of life will require rest to conserve energy, yet the disease itself may deny the patient the much-needed rest.

Encouraging the patient to express feelings and providing frequent human contact can promote the psychological comfort that enables the patient to rest adequately.

What can be done to assist patients in getting the rest and sleep that they desire? Time is an important element to be considered, since the patient's time is shortened by the disease. The patient and family anticipate death, and the how and when of the cessation of life may be pondered. The nurse is the team member who will be caring for and spending time with the patient as life grows shorter, and the nurse should encourage the patient and family to discuss their perceptions and concerns about the impending death. Sleep or rest may come easier after the patients verbalize their real concerns.

The questions that are frequently asked concern death itself? What is death like? Will it be painful or will I die alone? These are common concerns of the terminally ill elderly. Honesty is extremely important, and addressing the pain, the loneliness, and the fear of death itself should be done in a sensitive manner. Patients are relieved to know that death usually is not accompanied by pain, most expected deaths are peaceful, and usually there is somebody at their side at the time of death. Avoidance of these issues may cause undue stress and concern for the patient and family as well as the nurse. The human element, or therapeutic use of one's own presence, may facilitate rest and sleep. The presence of someone by the bedside assures patients that they are not alone. The touch of a hand, an embrace, or a gentle hug may provide the human element that will facilitate rest and sleep in the elderly.

Psychosocial Support

Comfort, caring, compassion, communication, and competence are all integral parts of hospice care. Comfort is usually associated with competent care that is medically directed, yet the hospice concept embraces the elements of empathy, kindness, gentleness, and compassion. The importance of these caring measures cannot be measured in patient outcomes, but they have a positive impact. Terminally ill elderly patients may feel rejected and isolated not only because of their disease, but also because of their age. Nurses struggle continually to reach a balance between objectivity and involvement in the delivery of care to the terminally ill elderly.

Touch sends a powerful message of caring.

One of the most effective tools to communicate caring is the warmth of human touch. The message of touch begins early in one's life, with the tender caress during infancy, the touch of the disciplining hand during the toddler stage, the embraces of adolescence, the intense caresses of young adulthood, and the supportive hugs of adult life. The message of touch conveys a deep sense of caring, and to the elderly, a sense of rejection can be changed to acceptance by the message of a tender touch.

Nonverbal messages of compassion are powerful. A quiet presence, a smile of acceptance, and a quiet tear—all silent communications—provide consolation for the dying. The impact of these silent messages is not certain, but the patient's response is usually one of acceptance and gratitude. Family members may need to be encouraged to express their feelings and emotions. The nurse should inform relatives that there are ways in which they may show their compassion and understanding. Loved ones may feel that touching the patient is inappropriate and may cause unnecessary discomfort; they need to be informed that most terminally ill patients want to be touched,

Hospice care emphasizes the importance of helping the patient live as fully as possible during his or her remaining life. Celebrations of holidays and participation in important family events should be encouraged.

and the elderly frequently long for the touch of a loved one. Family members should be encouraged to participate in patient care, if they so desire. Closeness of another person is so very important in the final stage of life. Family members should be encouraged to embrace the patient or get close in some other manner, such as sitting near or lying in bed with the patient. Living is still important for dying patients, and the celebration of events should be continued with the patient as a participant. Anniversaries and holidays are usually important to dying patients because they know that each celebration of the event may be their last.

A warm cordial environment is conducive to relaxation and to sharing of fears, apprehensions, doubts, and uncertainties. Family members, as well as patients, may have the need to talk about death, and they should be encouraged to do so. It is not unusual for elderly patients to express their feelings about funeral or memorial services, autopsies, and burial arrangements. Many of the elderly have prearranged funerals, consequently, the survivors are not overburdened at the time of death. Nurses may be asked to facilitate the making of these arrangements; they should be sensitive and move gently when dealing with these matters.

Reminiscence, a superb tool for persons of all ages, should be encouraged; it allows the elderly to relive past pleasures, disappointments, and resolved and unresolved issues. Patients who desire to leave a message, long or short, for their loved ones may use tape recording on days that they are feeling able. Taping not only provides for reliving but puts meaning in life that patients feel a need to pass on. Reminiscence allows for the patient and family to relive past events, to laugh and cry one more time.

> Taped reminiscence sessions can be an important gift that the dying person can leave to survivors.

Survivor Support

Death is not convenient at any time, and it is a stressful event. Loss of anything or anyone significant is followed by grief. Does grief for the elderly differ from the grief that the elderly themselves experience? Hospice care acknowledges the stress of death and provides bereavement care for the survivors of hospice patients. Family members and significant others are communicated with and supported for a 13-month period. Hospice recognizes that grief is a normal reaction to loss.

Survivors all grieve differently as they work through their loss. Some experience physical and emotional symptoms; some feel a sense of relief; and others feel anger, resentment, and guilt. All these emotions are normal grief reactions. Individuals with prolonged or unresolved grief may require counseling from a mental health professional. Consequently, the hospice program maintains contact with these individuals until resolution of the atypical grief is resolved. The elderly may have prolonged grief and never really resolve their grief, particularly if they have had a long relationship with the deceased. Patience, gentleness, tolerance, reminiscence, and therapeutic use of self are the most effective tools that nurses have readily available. The goal of resolution of grief is to make new relationships and to live, love, and laugh again.

Hospice programs in the United States started as demonstration and pilot programs with uncertain futures. Funding for hospice care comes from private as well as government sources. Currently some health insurance plans offer a hospice benefit. The federal government offers hospice care for its Medicare beneficiaries. The coverage is specific and has some restrictions, but it provides payment for hospice care for many of the terminally ill elderly in the United States. Hospice, a much-needed humanistic service, is a viable health care institution that acknowledges death, but whose focus is on the quality of living and on death with dignity.

REFERENCE   Kübler-Ross E: On Death and Dying. New York, Macmillan, 1969.

BIBLIOGRAPHY   Albert MVL, Steffl BM: Loss, grief, and death in old age. In Steffl BM (ed): Handbook of Gerontological Nursing, 73–87. New York, Van Nostrand Reinhold, 1984.

Baird SF: Helping the family through a crisis. Nurs 87, no. 9:66–67, June 1987.

Bass DT, Garland T, Otto M: Characteristics of hospice patients and their caregivers. Omega 16(1): 51–68, 1986.

Bonham GS: Hospice in transition: Kentucky, 1982–85. Am J Public Health 77(12):1535–1536, 1987.

Carolan M: Hospice care: Nursing the terminally ill. Am Assoc Occup Health Nurs J 35(4): 168–171, 1987.

Conrad NL: Spiritual support for the dying. Nurs Clin N Am 20(2): 415–426, 1985.

Daeffler R: A framework for hospice nursing. Hospice J 1(2): 91–111, 1985.

Forbis PA: Meeting patients' spiritual needs. Geriatr Nurs 9(3): 158–159, 1988.

Hastings Center: Guidelines on the Termination of Life-Sustaining Treatment and Care of the Dying. New York, Hastings Center, 1987.

Lynn DJ: Care near the end of life. In Cassel CK, Walsh JR (eds): Geriatric Medicine, vol. 2, 332–345. New York, Springer, 1984.

Marshall JR: The dying elderly patient. Am Fam Phys 28(5): 161–165, 1983.

Musgrave CF: The ethical and legal implications of hospice care: An international overview. Cancer Nurs 10(4): 183–189, 1987.

Richter JM: Support: A resource during crisis of mate loss. J Gerontol Nurs 13(11): 18–22, 1987.

Rose A: Care of the elderly dying patient. Geriatr Nurs Home Care 7(10): 18–19, 1987.

Stetz KM: Caregiving demands during advanced cancer: The spouse's needs. Cancer Nurs 10(5): 260–268, 1987.

Waters V: First impressions of grief . . . The nurse's attitude has a profound effect on bereaved relatives. Nurs Times 83(5): 46–47, 1987.

CHAPTER 21

Putting Widowhood in Perspective: A Group Approach Utilizing Family Systems Principles

Lynne R. Crouch

Chapter Objectives
At the completion of this chapter the reader will be able to:

1. Discuss the significance of widowhood to the affected individual.
2. List basic assumptions in conducting a widowhood group.
3. Describe the theoretical principles from Bowen's family systems theory that can be used in a widowhood group.
4. Outline the format and use of a genogram.

One of the major factors causing persons to realize their mortality as they grow older is the death of significant persons in their lives. The risk of death increases with every advancing year, and most deaths that occur involve an aged individual.

At a time in life when physical and emotional reserves are low and losses abundant, the death of a loved one can have profound effects—particularly if that loved one is a spouse. Imagine what it is like to lose that person who shared every day of your life for decades; in some cases more than a half century. No longer is that person sitting across the dinner table, sharing the news of the day. The place on the mattress that once was taken by a warm, familiar figure now is cold and empty. There is no one to cook for, shop for, or worry about, nor can you know the other person is worrying about you. Social affairs and holidays must be faced without the partner with whom they have always been shared.

Widowhood can have a dramatic effect on the physical, emotional, and social well-being of the surviving spouse. Widowed persons can suffer disruption to their activities of daily life and a loss of interest in living if they are unable to resolve their grief and adapt to this new role; therefore, interventions that facilitate their emotional healing and adjustment can have a significant impact.

Review of the Literature

Possibly because the theory utilized in conducting widowhood groups is relatively recent, the literature lacks specific writings dealing with the widow in the family system. Rather, the literature approaches widowhood from the perspective of the individual, often with a psychodynamic and psychoanalytical orientation. There are descriptions of how a widow experiences grief, but mention of the family is limited to emotional responses among family members rather than the family's response to the widow and her problem.

Despite the deficit in the literature some of the popular books on widowhood allude to the development of self. Wylie (1984) writes of grieving for the loss of the self that was defined by and invested in the deceased person. The widow is described as changing her emphasis: People become more important than things and routines; the widow herself, more important than conventional habits. Wylie notes that widows who reside with parents or children are better able to cope with widowhood than persons with no family support.

Raphael (1983) in *The Anatomy of Bereavement* speaks of one process necessary to beginning the development of self in the present: The finality of the loss must be accepted, and the bonds that built the relationship undone. She notes that the family and social network can have the most powerful influence in this process. If the family, in offering support and consolation, can permit the bereaved to accept and explore her grief as needed, they facilitate the type of review that allows a satisfactory mourning.

Supportive families are an asset to the widowed individual in accepting the loss of a mate.

George (1980) describes the death of a spouse as a highly visible life event that mobilizes the social network. Thus most widowed persons receive both specific task-oriented assistance and general emotional support from relatives and close friends. Moreover, widows turn to relatives, especially their children, for more support than they expect from friends.

Rado (1984) claims that the type of support the widow receives is based on how the widow and the deceased are valued by members of the social system. When the widow does not receive the compassion and support of significant others, she loses a vital aid in coping with the difficult confrontations demanded in grief work. The tasks of grief work require the encouragement, empathy, and sustenance gained from positive relationships.

The Solid Core of Self

Widows and widowers seem to do better accepting the loss of their mates when they have supportive family systems and an ability to develop the self. They recover more quickly emotionally, socialize earlier, find new meaning for their lives, and deal with the painful aspects of matelessness more readily than those who do not. Thus it is important early in the nurse-client relationship to assess the status of the family, its composition, and its importance to the widow or widower. Also important is listening for the individual's description of self and how he or she copes emotionally with the condition of being mateless.

That which one does, believes in, and supports is referred to as the solid core of self.

New widows and widowers are often not in touch with the solid core of self and have the task of developing that core. "Solid core of self" refers to those things the self does, believes in, and supports. There are many variables influencing the inability to know or develop one's self. For example, many widows have been absorbed in their mates' lives and career choices, failing to clearly delineate what they believe in or want for themselves, and many widowers allowed their mates to make many of the decisions related to household management. In families where peace in relationships is most important, thinking of self as a separately defined entity is discouraged. Also, many widows and widowers have been *other-* rather than *self*-focused all their lives, and that orientation can increase when the mate becomes ill.

Moreover, where caretaking is another added characteristic, the functional spouse feels obligated to take care of the mate. Caretakers can be thought of as people who take care of or do for the other to the exclusion of self. Thus it is difficult for caretakers to begin doing for themselves in widowhood; this way of behaving is foreign to their repertoire.

The Widowhood Group

The challenge of coping emotionally and developing a solid core of self in response to widowhood can be facilitated in a widowhood support group like the one conducted by the author. This group was created in 1983 to deliver mental health services at a community senior center. The group includes newly widowed people, as well as those widowed for some time.

As it has progressed, the group has become a forum to examine in detail the nature of family relationships, marriage, and self. Seniors who are mateless are encouraged to find answers to their own dilemmas of living single by learning from the experiences of others. Hearing of difficulties similar to their own decreases the sense of isolation and difference.

Group members are asked about the composition of their families of origin, their position in the birth order, the beliefs derived from their families, and the behaviors they are playing out from the past. Moreover, the quality and frequency of current relationships are assessed.

Some seniors have eventually examined and changed the nature of relationships with their children, in part as a result of beginning to examine these relationships more closely in the group. If people are severed emotionally from family members, and are fairly intense about this separation, they are not encouraged to reconnect with the family. However, if the widow or widower can handle the emotional intensity incurred by renewed contact and connection, reconnection with family members can be useful and healing.

Basic Assumptions Used in Conducting the Group

Many of the tenets of the group process were originated by Dr. Murray Bowen, author of *Family Therapy in Clinical Practice* (1983), and applied to this elderly population who are dealing with a life change or nodal event (the death of one's spouse and life thereafter).

Variations in Coping. The first basic assumption used in working with this group is that widows and widowers vary in how they cope emotionally and physically with the death of a spouse. The higher the survivor's level of chronic anxiety is, the more likely it is that the acute anxiety of widowhood will tend to overwhelm the person. Moreover, if this increase in anxiety is not managed, acute emotional symptoms or a life-threatening physical illness can result. Most elderly persons are not consciously aware of their anxiety levels, but know that anxiety can influence decision making. Family members themselves can sometimes raise the widowed person's level of anxiety in their attempt to be helpful.

In their attempt to be helpful, family members can raise the level of anxiety of the widowed person.

Exploring and learning to deal with anxiety in a group setting is not useful to all seniors. Many people who function fairly well are able to contain the anxiety resulting from the crisis of widowhood and adjust to being mateless on their own. They see widowhood as a natural part of the continuum of life. Other people become extremely anxious discussing death, the loss of their mates, and the negative aspects of widowhood. They do not want to wrestle with their anxiety. Their views must be respected. Those who can tolerate the anxiety generated by the topic of widowhood, however, go on to overcome psychological pain and often grow to be more mature human beings.

Older adults may not be familiar with psychological concepts or willing to discuss the psychological aspects of their lives.

Seniors often lack knowledge of psychological concepts and do not readily discuss psychological aspects of their lives. But if these same concepts can be presented in an understandable, nonthreatening way, these older people readily respond to questions of a psychological nature. Often, they view this kind of discussion as an open, freeing experience and hunger for it.

There are painless ways to introduce psychological topics to gain a fairly accurate picture of a person's emotional functioning. It is useful to listen for the emotional processes behind comments. "Emotional process" refers to the general hidden meaning behind what people say or do. For example, a widower may state that he had a good marriage, with no problems, and no arguments. The emotional-process message may be that he is denying any conflicts or differences and keeping the peace to prevent the differences from surfacing. The togetherness in the relationship may submerge the differences or the need to see them; that is, "to tell is to be disloyal." The emotional truth of the marriage may be different from the survivor's report after the spouse's death.

Caretaking. The second assumption used in the group is that certain people become "caretakers" by virtue of personality characteristics nurtured in the family of origin. In taking care of a chronically ill mate, the functional mate often becomes focused on the sick one to the exclusion of others. If caretaking becomes the primary activity in his or her life, the caretaker may face interpersonal dilemmas later. Caretakers usually have a difficult time assessing their own needs, giving themselves permission to spend money, or doing anything for themselves. This state of affairs makes being mateless a little more complicated: a long-term process yielding slow change.

It has been observed that widowed persons who maintain open relationships with family and friends and who pursue hobbies during the caretaking period adjust more easily to single life and grieve in a less isolated way. These same people have lifelong interests as well as centering mechanisms for themselves. Often, the emotional energy invested in caretaking gets refocused on children after the spouse's death. The responses to this refocusing depend on the ongoing relationships between parent and child and the ability of both parties to tolerate the shift in behavior.

> Spouses who excluded themselves from family and friends as they provided care for their mates may suffer more profound grief in widowhood than persons who maintained open relationships.

Wives and husbands who chose to let their spouses be cared for by other family members or paid caretakers seem to cope more effectively with widowhood if they have had an active role in care planning and frequent contact with the dysfunctional spouse. The widowed person who has allowed other caretakers to do too much of the decision making is likely to feel left out or guilty; this person often expresses regret at "not having done enough" for the spouse prior to the spouse's death.

Spouses in conflict, who got along poorly, form another category. This marital situation generates high overall tension and anxiety, and the functional spouse looks for someone to help with care, thereby detoxifying the emotional intensity of the marital relationship. Such survivors generally have more difficulty after the death of the spouse. In a group generally oriented to positive, loving, caring marital relationships, the spouse who had a negative relationship with conflict will need nonjudgmental emotional support from the group leader and group members. This person should be encouraged to express negative feelings without disapproval from the group.

> Widowed persons who had a negative relationship with their spouses need to be able to express their honest feelings without disapproval from the group.

Development of Self. One of the widowed person's biggest tasks is to work on defining a solid core of self and to see some worth in being self- rather than other-oriented. This process can occur naturally once the survivor has to face a myriad of decisions without an available spouse to consult. The assumption that variables influencing the development of self relate to one's sibling position underlies the group work. Responsibility and decision making come more easily to an oldest child than they do to a youngest child, who tends to be more dependent on others.

A second variable is whether one has been a "problem" youngest or oldest. The more problems the survivor has had as a youngster, the more problematic widowhood is likely to be.

A third variable is how introspective the survivor is. Today's seniors grew up in an era that did not emphasize self-focus or introspection. Seniors, however, can develop their ability to know themselves. Once seniors gain a better understanding of themselves, they have the potential of sticking to their beliefs and being better defined. For instance, in dating, they can be open and honest in their expectations and what they will tolerate. Likewise, they can maintain their parental status, even with adult children who want to reverse roles and tell their widowed parents how to live.

Mental Alertness. A fourth group assumption is that widowed seniors who continue to exercise their mental faculties and remain curious about their world tend to cope more effectively with the nodal event of widowhood. "Three types of personal resources have been related to adjustment in widowhood: income, social support and education" (George, 1980). Seniors in the group are encouraged to use their mental faculties for such activities as social groups, reading, puzzles, and hobbies. Deliberately maintaining mental alertness lessens the likelihood of a decline in mental functioning with advancing age. This observation remains true if declining physical health does not interfere in mental functioning.

Accepting the Challenge. The final group assumption is that some seniors view widowhood as a phase of life to be challenged and overcome—to discover new meaning. Typically, this group has put the death into perspective, remembering their spouses with cherished memories, but now turning their attention elsewhere. They also have begun investing their emotional energies in old, established relationships or new ones.

Purpose of the Group

The purpose of the group is to permit seniors an opportunity to come to grips with being widowed. Utilizing family theory as the background approach helps broaden people's view of this event in their lives. As family dynamics becomes more understandable, seniors often demonstrate a new level of insight about their particular lives and the influence of significant family relationships. Utilizing the larger family structure as the unit of orientation is different from the approach described in most literature on the grieving process. Family is alluded to but not considered in depth in most of the literature on widowhood. Instead, widowhood is discussed from the individual perspective. (See Table 21-1 for general suggestions about conducting a widowhood group.)

Theoretical Principles

Bowen's family systems theory has served as a blueprint for thinking about the group members and their stage of life (Bowen, 1983). This theory is composed of eight major concepts, but this chapter will deal with only five of them: triangles, differentiation of self, multigenerational transmission process, emotional cutoff, and sibling position.

TABLE 21-1. Dos and Don'ts for Conducting Widowhood Groups

Dos:

1. Maintain a healthy respect for the elderly.
2. Realize that you cannot take a senior's pain away.
3. Listen carefully—without having your mind on something else or what you will say next.
4. Have a tolerance for the various reactions and behaviors you may see related to the death of a spouse.
5. Respect a person's position and attitudes toward family and friends.
6. Know there are many sides and versions to happenings in families.
7. Encourage free expression of thoughts and feelings.
8. Make widows and widowers active participants in the group.
9. Be patient if a widow cannot immediately express herself in the group. With time, she will.
10. Intervene if others become judgmental regarding a person's attitude or family situation.
11. Reassure widowed people that they are not losing their sanity in the grief process, where necessary.
12. Recognize the critical therapeutic value of presence, or being there. How could you just be there and not do for the grieving person?
13. Feel comfortable mentioning the dead person.
14. Use the word "died" instead of terms like "passed away." But allow seniors to use whatever terms are comfortable for them.

Don'ts:

1. Don't expect a widow to be a certain place in the process of grieving on the basis of the time elapsed since the death.
2. Don't require widows to think differently about their families.
3. Don't let widows' situations overcome you. Often there are no easy answers to complex problems after a death.
4. Don't impose your religious views on the elderly or criticize them for not having any.
5. Don't take away the hope for a person to come to better terms with a death.
6. Don't be afraid to give your view on a problem.
7. Don't force a widowed person to accept your way of thinking.
8. Don't force them to stay in the group when the time comes for them to go on to other endeavors.
9. Don't forget to be your thoughtful self with them.

Triangle

In a triangle, or three-person relationship, the widowed person may communicate indirectly and not achieve the full relationship that is possible.

The triangle, a three-person configuration, is the molecule or the basic building block of any emotional system including a family (Bowen, 1983). Thus the smallest relationship in a family has three members, not two (Hall, 1983). A two-person relationship becomes unstable when the anxiety increases and a third person is then drawn into the emotional field. In periods of calm, the triangle is composed of a comfortably close twosome and a less comfortable outsider. In periods of stress, the outside position is more comfortable than the position of the tense twosome. People speak unknowingly of twosomes all the time. For example, they take sides with one member against another rather than remaining objective about the situation.

One of the most frequent examples of triangles is between a widowed parent, his or her child, and the child's spouse. For example, a widow may seek information about her son from a daughter-in-law rather than from the son directly. Triangulation, or pulling another person in where he or she is not needed, may diffuse anxiety, but it does nothing to develop person-to-person relationships. The widowed mother is better off directly confronting her son. In this manner, relationship lines are kept straight and clean. Triangles occur between in-laws and widows, widows and children, and widows and the extended family, and may even include the deceased person. Within the group, members are aided in identifying such triangles and encouraged to develop more direct means of communication.

Differentiation of Self

People emerge from their families with a fixed sense of themselves as individuals, separate from others. The degree to which individuals are dominated by their need for togetherness versus individuality is determined by the level of differentiation. Differentiation can also describe the way in which people function in relationships in terms of their ability to allow emotional autonomy in a relationship. When emotional autonomy is high, there is a greater capacity to be in a close relationship without having one's thinking, emotions, and behaviors governed by those relationships. The lower the level of differentiation, the greater the emotional need to have others think, behave, and feel according to one's desires (Kerr, 1984).

Differentiation of self is observed more than it is discussed among widowed persons. The degree of emotional bonding with others, the level of anxiety, and the degree of emotional cutoff with significant family members are assessed to determine the level of differentiation of self in a widow or widower. From discussions within the group, it can be determined if the widow is tangled in family emotional togetherness or fusion. If the widow or widower is beseiged with more chronic life problems and insistent that others' thinking should be consistent with his or her own, the individual is less differentiated. These individuals need assistance in finding effective ways to deal with their anxiety.

Multigenerational Transmission Process

By identifying how other generations within the family respond to crises, widowed persons can understand their own coping patterns.

This concept expands the emotional unit of the family from nuclear family to that of the larger family over generations (Kerr, 1981). The multigenerational transmission process demonstrates the strong tendency to repeat patterns of emotional behavior in successive generations, thereby creating a lower level of differentiation in some members of younger generations (Hall, 1983). This concept is used within the group to demonstrate to widows how their family members coped with widowhood so that they can understand their own coping patterns.

Emotional Cutoff

In an attempt to deal with togetherness or lack of differentiation in their intimate relationships, people may distance themselves from family members. This cutoff can be carried out geographically as well as psychologically by avoiding certain topics in the presence of family (Hall, 1983; Kerr, 1981). Bowen believes that the pattern of cutoffs is determined by how people handle their unresolved emotional attachment to their parents—all people have some degree of unresolved emotional attachments to their parents (Bowen, 1983). Finally, the concept deals with the way in which people disconnect themselves from the past in order to start their lives in the present.

Most group members know immediately what is meant by cutting a family member off emotionally or distancing that person for some time or forever. Often, group members will describe the process in which they renewed relationships with distant siblings even before the death of the spouse as a means of weaning themselves from their mates. Some cutoffs within families have been in place for generations, so the process of reconnecting can be difficult or unlikely. For instance, older siblings who have had a poor relationship and not spoken since their teen years may have no desire to develop a meaningful relationship much later in life. Assessing the kind of cutoffs in the widowed person's life can yield insight into the available support system.

Sibling Position

The theory that sibling position influences personality characteristics is used to understand how persons cope with widowhood. It is believed that oldest children will manage widowhood better than youngest children.

It is believed that personality characteristics are derived from a person's sibling position (Bowen, 1983). An oldest child, for instance, is believed to be more responsible and domineering than a youngest child. Families reinforce such expectations as well. Sibling position is important to assess in widowed persons. It has been noted in the group that youngest children frequently have a harder time dealing with widowhood; they have more difficulty making decisions and facing responsibility. Oldest children seem to be more responsible and deal more easily with the tasks of single life. Persons who came from a large family and lost many of their siblings before they were widowed may be prone to loneliness and desire close relationships and support of group members.

The Family Diagram, or Genogram

Use of the genogram (Figure 21-1) provides a framework that enables a person to organize a large amount of data related to family structure and dynamics. It broadens individuals' views of themselves and the unit from which they come. It can be a simple, organized "road map" of an ongoing life in a family across three or more generations.

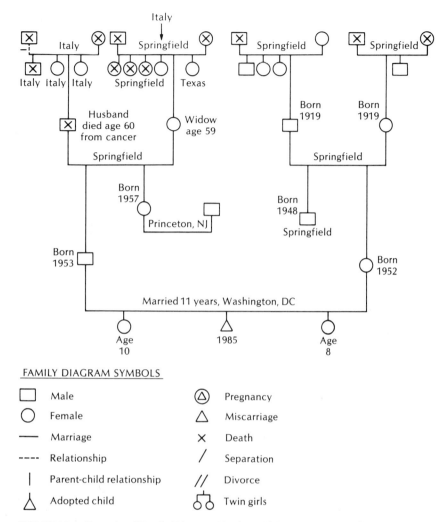

FIGURE 21-1. Example of Family Diagram, Used as Aid in Discussing Family Dynamics.

Factors such as physical, social, and emotional illnesses are recorded. Other information includes dates of births, deaths, severe illnesses, hospitalizations, marriages, separations, divorces, moves, and promotions. It charts when family members retire, when children leave home, how close family members live to each other, how often they have contact with family members, and the nature of contacts. It could also include such data as religious affiliation.

For a number of months the author compiled genograms with members of the widowhood group. Most seemed to enjoy and profit from this exercise. They easily made connections between facts and began to see dynamics among family members in new ways.

Summary

It should be noted that the use of family therapy takes considerable time to master and use appropriately. Anyone interested in using the family systems theory described in this chapter should become familiar with Bowen's *Family Therapy in Clinical Practice* (1983). It would also be advantageous to discuss these ideas with a professional who has utilized the theory.

It is difficult at best to superimpose family theory on group process. Family therapy was designed primarily to be used with one or only a few family members. It can be difficult to achieve individualized attention in the group setting. Likewise, some widowed persons have not viewed the family as a resource and may react negatively to this approach.

On the other hand, positive results often outweigh the disadvantages of conducting a widowhood group in this manner. Often, widows are helped to develop deeper, more meaningful relationships with their family members. They learn to express themselves more openly, and they benefit from reminiscing about family and the past. It is rewarding to see these individuals develop a stronger sense of self and face the world with new confidence. The family systems approach can help families to serve a crucial role in the healing process associated with widowhood.

REFERENCES

Bowen M: Family Therapy in Clinical Practice. New York, Jason Arson, 1983.

George LK: Role Transitions in Later Life. Monterey, CA, Brooks/Cole, 1980.

Hall MC: The Bowen Family Theory and Its Uses. New York, Jason Aronson, 1983.

Kerr ME: Family systems theory and therapy. In Gurman AS, Kniskern DP (eds): Handbook of Family Therapy, 226–264. New York, Brunner/Mazel, 1981.

Kerr ME: Theoretical Base for Differentiation of Self in One's Family of Origin. New York, Haworth Press, 1984.

Rado TA: Grief, Dying and Death. Champaign, IL, Research Press, 1984.

Raphael B: The Anatomy of Bereavement. New York, Basic Books, 1983.

Wylie BJ: Beginnings: A Book for Widows. New York, Ballantine, 1984.

BIBLIOGRAPHY

Gass KA: Coping strategies of widows. J Gerontol Nurs 13(8): 29–33, 1987.

Lindsay R: Alone and Surviving. New York, Walker, 1977.

Preston D, Grimes J: A study of differences in social support. J Gerontol Nurs 13(2): 36–40, 1987.

Rauckhorst LM: Health habits of elderly widows. J Gerontol Nurs 13(8): 19–22, 1987.

Remondet JH, Hansson RO: Assessing a widow's grief—A short index. J Gerontol Nurs 13(4): 30–34, 1987.

Richter JM: Support: A resource during crisis of mate loss. J Gerontol Nurs 13(11): 18–22, 1987.

Ryan MC, Patterson J: Loneliness in the elderly. J Gerontol Nurs 13(5): 6–12, 1987.

Valanis B, Yeaworth RC, Mullis MR: Alcohol use among bereaved and non-bereaved older persons. J Gerontol Nurs 13(5): 26–32, 1987.

Viorst J: Necessary Losses. New York, Simon & Schuster, 1986.

Whall AL: Family Therapy for Nursing: Four Approaches. New York, Appleton-Century-Crofts, 1986.

Whall AL: Therapeutic use of self. J Gerontol Nurs 14(2): 38–39, 46–47, 1988.

Yost E, Corbishley M: Group therapy. In Chaisson-Stewart M (ed): Depression in the Elderly: An Interdisciplinary Approach, 288–315. New York, Wiley, 1985.

CHAPTER 22

Adaptive Equipment Specialists: A Nurse-Owned Business to Promote Independent Living in the Community

LuRae Ahrendt

Chapter Objectives
At the completion of this chapter the reader will be able to:

1. List the types of assistance that can enable disabled persons to function in the community.
2. Describe how nurses can develop their own health-related businesses.

Increasing numbers of disabled elderly with a wide diversity of needs are choosing to remain in their homes rather than enter an institutional setting. Quite naturally, people feel more comfortable in their home environments and do not easily forfeit the possessions, relationships, and life-style that living in one's home provides. The cost of nursing home care or retirement community living may be beyond the means of many elderly individuals; thus living at home becomes an economic necessity.

The growing prevalence of disabled persons in the home setting also relates to changes in health care reimbursement. Lengths of hospital stays have significantly declined since the implementation of Diagnostic Related Groups (DRGs), and patients are being discharged more quickly than in the past and in sicker, more dependent states. There may be insufficient time for appropriate discharge planning; rarely do hospital staff have the ability to conduct a home visit to fully identify functional and accessibility needs of patients prior to discharge.

It may not be until patients return to their homes after hospital discharge that they become aware of the impact of their disabilities on their routine activities. They may not have considered how they would reach the top shelves in their kitchens, transfer in the bathtub, propel their wheelchairs down the steps to their yards, or prepare meals with one nonfunctional arm. Often, they may not be able to identify their needs for, or may be unaware of, assistive devices and environmental modifications that could improve their functional capacity. If they are knowledgeable enough to assess their needs, these disabled persons may then discover that community resources are lacking or difficult to coordinate.

Creating a Business Venture from a Community Need

Assistive devices and environmental modifications can make the difference for a disabled person between remaining in the community and entering an institutional setting.

Through their professional and community activities, the author, a registered nurse, and her husband, a physical therapist, witnessed numerous examples of the problems confronting disabled persons in the community as they tried to function in their homes. An enormous gap existed between the many assistive devices, special equipment, and structural modifications available to aid the disabled, and the disabled persons who needed them. The solution seemed simple: Bridge the gap through a special service that would bring resources and disabled persons together. This service became a business venture, Adaptive Equipment Specialists (AES).

As the name implies, the company provides *accessibility specialists* who are experienced in the creative use of medical equipment and structural modifications in relationship to a person's disabilities. The staff represents several disciplines, including rehabilitation nurses, physicians, physical therapists, occupational therapists, and social workers. The team offers expertise in assessment and care of the disabled, as well as knowledge of durable medical equipment. They maintain regular contact with many manufacturers to stay current with new and cost-effective equipment that could benefit clients.

In addition to professional staff, technicians are involved with the company. These individuals customize equipment and make necessary environmental modifications. As they are needed, plumbers, electricians, and carpenters are contracted for major renovations or installation of special equipment.

Services of AES

After AES has been contacted by the disabled person, family, or referring agency, services begin with assessment of the client and the home environment by the nurse and the durable medical equipment specialist. Evaluation of the physical environment of the home requires careful observation in order to identify any structural obstacles to accessibility and function. Findings are documented (Figure 22-1) for later review with the AES team.

Barriers to independent function are noted. Obstacles may include stairways, limited bathroom space, narrow doorways and hallways, and furniture. Adaptive equipment that the client is currently using, such as wheelchairs, ramps, and bathroom safety equipment, is evaluated for

Adaptive Equipment Specialists

Home Access and Use Assessment

I. General Information
   Customer _____ Date _____
   Address _____
   Contact person _____ Relationship _____
   Phone _____ (home) _____ (work)
   Patient profile _____
   _____
   _____
   _____

   Date of discharge _____ Agency _____ Age ____
   Health care team _____ Phone _____
   _____ Phone _____
   Type of wheelchair _____
   Prosthetic appliances _____

II. Home
   ____ Number of stories ____ Trailer ____ Apartment
   Own ____ Rent ____ Is remodeling possible? ____

III. Entrances   Front   Back
   A. Height of sill   ____   ____
       Number of steps   ____   ____
       Width of steps   ____   ____
       Height of steps   ____   ____
       Width of door   ____   ____
       Door opens (in/out)   ____   ____
       Ramping possible   ____   ____
   B. Other entrances _____

IV. Garage
   Clearance by car _____ Wheelchair accessible _____
   Accessible to house _____

V. Bedroom
   Width of hallway to bedroom _____ Door width _____
   Type of bed _____ Bed height _____ Clearance under bed _____
   Type of flooring _____ Closet type _____
   Room size _____ Width _____ Depth _____

VI. Bathroom
   Width of hallway to bathroom _____ Door width _____
   Room size _____ Width _____ Depth _____
   A. Tub height _____ Depth _____
      Tub door width of opening _____ Removable _____
      Describe faucet handles _____
   B. Shower stall _____ Width _____ Depth _____
      Threshold height _____ Describe faucet handles _____
      Shower nozzle _____ Hand spray _____
   C. Toilet height _____ Clearance sides of toilet ____ (L) ____ (R)
      Clearance under sink _____ Describe faucet handles _____

VII. Eating Areas
   A. Clearance under kitchen table _____
      Clearance under dining table _____
   B. Sink
      Describe faucet handles _____
      Cabinet height _____ Clearance under sink _____
      Cabinet depth _____

VIII. Stairwells _____
   Decks _____ Patios _____

IX. Summary

   Submitted by _____

FIGURE 22-1. Form for Documenting the Home Environment. (Reprinted with permission of Adaptive Equipment Specialists.)

effectiveness. Scattered rugs, the absence of smoke alarms, lack of handrails, poor telephone access, lack of emergency exit, unsafe adaptive equipment, and other hazards are identified. Also, the status of the living arrangement must be explored: Modifications for an apartment, an owned home, and a temporary residence belonging to a relative would differ.

The interview with the client and family offers valuable information that enables a total picture of the home situation to be obtained. During the interview, mental and physical limitations of the client become apparent, as do the client's and family's perceptions of the limitations. The need for clarification or education of prognosis and goals may be identified.

Findings and identified needs are reviewed with the client and family. Some immediate correction of environmental problems may occur—for example, removing scatter rugs or installing a battery in a smoke detector. Recommendations for equipment and structural modifications may be presented during the initial visit or later, after the AES team has discussed the client's unique situation.

Modifications to the home should be done in a manner that does not jeopardize the potential resale value of the property.

Structural modifications may be indicated when clients have long-term accessibility requirements and reside in their own homes. Every effort is made to assure that modifications maintain the integrity of the home and not destroy its potential resale value. If extensive modification to the home is warranted, it may be advantageous to build an addition to the home that will not only fulfill the requirements of the disabled person, but also increase the resale value of the home. In some rare instances, persons with multiple mental or physical disabilities may benefit from the purchase of a new home whose style is more appropriate for unique abilities and limitations.

Door widening is a simple adaptation that provides better mobility in the home for the wheelchair-bound person. Ramps on exterior doors provide effective accessibility for persons who are wheelchair-bound or who have limited mobility. Bathroom modifications are common; most disabled clients have limitations with independent bathing and toileting activities. The hard surfaces and slippery areas in the bathroom make this a high-risk area for injuries. Color-coded faucets, toilet seat lifts, and converted showers that allow a shower chair to be pushed from a dry surface into the shower area are among the useful bathroom modifications.

General safety tips are always shared with clients. Individuals with decreased mobility require extra time to vacate the premises in the event of an emergency. Strategically placed smoke and fire alarms can reduce the time necessary to warn the disabled person of a problem. The route and method of exit from the bedroom and main living area should be identified. Telephones should be accessible and have emergency numbers clearly visible.

Mobility within and outside the home is usually the client's primary concern. Ramps are often a good solution for wheelchair-bound individuals; they should have handrails and wheelchair guards built onto them.

Stairway lifts and wheelchair lifts are needed to provide stair access. Each type of lift has specific features to meet the accessibility needs of different disabled persons and various home settings. Stairway lifts are easily installed and adaptable to straight or curved staircases. In some units, the

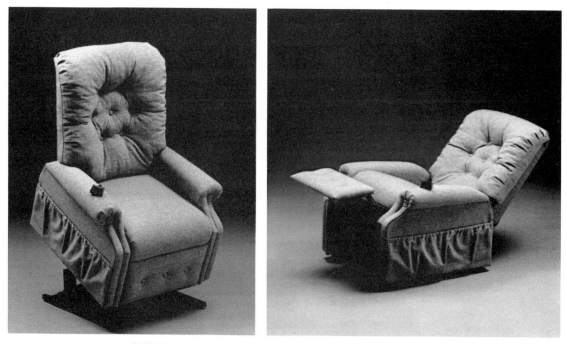

FIGURE 22-2. American Stair-Glide Easy-Lift Chair.

person rides sideways, and in others the person rides up the stairway backward. The stand-up lift is ideal for the person with hip or knee pain that makes sitting difficult. These stairway lifts have seat belts and pressure-sensitive foot plates as safety features. Matching the appropriate lift equipment with the special needs of the client is done by AES.

Stairway lift equipment can be rented for persons requiring only temporary assistance—persons recovering from surgery or a fracture, for example. These can also be considered by the client who is temporarily residing in a relative's home. Usually rental agencies offer clients a purchase option after three months' rental.

In addition to acquainting disabled persons with the wide variety of durable medical equipment available, AES advises clients about the need for the equipment to be prescribed by a physician or therapist and the potential and process for third-party reimbursement.

Assistive aids are manufactured for every activity of daily living. Lift chairs (Figure 22-2) are ideal for older people who have difficulty getting up and down from a seated position. Many hygiene and kitchen aids (Figure 22-3) are available for persons with weakness of the arm or hand. Hand-held showers are a popular product to assist with bathing. Blade handles make faucets easier for gripping. Electrical door closers are now available for private residences. Many of these aids are relatively inexpensive and very helpful to the elderly.

Safety in the home is of primary importance for the geriatric population. Installing grab bars in the toilet and bath area is one way of increasing

Many older persons without disabilities could benefit from environmental modifications and assistive devices that reduce their risk of injury.

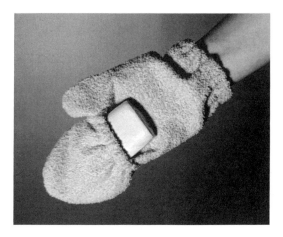

FIGURE 22-3. *Top left,* Maddak, Inc., Terry Cloth Wash Unit with Pocket for Soap. *Top right,* Maddak Special Cutlery. *Left,* Maddak Easiturn Faucet Handle.

safety. Various toilet equipment, like raised toilet seats and closed-front toilet seats, helps disabled persons use the toilet independently. A toilet for the disabled can be installed in most bathrooms, as can transfer benches to help persons transfer in and out of the shower or tub. Tub lift equipment (Figure 22-4) can promote bathtub safety. There should be handrails and good lighting at all stairways. Such specialized equipment allows the elderly person to be independent as well as safe in the home.

View of the Nurse-Entrepreneur

The role of the nurse in AES continues to grow and change with the expansion of the business. Clinically, the company's role is a dynamic one, and nursing holds an important place among the team of professionals. Nursing's holistic orientation provides the ability to assess how the disability affects mental, physical, and social health and plan strategies to maximize independence. Independent function, confidence, and hope are increased as clients are enabled to use their abilities, rather than be imprisoned within their disabilities.

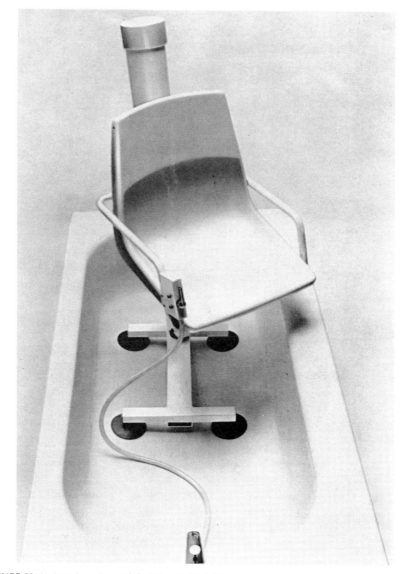

FIGURE 22-4. American Stair-Glide Tubmate Bath Lift.

Nurses possess a wide range of knowledge and skills that make them ideal candidates to develop health-related businesses. By owning a business, the nurse can control the quality of services delivered.

There are immense rewards in working with the family unit. By removing some of the barriers to optimum function, the caregiving load can be reduced and a normal household life-style preserved.

By being an owner of this business, the nurse has the ability to influence the quality of services provided. The philosophy and standards of care that the nurse believes in can permeate service delivery. There is the unique opportunity to develop a service model, as well as to serve as a resource to the community. New skills are gained as the nurse learns about business promotion, personnel management, budgeting, corporate taxation, and the many other details of operating a small business enterprise.

Nurses possess a wide range of special knowledge and skills that can be used to create exciting new service delivery models through private enterprise. Increased nurse-entrepreneurial activity offers new resources to the community and additional facets to the role of the nurse.

Appendix: List of Manufacturers

American Stair-Glide Corporation
Mr. Rick Thomas
4001 East 138th Street
Grandview, MO 64030
(816) 763–3100

Trans-Aid Corporation
Mr. Dave Marks
53 West Main Street
Turbotville, PA 17772
(717) 649–5174

Toce Brothers Manufacturing
Mr. John Toce
P.O. Box 447
Broussard, LA 70518
1–800–842–8158

Maddak, Inc.
Mr. Steve Levine
6 Industrial Road
Pequannock, NJ 07440–1993
(201) 694–0500

BIBLIOGRAPHY

Belk J: Federal policy and disabled people. Caring 6(8): 6–9, 52–54, 1987.

Coombs J: Living with the Disabled: You Can Help. New York, Sterling, 1984.

Neuberger J: New for the old . . . Better design of clothing and furniture for elderly patients. Nurs Times 82(41): 22, 1986.

Penn ND: Toilet aids. Brit Med J 296(6626): 918–919, 1988.

Pitsele SK: We Are Not Alone: Learning to Live with Chronic Illness. New York, Workman, 1986.

Staebler R: Community: A home and family for the disabled. Caring 6(8): 47–51, 1987.

Tynan C, Cardea JM: Community service home health hazard assessment. J Gerontol Nurs 13(10): 25–28, 1987.

PART THREE

Gerontological Nursing in Acute Care Settings

People age 65 and older constitute the greatest consumers of acute hospital services in the United States, and this pattern is expected to continue in the future. Hospitals have recognized that they are intensely involved in geriatric care and that their future fiscal viability may largely depend on the appropriateness and range of services they offer the elderly.

An important realization of acute care providers is that older individuals are different from adults of other ages. There are unique risks of illness and injury, altered presentations of symptoms and responses to therapy, and more complex psychosocial variables to address. To assure a high standard of care, age-related norms, treatment modifications, and a wide range of resources must be learned and used.

This part explores ways in which nurses in the acute sector can promote a high quality of gerontological care. A comprehensive review of the pre-, intra-, and postoperative care of older surgical patients offers specific facts and skills to assist nurses in assuring that more benefits than problems result from surgery. Concise guidelines for the recognition and initial management of common psychiatric problems are presented, as is a description of a geriatric assessment team that demonstrates one type of outreach service that hospitals can provide to the elderly.

Nurses who work in acute psychiatric, medical, surgical, and emergency care services must realize that gerontological nursing constitutes a large portion of their practice and become knowledgeable about the unique aspects of nursing the aged. By doing so, acute hospital nurses can assure not only that more years are added to an older adult's life, but also that the highest possible quality of life accompanies those added years.

CHAPTER 23

A Hospital-Based Geriatric Assessment Team

Lacy Flynn

Chapter Objectives
At the completion of this chapter the reader will be able to:

1. Describe the functions of a geriatric assessment team.
2. List the factors that are included in the multidisciplinary team assessment.
3. Discuss the types of problems that clients may present to the assessment team.

Geriatric clients frequently possess multiple problems requiring services that cross traditional boundaries (Moore et al., 1984). Communities are concerned with addressing these problems by providing services that can enhance the quality of life for elderly persons and their families. Such was the case in the Baltimore metropolitan area, where one hospital decided to address this service need by developing a multidisciplinary geriatric assessment team.

The hospital, Greater Baltimore Medical Center, had already demonstrated initiative in addressing the needs of the community's senior population by establishing a Center for Aging, responsible for the planning and oversight of geriatric services. When the concept of a geriatric assessment team was considered, the center developed a steering committee to survey the medical staff on this perceived need. Approximately 600 survey forms were sent to the medical staff, and the results not only supported the need for this service, but also revealed specific problems encountered by physicians as they worked with older clients. Interestingly, the most common of these problems were nonmedical in nature, for example, companionship, socialization, transportation, custodial care, support systems, evaluation for nursing home placement, and supervision of medication administration. The survey findings demonstrated a compelling need for a multidisciplinary approach to the medical, psychiatric, physical, and social needs of geriatric clients, and indicated the medical staff's support of this approach.

With the mission established, a literature search was conducted to learn about existing services that provided outpatient geriatric assessment and rehabilitation. It was discovered that there was little research in the area of outpatient geriatric assessment, although there was support for the judgment that an assessment service can influence a reduction in the need for institutionalization.

Most assessment teams consist of a physician, registered nurse, social worker, and, in some cases, a dietitian. The hospital decided to develop a similar structure, but also to include a pharmacist and physical therapist in recognition of the significance of drug-related problems and the need for astute functional assessment. The professionals on the team were selected for their interest in improving the quality of life of older persons and their caregivers. Members of the team adhere to the philosophy that the geriatric assessment team has the potential to have an impact on clients' quality of life by dealing with medical and psychosocial problems, the relationship between the client and the family or caregiver, and the environment (Riley, 1987).

The Intake Process

The program was designed to accommodate referrals from a variety of sources in the community. Clients are referred from primary physicians, social service agencies, home health services, retirement communities, public health and aging services departments, family members, friends, and clergy. (The experience of the program has been that most clients are referred from local county agencies.) Appointments are scheduled through the outpatient department of the hospital. When the appointment is scheduled clients are requested to bring with them all the medications they are using, including over-the-counter drugs. Clients and caregivers are prepared for the fact that the total assessment process will take approximately five hours.

Clients are advised that when they come for their assessment they should bring all prescription and nonprescription drugs used.

Clients are scheduled to arrive early in the morning, usually staggered at 8:00, 8:15, and 8:30. It has been found that often the frail older clients are accompanied by elderly offspring, and both are genuinely concerned, apprehensive, and occasionally angry about the day. The nurse plays a significant role by greeting clients, caregivers, and family members, explaining the routines, answering questions, and making them feel comfortable. Volunteers have proved beneficial in spending time with clients to assist them in being comfortable, and in recognizing and alerting staff to client problems, such as inappropriate behavior and poor family interactions.

Nursing Assessment

The nurse is the first team member to assess the client; therefore, he or she holds a strategic position on the team. The team nurse must be a competent and sensitive practitioner, preferably certified in gerontological nursing by the American Nurses' Association. In addition, some management skills are useful for the nurse to possess, since she or he must serve as a coordinator of team services. Not to be forgotten, also, are efficiency, compassion, and a good sense of humor.

During the nursing interview the tone is set for the entire assessment process.

The nursing interview sets the stage for the entire day and begins by acquainting the client and caregiver with the process, expected time frame, restroom facilities, and multidisciplinary team members who will be encountered. The nurse explains that there may be repetition in the questions various team members ask, but that each discipline will have a different reason for asking the question. Clients and caregivers are strongly encouraged to ask questions and clarify information. The investment of time in this preparation is beneficial in promoting trust and relaxation during the day.

The nursing assessment includes a review of systems, functional capacity, and mental status (similar to that outlined in Chapter 3). The nurse will explore the circumstances that led to the client's coming to the assessment service, together with feelings and expectations concerning the assessment process. The role and expectations of the caregiver are also reviewed. Self-care capacity is determined, as are the mechanisms used to manage deficits.

In addition to performing the nursing assessment, the nurse serves as a vital link among team members by alerting them to significant covert problems, such as a spouse's clue that her husband's memory problems are associated with alcohol abuse, or the client's hesitancy to speak openly in front of the caregiver. Also, other disciplines can be alerted to questions or areas of concern that should be explored during their assessments.

Multidisciplinary Assessment

What are the dynamic processes of clients' social situations that have shaped the course of their lives and those who care for them? What role structures have affected their lives as they have aged, such as motherhood, widowhood, and retirement? These are the areas explored by the social worker, who will ascertain the social situation of the client and interactions among the client and family members, and make recommendations to improve life-style. Some of the areas reviewed by the social worker include the client's primary contact in an emergency, social network, friends, neighbors, family dynamics, community agencies being utilized, home environment, economic resources, interests, former occupation, and ability to manage stress. Interventions and service needs arise from deficits discovered; however, the team has found that clients often are reluctant to utilize community resources. To this proud generation of self-sufficient persons who survived two world wars, the Great Depression, and many other hardships, the

Older adults may reject social services because of their belief in self-sufficiency or unwillingness to change behavioral patterns.

use of social services is often associated with charity or welfare. Also, clients and caregivers may reject social services because they threaten to "rock the boat" and change known patterns of behavior in their lives. The social worker will clarify the intent of services and explain the relationship of services to independent living in the community. If the client or caregiver persists in refusing social services, this choice is respected, but a door is left open for future contact if there is readiness for service utilization at a later time.

The elderly's unique responses to drug therapy, the prevalence of polypharmacy, and the serious consequences of drug misuse justify the vital role of the pharmacist in the assessment process. The clinical pharmacist obtains a thorough medication history and counsels and educates when problems are identified. Areas that are reviewed include prescription and over-the-counter drugs being used (including medications and remedies purchased in health food stores); how and when medications are taken; the client's understanding of medication use; signs of side effects and adverse reactions; and alcohol, tobacco, and caffeine use. If the pharmacist sees notations of client complaints or problems detected during the nursing assessment, the client is questioned as to the management of these problems to detect self-medication practices. By having the pharmacist's review prior to the physician's assessment, recommendations for alternative medication regimens or the potential need for medication can be proposed for the physician's consideration.

The assessment of frail elderly who have deteriorating functional abilities needs careful attention as it influences the determination of the elderly's success in maintaining independent living in the community (Rubenstein, 1981). Physical therapy assessment aids in identifying reasons for decline (be they physiological, social, environmental, or psychological) and developing a plan by which the highest level of independent functioning is maintained or promoted. This evaluation will also assist in assuring that the best placement and support are afforded to the individual. The physical therapist's assessment includes evaluation of functional capacity (ability to engage in activities of daily living), determination of gross range of motion, gross manual muscle testing, and screening for gait problems. The physical therapist will use the assessment data from other disciplines to identify possible causes for functional deficiencies, for example, the impact of polypharmacy on mobility. Follow-up rehabilitation in the form of physical, occupational, or speech therapy may be recommended and can prove valuable in decreasing dependency, reducing isolation, and revitalizing the client and family.

> Clients and their family members actively participate in the team conference to discuss findings and develop plans.

The last team member to see the client is the physician, who will conduct a complete history and physical, and review lab studies (urinalysis and SMAC) that were performed earlier in the day. After the multidisciplinary evaluation, the entire team meets to review findings, identify care needs, make recommendations, and establish long- and short-term goals. If additional services at a later date are deemed necessary, the client may be referred for such services as dietetic counseling, speech assessment, psychiatric consultation, and diagnostic studies (Table 23-1). The final part of the process is the most significant: the team conference with the client and caregiver. The conference is conducted in a comfortable room with uninterrupted privacy. The team presents their findings and recommendations, and encourages feedback and suggestions from the client and caregiver. Frank, open, mutual interaction is promoted.

TABLE 23-1. Types of Problems Presented by Clients and Follow-up

Problem	Follow-up
Chronic depression related to double amputation	Referral to physical and occupational therapists, counseling services.
Social isolation	Referral to local senior center, physical therapy assessment of arthritis problem to determine if function could be enhanced.
Occasional urinary incontinence	Educational sessions for muscle strengthening exercises, recommendation of use of adult briefs, discussion of ways to avoid falls and skin breakdown.
Inappropriate drug use	Counseling by pharmacist, discussion with primary physician about need for close monitoring.

With the client's written permission, the diagnostic/therapeutic plan is sent to the client's primary physician and referring agency. The team's physician will telephone the client's physician to discuss findings and recommendations; this practice has been found to enhance continuity and client compliance.

Evaluating Efforts

Follow-up with the client approximately one month after the assessment aids in evaluating the effectiveness of the service.

As a quality assurance measure, a follow-up questionnaire was devised to assess the impact of the team. Approximately three to four weeks after the visit, the nurse, physician, or social worker will call the client and caregiver and ask for feedback about the benefit of the service. Questions included the following:

1. Do you feel that your reason for coming to the Geriatric Assessment Service was addressed and resolved to your satisfaction?
2. Were you able to utilize the recommendations and follow through on your own or with family help? If not, what problems were encountered? What help did you receive and from whom?
3. Did team members follow up promptly and effectively on what they said they would do?
4. Did you learn of any new health or other types of problems as a result of the evaluation?
5. Have you made any changes in your life as a result of the evaluation?
6. Would you recommend the service to others?
7. What was most helpful about the evaluation?
8. What would you suggest to improve the service?

Team members are asked to complete an evaluation for each encounter relative to the following:

1. Was institutionalization prevented if the client was at risk?
2. How was life-style affected? Was there a resumption on the part of the

client of normal activities? Was socialization increased? Independence increased? Improvements achieved in the manner of taking medications?

3. Recommendations:

Were they followed and effective?

Was team follow-up timely and adequate?

CASE EXAMPLES

MR. F.

This case presentation deals with social isolation exacerbated by sensory deficits. Mr. F. is a 78-year-old male who is able to perform all of the necessary activities of daily living. He lives in an apartment with his wife, upon whom he appears to be quite dependent. During Mr. F.'s evaluation a profound hearing loss was noted, making it difficult to make a valid assessment of his mental status. He was found to have an irregular heartbeat and demonstrated an unsteady gait. Ankle edema was present and, from the history obtained, seemed to be related to the client's pattern of spending a great deal of time sitting with his legs hanging over the side of an armchair. No medications were being used by him. His wife claimed that Mr. F.'s memory had become poor and that he sometimes appeared confused. The social work evaluation indicated that his social isolation and boredom certainly reduced his functional status. Based on the findings, the team developed the following recommendations:

1. Otolarnygology evaluation. *Mr. F. most definitely needed to be evaluated to determine if there was a reversible component. If hearing could be improved, a more valid appraisal of mental status could also be gained.*

2. Physical therapy evaluation. *The reason for the abnormal gait needed to be determined and recommendations made as to the appropriateness of mobility aids.*

3. Cardiology evaluation. *The team physician notified Mr. F.'s primary physician, who was expected to begin medical evaluation and arrange referral as desired. In the interim, Mr. F. was counseled to elevate legs and reduce sodium intake.*

4. Geriatric day care. *To increase socialization, Mr. F. was informed of the local day-care programs and instructed in admission procedures.*

5. Assistive devices. *In light of Mr. F.'s deafness, he and his wife were acquainted with resources for the hearing impaired, such as the Lifetime Telephone Emergency System.*

The major issues and recommendations were discussed with the family. Through the discussion it was revealed that Mrs. F. encourages her husband to be totally dependent upon her, to the detriment of his own independent status. Mrs. F. manages the finances, shopping, meals, transportation, and laundry, leaving Mr. F. with little else to do but sit and watch television (even though he cannot hear it). Mrs. F. needed to feel assured that her hus-

band's well-being would not be jeopardized by increasing his independence and responsibilities.

In the follow-up with Mr. F. no major cardiovascular problem was discovered, although the recommended practices of a low-sodium diet and leg elevation were reinforced. Mr. F.'s gait improved as his ankle edema subsided and strength improved through increased activity; no mobility aid was deemed necessary at this time. Perhaps the most significant outcome to Mr. and Mrs. F. was the improvement in hearing capacity. The ear evaluation resulted in the discovery and removal of a deep cerumen impaction and the prescription of a hearing aid. The subsequent improvement in hearing made a profound difference to Mr. F.'s mental acuity and socialization. At this point, Mr. F. does not want to attend day care, but he has arranged to join the local senior center.

MRS. B.

The case of Mrs. B. demonstrates the significance of follow-up evaluation. Mrs. B., a physically healthy 75-year-old, lives with her employed daughter and retired son-in-law. Her appointment with the Geriatric Assessment Service was scheduled by her daughter, who is concerned by her mother's declining mental function and weight loss. Mrs. B.'s daughter shared a written evaluation done by a community psychiatrist that indicated his conclusion that Mrs. B. was suffering from a dementia, most probably Alzheimer's disease; the daughter fully understood this. Mrs. B. is able to perform activities of daily living that are pertinent to her personal care and hygiene, but is unable to perform the independent skills required for money management, shopping, or transportation. During the nursing and social work evaluations, information was obtained that indicated the family was struggling to maintain Mrs. B. at home. She was argumentative, insistent in doing chores that posed serious safety hazards for the family (e.g., turning on the gas to cook and forgetting to turn it off), and increasingly wandered outside, forgetting how to find her way home. The son-in-law, although retired, had many interests that took him away from the home and felt resentful at having to forfeit his activities to "baby-sit" his mother-in-law while his wife worked. The daughter did not feel she could leave her job to care for her mother because of the retirement income she would jeopardize and the resulting financial burden for her family. Mrs. B. had no other children or family members to assist with the situation. The family had attempted using home aides to supervise Mrs. B. while her daughter worked, but Mrs. B. behaved so violently with them that none would stay after a few days. Physical findings were unremarkable, except for a mild high-frequency hearing loss.

The team's findings were consistent with the previously established diagnosis of dementia, and their major focus was to maintain the well-being of all family members. The family had attempted every means of home management of Mrs. B., and tensions were mounting at the increased disruption she was causing to the household. In addition to the concern for the quality of life of the daughter and son-in-law, the safety of all household members *had to be considered. The team supplied Mrs. B.'s daughter with information on support services for Alzheimer's disease victims and caregivers, as well as local day-care programs. Also, the team introduced the idea that the family begin planning for the potential need for institutional care of Mrs. B. Mrs. B. became quite agitated with the recommendation, her daughter became tearful, and the son-in-law expressed interest. The team felt that the introduction of this very difficult recommendation from an objective third party could relieve some of the burden on the family in reaching this conclusion. The daughter responded, "I could never do that to my mother," and prepared to leave; the son-in-law showed disappointment with his wife's decision. As the family left, they were reassured that the team was available to assist the family in the future.*

In order to assess the team's success with compliance, a follow-up telephone call was made several weeks after Mrs. B.'s visit to the assessment service. The call was answered by the very depressed sounding son-in-law, who frantically urged the team to call his wife at work. (Loud, incoherent speech from Mrs. B. could be heard in the background.) Mrs. B.'s daughter was called and admitted to increased destructiveness of the home environment. Day care had not been successful because of Mrs. B.'s violent attacks on other participants. The daughter's sleep was interrupted by her mother's night wandering, and her marriage was being strained by her husband's resentment, frustration, and unhappiness. The reality of the risks to everyone's physical, emotional, and social health outweighed the daughter's guilt, and she requested the team's assistance in seeking nursing home care for her mother.

In its several years of existence, the Geriatric Assessment Service has had an impact on the lives of hundreds of individuals by identifying and correcting problems, improving the management of problems that are not reversible, and matching geriatric clients with services specific to their needs. It is felt that the quality of life of clients and their caregivers has improved as a result. In addition, the community has an important resource that offers an easy, single point of entry for multidisciplinary assessment, care planning, and referral. By charging a fee that covers staff time and laboratory services, the hospital was able to create this service without compromising its existing resources. It is hoped that other hospitals will see the benefit of a geriatric assessment service and assume leadership in adding this program to the existing continuum of community geriatric services.

REFERENCES

Moore JT, Warshaw GA, Walden L: Evolution of a geriatric evaluation clinic. J Am Geriatr Soc, 32(12): 900–905, 1984.

Riley A: Personal interview, Greater Baltimore Medical Center, Baltimore, MD, 1987.

Rubenstein LZ: Specialized geriatric assessment units and their clinical implications. Western J Med, 136(6): 497–501, 1981.

BIBLIOGRAPHY

Baurret E: Improving patient care for the elderly through a geriatric consultation team. Perspectives 10(4): 11–12, 1986.

Black S: The needs of the well elderly. Health Visit 60(8): 266–267, 1987.

Campion EW: The merits of geriatric consultation. JAMA 257(17): 2336–2337, 1987.

Eliopoulos C (ed): Health Assessment of the Older Adult. Menlo Park, CA, Addison-Wesley, 1989.

Howie C: Helping the aged. Nurs Times 83(5): 40–42, 1987.

Parker M, Secord LJ: Private geriatric case management: An overview. Caring 6(12): 20–23.

Stanhope M, Lancaster J: Community Health Nursing: Process and Practice for Promoting Health, 2nd ed. St. Louis, CV Mosby, 1986.

Torr P: A step in the right direction: The liaison nurse within a hospital for the elderly. Geriatr Nurs Home Care 7(5): 21–22, 1987.

CHAPTER 24

Care of the Older Surgical Patient

Martha Anne Palmer

Chapter Objectives
At the completion of this chapter the reader will be able to:

1. List the components of the nursing assessment of the older surgical patient.
2. Discuss the fears that the elderly may have concerning surgery.
3. Describe ways in which the nurse advocates for the older surgical patient.
4. Outline essential preoperative teaching that should be provided.
5. Describe the nutritional needs of the surgical patient.
6. Identify the unique intraoperative risks for older patients.
7. Describe postoperative assessment, care, and risks.

More than 5 million persons over age 65 are hospitalized yearly. Though the largest percentage of hospitalizations of the elderly are for medically related conditions, 35% of inpatient admissions are for surgical services. The most common surgical admissions of elderly women are for lens extractions, reduction of fractures, cholecystectomy, and hip replacements. For older men, prostatectomy, inguinal hernia repair, and lens extraction are the most frequently performed surgeries (National Center for Health Statistics, 1985).

More elderly persons are undergoing surgery than ever before. Prior to the 1960s surgical mortality was two to five times higher for older persons; thus elective surgery was avoided. In the past ten years improved surgical and anesthesia techniques, advanced monitoring systems, and more thorough preoperative assessment of risk factors have contributed to significant decreases in surgical mortality rates for older adults. Surgery is now seen as an important means to improve function and the quality of life of the elderly.

Surgery not only may add years to life, but also promotes more function and a better quality of life in those years.

Nevertheless, the elderly remain at higher risk for postoperative complications than younger persons, and mortality rates for surgery increase with each decade (Ziffren, 1979). Mohr states that patients over age 70 are to be considered at higher risk but should not be refused surgery on the basis of age alone, pointing to the importance of assessing all risk factors in determining outcome (Mohr, 1983).

Preoperative Nursing Care

Nursing Assessment

Nurses play a key role in preoperative assessment of older adults. The nursing data base takes into consideration the objective information contributed by other health care team members. The nurse will perform a broad health assessment that encompasses all areas of functioning and focuses on a wellness model, with the goal of returning patients to their optimal level of functioning. The assessment should include mobility and activity levels, social functioning, family systems and significant relationships, morale, sensory impairments, prosthetic aids used, economic resources, home environment and management, and availability of community resources that could provide assistance after discharge. Stressors, such as recent loss of spouse or economic hardship, should be recorded.

Careful history taking is important to identify preexisting conditions and medications that may affect the course of surgery. Carrick (1982) emphasizes questioning the patient concerning previous angina, myocardial infarction, edema, palpitations, asthma, pneumonia, chronic lung disease, diabetes, and transient ischemic attacks.

Physical assessment of body systems should include baseline vital signs, height and weight, and an examination of all organ systems. It is important for nurses to allow ample time for the assessment or divide it into two shorter sessions, allowing for slowed reaction time and illness-related fatigue. Skill is required to differentiate normal aging changes (see Chapter 3) from pathology and to assess present physical findings in comparison to prior level of functioning.

Documentation of medications should include allergies and over-the-counter remedies, which many elderly do not consider as medication because they were not prescribed by their doctors. Prescription drugs may combine with over-the-counter drugs to produce harmful effects (Shomaker, 1980). Tranquilizers and other psychotropic medications have a cumulative effect, and with the impaired renal excretion of drugs from aging kidneys, may remain in the system and interact with anesthetic agents during surgery (Luckman and Sorenson, 1980).

Assessment of Risk Factors

Preoperative evaluation requires team effort. Existing medical conditions of surgical patients must be evaluated. Creatinine clearance, serum glucose, electrolytes, complete blood count, hepatic and renal function, total plasma proteins, arterial blood gases, and cardiac enzymes are analyzed. Visual acuity, auditory threshold, and hand grip strength are also important to assess (Stephen, 1984). A baseline chest X ray is considered standard practice as part of the preoperative evaluation. Pulmonary function testing is indicated for patients with a history of smoking, obesity, and existing pulmonary disease (Feigel and Blaisdell, 1979; Tisi, 1979; Robbins and Mushlin, 1979).

Assessment of cardiac status is most important preoperatively. Patients with a history of recent myocardial infarction are at the greatest risk for postoperative cardiac death (Goldman et al., 1978). Nurses may find increasing numbers of older surgical patients who have had arterial lines inserted as a means to monitor cardiac status (DelGuercio and Cohn, 1980).

Assessment of Nutritional Status

A malnourished state upon admission can make the older adult less able to manage the stresses associated with surgery successfully.

The importance of thorough preoperative nutritional assessment for elderly patients cannot be overemphasized. The elderly are known to be commonly deficient in protein, vitamins A, C, D, and E, thiamine, folic acid, and iron (Tideiksaar, 1983). Studies of hospitalized medical and surgical patients have found evidence of protein-calorie malnutrition as high as 50% (Bistrian et al., 1974; 1976). Further, if malnutrition was present on admission, 69% of the patients surveyed were more severely malnourished 20 days later. Of patients whose nutritional status was normal on admission, 75% were found to be malnourished at the time of discharge (Bonner, 1985). Such studies emphasize the stressful effect of illness, surgery, and anesthesia on increasing metabolic demand (Long, 1984). Nurses should assist in identifying nutritional problems and improving or maintaining nutritional status of older surgical patients during their hospital stay.

Preoperative nutritional assessment should include height and weight, standard anthropomorphic measures such as midarm circumference and triceps skin fold, lymphocyte count, serum albumin, hemoglobin, hematocrit, transferrin, TIBC, creatinine/height index, and a detailed diet history (Van Landingham et al., 1982; see Table 24-1). The standard measures used for assessing nutritional status may not be valid in the elderly, however, and more sophisticated techniques, such as carbon dioxide consumption, neutron activation, and sodium and potassium balance may be employed (Koetting and Schneider, 1985).

TABLE 24-1. Indicators of Depleted Nutritional Status

Height/weight	>10% loss
Middle arm circumference	80–85% of standard
Triceps skin fold	80–85% of standard
Total lymphocyte count	1,000–1,500/mm^3
Albumin	2.5–3.5 g/100 ml
Prealbumin	10.1–15 mg/100 ml
Retinol binding protein	2.1–3 mg/100 ml
Hemoglobin	<10.0 g/dl
Hematocrit	<30–35%
Serum transferrin	100–175 mg/dl
Total iron binding capacity	<250 mcg/100 ml

Assessment of Mental Status

Emotional problems can be exacerbated from the stress of surgery. A careful mental status evaluation can aid in identifying high-risk individuals.

An assessment of patients' psychological condition and mental status is important. Age-related losses contribute to a high incidence of depression in the elderly. The stress of surgery may exacerbate an endogenous depression or contribute to a reactive depression. Elderly persons with dementia, intellectual impairments, depression, and personality disorders are considered at high risk during surgery (Grossberg, 1984). Use of assessment tools such as the Zung Depression Scale (Zung, 1980) and Pfeiffer's Short Portable Mental Status Questionnaire (Pfeiffer, 1975) can assist nurses in identifying high-risk individuals prior to surgery, so that management strategies can be implemented.

The nurse will combine subjective and objective data to develop a care plan for the patient, taking into consideration both physical and psychosocial needs. Coping abilities and strengths should be listed. Potential risks, such as "potential for impairment of skin integrity," should be included in the preoperative care plan so that preventive measures can be implemented before surgery. Areas requiring education should be outlined and family members contacted early to assist with teaching at home. Referral to social service or home health agencies is an important aspect of early discharge planning. Available community resources should be identified early to provide support following discharge.

Emotional Support

Many elderly fear hospitalization and surgical intervention. Fears that hospitalization will result in loss of function and thus force dependency on others are a major source of concern. Many believe that being hospitalized will lead to nursing home placement and worry about whether they will ever return home. Concern over family members or pets at home adds to stress levels.

Fears of the unknown, of pain, mutilation, separation, and destruction of body image are experienced to varying degrees. Providing information and teaching about what to expect during surgery and the postoperative period will help to reduce anxiety and stress (Dziurbejko and Larkin, 1978). Grossberg (1984) maintains that before surgery the elderly will want to put their lives in order, perhaps update their wills, and need to spend time in life review. Some elderly have reported bad dreams before surgery (Grossberg, 1984). Many may request visits from clergy.

Patients facing surgery employ various coping mechanisms to deal with stress, and denial is most common. For many elderly, the denial may be adaptive, a mechanism to protect the ego from experiencing the stressful event. For such patients it may be more healthy not to want a lot of information. It is important to allow ample time to give explanations; find out what the patient wants to know and respond only to those questions. Others may have their anxiety lessened by knowing what to expect. Explanations should include whether or not the patient will wake up in the ICU, be hooked to breathing machines, and have intravenous lines in place, along with reassurance that the use of such devices does not necessarily mean there is a problem or complication. An explanation of the roles of members of the health team can lessen confusion.

Patients may worry about having pain and need to know that while it is to be expected, medication to relieve pain is available and will be given as needed.

Elderly individuals may experience anger at being ill or incapacitated, or losing a body part. Others may be experiencing depression related to the multiple losses of aging and need empathy, support, and encouragement. Patients may regress and become dependent on staff. Such behavior requires nurses to confront in a kind way, set limits, and utilize behavioral interventions.

Nurses should evaluate cognitive function in patients facing surgery, take extra time to listen, aid with reminiscence and life review, and assure that patients fully understand the implications of the surgery for which they have given consent.

The stress associated with impending surgery and the relocation to the new environment of the hospital can lead to confusion in some older patients.

Emotional support in the preoperative period is an extremely important nursing intervention with elderly patients. The relocation of hospitalization is traumatic and is compounded by the stress of illness and fear of surgery. A new environment contributes to confusion in older adults (Wolanin and Phillips, 1981). Sensory losses increase the risk of confusion. The hospital stay is filled with fear, anxiety, pain, confusion, and loneliness. The high-tech, busy hospital will seem less cold and impersonal if nurses just take a few extra minutes to provide reassurance and care.

Advocacy

Physicians have a legal duty to make certain their patients understand the nature of the surgery being consented to, the attendant risks and benefits, problems that may be encountered while recovering, and what to expect in the postoperative period (Pomorski, 1983). While family members and patients may disagree on whether surgery should be performed, the decision ultimately rests with the patient unless competency becomes an issue. Explanations are necessary even if the patient appears fearful, forgetful, or neurotic. Nurses can encourage patients and families to ask questions; they can clarify misunderstandings and communicate openly with the surgeon.

Precedents in the law have clearly defined the physician's role in the issue of informed consent (*Schoendorf* v. *Society of N.Y. Hospital; Natanson* v. *Kline; Salgo* v. *Leland Stanford Board of Trustees; Jones* v. *Regents of California*). Patients have a legal right to enough information to make a decision, and physicians who fail to provide adequate, truthful facts can be held liable (Curtin and Flaherty, 1982).

A nurse may deliver consent forms to the patient, witness the signature, and help translate medical terminology. The nurse is not legally authorized to explain the surgery for the physician and, furthermore, must contact the

The nurse should ensure that patients thoroughly understand procedures to which they consent. At no time should the nurse allow patients to grant consent without full comprehension or to be pressured into granting consent.

physician if he or she believes the patient does not understand the procedure and needs more information. A nurse may not independently obtain a patient's signature on a consent form. Curtin and Flaherty (1982) state that, if a physician has failed to obtain informed consent or refuses to do so, it is the nurse's duty to refuse to explain a procedure to a patient or persuade her or him to sign a consent form. In such instances, the nurse is professionally within the scope of nursing practice and serving an advocacy role for the patient as well.

Teaching

Preoperative teaching for elderly patients should begin as early as possible. Surgery disrupts the body's homeostatic response. Aging changes in organ systems and preexisting medical conditions leave a slim margin of physiologic reserve to aid the healing process. The stress of hospitalization and anxiety about the pending surgery may impede the learning process. These factors necessitate frequent practice sessions to improve functioning preoperatively in order to avoid complications in the postoperative period.

In the respiratory system, decreased vital capacity, increased residual volume, impaired gas exchange, and reduced bronchopulmonary movement are normal aging changes (Tichy and Malasanos, 1979). The depressant effect of pre- and postoperative medications and anesthesia increase the risk for pneumonia and other respiratory complications (Podjasek, 1985).

It is recommended that patients cease smoking at least one week before surgery. Use of the incentive spirometer prior to surgery will help improve pulmonary function. Patients should be encouraged to increase the amount of sustained, maximal inspiration and to practice taking ten inhalations every one to two hours. Nurses may need to assist patients in learning to perform the exercise correctly and to observe them actually using the spirometer rather than offering reminders and expecting the patient to practice independently. Repeated explanations may be necessary.

Pulmonary function can also be improved with yawning and deep breathing exercises. Luckman and Sorenson (1980) suggest teaching deep breathing in the following steps:

1. Lie on back or side with knees flexed, or take a sitting position.
2. Place hands on lateral midabdomen.
3. Inhale through nose; upper abdomen should balloon outward; hold inspiration one to three seconds.
4. Exhale through mouth; squeeze air out by contracting abdominal muscles.

The exercise should be practiced five to ten times hourly.

Coughing exercises are traditionally taught preoperatively, but may be contraindicated for elderly patients, particularly if undergoing abdominal surgery. Vigorous coughing can rupture wounds and interfere with the wound-healing process. An abdominal incision, with resultant edema near the diaphragm, will prevent full inspiration and exhalation, contributing to poor movement of air in the lower lobes of the lungs. An abdominal incision also makes forced expiration difficult (Podjasek, 1985). Thus coughing exercises must be taught judiciously using the following steps (Luckman and Sorenson, 1980):

1. Following deep breathing exercise, lie on back or side, or take a sitting position.
2. Splint abdomen by lacing hands across abdomen over a pillow or folded towels.
3. Inhale through nose.
4. Exhale through mouth, giving two short coughs with tongue extended. This step will assist in loosening and moving secretions from the base of the lungs.

Turning exercises will help to prevent respiratory complications and venous stasis, and decrease flatus and abdominal pain. Teach the correct method of turning in bed to patients preoperatively and encourage them to practice turning without assistance every hour:

1. Lie on back with bed's side rails up.
2. With arm farthest away reach for the opposite rail.
3. Pull toward rail and turn on side.

Patients should also practice moving into a sitting position without straining abdominal muscles.

Leg exercises complete the series of preoperative exercises. Use of these exercises can facilitate venous return to the heart and prevent thrombophlebitis, a serious complication of immobility. Teach patients the following:

1. Rotation of each foot in a circular motion.
2. Flexion and extension of the ankles.
3. Flexion and extension of the knees.
4. Flexion and extension of the hips.
5. Abduction and adduction of the hips.

Nutritional Preparation

Delayed immune response and slowed healing in the defense, reconstruction, and maturation phases of wound healing are age-related processes. The poor nutritional status of many elderly patients further increases the risk for infection, wound dehiscence, wound evisceration, fistulas, herniation, and skin breakdown after surgery (Bruno and Craven, 1982; Schilling, 1975; Croushore, 1979). Table 24-3 relates the effect of aging changes and nutrient intake to the process of wound healing.

Adequate nutritional preparation prior to surgery is often difficult, particularly in emergencies when there is little time to assess deficiencies and implement nutritional support.

Nutritional status is further depleted after admission by factors such as withheld oral intake for diagnostic tests, prolonged use of intravenous saline or glucose, inadequate workup of nutritional status, failure to recognize the importance of nutrition in wound healing and prevention of infection, failure or inability to delay surgery until nutritional status is improved, and delay in implementing nutritional support until the patient is severely depleted.

Surgical patients have varying nutritional needs depending on age, the type of operation, preoperative nutritional status, and the expected extent of postoperative losses. Recommended daily intakes of nutrients include the following (Robinson et al., 1986):

Protein: 1.0–1.5 g/kg body weight, or about 100 g protein.

Energy: 35–45 calories/kg body weight.

Vitamins: Increased amounts of vitamins C and K.

Minerals: Additions of phosphorus, potassium, sodium, and chloride to intravenous fluids as necessary to correct electrolyte imbalances; iron tablets or transfusions to correct hemoglobin level; zinc.

Fluids: 35 ml/kg body weight; may need as much as 3–4 liters daily to flush out toxins.

Nurses need to confer with the physician and dietitian to help ensure improved nutrition for their elderly surgical patients. Parenteral fluids given preoperatively cannot fully meet the body's nutritional needs. It is important to remember that without the addition of vitamins or electrolytes there are few nutrients in a liter of intravenous fluid. Further, 100 cc of dextrose or normal saline contains only 180–200 calories. Salmond (1982) estimates that hospitalized patients need 2,000–2,500 calories daily, 3,500 calories for uncomplicated surgical conditions, and as high as 10,000 calories in cases of sepsis or burns. Supplemental feedings are important to improve nutritional status.

Many hospitals have formed nutritional assessment teams that have developed criteria for determining which patients could most benefit from total parenteral nutrition (TPN). Van Landingham and colleagues (1982, 323) advise that TPN is indicated for trauma, severe burns, respiratory failure, pancreatitis, inflammatory bowel disease, inanition due to illness or chemotherapy, and anticipation of paralytic ileus, as well as in surgical cases where the gastrointestinal tract is unavailable. In relation to fluid needs for elderly surgical patients, nurses must be cognizant of the risk for fluid overload. If patients are receiving supplemental feedings by nasogastric tube, it is important to monitor total daily water intake. A liter of Ensure contains only 850 cc of water, so an extra 50 cc of water may be used to flush tubing after medication administration or every four hours as needed to provide adequate fluids. Patients must be monitored carefully for signs of fluid overload or dehydration. Skin turgor is best assessed by pinching the skin over the sternum or forehead (Mezey et al., 1980). Serial measures of height and weight, daily intake and output, and laboratory values will indicate improvement in nutritional status (see Table 24-2).

(*Text continues on page 360*)

TABLE 24-2. Common Complicating Conditions in Elderly Surgical Patients

Complicating Condition	Medical/Surgical Factors	Aging Processes	Nursing Interventions
Fluid and electrolyte imbalance	Blood, fluid losses during surgery, cool operating room, fluids evaporate from tissues, surgery and anesthesia stimulate ADH and aldosterone, overhydration with IV infusion.	Decreased renal function—nephron loss, GFR, decreased renal blood flow and creatinine clearance; decreased cardiopulmonary function.	Careful monitoring I and O, assessment skin turgor—over sternum or forehead, assess for signs of hypervolemia and hypovolemia, determine urinary status, note nonmeasured fluid losses such as diaphoresis, assess for sacral edema, correct imbalances with isotonic IV infusions and electrolytes.
Malnutrition	NPO for test preparations, decreased intake postoperatively, psychosocial influences, operative site, stress of surgery increases nutritional needs.	Decreased secretion, motility, and absorption; decreased basal metabolic rate; loss of taste buds; loss of appetite; reduced absorption of iron, B_{12}, calcium; sensory losses.	Preoperative nutritional assessment, monitor weight, fluid balance, food intake and laboratory values, preoperative nutritional preparation, calorie and protein increases postoperatively, hyperalimentation if indicated, use of nutritional support team, maintain positive nitrogen balance postoperatively; vitamin/mineral supplements.
Pneumonia, atelectasis	Heavy smokers with cough, obesity, bronchitis, chronic pulmonary disease, thoracic or upper abdominal surgery, anesthesia and pain medication reduce functional residual capacity, lung expansion and gas exchange.	Reduced bronchopulmonary movement, decreased pulmonary function–tidal volume, vital capacity, increased residual volume, loss of protective airway reflexes.	*Preoperatively*—cease smoking one week, weight reduction, pulmonary function testing; if bronchitis present, give antibiotics, expectorants and bronchodilators, teach pulmonary maneuvers; cough (tongue extended to loosen secretions), deep breathing, incentive spirometer. *Postoperatively*—position change hourly, monitor blood gases, off ventilator as soon as possible, continue pulmonary maneuver; O_2 to ensure adequate oxygenation, early ambulation, chest physiotherapy.
Pressure ulcers	Malnutrition; chronic disease, e.g., diabetes, CHF, PVD; length of time on OR table.	Moisture loss, thinning epidermis, capillary loss in dermis, loss of sensory receptors, loss of subcutaneous fat.	Frequent turning, correct positioning, pressure relieving devices, avoidance of shearing forces, early movement and ambulation, good skin hygiene, lotions, gentle massage, nutritional supplements, increase fluid intake, high-protein, high-calorie diet.
Wound dehiscence, wound evisceration	Malnutrition; large, sudden weight loss.	Delayed immune response, delayed wound healing—slowing of inflammatory response, mitosis, cell proliferation, abnormal collagen formation causing poor tensile strength in wound, decreased muscle strength.	1–3 weeks preoperative nutritional preparation, hyperalimentation, vitamin supplements, strict aseptic wound care, encourage rest—slow-wave sleep aids wound healing, inspiratory breathing exercises, coughing only if secretions present,

TABLE 24-2. (*Continued*)

Complicating Condition	Medical/Surgical Factors	Aging Process	Nursing Interventions
			prevent/reduce vomiting; discharge teaching, proper wound care and observation for complications, diet instructions.
Incidental hypothermia	Cold operating rooms, room temperature infusions, exposure of skin for draping and preparation, exposure of peritoneum/pleura during surgery, peripheral vasodilation.	Impaired thermoregulatory mechanisms, decreased cardiopulmonary reserves, impaired ability to increase basal metabolic rate.	Temperature monitoring in OR, careful cardiac monitoring, hyperthermia blanket, warm top blankets after incision closure, warm IV fluids, transfer from OR quickly, thermal top blankets in RR, transfer blankets with patient to surgical unit.
Joint stiffness, contractures	Presence of degenerative joint disease, osteoporosis, reduced mobility during preoperative preparation, immobility during surgery, pain limiting motion in postoperative period.	Decreased muscle strength and wasting, decreased bone mass, ossification of cartilage in joints, flexion of joints, stooped posture, slowed movement, gait changes.	Assess prior functioning level, leg exercises preoperatively, early ambulation, proper positioning and movement in bed, active/passive range of motion, encourage active movement by patient.
Acute confusional states, delirium	Type of anesthesia, penetration of blood/brain barrier by certain drugs, presence of preexisting depression or dementia, environmental factors, number of medications taken, hypoxemia, psychosocial factors.	Loss of neurons, brain atrophy, decreased cerebral blood flow and oxygen consumption, decreased renal function, slowed clearance of drugs from system, sensory losses, decreased cardiopulmonary reserves.	*Preoperatively*—baseline assessment of mental status and emotional state, psychological support, allow time for questions and verbalization of fears, provide pastoral care if desired, correct electrolyte imbalances, anemia. *Postoperatively*—monitor level of consciousness, avoid restraints, provide calm environment, avoid use of indwelling catheters, orient to environment, progressive mobility, small doses of Haldol if organic causes, reassurance from all staff, need special attention if have hearing loss, monitor electrolytes and fluid balance, ensure adequate oxygenation.
Cardiac failure	Existing cardiac disease, hypertension, anesthesia effects on blood pressure, stress of surgery increases metabolic needs and increases workload on heart.	Decreased cardiac output, altered O_2 transport, fatty accumulations in heart valves, atherosclerosis and arteriosclerosis of vessels, widening pulse pressure.	*Preoperatively*—risk assessment, correct, treat existing conditions; low dosage heparinization; improved nutritional status will improve cardiac function. *Postoperatively*—continuous CVP monitoring, assess JVD and breath sounds hourly; continuous ECG monitoring; close observation of vital signs, level of consciousness and urinary output; maintain infusion rates; check I and O; observe peripheral circulation, color; maintain cardiovascular functions; careful, early mobilization, rest periods.

Intraoperative Nursing Care

Preanesthetic medications must be carefully prescribed for the elderly. Decreased cerebral blood flow and oxygen consumption, slowed metabolism, and delayed excretion of drugs require lowered dosage of narcotics, barbiturates, tranquilizers, and anticholinergics. Overdose of narcotics may cause respiratory and circulatory depression and inhibition of the cough reflex. Barbiturates are contraindicated for agitated patients and those with cardiovascular or hepatic disease, emphysema, and cachexia. The sedative effect of tranquilizers administered before surgery makes careful observation of patients necessary. The nurse must watch for signs of hypotension and cardiovascular, respiratory, and central-nervous-system depression. The anticholinergic drugs are given to decrease parasympathetic activity such as bradycardia, salivation, and bronchial secretions. Scopolamine is not recommended for the elderly. Atropine 0.2–0.3 mg IV or IM is the preferred preanesthetic medication; this drug is contraindicated in patients with glaucoma. Carrick (1982) states that a small dose of chloral hydrate is often adequate for sedation the night before surgery. In general, caution must be exercised in prescribing preoperative sedation and should be limited to the lowest possible therapeutic dose.

Cool Operating Rooms

Hypothermia is a significant threat to the elderly during surgery. Close monitoring of body temperature during operative procedures and in the recovery room phase is crucial.

Temperatures in operating rooms generally range around 36–38° C and can place elderly patients at risk for hypothermia. The cool room causes shivering, which increases oxygen demand as much as 300–500%. An increased oxygen demand leads to increased cardiac output and ventilation, causing tissue ischemia in the heart and brain.

The lower temperature delays wakening and return of reflexes. The elderly have lowered ability to combat hypothermia and take longer for body temperatures to return to normal. In a study by Vaughan and colleagues (1981), 60% of patients were found to have hypothermia when admitted to the recovery toom. Temperatures remained significantly lower during their 90-minute stay, and were lower on discharge from the recovery room (Vaughan et al., 1981).

Basal metabolic rate falls 6–7% for each degree centigrade drop in body temperature. While this drop might serve a protective function in the central nervous system, Stephen (1984) states that hypothermia acts as an anesthetic; so amounts of other drugs must be reduced to avoid overdosage. Hypothermia can be prevented or reduced by warming the operating rooms, warming intravenous fluids, using hyperthermia blankets, placing a heating mattress under the patient, and protecting and warming exposed peritoneum with warmed saline pads. During surgery and in the postoperative recovery room period, it is important to monitor body temperature closely (with rectal or esophageal probes), as well as cardiac function (Heymann, 1977).

Anesthesia Effects

The numerous drugs used in conjunction with surgery serve various functions including decreasing anxiety, relief of pain, relaxation of muscles, and induction and maintenance of anesthesia. "An overriding principle in the administration of anesthetic drugs to geriatric patients is that a little bit goes a long way" (Stephen, 1984, 238). One of the serious effects of many anesthetic drugs is a dose-dependent drop in blood pressure, while others may cause tachycardia. Both conditions should be avoided. Tachycardia increases the workload of the heart, and studies have correlated sudden drops in blood pressure with increased morbidity and mortality.

The decision to use general or regional anesthesia is determined by the patient's age, medical conditions, site of operation, and type of surgery performed. General anesthesia may have an advantage when used for confused, disoriented, and agitated patients who are uncooperative. Certainly for tense, anxious patients, the sedation of general anesthesia will produce better tissue relaxation, prevent pain, and lessen fear, since they will not worry about being awake in the operating room. Under general anesthesia there is a better ability to control sudden cardiovascular changes by changing the depth of anesthesia.

Although studies do not conclusively show a decrease in mortality with use of regional anesthesia, there appear to be some advantages in its use. Because little or no sedation is used with regional anesthesia, there is less postoperative confusion than with general. Other advantages of regional include low incidence of neurologic complications, less blood loss, lower incidence of deep vein thrombosis and pulmonary embolus, an extended period of pain relief, and better ventilation and control by the patient. The level of the regional anesthesia is a factor allowing the patient unrestricted expansion of the lung and clearing of secretions (Sullivan and Siker, 1986).

Disadvantages of regional techniques include hypotension in spinal anesthesia, as well as technical difficulty in performing the procedure because of arthritic changes and calcium deposits along the vertebral column. If epinephrine is added to the local anesthetic used, there is a lengthening of the period of hypotension; thus this drug should be used carefully and recovery room personnel alerted to insure close monitoring (Carrick, 1982; Sullivan and Siker, 1986).

Fluid Replacement

Older hearts are less able to manage excess fluid loads. Intravenous fluids must be carefully administered to minimize the risk of pulmonary congestion.

Fluid replacement during surgery is required to replace blood and fluid lost through evaporation at the operative site and to maintain electrolyte balance. Transfusion of a single unit of blood may even be necessary for elderly patients if more than 500 cc is lost, in order to compensate for limited cardiac reserve. There is a danger of fluid overload and pulmonary congestion postoperatively if too much fluid is administered intraoperatively. If there is an accumulation of extracellular fluid, intraoperative fluids should be lowered to avoid complications (Hartsuck, 1975).

Infection Control

Although age is not an independent risk factor in the incidence of surgical infection, the prevalence of medical conditions such as diabetes, heart disease, pneumonia, and urinary tract infections predisposes the elderly to higher risk for wound infection. Delayed wound healing, diminished immune response, and poor nutritional status increase the risk.

The longer a patient is in the hospital before surgery, the higher the rate of infection will be, because of exposure to various bacteria on the units. It is known that the infection rate of clean wounds doubles with each hour of surgery because there is more time for contamination to occur in the operating room, and the open incision loses its local resistance as bleeding continues and tissues become ischemic.

Patients may be a major source of their own infection. Goldman (1985) cites a study in which the infection rate was reduced from 17.5 to 8% by three preoperative washings. The following preventive measures may help reduce infection in elderly patients:

Avoid placing preoperative patients in the same room with infected patients.

Perform preoperative shaving as close to the time of surgery as possible.

Patients who come in one day before elective surgery should follow the antiseptic shower/bath protocol of
    Shower or bath on admission.
    Second shower or bath at bedtime.
    Third shower or bath on the morning of surgery.

This schedule of three consecutive bathings can be planned for patients admitted for longer preoperative workups once the day of surgery is known.

Postoperative Nursing Care

Postoperative care of the elderly, while similar to routine postoperative care, must take into consideration the greater risk for complications resulting from physiological processes of aging, altered homeostatic balance, anesthesia, and the surgical procedure.

Goals for postoperative care include the following:

- Maintenance of adequate cardiovascular function and tissue perfusion.
- Maintenance of adequate respiratory function.
- Maintenance of adequate fluid and electrolyte balance.
- Maintenance of renal function.
- Promotion of wound healing.
- Maintenance of adequate nutrition and elimination.
- Promotion and maintenance of early ambulation and movement.
- Promotion of comfort, rest, and safety.
- Provision of psychological support for patient and family.
- Promotion of optimal cognitive functioning.

- Provision of adequate teaching for life after discharge from hospital.
- Recognition and prevention of postoperative complications.

The postoperative complications most common in elderly patients and appropriate nursing measures are listed in Table 24-2.

Assessment

Vital Organ Functions. Elderly patients with preexisting heart disease are most prone to myocardial infarction postoperatively. Patients with chronic hypertension may have problems with high blood pressure immediately after surgery. Arrhythmias occur if potassium levels are abnormal. Tachycardia results from hypoxia and blood and fluid losses. Myocardial depression and hypotension are two serious complications of the immediate postoperative period. Both are a result of the cumulative effects of anesthesia, overdose of preoperative medications, blood and fluid loss, and peripheral pooling of blood.

Myocardial depression and hypotension are the most significant complications during the immediate postoperative period. Changes in the rate, rhythm, and quality of pulses and systolic blood pressure reductions should be promptly recognized and reported.

Careful monitoring of vital signs is important. Blood pressure should be checked in both arms. Systolic drops greater than 20 mm Hg, drops with each reading of 5 to 10 mm Hg, or pressure falling below 80 mm Hg are indicators of problems. Readings should be compared with preoperative and intraoperative levels—trends over time are more significant than a single reading.

Assess the rate, rhythm, and quality of pulses. In elderly patients, in addition to radial pulse measurement, an apical pulse rate should be determined for one full minute. Observe skin for color and temperature. Check peripheral circulation by assessing the temperature and appearance of extremities. Patients should be moving their legs and flexing their feet as soon as they are awake (McConnell, 1983).

In high-risk patients, monitoring of cardiac status by electrocardiogram, CVP lines, and arterial blood gases may be indicated for several days. Djokovic and Hedley-Whyte (1979) encourage careful, rapid postsurgical mobilization and posit that elderly patients continue to be at risk for myocardial infarction as cardiac work resumes in the postoperative period.

Correcting fluid and electrolyte imbalance is also important. Hyponatremia may result from overadministration of intravenous fluids or too much water orally. The danger of fluid imbalance in the elderly has been discussed earlier. It is important to check the patient's anesthesia record to determine the amount of fluid given during surgery and adjust the IV rate so that 24-hour fluid needs are met. Hypovolemia may impair renal function, already diminished by 50% in the elderly, and lead to necrosis of renal tubules. Decreased urinary output may be an indicator of this serious complication; intake and output should be carefully monitored. Insertion of Foley catheters should be avoided unless there are indications of renal failure. Voluntary voiding should occur within six to eight hours. Because of blood and fluid losses during surgery and increased secretion of antidiuretic hormone, low output may be expected in the first 24 hours. A patient with a catheter should have a continuous flow of urine at a rate of 30 cc per hour. Diuresis may occur on the second and third day after surgery (Carrick, 1982; Croushore, 1979; McConnell, 1983).

Early recognition and management of circulatory problems and the correction of fluid and electrolyte balance can prevent serious complications such as shock and myocardial infarction in the postoperative period.

Airway obstruction and hypoxia are common respiratory complications. Aging changes in pulmonary function, poor gas exchange, and the effects of anesthesia and preoperative medications lead to respiratory depression. Intubation and artificial ventilation may be necessary, although extended time on a ventilator doubles the risk for upper airway gram-negative infections (Djokovic and Hedley-Whyte, 1979). Elderly patients are at risk for pneumonia and atelectasis; patients with peripheral vascular disease and those immobile with hip fractures are at risk for pulmonary emboli. Djokovic and Hedley-Whyte (1979) recommend low-dose heparinization preoperatively as a preventive measure.

Nurses must observe for signs of obstruction along the respiratory tract; administer oxygen as ordered; monitor arterial blood gases; assess rate, rhythm, and depth of respirations; and properly position the patient to ensure lung expansion. Patients may be comfortable turned on the side with a pillow supporting the back, knees flexed, chin extended, and the upper arm elevated on a pillow to allow maximum lung expansion. Pulmonary exercises taught preoperatively should be continued postoperatively.

In the elderly, small, seemingly insignificant changes in vital signs or behavior may be early signs of impending problems; so skilled observation is imperative. For example, elderly patients may normally have a lower body temperature and, as discussed earlier, be prone to hypothermia in the operating room. A slight rise in temperature above normal for such patients may indicate wound infection or pneumonia.

Comfort Measures. Restlessness may signal discomfort rather than confusion (Kruczek, 1986). Pain is experienced subjectively and influenced by sociocultural, psychological, and physical factors. Many elderly have learned to tolerate and cope with chronic pain lasting for years. They tend to report pain less frequently when hospitalized, expecting to tolerate acute pain as they learned to bear their daily pain (Wachter-Shikora and Perez, 1982).

Nurses must be aware of nonverbal signals of pain such as clenched fists, rigid body position, strained facial expression, or silent shedding of tears. Question elderly patients during the recovery period, and do not assume that silence means they are not in pain. Unrelieved pain may impair cognitive function.

Careful assessment of pain level is necessary, because narcotics given for pain relief dull medullary centers, depressing respirations and cough reflexes. Pain medications potentiate the effects of anesthesia. Some anesthetic agents, such as halothane, are not secreted rapidly, and the cumulative effect causes central-nervous-system depression. Tachycardia, shallow, sighing

The profound effects of narcotics in the elderly reinforce the importance of using massages, frequent position changes, diversional activities, and other nonnarcotic comfort measures to manage pain.

respirations, and diaphoresis must be evaluated with any changes in laboratory values to determine whether these are symptomatic of pain or complications. Alterations in renal function may prevent the use of large doses of narcotics to relieve pain. Individual dosages may need to be reduced as much as one-quarter to one-third (McConnell, 1983); mobilization and pulmonary exercises should be continued to avoid pneumonia and other complications. Schilling (1975) states that early ambulation can promote stronger, less painful wounds. Pain should lessen after the first 48 hours (Croushore, 1979).

Try nonnarcotic comfort measures such as frequent position change, ambulation, use of pillows and heating pads, a warm drink, relaxation exercises, diversional activities and music to refocus attention, back rubs, massage, and use of humor. Often the presence and reassurance of the nurse and supportive visits from family and friends can do much to relieve the anxiety and tension that contribute to the perception of pain (Wachter-Shikora and Perez, 1982).

Cognitive Function. Elderly patients require more time to recover mentally as well as physically from the stress of surgery. Changes in behavior or impairments in mental functioning may affect as many as one-third of those undergoing surgery. Those who are over age 80, have a malignant disease, and take five or more drugs are especially at high risk for developing changes in mental status after surgery (Millar, 1981). Postoperative psychiatric disorders may be affective, such as depression related to concerns about illness, or organic, such as acute delirium reactions. Acute delirium states may be superimposed over preexisting chronic, organic brain disease. (The importance of a preoperative assessment of mental function was stressed earlier in this chapter.) Mental status changes may be the earliest sign of impending complications.

The older surgical patient can develop confusion from physiological disturbances, medications, and sensory overload or deprivation. Restoring physiologic homeostasis, providing orienting devices, assuring that eyeglasses and hearing aids are used, and allowing maximum control over the environment and activities can aid in reducing confusion.

The causes of impaired mental function include social and environmental factors as well as organic, hereditary, and psychologic ones. Age-related changes in sensory organs cause perceptual problems, which are compounded by stressors in the hospital environment. Frequent room changes, windowless intensive care units, continuous noise of monitors, glaring lights, use of medical jargon by personnel, interruptions, and frequent wakings in recovery rooms and intensive care units cause sensory deprivation or sensory overload. Reversible, organic causes are numerous, and include electrolyte and metabolic imbalance, decreased oxygen supply to the central nervous system as a result of decreased cardiac output, anemia, infection, fever, hypotension, and compromised pulmonary function; urinary retention or infection; impaired renal or hepatic function; constipation; adverse drug effects, particularly from tranquilizers and sedatives; and specific surgical stressors. Surgery lasting more than four hours, emergency surgery decided upon and performed within 24 hours, and postoperative hemorrhage contribute to acute delirium states. Confusion may be a symptom of alcohol or drug withdrawal.

A family history of psychosis, impaired ego functioning, and the emotional disposition of some personalities increase vulnerability to postoperative mental changes. Williams and colleagues (1979) found confusion on admission or during the preoperative period the most consistent predictor of postoperative confusion. Coping mechanisms used prior to surgery may break down, particularly in patients with minimal dementia. Usual personality traits, both desirable and undesirable, may become exaggerated. Depression may result from fear of death or physical disfigurement, or from anger related to being dependent on others. Many patients feel helpless and lose the will to recover. Depressed patients may exhibit symptoms such as withdrawal from interaction with nursing staff or family, increased complaints, sleeplessness, sadness, low self-esteem, and poor appetite (Thompson and Feinberg, 1980). Elderly patients may welcome visits by clergy or members of the pastoral care department, who can reassure patients and allow them to ventilate fears and concerns.

When assessing patients with impaired mental functioning, it is helpful to compare current mental status exams with preoperative baseline data, and review body systems, drugs and anesthesia used during surgery, and current and preoperative medications.

Nurses can initiate many measures to help decrease postoperative mental impairments. In a study by Williams and colleagues (1979) improved cognitive functioning correlated highly with increased activity, use of orienting devices, freedom from urinary problems, private rooms, and frequent explanations, reassurance, and orientation.

Activity can be increased by having patients turn frequently, helping them get out of bed and walk, and having them move about in the hospital to get different sensory input. Orienting devices include calendars, clocks, radio, television, familiar objects or pictures from home, newspapers, and magazines. Prosthetic aids such as eyeglasses and hearing aids help patients relate more clearly to the environment. Patients with hearing problems need special attention. If language is a barrier to communication, use of an interpreter can help with orientation. Frequent touch is reassuring and provides tactile stimulation. Judicious use of restraints is advisable. Increased stimuli at night can help to avoid "sundowning," or evening confusion (Trockman, 1978).

Providing opportunities for patients to exert some control over the environment of a critical care unit can help to reduce stress levels. Allowing patients control over the arrangement of cards and plants, as well as decisions about bath schedules, and allowing them to choose to listen to the radio, watch television, or read resulted in improved mood and greater perception of control in a study by Kallio (1980).

Restraints should not be used unless absolutely necessary on confused elderly patients, and antipsychotic drugs must be prescribed sparingly. Thompson and Feinberg (1980) suggest low doses of haloperidol for extreme agitation that is organic in nature. Surgery is a frightening experience for elderly patients, and nurses can intervene to reduce the incidence and decrease the length of transient cognitive impairment.

TABLE 24-3. Interaction of Nutrients and Aging Processes on Wound Healing

Stages of Wound Healing	Aging Processes	Essential Nutrients
I. *Defense*—day 1 to day 4		
Vasoconstriction Platelet aggregation, clot formation	Decreased gas exchange and pulmonary function. Decreased cardiac output, altered O_2 transport. Atrophy, arteriosclerosis of blood vessels of dermis. Decreased peripheral circulation.	Vitamin K—synthesis prothrombin and clotting factors, promotes clot formation. Iron—red blood cell formation, transport O_2 to wounds.
Inflammation Vasodilation, edema, pooling of H_2O proteins, electrolytes, antibodies, complement	Diminished immune response. Diminished inflammatory response. Altered protein synthesis. Decreased homeostatic response.	Vitamin A—assists in immune response and resistance to infection. Vitamin B complex—enzyme and antibody production. Vitamin C—necessary for immune response and resistance to infection. Proteins—required in immune response. Albumin—prevents wound edema.
Cell migration Neutrophils, monocytes, red cells migrate to wound Macrophages debride wound, remove infection	Impaired cell migration. Disrupted sleep patterns—decrease in slow-wave sleep. Decreased production of neutrophils and lymphocytes.	Vitamin A—enhances functioning of white blood cells. Iron—enhances bactericidal activity of white blood cells. Proteins—assist in white blood cell formation and phagocytosis. CHO—maintains energy requirements of white blood cells.
II. *Reconstruction*—day 4 to day 21		
Cell multiplication Fibroblast formation	Slowed rate of cell proliferation. Slowed mitosis.	Fats—build cell membranes. Zinc—stabilizes cell membranes, assists in cell multiplication.
Collagen synthesis, cross-linking, remodeling	Decreased collagen and elastic synthesis.	CHO—maintains energy requirements of fibroblasts. Proteins—assist in fibroblast and collagen formation and wound remodeling. Vitamins A and C, copper, ferrous iron, CHO, trace metals, zinc—collagen formation, cross-linking.
Epithelialization of wound		Zinc, vitamin A—assist in epithelialization.
III. *Maturation*—day 21 to 2 years		
Collagen synthesis stabilizes	Abnormal configuration of collagen and cross-linkages.	
Collagen cross-linking continues	Increase in elastin fibers.	
Tensile strength of wound increases scar formation	Less tensile strength in wounds.	Proteins—add tensile strength to wound.

TABLE 24-4. Guidelines for Teaching Elderly Patients

1. One-on-one sessions are most effective and need to be individualized.
2. Involve patient in setting goals and planning self-care routines.
3. Short-term goals that can be quickly accomplished provide reinforcement and enhance self-esteem.
4. Adapt medication schedules for patient's daily routine of meals, naps, and activities.
5. Schedule frequent, brief teaching sessions at intervals throughout the day.
6. Present material to be learned at a pace acceptable to the patient.
7. Allow time to master the task—repetition will help retention and recall.
8. When teaching a new skill, verbalize each step as you demonstrate it and follow with a practice session.
9. Simulate as near as possible the conditions in which the skill will be performed at home.
10. Speak slowly, in concise, short, concrete sentences, deleting unnecessary information.
11. Match vocabulary to learner's level.
12. Associate new information with past knowledge and experience.
13. Use cues—phrases or single-word cues help recall.
14. Use teaching aids to stimulate both the visual and auditory senses. Examples: teaching tapes if vision is poor, charts to illustrate oral presentation.
15. Speak in a low-pitched tone and make sure hearing aid is inserted and working properly.
16. Check for adequate lighting sources and make sure glasses are clean and worn for teaching sessions.
17. Use large-print materials—large, bold letters with wide spacing of words, written with a black, felt-tip pen. Lowercase letters are easier to read.
18. Minimize environmental noise and distractions.
19. Include sessions for family members so they can reinforce teaching at home.
20. Positive reinforcement, acceptance, and genuine caring will support your patient's growth and willingness to learn.

Wound Healing. A variety of aging processes that can delay all stages of wound healing are outlined in Table 24-3. The compromised nutritional status of many elderly patients further increases the risk from wound complications and pressure ulcers.

Hemorrhage may occur in the defense stage of wound healing, related to decreased synthesis of prothrombin and other clotting factors. Nurses should observe for signs of shock and profuse drainage of bright blood during the first 48 hours after surgery. Proper placement of drains will help remove excess fluid and purulent drainage from the incision site and accelerate the healing process. Pressure dressings applied too tightly can constrict blood vessels. Circulation of surrounding tissue, changes in sensation, and discomfort must be checked frequently. An incision that is inflamed, warm, and tender indicates the presence of infection. It is important to check laboratory values, temperature, and urinary output, to maintain fluid and electrolyte balance, and to replace blood losses. Strict, aseptic wound care should be practiced.

Discharge Planning and Teaching

As stated earlier, plans for discharge must begin early in the hospital stay. A major concern for surgical patients is activity tolerance in relation to home environment. It is important to assess support systems early, particularly if the patient is living alone, and make adequate arrangements for personal care, food management, and general household maintenance.

In planning discharge, the nurse should help the patient schedule follow-up appointments to see the physician and surgeon. Part of this process may entail helping the patient find transportation through community service agencies. Continued teaching and assistance to the patient can be provided through home health nurses.

Changing the life-styles and habits acquired over many years to incorporate more healthy practices is difficult for elderly persons. Patience, confidence in their abilities, and extended time are needed to ensure success. Helping an elderly patient learn a new skill and seeing the improved self-esteem that comes with independence are extremely rewarding for the nurse who has invested time in teaching. Special interventions and techniques for effectively teaching elderly patients in the hospital are listed in the guidelines in Table 24-4.

Growing numbers of elderly individuals will take advantage of surgical techniques that can not only add years to their lives, but also improve their functioning in their remaining years. By strengthening older adults' physical and psychological status prior to surgery, recognizing and minimizing risks, and facilitating a prompt return or improvement of function postoperatively, nurses can assure that maximum benefit from surgery will be achieved.

REFERENCES

Bistrian BR, Blackburn GL, Hallowell E, et al.: Protein status of general surgical patients. JAMA 230(13): 858–860, 1974.

Bistrian BR, Blackburn GL, Vitale J, Cochran D, Naylor J: Hospitalized surgical patients. JAMA 235(5): 1567–70, 1976.

Bonner M: Nutritional deficiencies. Lecture on Clinical Aspects of Aging, Medical Grand Rounds, Johns Hopkins University School of Medicine, March 2, 1985.

Bruno PB, Craven RF: Age challenges to wound healing. J Gerontol Nurs 8(12): 686–691, 1982.

Carrick L: Considerations for the older surgical patient. Geriatr Nurs 3(1): 43–47, 1982.

Croushore TM: Postoperative assessment: The key to avoiding the most common nursing mistakes. Nurs 79, 9(4): 47–51, 1979.

Curtin L, Flaherty MJ: Nursing Ethics: Theories and Pragmatics. Bowie, MD, RJ Brady, 1982.

DelGuercio LRM, Cohn JD: Monitoring operative risk in the elderly. JAMA 243(13): 1350–1355, 1980.

Djokovic JL, Hedley-Whyte J: Prediction of outcome of surgery and anesthesia in patients over eighty. JAMA 241(21): 2301–2306, 1979.

Dziurbejko MM, Larkin JC: Including the family in preoperative teaching. Am J Nurs 78(11): 1892–1894, 1978.

Feigel DW, Blaisdell FW: The estimation of surgical risk. Med Clin N Am 63(6): 1131–1143, 1979.

Goldman DA: Infection prevention in clean surgery. Conversation in Infection Control 6(2): 1–12, 1985.

Goldman L, Caldera DL, Southwick FS, et al.: Cardiac risk factors in non-cardiac surgery. Medicine 57:357–370, 1978.

Grossberg GT: Psychological aspects of aging. In Krechel SW (ed): Anesthesia and the Geriatric Patient, 63–72. Orlando, FL, Grune and Stratton, 1984.

Hartsuck JM: Fluid and electrolyte therapy. In Greenfield LJ (ed): Surgery of the Aged, 39–52. Philadelphia, WB Saunders, 1975.

Heymann AD: The effect of incidental hypothermia on elderly surgical patients. J Gerontol 32(1): 46–48, 1977.

Kallio JT: The effect of induced control on the perceptions of control, mood state, and quality of nursing care for clients in a critical care unit. Adv Nurs Sci 2:105–107, 1980.

Koetting CA, Schneider PJ: Pros and cons of anthropomorphic measurements. Infusions 9(6): 184–186, 1985.

Kruczek TM: How hospitals hurt old people. RN 49(2): 17, 19, 1986.

Long CL: Energy and protein requirements in stress and trauma. Critical Care Nursing Currents 2(2): 7–12, 1984.

Luckman J, Sorenson KC: Medical-Surgical Nursing: A Psychophysiologic Approach. Philadelphia, WB Saunders, 1980.

McConnell EA: After surgery: How you can avoid the obvious and the not so obvious hazards. Nurs 83, 13(2): 74–78, 1983.

Mezey MD, et al.: Health Assessment of the Older Individual. New York, Springer, 1980.

Millar HR: Psychiatric morbidity in elderly surgical patients. Brit J Psychiatry 138:17–20, 1981.

Mohr, DN: Estimation of surgical risk in the elderly: A correlative review. J Am Geriatr Soc 31(2): 99–102, 1983.

National Center for Health Statistics: Health, United States, 1985. Pub. No. (PHS) 86–1232, Public Health Service. Washington, DC, Government Printing Office, December 1985.

Pfeiffer E: A short portable mental status questionnaire for the assessment of organic brain deficit in elderly patients. J Am Geriatr Soc 23:433–441, 1975.

Podjasek JH: Which post-op patient faces the greatest respiratory risk? RN 48(9): 44–53, 1985.

Pomorski ME: Surgical care for the aged patient: A decision-making process. Nurs Clin N Am 8(2): 403–410, 1983.

Robbins JA, Mushlin AI: Preoperative evaluation of the healthy patient. Med Clin N Am 63(6): 1145, 1979.

Robinson CH, Lawler MR, Chenoweth WL, Garwick AE: Normal and Therapeutic Nutrition, 17th ed. New York, Macmillan, 1986.

Salmond SW: Recognizing protein caloric malnutrition. Critical Care Update 1:5–6, January 1982.

Schilling JA: Wound healing and the inflammatory response in the aged. In Greenfield LJ (ed): Surgery of the Aged, 24–38. Philadelphia, WB Saunders, 1975.

Shomaker DM: Use and abuse of OTC medications by the elderly. J Gerontol Nurs 6(1): 21–24, 1980.

Stephen CR: The risk of anesthesia and surgery in the geriatric patient. In Krechel SW (ed): Anesthesia and the Geriatric Patient, 231–246. Orlando, FL, Grune and Stratton, 1984.

Sullivan DR, Siker ES: The pros and cons of regional anesthesia. In Stephen CR, Assaf RAE (eds): Geriatric Anesthesia: Principles and Practice, 277–290. Boston, Butterworth, 1986.

Thompson TL, Feinberg LE: Evaluation of postoperative changes in mental status. Post-Graduate Medicine 67(3): 272–287, 1980.

Tichy AM, Malasanos JL: Physiological parameters of aging, Part 1. J Gerontol Nurs 5(1): 42–46, 1979.

Tideiksaar R: Factors that affect nutrition in the elderly patient. Physician Assistant and Health Practitioner 7(2): 23–28, 1983.

Tisi GM: Preoperative evaluation of pulmonary function. Am Rev Respir Dis 119: 293–310, 1979.

Trockman G: Caring for the confused or delirious patient. Am J Nurs 78(9): 1495–1499, 1978.

Van Landingham SB, Key JC, Symmonds RE: Nutritional support of the surgical patient. Surg Clin North America 62(2): 321–331, 1982.

Vaughan MS, Vaughan RW, Cork RC: Postoperative hypothermia in adults: Relationship of age, anesthesia, and shivering to rewarming. Anesthesia and Analgesia 60(10): 746–751, 1981.

Wachter-Shikora N, Perez S: Unmasking pain. Geriatr Nurs 3(6): 392–393, 1982.

Williams MA, Holloway JR, Winn ME: Nursing activities and acute confusional states in elderly hip-fractured patients. Nurs Res 28(1): 25–35, 1979.

Wolanin MO, Phillips LRF: Confusion. St. Louis, CV Mosby, 1981.

Ziffern SE: Surgical mortality rates according to age groups. J Am Geriatr Soc 27(10): 433–437, 1979.

Zung WWK: A self-rating depression scale. Arch Gen Psych 12(1): 63–67, 1980.

BIBLIOGRAPHY

American Society of Anesthesiologists: New classification of physical status. Anesthesiology 24:111, 1963.

Cockram P: Anesthesia and the aged. AARN 52(2): 156–163, 1984.

Doering KJ, LaMountain P: Flowcharts to facilitate caring for ostomy patients, Part 1: Preoperative assessment. Nurs 84, 14(9): 47–49, 1984a.

Doering KJ, LaMountain P: Flowcharts to fscilitate caring for ostomy patients, Part 2: Immediate post-op care. Nurs 84, 14(10): 47–49, 1984b.

Doering KJ, LaMountain P: Flowcharts to facilitate caring for ostomy patients, Part 3: Recuperative care. Nurs 84, 14(11): 54–57, 1984c.

Drain CB, Cristoph SS: The Recovery Room: A Critical Care Approach to Post Anesthesia Nursing, 2nd ed. Philadelphia, WB Saunders, 1987.

Fowler E: Pressure sores: A deadly nuisance. J Gerontol Nurs 8(12): 680–685, 1982.

Goldman L, Caldera DL, Nussbaum SR, et al.: Multifactorial index of cardiac risk in non-cardiac surgical procedures. Northeast J Med 297(16): 845–850, 1977.

Hallburg JC: The teaching of aged adults. In Stilwell EM (ed): Readings in Gerontological Nursing, 225–233. Thorofare, NJ, CB Slack, 1980.

Jackson MF: High risk surgical patients. J Gerontol Nurs 14(1): 8–15, 40–42, 1988.

Keithley JK: Wound healing in malnourished patients. AORN J 35(6): 1094–1099, 1982.

Lincoln R, Maddox A, Patterson C: Use of the Norton pressure sore risk assessment scoring system with elderly patients in acute care. J Enterostom Ther 13(4): 132–138, 1986.

Lueckenotte AG: Sharpen skills in hospital settings . . . . The older hospitalized patient. J Gerontol Nurs 13(3): 12–19, 1987.

May JR: Drug interactions in surgical patients. Am J Surg 153(3): 327–335, 1987.

McDowell DE: The special needs of the older colostomy patient. J Gerontol Nurs 8(12): 680–685, 1983.

Pritchard V: Preventing and treating geriatric infections. RN 51(3): 36–38, 1988.

Schultetus RR: Intraoperative awareness. Today's OR Nurse 9(9): 22–27, 34–35, 1987.

Stephen CR, Assaf RAE (eds): Geriatric Anesthesia: Principles and Practices. Boston, Butterworth, 1986.

White NE: Surgical conditions in the elderly. In Steffl BM (ed): Handbook of Gerontological Nursing, 286–300. New York, Van Nostrand Reinhold, 1984.

Whitney JD, Fellows BJ, Larson E: Do mattresses make a difference? J Gerontol Nurs 10(9): 21, 24–25, 1984.

CHAPTER 25

Psychiatric Emergencies of the Elderly

Mary Jane Lucas-Blaustein

Chapter Objectives

At the completion of this chapter the reader will be able to:

1. State examples of acute psychiatric emergencies in the elderly and related nursing actions.
2. Outline the components of a mental status evaluation.
3. Describe physiological and environmental factors that can influence mental function.

Psychiatric disorders are not uncommon in the elderly population. It is estimated that approximately 4 million persons over age 65 in the United States have suffered moderate to severe psychiatric impairment secondary to cerebral arteriosclerosis, dementia, functional psychosis, alcoholism, or other conditions (Stuart and Sundeen, 1983, 890). The prevalence of psychiatric disorders in late life and the life crises that affect older adults increase the risk of psychiatric emergencies. Psychiatric emergencies can occur in any setting; thus all professional nurses should know how to prevent, recognize, and intervene in these problems.

A psychiatric emergency is any mental and behavioral disorder that warrants prompt attention. Because the patient may not recognize the nature of the emergency or the immediate need for the intervention, nurses must be equipped with the knowledge and skill to make informed psychiatric judgments, often on the spot. Elderly people tend to be reluctant to seek psychiatric help or help that has the mental health label, and a number of studies show that they avoid such assistance (Altshuler, 1985, 454). Often it is the action of family members or professionals that causes the older adult to seek help for psychiatric problems.

While suicide and homicide are the most dramatic psychiatric emergencies, there are many other more common kinds of problems that can be life threatening; these are often recognized by others. For example, prolonged refusal to eat or drink, reclusiveness, combativeness, withdrawal, confusion, and general cognitive dysfunction are potentially life-threatening situations.

Some psychiatric emergencies are secondary to major mental illness, and others may be secondary to situational disorders, drug toxicity, or alcohol abuse.

Mental Status Assessment

The mental status examination is the first basic tool of the nurse faced with a psychiatric emergency (Lucas, 1984, 170). The purpose of the mental status examination is to identify evidence of mental disorders and abnormal mental states that adversely affect the elderly person's ability to cope with life stresses and deal with problems in an appropriate manner. Although it is beneficial to complete the entire examination as soon as possible, in an emergency situation the patient may be unwilling or unable to cooperate. Therefore, initial evaluation may be limited to careful observation and description of behavior. A thorough mental status evaluation should be done as soon as possible because it is indispensable to formulating an effective plan of intervention.

The following outline shows the type of data that should be evaluated during the mental status evaluation:

General behavior and appearance:

- Dress and grooming
- Posture and mobility
- Facial expressions and gestures
- General health status
- Response to situations and demands
- Tics, mannerisms, unusual gestures
- Attitude toward examiner and others

Speech:

- Tone of voice
- Rate and amount of speech
- Unusual words or jargon
- Coherency
- Spontaneity
- Sudden change in topic

Mood:

- Sad or hopeless
- Cheerful
- Euphoric
- Bored
- Hostile
- Labile
- Constancy of mood
- Appropriateness in relation to situation

Delusions:

- Attitude toward people in environment
- Distorted meaning of events or experiences
- Feelings of being persecuted or harmed
- Victim's belief that he or she is special

Hallucinations:

- Hears voices (describe content)
- Sees visions (describe)
- Smells unusual odors (describe)
- Tastes odd or peculiar things (describe)
- Feels odd skin sensations (describe)

Cognition:

- Orientation: name, time, place, date
- Memory: recall of three words in 3–5 minutes
- Attention span
- Calculation: subtract serial 7s from 100, spell "world" backward

Insight and judgment:

- Attitude toward present state
- Recognition of need for help
- Ability to make decisions, participate in plan

Physical Assessment

Many psychiatric disorders can stem from physiological problems; thus a comprehensive physical examination is essential for the patient demonstrating a psychiatric emergency. The physical assessment includes an examination of the patient for signs and symptoms of pathology, taking into account normal age-related changes (see Chapter 3). Consideration should be given to the fact that sensory activity and organ physiology are compromised in the elderly individual. The nurse should be alert to signs of dehydration, starvation, injury, abuse, and incompetence in self-care. Vaginal bleeding or any signs of trauma to the perineum are signs of possible sexual abuse.

The initial physical evaluation of the patient should include a review of the following:

Neurological status
  Gait
  Pupil reaction
  Strength
  Symmetry of facial features
  Level of consciousness

Vital signs

Skin condition

Hygiene

Hydration, nutritional status

Evidence of injury

Medications used

As soon as feasible a more complete physical examination, including laboratory evaluation of blood and urine, should be performed.

Assessment of Environment

Environmental assessment supplements the physical and mental state examinations. It can be useful in determining the resources available to assist in the emergency situation. The following factors are important to consider:

- Location of the patient: hospital, nursing home, home, on the street.
- Availability and reliability of people in the immediate environment.
- Availability and accessibility of community services: police, ambulance, social service agencies, hospital, mental health center.
- Immediate dangers or barriers in the environment: steep stairs, passing traffic, guns, throwable objects, drugs.

Environmental factors that may have contributed to the psychiatric crisis should be explored, such as recent burglary, rent increase, need for repairs, loss of neighbor or pet, inability to manage household, and new living arrangement.

Examples of Psychiatric Emergencies

Delirium

Delirium is a mental disorder characterized by an acute change in mental state, causing impaired intellectual functioning and an observable alteration in level of consciousness. Delirious patients may be slightly drowsy to comatose, or they can be hypervigilant and agitated. Often the symptoms that necessitate emergency action are reactions to vivid hallucinations, delusions, and severely impaired judgment that cause the patient to be restless, fearful, panicky, agitated, or violent.

Delirium is characterized by alterations in cognitive function and level of consciousness that stem from disturbances in homeostasis.

Delirium can be caused by any disruption in metabolic homeostasis, such as drug toxicity, alcohol abuse, malnutrition, urinary tract infections, and hypoglycemia. The elderly are particularly vulnerable to delirium from relatively trivial metabolic insults, which for the younger person would not be as serious.

Delirious patients are at risk for irrational, dangerous behaviors such as

TABLE 25-1. Initial Interventions for Patients Experiencing Confusion

- Obtain prompt comprehensive examination to identify causative factors; focus nursing actions on treatment plan to correct cause, if possible.
- Place patient in a supervised environment with minimal stimulation (e.g., low noise level, soft lighting, stable room temperature of about 75° F, away from traffic flow).
- Remove hazards from environment, such as chemicals, equipment.
- Contact reliable historian to provide information about patient.
- Orient patient to person, place, time; clarify misperceptions.
- Assign care to one staff member; attempt to limit number of staff who have contact with patient.
- Monitor intake and output.
- Evaluate patient's skin integrity, nutritional status, vital signs; report problems to physician.
- Assure physical needs are met (e.g., offer toileting, keep patient warm, provide fluid).
- Supervise patient to prevent injury.

violence, jumping from windows, and dehydration and starvation from their refusal of fluid and food. The mortality rate for delirious elderly persons is high. Once recognizing the presence of delirium, the nurse must do a physical examination, mobilize help to keep the patient safe, and seek the assistance of a physician to determine and treat the underlying cause. The basic principles of caring for confused patients are applicable to the patient who is delirious (Table 25-1).

Depression

Dulled cognition, apathy, and inattention to personal hygiene and grooming can cause the depressed person to mistakenly be viewed as demented.

Depressive syndrome usually includes a sustained low mood with an alteration in the patient's self-attitude, ranging from apathy and dullness to worthlessness and guilt. Sometimes, irritability, slowness of thought, and problems with memory and concentration are associated with depression and can be mistaken for dementia. Sleep and appetite disturbances are common, and suicidal thoughts and plans may be present. Constipation and somatic preoccupations, such as general aches and pains, are often present in elderly depressed patients. Depressed patients also may experience auditory hallucinations and delusions, including somatic delusions that are frightening to patients and family members.

Suicide rates among the elderly are high, constituting 25% of the suicides reported each year in the United States. A number of researchers have found that the likelihood of completed suicide in depressed people is related to feelings of hopelessness and negative expectations about the future (Atchley, 1980). Epidemiological data indicate that the white male over the age of 45 who is unemployed and without family resources is in the highest risk group for completed suicide.

All depressed patients should be carefully quizzed about suicidal thoughts, and any plans and means available to the patient should be evaluated. If in the nurse's clinical judgment the patient is believed to be potentially suicidal, precautions should be taken not to leave the person alone under any circumstance. Appropriate action to see that someone is with the

TABLE 25-2. Suicide Precautions

- Provide one-to-one observation.
- Remove objects that could be used for self-destruction and other means of injury from environment.
- Notify family and other responsible parties of suicide risk and treatment plan.
- Mobilize appropriate resources (psychiatrist, police, other staff).
- Monitor intake and output, elimination, rest, and sleep.
- Promote positive therapeutic alliance with patient.
- Encourage expression of feelings.
- Reassess mental state regularly.

patient, even if the patient objects, is indicated. Early intervention is crucial in the treatment of elderly depressed patients (Table 25-2).

Mania

Elderly manic patients are at significant risk for emergency situations because of extreme elevation of mood, grandiosity, and delusional thinking. Sleeplessness and inability to eat are symptoms that often accompany manic states. Frequently observed are sudden changes in mood to anger or depression. Hallucinations and delusions, accelerated speech, inappropriate sexual behavior, and evidence of impaired judgment signal the need for intervention. Irrational behavior can escalate into violence and may become a psychiatric emergency in the unrecognized or untreated manic elderly patient. In addition, cardiopulmonary stress can be significant in the patient who is agitated and unable to sit still, sleep, eat, or drink. Symptoms of mania can range from moderate to severe, have an acute onset, and worsen if no intervention is implemented. The manic patient requires immediate attention. Emergencies can be avoided by early recognition of mental status changes, such as escalation of mood and behavior, before a crisis point is reached (Table 25-3).

Dementia

Dementia is a neuropathological syndrome characterized by a decline in intellectual ability in a person who is alert with a clear state of consciousness. The etiologies of dementia are multiple, and though some are reversible, the majority of dementia syndromes are due to irreversible diseases. Alzheimer's disease, the most common cause of dementia in the elderly, is often accompanied by other psychiatric symptoms such as depression, delusions, and hallucinations. Multi-infarct dementia is the second most common type, followed by other chronic neurological diseases such as parkinsonism and its variants, Pick's disease, Huntington's disease, and spinocerebellar degenerations.

Dementia results in defects in the patient's capacity to solve problems, understand instructions, and grasp the nature of the environment, including

TABLE 25-3. Initial Interventions for Patients with Mania

- Place patient in supervised environment with minimal stimulation (e.g., low noise level, soft lighting, stable room temperature of 75° F, away from heavy traffic flow).
- Attempt to limit number of persons who have contact with patient.
- Provide short explanations and simple directions.
- Offer fluids and easy-to-eat nutritious snacks frequently (unless contraindicated).
- Monitor intake and output, vital signs, activity level.
- Encourage rest.
- Prevent patient from injuring self or others.

Poor judgment and reduced capacity to communicate increase the dementia victim's potential for injury.

the dimensions of time and space. The capacity to manipulate the body to perform such simple tasks as dressing or eating, and the ability to recognize familiar faces, objects, and situations are similarly impaired. A demented individual could wander into the street, go into the cold without proper dress, accidentally ingest poison, set fires, and perform other acts that constitute an emergency. The demented person also is unable to communicate reliably, further increasing the potential for injury. This person may be an easy victim of abuse. The general principles of caring for the confused patient (Table 25-1) are applicable to the demented person. Referrals to agencies that can provide ongoing supervision and evaluation of the patient are important.

Schizophrenic Disorders

Schizophrenia is a chronic episodic mental disorder usually having its onset in adolescence or early adulthood. Its etiology is still unknown, though current hypotheses suggest that heredity, biochemical abnormalities, disrupted relationships, and environmental factors contribute to the development of this condition. The social functioning of the schizophrenic patient is severely impaired, as is communication and, often, self-care. Acute episodes are characterized by persecutory delusions, auditory hallucinations, illogical thinking, disordered verbal communication, impaired judgment, and other grossly disorganized behaviors.

Although the behaviors of the schizophrenic individual seldom constitute a psychiatric emergency, homelessness and other social problems that the person may experience can lead to dangerous situations that can threaten well-being.

Many elderly schizophrenic patients are being discharged from state mental hospitals into the community and nursing homes after years of institutionalization and treatment with neuroleptic drugs. Chronic schizophrenic patients in the nursing home setting rarely present emergencies because they are often severely functionally disabled by the permanent side effects of neuroleptics, such as tardive dyskinesia. They exhibit highly institutionalized, dependent behavior, impaired social functioning, and behavioral oddities that may pose a challenge to nurses, but rarely present as psychiatric emergencies. On the other hand, the old chronic schizophrenics in the community can be found in dangerous situations like homelessness, making them vulnerable to victimization, malnutrition, and hypothermia. Intervention in such cases requires a coordinated effort among nurses, social service agencies, mental health facilities, and the police.

TABLE 25-4. Initial Interventions for Patients with Schizophrenia

- Place patient in supervised area with minimal stimulation.
- Assign one staff member to patient.
- Make sure that staff are sensitive and understanding of patient's behavior.
- Evaluate for secondary problems, such as malnutrition, poor hygiene, injury.
- Clarify misperceptions; orient to reality; do not foster delusions.
- Afford maximum opportunities for patient to make decisions and be in control.
- Initiate referrals for ongoing assistance, such as mental health clinic, free or low-cost meals, shelters, or other forms of safe housing. Even if patient rejects service, provide with information on available resources for potential future use.

Much less common than the early-onset variety, late-onset schizophrenia is sometimes called paraphrenia. Paraphrenia has its onset after the age of 55. These patients exhibit the same thought disorder, impaired social functioning, and bizarre behavior as patients with an early onset, but tend to be less dysfunctional than older persons who have suffered with the condition for many years. These patients can become reclusive, sometimes living under highly undesirable, unhygienic conditions, deluded, and unwilling to allow anyone to intervene; they also require coordinated efforts to arrange appropriate care (Table 25-4).

Paranoid Disorder

Sometimes in middle to late life, a paranoid disorder can occur, usually characterized by a highly systematized persecutory delusional system that is not due to any other mental disorder. The etiology is as yet unknown, and the condition is rather rare, but certain stressors, like deafness and visual impairment, are known to contribute to the development of this disorder.

These patients are difficult to evaluate and refer to treatment because they are suspicious, delusional, and often angry and uncooperative. If, in the nurse's judgment, the patient's situation is dangerous (for example, being barricaded in a house or locked in a bathroom in a nursing home), an organized coordinated plan of intervention is necessary. Table 25-5 outlines basic approaches in managing paranoid behaviors.

Violence and Aggression

Patients who are experiencing delirium, paranoia, and visual agnosia are at particularly high risk for aggressive behaviors.

Violence and aggression are behaviors that are secondary to any number of mental disorders, and they are always symptoms of some kind of underlying disorder. Precipitants of violent behavior include a preexisting psychopathology, as well as people and elements in the environment. The assessment of violence and aggression must include the evaluation of cognition, level of consciousness, emotional state, physical status, and environment. The episodes of violence should be evaluated by noting their frequency, duration, time of day, nature of the aggression, and circumstances under which they occur. Patients suffering from delirium, visual agnosia, and paranoia are at particularly high risk for aggressive behavior. Although some violent behav-

TABLE 25-5. Managing Paranoid Behaviors

- Evaluate patient for sensory deficits; compensate for or correct sensory deficits (e.g., have patient use prescribed eyeglasses or hearing aid, adjust lighting to prevent shadows, place patient in area away from intercoms and paging systems).
- Assign one staff member to patient; attempt to minimize number of persons who have contact with patient.
- Use consistent approaches.
- Offer explanations; prepare patient for procedures, activities.
- Ensure that staff understands that rational explanations usually do not correct patient's suspiciousness and could cause additional emotional distress for patient; support, warmth, honesty, and patience will promote a therapeutic relationship.
- Prevent patient from harming self (e.g., malnutrition resulting from suspicion about food, worsening of medical condition caused by refusal to take needed medication).
- Follow prescribed psychiatric treatment plan.

ior occurs without warning, other episodes may be preceded by verbal expressions of anger, pacing, and threats of violence before the actual striking out. Violent episodes are followed by what is considered a refractory phase during which the patient calms down.

Some guidelines for handling violent patients are that the nurse should be calm, rational, and nonpunitive, and should plan interventions utilizing the multidisciplinary team and other available resources. Self-protection is a concern when nurses work with a potentially violent patient. Nurses should never risk being hurt by failing to take adequate precautions for their own safety (Stuart and Sundeen, 1983, 421). Neither chemical nor physical restraints should be used unnecessarily, although they sometimes are required. Calm, verbal communications and behaviors that are not threatening to the patient but reflect that the nurse has the situation under control are useful. Removing objects from the environment that can be thrown or broken can reduce injury risks. Psychopharmacology, used judiciously, often benefits these patients. Any patient who has repeated violent episodes requires a treatment plan to prevent further episodes.

Crises Secondary to Situational Problems

It is well known and obvious that aging persons experience gradual changes and losses of many kinds, including decreased physical strength, reduced functional capacity, changes in social status and contact, and the loss of friends and loved ones through death. Some people will cope well with this stage of life, but others will experience profound difficulty progressing through the years. The ability to deal with aging and its inevitable consequences is often rooted in the following factors:

- The quality of life experiences and strength of relationships.
- The availability of meaningful sources of personal contact through family, friends, neighbors, and community.
- Financial security.
- Personal comfort.

TABLE 25-6. Example of the Problem-Solving Process in an Emergency Situation: Severe Dehydration in a 75-Year-Old Woman Caused by Her Refusal of Food and Water

Possible etiology	Difficulty in swallowing caused by neurological disease.	Drowsy, confused, visual hallucinations, fever resulting from infection.	Anorexia resulting from sadness, helplessness, hopelessness, and desire to die.	Suspicious, afraid food and water are poisoned.
Nursing diagnosis	Alterations in nutrition: less than body requirements related to swallowing difficulties.	Alterations in nutrition: less than body requirements related to altered thought processes and altered level of consciousness.	Alterations in nutrition: less than body requirements related to ineffective coping.	Alterations in nutrition: less than body requirements related to altered thought processes.
Medical diagnosis	Dysphagia	Delirium	Depression	Paranoia
Intervention	Change in nutritional route or preparation of food, neurological evaluation.	Constant observation, physical assessment, intravenous therapy.	Suicide precautions, hydration, psychiatric consultation.	Initiate therapeutic alliance, IV or NG feeding, psychiatric consultation.

People who have had lifelong histories of difficult and conflicted relationships usually continue to have this pattern in late life; therefore, information about the life history will enhance the nurse's ability to comprehend the present situation adequately.

Crises can occur in later life related to natural changes in role, such as retirement, or situational crises, such as a response to the death or illness of a spouse. The course of grief and bereavement can often be positively influenced by the nurse who recognizes the need for intervention that can prevent prolonged, protracted reactions. The availability of the nurse by telephone and direct visits, therapeutic use of the empathetic approach that promotes a supportive alliance with the patient, and the mobilization of community resources can greatly enhance the satisfactory resolution of grief. For those people whose lives have been replete with conflicts and problems, the nurse may need to implement a plan for referral for specialized treatment, such as crisis intervention.

The use of the nursing process is imperative in dealing with the elderly patient who presents a psychiatric emergency. Thus the management depends on an organized assessment of the patient's mental and physical states, environmental factors, and the availability of resources to implement an orderly plan. Table 25-6 demonstrates the manner in which the nursing process flows for a problem presented by one older patient.

REFERENCES

Altshuler KZ: Psychiatric treatments for the aged: 2000 and beyond. In Samoraysle T (ed): Aging 2000: Our Health Care Dealing. New York, Springer, 1985.

Atchley R: Aging and suicide: Reflection of the quality of life? In Haynes S, Feinleib M (eds): Epidemiology of Aging, Second Conference. Washingtion, DC, US Department of Health and Human Services, 1980.

Lucas MJ: Assessment of mental status. In Eliopoulos C (ed): Health Assessment of the Older Adult. Menlo Park, CA, Addison-Wesley, 1984.

Stuart G, Sundeen S: Principles and Practice of Psychiatric Nursing, 2nd ed. St. Louis, CV Mosby, 1983.

BIBLIOGRAPHY

Beck CK, Rawlins RP, Williams SR: Mental Health–Psychiatric Nursing: A Holistic Life-Cycle Approach, 2nd ed. St. Louis, CV Mosby, 1988.

Brady PF: Labeling confusion in the elderly. J Gerontol Nurs 13(6): 29–32, 1987.

Brannan P: Using nursing skills instead of restraints. Geriatr Nurs 9(2): 114–115, 1988.

Coyle MK: Organic illness mimicking psychiatric episodes. J Gerontol Nurs 13(1): 31–35, 1987.

Gomez GE, Gomez EA: Delirium. Geriatr Nurs 8(6): 330–332, 1987.

Kermis M: Mental Health in Late Life: The Adaptive Process. Boston, Jones and Bartlett, 1986.

Lucas MJ, Steele C, Bognanni A: Recognition of psychiatric symptoms in dementia. J Gerontol Nurs 12(1): 11–15, 1986.

Mace N: Facets of dementia: Using mental status tests. J Gerontol Nurs 13(6): 33, 1987.

Ronsman KM: Pseudodementia. Geriatr Nurs 9(1): 50–53, 1988.

Struble LM, Sivertsen L: Agitation behaviors in confused elderly patients. J Gerontol Nurs 13(11): 40–44, 1987.

Whall AL: Geropsychiatry: Assessing suicidal intent. J Gerontol Nurs 13(8): 36–37, 1987.

PART FOUR

Gerontological Nursing in Long-Term Care Settings

Nursing in long-term care facilities may be among the least understood and most underestimated practices in existence. Misconceptions prevail that nursing home nursing is an easy, simple job; that working with nursing home patients is depressing and boring; and that nurses who work in this setting are not competent enough to be employed in other settings. In reality, nursing home nursing is fast becoming one of the most complex and exciting practice opportunities. A broad knowledge base and ability to use highly technical skills are required to meet diverse clinical problems—problems that must be faced without physicians or an abundance of other professionals with whom to consult. Unique personnel and consumer issues make managerial and human relations skills prerequisites for effectiveness. Limited resources challenge nurses with finding creative, innovative approaches to achieve a high quality of care.

Despite these demands, nurses in long-term care facilities can find satisfactions that are available in few practice settings. Long-term relationships with patients and families allow for strong bonds to be established and goals to be reached. Nursing is the backbone of nursing home services, and nurses have freedom to practice nursing in an independent form. Most importantly, the practice setting affords the opportunity not only to perform therapeutic procedures to manage illness, but also to affect the quality of life so that patients' remaining years have comfort, meaning, and satisfaction.

This part provides a chapter that helps nurses understand the special needs of patients and families as they select and adjust to nursing home care. The challenges of nursing administration in the nursing home are reviewed with a special emphasis on the importance of nurse managers in influencing the overall quality of services. Last, the emerging new role of the psychiatric nurse specialist in the nursing home is presented to highlight an important resource for long-term care facilities as they address the needs of a growing chronic geropsychiatric population.

CHAPTER 26

Selecting and Adjusting to Nursing Home Care

Charlotte Eliopoulos

Chapter Objectives
At the completion of this chapter the reader will be able to:

1. Discuss the realities of nursing home care and the problems it may cause for patients and families.
2. Outline the factors that consumers should evaluate in selecting a nursing home.
3. Describe the reactions to institutionalization that patients and families may experience.
4. List ways that families can make their visits more meaningful.
5. Describe an example of a family support program that can be developed in the nursing home setting.

Increasing numbers of families are facing the need for institutional care of aging relatives. Although less than 5% of the elderly population reside in any institutional setting at a given time, one in four will spend some time in a nursing home at the ends of their lives. Institutionalization becomes more of a possibility with each decade after age 65 (Table 26-1), and more people are surviving to those later decades. Behavioral impairments, arteriosclerosis, heart disease, arthritis, digestive disorders, and elimination problems are the major problems found among nursing home residents, but even more important are the functional impairments these people display (Table 26-2). Behavioral problems and incontinence especially exhaust family resources and limit the older individual's ability to remain at home.

The decision to seek nursing home care is rarely an easy choice or a first choice, and often it is a traumatic experience for the entire family unit. Older patients and their families need to

- Understand the realities of nursing home care.
- Know how to select an appropriate facility.
- Recognize and deal with the emotional reactions involved.
- Learn to maintain meaningful relationships.
- Identify and seek resolution of problems.

TABLE 26-1. The Risk of Institutionalization with
Advanced Age

Age	Percentage of Group Institutionalized
65–74	1.2
75–84	5.9
85 +	23.7

TABLE 26-2. Functional Impairments of Nursing
Home Residents

Impairment	Percentage of Nursing Home Residents
"Senility"	63
Bedfast or chairbound	31
Incontinent	35
Cannot see to read newspaper	49
Cannot hear conversation on telephone	35
Impaired speech	24

Source: National Center for Health Statistics: National Nursing Home Survey,
1977: Summary for U.S. Hyattsville, MD, U.S. Department of Health, Education, and Welfare, 1979.

Realities of Nursing Home Care

Few consumers have a realistic understanding of nursing homes. Perceptions of nursing home care may have been influenced by publicized scandals or the opinions of friends and neighbors.

People who have never been involved with nursing homes have many misconceptions about them. Exposed to tales of poor conditions and front-page
exposés, some persons view nursing homes as "snake pits" that neglect and
abuse the unfortunates who depend upon their services. Other people perceive nursing homes as rest homes that provide room and board for old
people. Still others believe these facilities can provide more intense personal
care and attention than the older person could receive at home from the
family. Few people understand that most long-term care facilities provide
good services to an increasingly ill and frail population with a fraction of
the resources of the acute sector.

Although it provides health services and serves as a permanent residence for most of its patients, a nursing home is neither a hospital nor a
home. A nursing home can be expected to provide personal care, routine
treatment, professional supervision of care, a safe environment, special diets,
activities, and management of emergencies for its clients. Rehabilitative and
other services can be available as well. Most long-term care facilities are not
equipped or staffed to provide intense services to the patient who requires
highly skilled interventions (e.g., cardiac monitoring, ventilators) or who is
medically unstable. In addition to physical plant limitations (e.g., lack of
wall oxygen or monitoring stations), staffing may prohibit the nursing home
from providing hospital-type services. Although nursing home beds outnum-

TABLE 26-3. Comparison of Nursing Home and
Hospital Costs

	Nursing Homes	Hospitals
Total facilities	25,849	6,888
Beds (1,000)	1,642	1,350
National expenditures (in billion $)	32	157.9
Per capita private consumer expenditures ($)	66	293

Source: U.S. Department of Commerce: Statistical Abstract of the United
States, 1986, 106th ed. Washington, DC, Bureau of the Census, Nos. 148,
149, 171, and 178.

ber acute hospital beds, only 17% of all health care workers are employed
in nursing homes. Of those,

9% are registered nurses.

9% are licensed practical nurses.

39% are nursing assistants.

12% are food service workers.

8% are housekeepers.

When the employee-to-patient ratio is compared, there is a 3.6:1 ratio in
hospitals, while nursing homes average 0.57:1 (U.S. Department of Commerce, 1986). Reimbursement also contributes to a difference between hospitals and nursing homes: In 1986 expenditures for hospital care were more
than four times as high as for nursing homes (Table 26-3). Patients and
families accustomed to the intensity of services and staffing level in a hospital may have difficulty understanding the differences when they confront the
nursing home setting. It may be unrealistic to expect staff to provide one-to-
one supervision on a 24-hour basis, spend 1½ hours to coax someone to eat
each meal, regularly manicure and polish patients' nails, play card games
with them every afternoon, or answer call lights within 15 seconds. Although this level of service may be provided occasionally, expecting it on a
routine basis in the average long-term care facility can lead to disappointment. Families and patients should be prepared for the reality that institutional care will seldom provide the degree of special attention that was afforded by loved ones in one's own home.

Nursing homes cannot be expected to provide the same intensity and scope of services as a hospital, or the personal attention that one would receive from family caregivers in the community.

To use the word "home" in nursing home care can be misleading and
give rise to another set of unrealistic expectations. "Home" typically is associated with a pleasant, safe refuge from an uncertain world—a place that is
familiar, where one can be oneself and comfortably express individuality
and freedom. In an institutional setting, "home" hardly portrays a similar
picture.

Upon entering a nursing home, patients must adapt to a new environment with furnishings, decorations, noises, and odors that bear no resemblance to those known in one's household. The personal items that reflected

individuality and carried a history are absent. After decades of sleeping alone or with a spouse, patients must share a bedroom with a stranger who may or may not be to their liking. They must learn to conform to bathing, sleeping, and activity schedules that facilitate efficiency more than individual preference. There is limited control over the time and content of meals, and the act of obtaining a favorite snack from the refrigerator when desired becomes a monumental or impossible task. Privacy shrinks as nursing staff poke heads in the bathroom to make sure "all is well"; housekeepers clean drawers and discard what they judge to be useless; and confused patients wander in and out. Adjusting to this new version of home can be stressful and, in fact, can lead to relocation trauma.

Whether in a camp, dormitory, or nursing home, group living is not an easy task. New nursing home residents must adjust to a variety of fellow residents. These residents may represent different ethnic and racial groups, as well as various personality types. They may possess deformities or demonstrate unusual behaviors. New residents may perceive the others as very different from themselves, and for that reason new residents may feel out of place, frightened, or anxious. Honest explanations and preadmission visits can reduce some of the element of surprise and adverse reactions.

Selecting the Facility

Rarely do elderly individuals and their families explore nursing home care unless faced with a crisis. The pressure to discharge the patient from the hospital or relieve the family of an overwhelming care burden can lead to the acceptance of "any available bed" rather than selection of a facility best suited to the patient's and family's needs. Ideally, consumers should become acquainted with the various nursing homes in their communities, as they would become familiar with other types of consumer services.

Gerontological nurses should ensure that all available options for care are made known to patients and families and, when nursing home care is decided upon, that the most appropriate facility is selected.

When faced with the need for nursing home care, a family's first question should be, Is nursing home care really needed? Such concerns as a lack of knowledge about how to care for a debilitated person and responsibility for the ill person while family members are working understandably can cause families to feel that caregiving responsibilities are beyond their capabilities; institutionalization may be the only option known to them. Knowledge about the assistance provided by home health agencies, geriatric daycare programs, family support groups, sheltered housing, and other community services could help caregivers view their responsibilities as less frightening and overwhelming. In some cases, home management of the patient may be possible.

When family and community services cannot meet the patient's care requirements and nursing home care is judged necessary, proper selection is necessary. To assist their exploration, consumers need explanations regarding differences in the levels of care provided and reimbursement mechanisms. Medicare, for instance, pays only for skilled nursing care for a limited period of time. Intermediate care facilities provide less intense professional services than do skilled facilities. Facilities may be certified to accept patients on Medical Assistance, those on Medicare, or both. Local health departments, social services offices, or hospital or nursing home associations can provide lists of nursing homes; even the telephone directory can be a source of information regarding local nursing homes. Often, telephone inquiries can be made to determine whether the facility can provide the level of care required, whether it will accept the reimbursement mechanism, and whether it has a bed available. This initial "telephone visit" can save considerable time and energy.

The family seeking nursing home care for a relative should, if possible, investigate several nursing homes to allow an adequate comparison. Important background information on a facility can be gained by reviewing health department survey reports available for public review from local and state health departments. Consumers should be prepared for the reality that deficiencies are not unusual—few facilities are perfect.

More important is the nature of the deficiencies. Recurrent problems, chronic understaffing, poor infection control techniques, inadequate dietary supervision, medication errors, and inattention to restorative care are among the red-flag items that should give rise to concern. These preliminary evaluation measures will be assets in more selective on-site visits.

A good nursing home has nothing to fear from opening its doors to the public. Consumers should schedule appointments to visit a facility, preferably when routine activities and meal times can be observed. The types of items that should be evaluated include the following:

Philosophy of care. Are independence and individuality promoted? Are residents treated with respect, as active partners in their care?

Availability of special services. What arrangements are made for podiatry, speech, occupational, and physical therapies?

Staffing pattern. How many RNs, LPNs, and nursing assistants are on duty each shift?

Attitude and image portrayed by staff. Do staff acknowledge residents, smile, make eye contact, act courteously?

Attitude and image portrayed by residents. Are residents clean, in street clothes? Do they interact freely?

Layout. Where are bathrooms, dining rooms, and recreational areas located in relation to patient rooms? Are patients' rooms and activities areas visible from the nursing station?

Activities. What is the range and frequency of activities? How can families be involved? Is there a resident council?

Care management. How are incontinent patients managed, behavioral problems dealt with?

Religion. Does the facility adhere to the practices of any particular faith? How are religious needs met?

Physical facility. Is the facility clean, attractive, odor free? How much ease would a handicapped person have traveling to all areas, including the outdoors?

Visitation. Are visitors present? What are visiting hours? Can children visit? Are there areas of privacy for visitation?

If possible, the patient should visit the facility before admission to participate in the selection process and become familiar with his or her new home.

Dealing with Reactions

No matter how much one prepares for it, the actual day of admission can be quite difficult. For the individual being admitted, a significant role transition occurs. The status, importance, and privilege that accompanied one's family or work roles fade as the nursing home patient learns that compliance with facility rules and cooperation with staff are requisites for survival. Clients may find that their recommendations to staff about how operations could flow more smoothly are unappreciated and unwelcomed. It is not surprising that patients become frustrated, depressed, and angry, as demonstrated through such mechanisms as these:

- Accusing family of being uncaring and cruel for placing them in the facility.
- Refusing to participate in activities.
- Regressing in self-care capabilities.
- Crying, eating or sleeping poorly.
- Complaining more of physical ailments.

Patience is required in the face of such behavior. Families will discover that trying to rationalize or becoming defensive with patients may be less helpful than listening and supporting them through the emotionally difficult period.

Institutional life itself can cause unfortunate reactions. Without knowing the unique history of the person before them now, staff interaction with this person is based on how they perceive him or her. The patient risks becoming less of an individual and developing coping behaviors that further separate him or her from the larger world. Reactions to institutionalization were astutely described nearly three decades ago by Erving Goffman (1961) in his book *Asylums,* and these reactions can be applicable to today's nursing home resident:

Humiliation. Toileting, a drink of water, and other necessities must be requested.

Regression. A disculturation to the larger world occurs as the norms of the nursing home world are adopted.

Depersonalization. The patient may become viewed as a task or diagnostic problem—e.g., the total feed, the MI in Room 100—rather than an individual.

Abnormality. Normal behaviors, such as sexual expression, may need to be forfeited to conform with institutional rules.

Families can aid in reducing such consequences by helping staff to understand the individual within "the patient." This understanding can be accomplished by sharing some of the patient's history, such as previous occupations, hobbies, accomplishments, and number of children and grandchildren. Decorating a wall or bulletin board in the patient's room with photographs and memorabilia can serve as a constant reminder of the patient's uniqueness and be a stimulus for conversation. Encouraging continued interest and participation in hobbies and family and community functions can be beneficial. As much as realistically possible, the family should help the patient remain involved in the noninstitutional world.

Family members have their own reactions stemming from a loved one's entering a nursing home. Regardless of how clearly they understand institutional care to be necessary, it is not uncommon for them to feel tremendous guilt, which can be exacerbated by the patient's feelings about nursing home placement. The family may feel depressed or inadequate at not being able to care for the patient themselves. Inability to change the situation or the shouldering of additional burdens (cost of care, inconvenience of visitation, responsibility for decision making) may cause anger to surface. The family's social world may need readjustment as they plan activities around the nursing home schedule, or, if they had to forfeit activities in the past because of caregiving responsibilities, the family may need to reestablish social roles. These feelings can be displayed in families in many ways, including the following:

- Clinical signs of depression, declining health.
- Angry outbursts and excessive complaining to staff.
- Decreased visitation.
- Excess visitation (at the expense of their own physical, emotional, and social well-being).

Relatives of the patient require assistance and support as they face the emotional stress of having a loved one enter a nursing home. Monitoring their feelings and guiding them in maintaining active involvement with the patient are important nursing measures.

Families need special attention as they adjust to the nursing home experience. Ideally, they should be confronted with the realities of nursing home life and anticipated reactions before the patient is admitted. Family "orientation sessions" conducted by a professional skilled in group work can provide information, offer a ventilation mechanism for feelings, and promote networking and support among residents' families (see the chapter appendix describing the "In Touch" program). To hear a professional say that it is normal to feel depressed, guilty, and angry, and to learn that other families share similar feelings may lift the emotional burden somewhat.

Families should be encouraged to maintain their own physical, emotional, and social health and guided as they develop a new dimension to their relationship with the patient. It can prove useful to offer assistance to families as they pass through the normal emotional valleys of the nursing home experience.

Maintaining Meaningful Roles

Visitation in a nursing home can be an awkward and uncomfortable situation for family members. In addition to adjusting to the status of their loved one, families are faced with a wide range of sights, scents, and sounds. Privacy may be limited. With a limited social world patients may have little to discuss other than their ills and bodily functions or those of fellow residents, which can be uncomfortable or uninteresting for the visitor. Worse still, there may be nothing to discuss, and the silence can make the visit become painfully long and cumbersome. Families should be guided in how to make their visits a meaningful experience for the patient and themselves. Here are some suggestions:

Maximize sensory function. When speaking to the patient, sit at eye level, avoid settings with high glare, speak clearly and loudly.

Touch. Hug, hold hands, comb hair, and find other ways to promote contact.

Visit outside the patient's room. If possible, go to a lounge, cafeteria, or outdoors. (Doing so can make the visit more comfortable for patient and visitor.)

Plan ahead for topics to discuss. Family news, community activities, and gossip aid in maintaining a link with the larger world.

Bring an activity. Games, puzzles, photo albums, and magazines can be stimulating and meaningful. A visiting pet can be a pleasurable diversion. Grooming activities can pass the time and boost the patient's self-concept.

Take the patient out. A visit home, lunch at a local restaurant, or a drive can be a welcome experience.

Allow the patient to ventilate feelings. Complaints, dissatisfactions, and frustrations are to be expected and need active listening. Offer support and attempt to identify real and serious problems.

Meaningful visits are significant to both patients and visitors.

Dealing with Problems

In any human services organization negative situations can occur. Most of these incidents are out of the ordinary or due to unusual circumstances—for example, a personal garment not returned from the laundry, a medication not administered in a timely fashion, or a disagreement with a fellow resident. At times, serious or chronic negative issues surface, such as food served at improper temperatures, inattention to care needs, or abuse. Families need to listen carefully to complaints and separate unusual or minor problems from major or ongoing ones. Complaints should not be ignored, nor should they be silenced out of fear of offending staff.

An attempt should be made to solve problems constructively by approaching the staff closest to the problem. For example, if a nursing assistant repeatedly places the patient's call bell out of the patient's reach, the assistant should be confronted first and asked to make sure the patient has access to the bell. If dealing directly with the party involved does not prove satisfactory, the next line supervisor should be approached. If no satisfaction is gained, the next level of authority should be sought. Patients and families should understand the chain of command in the facility—for example, from charge nurse, to head nurse, to supervisor or assistant director, to director of nursing, to administrator. Staff should be given a reasonable time to resolve the problem. If satisfaction is not obtained from facility staff, external sources can be sought for assistance:

- The nursing home advocate or ombudsman in the state or area agency on aging.
- Nursing home licensing and certification divisions of state or local health departments.
- State board of nursing home administrators in the state health department.
- State Medicaid or Medicare agencies (if facility is certified for those programs).
- The Joint Commission for Accreditation of Hospitals (if facility is JCAH accredited).

Nursing homes should have the complaint procedure posted in a highly visible location. This poster will contain information regarding the specific local agency and telephone number for complaint reporting.

Although nursing home placement can be difficult, the negative effects can be minimized by adequate preparation, realistic insight, and support in learning the new roles associated with nursing home resident and visitor. With family caregiving responsibilities lifted, relatives' burdens may be lightened, and the family may be able to focus on more meaningful involvement with the patient. Benefits to their own physical, emotional, and social well-being may also be gained. The patient may enjoy a different relationship with loved ones, knowing that he or she is not depending upon them or being a burden. With these changes, an improved quality of family relationships may emerge.

REFERENCES

Goffman E: Asylums. New York, Doubleday, 1961.

U.S. Department of Commerce: Statistical Abstract of the United States, 1986, 106th ed. Washington, DC, Bureau of the Census, 1986.

BIBLIOGRAPHY

Aasen N: Interventions to facilitate personal control. J Gerontol Nurs 13(6): 20–28, 1987.

American Association of Retired Persons: Knowing Your Rights. Washington, DC, AARP, 1986.

Carter MA: Professional nursing in the nursing home. J Professional Nurs 3(6): 325, 376, 1987.

Eliopoulos C: Nursing Administration of Long Term Care. Rockville, MD, Aspen Systems, 1983.

Elizabeth C: Coping with the difficult family member: A model. Contemporary Long Term Care's D.O.N. 10(12): 32–33, 1987.

Ernspiker KR: Fostering new residents in nursing homes. Contemporary Long Term Care's D.O.N. 11(8): 21, 27, 1988.

Goto L, Braun K: Nursing home without walls. J Gerontol Nurs 13(1): 6–9, 1987.

Johnson C, Grant L: The Nursing Home in American Society. Baltimore, MD, Johns Hopkins Press, 1985.

McCracken A: Emotional impact of possession loss. J Gerontol Nurs 13(2): 14–19, 1987.

Roberts KL, LeSage J, Ellor JR: Quality monitoring in nursing homes. J Gerontol Nurs 13(10): 34–40, 1987.

Rossi T: Step by Step: How to Actively Ensure the Best Possible Care for Your Aging Relative. New York, Warner, 1987.

Sommers T, Shields L: Women Take Care: The Consequences of Caregiving in Today's Society. Gainesville, FL, Triad, 1987.

Appendix: Family Support in the Nursing Home Setting: The "In Touch" Program

Kay Kness

In Chapter 26, Eliopoulos mentions the importance of helping families to confront the realities of nursing home care. One mechanism that can be effective in this process is the use of family orientation sessions. This format has been used with success by the Manor Health Care Center in Ruxton, Maryland, as part of their "In Touch" program, which can serve as a model to other facilities that wish to implement family support and orientation programs.

Description of Program

As part of the In Touch program, families are encouraged to attend a monthly group meeting for the relatives of newly admitted residents (Figure 26-1). Key personnel with whom family members have had contact are present to facilitate the group, and they provide familiar faces to alleviate some of the anxiety of entering the group. Although a staff member is designated as the group leader, other staff take an active role in providing information and answering questions.

The group is conducted using a combined group therapy and educational model. Typically, initial sessions focus on clarifying myths associated with nursing home placement, such as the misconception that nursing

Love is doing what people need—
not just what *they* want;
Love is doing what people need—
not just what *we* want.

One of the most difficult experiences you will ever face is the aging of a loved one. Becoming in touch with the reality of your feelings will allow you to encourage, enjoy, and share in the day to day living of the one you love.

IN TOUCH offers an organized yet informal setting where families may recognize the difficulties of the decisions ahead, identify family strengths and develop coping skills; all of which offer a positive approach to a difficult experience.

One evening each month, this nursing center hosts an hour-and-a-half gathering led by a professional consultant experienced in gerontology. Members of the nursing center staff also attend this gathering. An open format in a casual atmosphere allows discussion of specific problems and feelings, and written and verbal material regarding anticipated experiences is provided as well.

Your adjustment and smooth transition to the changes in the life of your loved one will ultimately enable you to assist in their personal acceptance of those changes. Your love is essential—but to be effective it must be accompanied by intelligent and realistic knowledge and understanding.

Achieving success and fulfillment in this difficult period of change requires a firm approach to both decision-making and personal feelings. IN TOUCH is designed to make the adjustment to nursing center life less frustrating and perhaps even rewarding.

AVAILABLE FOR:

Anyone closely associated with an elderly person experiencing changes in their previous lifestyle.

Anyone faced with the decision of nursing center placement.

Ministers, counselors, social workers, or anyone who has the occasion to counsel those involved in this decision-making process.

IN TOUCH meets at

_____

_____

Please call in advance.

THE GOALS:

To offer a positive means for family adjustment.

To investigate the myths and social stigmas surrounding nursing centers and the lives of their residents.

To prepare families to make the best decision for their personal situation.

To meet geriatric professionals who understand your situation.

To offer an opportunity to meet and interact with other family members facing similar experiences.

To offer a constructive situation in which you can face your feelings of guilt, frustration, and anger so that you may then assist your loved one in enjoying the highest quality of life possible.

For more information:

FIGURE 26-1. Invitation to the In Touch Program of the Manor Health Care Center, Ruxton, Maryland. (Reprinted with permission.)

homes are a place to die or that families abandon their relatives who are placed in nursing homes. These are relatively "safe" and comfortable topics for families to discuss as they gel as a group and gain trust.

As the group progresses, family members are encouraged to express personal feelings and reactions, such as their guilt, anger, and frustration. The experienced group leader guides the discussion, encouraging members with similar feelings to share them and offer personal insights on how they manage these feelings. By hearing other family members describe similar reactions, families do not have to feel that their feelings are abnormal or "bad." Through mutual support, families can attain a healthy resolution of their reactions and a level of emotional comfort that aids them in achieving satisfying relationships with their institutionalized loved ones.

A frequently witnessed outcome of the formal group is the friendships that develop between members of different families. These friendships enable families to have a wider base for socialization during visitations and ongoing peer support. Some of these friendships continue even after the patients are deceased.

In summary, the structured, informational group meetings assist families of nursing home residents to

Share experiences.

Express concerns.

Obtain information.

Improve coping skills.

Receive a wider network of support.

Develop and maintain a satisfying relationship with their institutionalized relatives.

Informal Support System

In addition to the group sessions, staff must be sensitive to other situations that warrant special intervention and support to families. Often, such intervention begins prior to admission to the center, when family members first tour the facility and are confronted with the reality of nursing home life, as in the following example:

Mrs. B. and her husband visited the nursing center to make arrangements for the admission of Mrs. B.'s mother. They were shown several rooms, none of which was satisfactory to Mrs. B. As the room inspection continued, Mrs. B. started crying and then became almost hysterical. Going off to a quiet room, the social worker explored the reasons for this reaction with Mrs. B. After nearly one hour, Mrs. B. was finally able to communicate that five years earlier, when her mother first became ill, she had promised her mother that she would never place her in a nursing home. Although her mother's care requirements exceeded her ability to fulfill them,

Mrs. B. carried tremendous guilt about breaking this promise. Once this "secret" was released and a realistic understanding of the need for nursing home care was established, Mrs. B. was able to progress with the arrangements for admission.

Imagine the emotional turmoil within Mrs. B. and the potential displaced feelings to staff if Mrs. B.'s feelings had not been identified and addressed at that time.

It has been indicated that when a protective silence is used in facing a crisis, "This form of communication can lessen family functioning and result in dysfunctional behavior in family members" (Orcutt, 1977). On the other hand, "When family communication remains open, less psychic energy will have to be directed to keeping a protective lid on expression of feeling and more energy can be directed to mutual support of one another" (Northouse, 1980). As early as the first contact, staff need to begin the process of developing a trusting relationship with families and conveying acceptance of the expression of their feelings.

Adjustment Process

Families must be advised that adjustment to this new environment takes at least three months for both resident and family, who are faced with multiple losses. The adult child has lost the healthy, active parent. The spouse has lost the partner to share daily life. The patient faces the loss of health, independence, role, status, possessions, and decision-making ability. For all, these losses bring a sense of fear and sadness. Through these losses both resident and family must be allowed the time to process their grief in order to reach a healthy state of mind. The shock of loss at first places one in a daze. The realization of the event can lead to sadness, depression, rejection, and guilt. As a reaction to the loss, anger is often experienced. It is imperative that anger be allowed expression in order to reach a recovery (acceptance) phase.

A daughter who had placed her mother in the center was not able to visit her mother for three weeks following admission. With the help of the orientation group, she was given encouragement to visit her mother that night and express her feelings. The daughter was told not to attempt to "talk her mother into liking the center," but only to acknowledge her feelings and needs. The group provided reassurance and support to the daughter. She indeed visited her mother that evening, speaking openly of her feelings, and began the process of working through her guilt.

Families are encouraged to be active listeners and recognize covert feelings and needs. Clues to the elderly's feelings and needs can be gained through body language and choice of words, as well as voice inflections.

Northouse (1980) tells us that families need a sense of control. To increase control, families are provided with information, timely answers to their questions, and vehicles to obtain additional information. This information enables them to feel in control and identify their role within the institutional setting. This improved communication also clarifies the goals of the families for the staff.

The key words in making this and other family support systems work are "open communications." Professionals should always recognize that need.

Summary

There are numerous positive effects of family support:

1. The role of the family in an extended care facility is identified.
2. Families are able to better understand long-term care and the aging process.
3. A sense of trust is created between family and staff.
4. The staff act as guides, not decision makers for the family.
5. Improved communication is developed between staff and family.
6. The needs and concerns of the family are identified, so that the staff may better meet these needs.
7. Common concerns among other family members with similar experiences may be identified.
8. Families are able to relinquish physical care to the nursing center and provide increased time for the emotional support of the resident.
9. There is a decline in feelings of guilt and acceptance of the need for long-term care.

The nursing home admission can be viewed as a "gift of time" for families whose loved ones may have a few weeks or a few years to live. The family can relinquish the physical care burdens to the nursing staff and have time for life review, resolving old hurts, and closure. Once a person dies, the family is robbed of these opportunities. At the same time, they may ask advice and share plans with the elderly. These activities continue a sense of family and promote a sense of worth for the resident.

REFERENCES

Northouse LL: Who supports the support system? J Psych Nurs Mental Health Serv 18(5): 11–15, 1980.

Orcutt B: Social work with the dying patient and the family. New York, Columbia University Press, 1977.

BIBLIOGRAPHY

Brody EM: Women in the middle and family help to older people. The Gerontologist 21(5): 471–479, 1981.

Brotman HB: Every ninth American. In U.S. Senate Special Committee on Aging: Developments in Aging, 1979, Part 1. Washington, DC, U.S. Government Printing Office, 1980.

Hayter J: Helping families of patients with Alzheimer's disease. J Gerontol Nurs 8(2): 81–86, 1982.

Hirst S, Metcalf F: Learning needs of caregivers. J Gerontol Nurs 12(4): 24–28, 1986.

Johnson E, Bursk B: Relationships between the elderly and their adult children. The Gerontologist 17(1): 35, 1977.

Kaplan D, Grobsteen R, Smith A: Severe illness in families. Health and Social Work 1(3): 72–81, 1976.

Neugarten BL: The future and the young old. Part II. The Gerontologist 15(1): 4–9, 1975.

Olsen JK: Helping families cope. J Gerontol Nurs 6(3): 152–154, 1980.

Shanas E: The family as a social support in old age. The Gerontologist 19(2): 169–174, 1979.

Smith KF, Bengtson V: Positive consequences of institutionalization and solidarity between elderly parents and their middle-aged children. The Gerontologist 20(6): 656–660, 1980.

Stafford F: A program for families of the mentally impaired elderly. The Gerontologist 20(6): 656–660, 1980.

Treas J: Family support systems for the aged: Some social and demographic considerations. The Gerontologist 17(6): 486–491, 1977.

York J, Calsyn R: Family involvement in nursing homes. The Gerontologist 17(6): 500–505, 1977.

CHAPTER 27

Nursing Administration in the Nursing Home Setting

Charlotte Eliopoulos

Chapter Objectives
At the completion of this chapter the reader will be able to:

1. Trace the growth of nursing homes in the United States.
2. Describe nursing's role in the history of nursing homes.
3. List the changes that long-term institutional care is experiencing.
4. Outline the diverse roles of the director of nursing in the nursing home setting.

Unless they are among the minority of nurses employed in this setting or are faced with utilizing this form of care within their family circumstances, nurses often misunderstand and underestimate the nursing home setting. Nursing homes rank high in the health care industry for their rapid growth and profound transformation, and they will continue to demonstrate dramatic changes as they meet the challenges of future nursing home consumers. Growing numbers of nurses will be employed in nursing homes, and others will interact with these facilities as they plan and coordinate care; thus a realistic understanding of nursing leadership in this setting is essential.

Growth of Nursing Homes

Nursing homes outnumber hospitals by nearly three to one, with correspondingly more patient beds and patient days than their hospital counterparts (U.S. Bureau of the Census, 1986, 107). Approximately $30 billion is spent on nursing home care annually (ibid.). One would imagine that such a large industry grew under the direction of a carefully laid long-term care policy, but such was hardly the situation. Today's nursing home evolved from several different types of facilities, most of which originated to serve the poor. In colonial days public interest in caring for the poor and needy led to the development of orphanages, almshouses, poor farms, and similar forms of institutional care. By the early 1900s religious organizations and other private charitable groups—the seeds of today's private nonprofit facilities—founded homes for the homeless and ill aged. These public and private institutions operated on shoestring budgets, frequently causing the service they delivered to be basic, at best; consequently, these facilities were an option of last resort.

Perhaps the first major change to have an impact on institutional services to the elderly was the 1935 passage of the Social Security Act. With Social Security income the elderly had the resources to purchase care and did not have to rely on charitable or government institutions. In response to the growing demand for care and the elderly population's new ability to pay for it, private homes for the aged were established. Interestingly, many of these homes were owned and operated by nurses (or lay persons calling themselves nurses) who provided room, board, and limited personal care in return for all or a portion of clients' Social Security income. In 1946 the Hill-Burton Act influenced another major landmark in the growth of nursing homes by providing federal aid to build and operate these facilities (Dunlop, 1979). The 1,200 nursing homes with 25,000 beds that existed in 1940 multiplied to 9,582 facilities with 290,000 residents by 1960.

Perhaps the most significant factor affecting the nursing home industry was the passage of Medicare and Medicaid in 1965. With a guaranteed form of reimbursement, nursing homes became an attractive business venture for many persons outside the health care profession. The business community promoted nursing homes as excellent investments, and in fact, these were profitable enterprises for the many individuals who became millionaires in this growing industry. The economic incentive for the business community and the growing number of older persons in society facilitated a significant increase in nursing homes. In the decade between 1960 and 1970 the number of nursing homes more than doubled, and the number of residents tripled (Table 27-1), with most of that growth occurring in the private sector. Along with more nursing homes came a profound increase in health care expenditures for nursing homes, rising from $500 million in 1960 to $4.7 billion in 1970, and now exceeding $30 billion.

Many persons are familiar with the scandalous past of the nursing home industry. Some owners' efforts to maximize profits by cutting corners, paying low wages, and meeting only minimal standards, combined with government reimbursement for only minimal care and poor monitoring, led to unfavorable conditions. Abuse, inattention to care, lack of basic supplies, mismanagement of funds, violation of patients' rights, and incompetent, un-

TABLE 27-1. Growth of Nursing Homes, 1960–1980

	1960	1970	1980
Total facilities	9,582	22,004	30,111
Residents (1,000)	290	1,076	1,396
Expenditures ($ billion)	0.5	4.7	20.4

Source: U.S. Department of Commerce, Bureau of the Census: Statistical Abstract of the United States, 105th ed., Hospitals and Nursing Homes, Summary and Characteristics, No. 165. Washington, DC, U.S. Bureau of the Census, 1986.

FIGURE 27-1. Vicious Cycle of Poor-quality Nursing in Nursing Homes.

caring staff were well publicized. Although these did not reflect the conditions in most facilities, public perception of nursing homes was highly negative.

Nursing and Nursing Homes

In the past, the lack of nurse power in nursing homes influenced the quality of care and the status and financial rewards of nursing home nurses.

As was mentioned, nurses played a significant role in the history of nursing homes—that is, until they became profitable for others! Few nurses of the past were entrepreneurial in nature. They became nurses to "help others," not to earn big dollars. Viewing nursing homes as profitable investments, entrepreneurs who were not nurses seized the opportunity to own and operate nursing homes. Increasingly, nursing's status, impact, and power in nursing homes decreased. Salaries for nursing directors often did not match those of staff nurses in acute hospitals; nursing policies, practices, and budgets were established without nursing input; staffing levels were minimal and primarily consisted of nonprofessionals with minimal training and experience. The director of nursing may have been one of a few RNs—if not the only one—in the facility, with a staggering scope of responsibility. Obviously, these conditions were not attractive to many highly professional nurse leaders who could enjoy significantly better status, salary, and working conditions in community health or hospital settings. Although many fine professionals were employed in nursing homes, most of the RNs attracted to this setting were there for all the wrong reasons. The result was the vicious cycle diagramed in Figure 27-1.

Changes

A variety of factors have bombarded the long-term care sector, forcing long-needed changes. These factors include the following:

Stringent regulations. The scandals and exposés of the 1960s and 1970s caused public outcry and pressured legislators to effect tougher standards and regulation. Nursing homes were forced to improve or discontinue operations.

Increased consumer expectations. As families and residents became more exposed to the problems that existed in nursing homes and more aware of their rights, they were in better positions to advocate improvements and seek recourse for questionable practices.

Increased interest in gerontological nursing. Once viewed as a specialty for "over the hill" nurses or "rejects" from acute care, gerontological nursing began attracting nurses as an exciting young specialty. Many nurses found that having the opportunity to utilize a wide range of knowledge, have a significant impact on patient care, and contribute to a developing specialty was a rare and fulfilling experience. Of course, changes in the acute-care job market have displaced some nurses who might not have otherwise opted for nursing home nursing. These changes not only eased some of the recruitment problems, but also increased the professional pool available for nursing home care.

The need for highly skilled nurse leaders in the nursing home setting is growing.	*Changing patient populations.* Many nursing homes now look similar to acute medical hospitals in terms of patient acuity. Residents are sicker, older, and more dependent than ever before. Staff skills, supportive services, medical involvement, and technology within the nursing home are progressively increasing.

If the nursing home of today is different from the facility of the past, the nursing home of the future may bear no resemblance to what we know at present. As the changes continue, one thing will be certain: Highly skilled nursing administrators will be essential in the nursing home setting.

The Nursing Director Role

Figure 27-2 presents a typical job description for director of nursing of a long-term care facility. In reviewing the components of this job description, one can realize the tremendous responsibility associated with the director of nursing role. The nursing director must wear many hats, and the quality of the clinical services is significantly determined by how successfully these various job responsibilities are achieved. The responsibilities associated with this position can be categorized under the following roles.

Leader

By virtue of the title, the director of nursing is viewed as the leader of the nursing department. However, having the title does not guarantee that others will necessarily follow, or that there will not be other staff challenging the director's leadership. Informal leaders exist in most organizations and derive their power in many ways (Eliopoulos, 1983, 125):

- Develops and assures conformance to nursing service standards, goals, policies, procedures, and job descriptions.
- Coordinates nursing service activities with those of other departments.
- Assures that there is a nursing assessment performed and plan of care developed for each resident.
- Screens potential residents for appropriateness for facility.
- Assigns and evaluates responsibilities for assuring that residents' nursing needs are fulfilled.
- Assures that nursing documentation requirements are met.
- Reports or assures that there is reporting of all significant clinical information to the physician.
- Recruits, screens, and hires nursing personnel.
- Evaluates the performance of nursing personnel.
- Counsels, disciplines, and fires nursing personnel when necessary.
- Assures that nursing personnel have valid licenses and function within scope of practice.
- Assures that required in-service education and orientation programs are planned, presented, and documented.
- Determines staffing needs for department and assures that daily staffing is sufficient to meet residents' needs.
- Prepares and negotiates budget for department.
- Monitors incidents and accidents.
- Develops and assures compliance with quality assurance plan for department.
- Serves as a liaison between administration and nursing employees.
- Represents nursing on various internal and external committees and for various official activities.
- Handles problems and complaints of residents, families, and staff.
- Assures positive public relations between nursing service and consumers.
- Conducts research, writes reports, and analyzes data pertaining to nursing services.
- Performs other functions as assigned.

FIGURE 27-2. Sample Job Description for the Director of Nursing of a Nursing Home.

- *Role.* Certain positions or titles traditionally have been granted power—for example, physician, union delegate, chairman of the board.
- *Expertise.* The knowledge and skill possessed by persons can give them power—for example, the ward clerk who knows how to process insurance forms or the LPN who knows staff capabilities and preferences in patient assignments.
- *Information source.* There are some people viewed as powerful because they can obtain and communicate information effectively—for example, the supply clerk who travels to all units, exchanging information along the way.
- *Association.* Being close to a powerful person elevates one's power—for example, the medical director's secretary, or the orderly who happens to be the nephew of the administrator.
- *Control of rewards.* Persons who can manipulate resources command power—for example, the supervisor who can influence one's raise or the fiscal officer who will determine if a purchasing request should be approved.

- *Personality*. Charisma, appearance, and other personal attributes can increase one's power—for example, the nursing assistant whom everyone likes or the maintenance man who emits sensuality.

Leadership effectiveness is influenced by how well the nursing director manages and utilizes all sources of power. For example, if the nursing director wishes to implement a new program, he or she will increase the odds for success by first gaining the support of key power brokers (medical director, supervisors, popular staff) before widespread introduction of the idea.

Analyzer

Data analysis and planning are essential to effective nursing administration. Time must be allocated for these important tasks.

The director of nursing needs to be sensitive to all sources of information and their significance. There are many sources of information providing feedback into problems, needs, and trends, such as incident and accident reports, absentee and turnover rates, supply usage, overtime usage, patterns of complaints and compliments, decubitus rates, resident level of care, infection rates, and health department survey findings. In addition, the director can conduct audits to evaluate specific issues. Rather than store these data, the director must determine whether changes or new findings are present and find the reason for them. For example, the director may discover that one month's sick time usage was a total of 98 days for the department. In reviewing records it may be noted that over the past four months sick time usage has been progressively increasing; thus a trend is detected. Further exploration may reveal that a majority of the increased sick time usage can be attributed to one of the nursing units. The director knows that the unit received a new head nurse four months ago. This fact implies to the director the need to investigate further to determine whether the staff is testing the new head nurse, the head nurse is monitoring sick time usage, a flu or other illness has affected the staff, or other factors are responsible for the trend.

Planner

In addition to the day-to-day problem solving, guiding the department to achieve specific goals is a necessary function of the nursing director. There is a need to plan many aspects of the department's functioning, including staffing levels, schedules, supply needs, staff development, employee motivators, evaluations, and new programs. The director who lacks a plan for the department and instead functions as a crisis manager will waste time and resources, and seldom create a dynamic service. A realistic plan, based on the previous year's evaluation of assessed needs and desired outcomes for the next year, is an essential working tool. From this plan, resource requirements (time, material, staff) can be derived. The director may discover after evaluating resource needs for a plan that it is unrealistic or unachievable. For example, the director may plan to upgrade 50 nursing assistant I (NA I) positions to NA II positions because this change will expand the staff's capabilities and be a form of career mobility for the NAs. Upon planning, the director may discover several things: In order to have the NAs attend the training sessions, unit staffing will be depleted and resulting overtime will exceed the budgeted level; budgeted funds provide only for the upgrading of 15 positions; and resident care needs are such that less than one NA for each of the eight units will have the opportunity to utilize the advanced NA II skills. Imagine the credibility and morale problems that could have resulted if the director had promised to upgrade the positions before plotting the plans! Another important advantage to developing plans is the ability to prioritize activities so that time can be managed effectively.

Educator

Federal regulations require that mandatory in-service education programs be presented annually on the topics of infection control, fire and safety, accident prevention, confidentiality of patient information, and preservation of patient dignity. Other topics are to be included based on the staff's educational needs and interests. In addition, staff must be well oriented, have skills maintained and upgraded, and be exposed to current practice concepts. Ideally, the director will have a staff development instructor available to plan, coordinate, teach, and maintain records on in-service programs. The director also will use opportunities to educate staff formally and informally using mechanisms such as circulating articles, discussing new ideas over a lunch table, writing newsletters, bringing in speakers, presenting lectures, conducting nursing rounds, and being a role model for desired behavior.

Resource Gatekeeper

Cost containment is vital to the survival of any health care facility. The use of human and material resources must be carefully planned and monitored; even minor oversights can be costly. For example, a unit may have 20 residents requiring disposable underpads to protect their bedding. These pads cost 15 cents each and are changed an average of seven times a day, for a daily cost of $1.05 for each resident using them or, in the case of this unit, $21.00 a day. If the staff uses two pads when one would suffice, the unit cost increases an additional $21.00 a day. This may not seem significant until the annual impact is realized: an additional cost of $7,665.00 (for only 20 residents!). Likewise, if each of six units had one nurse working two hours of overtime daily at an hourly time-and-one-half rate of $12.00 the cost to the facility would be $144.00 a day, or $52,560.00 annually. Often it is the small amount of unbudgeted, unauthorized overtime and minor misuse of supplies—items easy to overlook—that result in budgets going in the red. Daily monitoring of nonproductive time and monthly review of supply usage, preferably by unit, can be helpful in identifying problems before they get out of control.

Personnel Manager

Assuring and maintaining the appropriate quality and quantity of nursing staff is a major responsibility of the nursing director. The necessary patient acuity level must first be assessed to determine the number of full-time-equivalent (FTE) positions needed. For example, if the 34 patients on Unit A require 2.8 hours of nursing care daily the number of FTEs would be calculated as follows:

$$\begin{array}{rl} 34 & \text{number of patients} \\ \times\ 2.8 & \text{hours of nursing care per patient} \\ \hline 95.2 & \text{hours a day needed for the unit} \\ \times\ 365 & \text{days} \\ \hline 34{,}748 & \text{nursing hours required for the unit in a year} \end{array}$$

This is only a preliminary number because nonproductive hours (sick time, workshop days, vacations, holidays) must be considered. By examining leave policies and past usage the average amount of nonproductive time per employee can be calculated. For example, it may be found that the facility's employees annually average the following number of days:

$$\begin{array}{rl} 5 & \text{sickness} \\ 13 & \text{vacation} \\ 10 & \text{holidays} \\ 1 & \text{workshop attendance} \\ 1 & \text{funeral leave, jury duty, other} \\ \hline 30 & \text{nonproductive days annually} = 240 \text{ hours} \end{array}$$

Thus the actual productive hours per employee is

$$\begin{array}{rl} 2{,}080 & \text{potential productive time (52 weeks} \times 40 \text{ hours)} \\ -\ 240 & \text{nonproductive hours} \\ \hline 1{,}840 & \text{productive hours per employee} \end{array}$$

Dividing:

$$\frac{34{,}675 \text{ total number of hours needed on unit}}{1{,}840 \text{ productive hours per employee}} = 18.9 \text{ FTEs}$$

Rounded, 19 positions are required for the unit. Before accepting this figure as the staffing need for the unit, the director must plot the positions on a schedule. Often, when practices such as giving every other weekend off or not working employees more than five consecutive days are considered, it is found that additional staff may be needed. The staffing for this unit potentially could be increased 1.5 positions when these factors are considered.

The next step is to determine what level of staff will fulfill the FTE requirements. In addition to patient acuity and the nursing director's preference, budget constraints may determine the mix. For example, a staff of all

Unit size: 34 beds
Total staff required: 19 FTEs
Annual salaries & fringes: $23,000 RN; $17,000 LPN;
$11,000 NA (Nursing aide)

	I	II	III
RN			
#	2	4	19
%	10	20	100
$	46,000	92,000	437,000
LPN			
#	4	6	
%	20	30	
$	68,000	102,000	
NA			
#	13	9	
%	70	50	
$	143,000	99,000	
TOTAL UNIT COST ($)	257,000	293,000	437,000

FIGURE 27-3. Impact of Various Staffing Patterns on Nursing Budget.

registered nurses could cost 70% more than a staff that is 70% unlicensed (Figure 27-3).

Once the necessary positions have been funded, the nursing director must ensure that they are filled with the most competent staff possible. During the recruitment process, potential employees should be evaluated for ability to fulfill the responsibilities outlined in the job description, as well as their experience, education, attitude toward nursing home residents, communication skills, appearance, and impression made. Although some subjective evaluation is made during the hiring process, discrimination based on sex, age, race, national origin, and handicaps must be avoided. Any testing performed as a prehiring screening measure must be based on skills required in performance of the job and administered to all applicants for the position.

Reference checks are essential. Written permission for references must be obtained from the applicant, and all communication pertaining to references should be in writing. Calling a nurse friend for whom the applicant once worked and asking about the applicant is inappropriate and could result in legal problems. (Likewise, a director cannot volunteer to another agency that a former employee, who is now seeking employment with them, was a problem unless the employee granted permission for the reference.) Legally, nothing is wrong with stating on a requested reference that the employee had problems, provided that they are facts, not suppositions. Saying the employee was terminated for being found guilty of carrying facility linens off the premises is acceptable, but stating that the employee also was responsible for a rash of patient thefts is inappropriate if it is just a suspicion.

A thorough orientation of all employees prior to their assumption of job responsibilities is a safeguard for the facility and a benefit to employees themselves. Personnel and patient care policies and procedures should be reviewed, key personnel introduced, and the location of resources learned. The philosophy of care and attitude of management toward employees can be conveyed during this process. Also, the orientation serves as an opportunity for further assessment of new employees.

Close supervision of staff is extremely important, particularly with the large number of nonprofessional staff employed in the nursing home setting. Supervision entails following through on assignments to ensure correct completion, observing staff in caregiving activities, and being available for problem solving. If possible, daily anecdotal notes, highlighting desirable and problem behavior, should be maintained and analyzed at intervals. Employees should receive regular feedback regarding their performance, accompanied by corrective action plans when necessary. Regularly collected data feeds into the annual performance evaluation given to each employee.

Communicator

Direct communication with staff can prevent misinformation that results from messages being filtered through various levels. This contact with staff also reflects a caring, open attitude.

The nursing director is in a strategic position for the flow of information. The director communicates a great deal of information, including organizational goals, administrative mandates, practice changes, consumer response, quality of services, and needs. By sharing information with staff in a timely manner, considerable misperception, anxiety, and wasted effort can be avoided. Directors soon learn that every additional layer through which information must travel increases the likelihood that the original message may be distorted; therefore, they are wise to use as many opportunities as possible to communicate with staff directly. Small group meetings, memos distributed with paychecks, in-house publications, and announcements on bulletin boards are mechanisms for direct communication between the director of nursing and the staff.

Receiving information from staff is also part of the communicator role. Employees need access to the director to clarify misperceptions, share problems, and make recommendations. Be it through designated "open-door" times or rounds through the facility, the director should offer times when staff can freely communicate.

In addition to the exchange of information within the nursing department, the nursing director should maintain open communication with other departments. Interdepartmental communication promotes constructive problem solving, coordinates actions toward common goals, and facilitates positive working relationships.

Communication with the community is important also. The professional and lay community should be kept abreast of new programs, improvements, and changes. The community should know that their opinions, questions, and feedback are welcomed as well. For instance, nurses at the local emergency room may be unhappy with the nursing home staff because patients are transferred without charts or medical histories. If the nurses know they can pick up the telephone and call the nursing director of the facility, the problem could be prevented from happening again, or the ER nurses may learn that this was a highly unusual circumstance. Without the contact with the director, the nurse may believe that the nursing home is disorganized and uncaring—or worse still, convey this misconception to others.

Not to be forgotten is the importance of communicating with the facility's administrator. The director of nursing needs regular contact with the administrator to keep abreast of issues, offer feedback, and keep the administrator advised.

Advocate

Nursing administrators must be advocates of good care for patients, adequate resources for staff, and improvement in the overall status of long-term care.

Nursing directors must advocate on several fronts. They first must advocate practices that support the highest possible quality of patient care; this advocacy can involve lobbying for improved reimbursement or developing standards for staff to follow. They also must advocate the advancement of the specialty by such activities as educating nurses in other settings regarding the realities of nursing home nursing and supporting research to enhance the specialty. Recognizing the political nature of health care organizations, nursing directors must be advocates for themselves through negotiating salaries reflective of their levels of responsibility and assuring their continued professional growth.

Opportunist

Like any executive, nursing directors must learn to capitalize on opportunities to benefit their facilities and themselves. For example, the director may assess that some of the individuals who investigate potential admission to the facility could remain in the community if adequate services and family respite were provided. From this, the director can identify the need for a new service, such as geriatric day care, that would meet a community need and generate revenue for the facility. Such intrapreneuring (creating new business opportunities within the organization) is a feature of successful organizations and successful executives. Nurses also must discover that using opportunities for one's own advancement or benefit is not bad or inappropriate. For example, the director may see that several of the new outreach programs sponsored by the nursing home lack coordination and leadership, and propose that a new position be created to administer those programs; of course, the nursing director could describe how he or she is the ideal candidate to fill this role.

Certainly there are numerous other roles left unmentioned, such as that of consultant, negotiator, motivator, change agent, and spokesperson. The few roles that have been discussed demonstrate that the diversity, complexity, and multiple responsibilities of the nursing director position are significant and demand considerable expertise. The challenges of this role will only multiply as the nursing home becomes a more complex care environment. Nursing directors will need to be more than a "required license" or "the nurse in charge": They must be executives able to plan, negotiate for, administer, and evaluate a complex nursing system and its interaction with the entire facility. Some of the best talent the profession has to offer will be needed in the nursing home setting. Nursing is at the crossroads of either repeating a history laced with lost opportunities and minimal influence, or exercising control over the molding of a different and dynamic style of practice in the nursing home setting.

REFERENCES

Eliopoulos C: Nursing Administration of Long-Term Care. Rockville, MD, Aspen Systems, 1983.

Dunlop BD: The Growth of Nursing Home Care. Lexington, MA, Lexington Books, 1979.

U.S. Department of Commerce: Statistical Abstract of the United States, 105th ed. Washington, DC, U.S. Bureau of the Census, 1986.

BIBLIOGRAPHY

Blancett SS: Classics for JONA: Readings in nursing administration. Philadelphia, JB Lippincott, 1988.

Carter MA: Professional nursing in the nursing home. J Professional Nurs 3(6): 325, 376, 1987.

Douglas LM: The effective nurse leader manager, 3rd ed. St. Louis, CV Mosby, 1988.

Evashwick CJ, Weiss LJ: Managing the Continuum of Care. Rockville, MD, Aspen Systems, 1987.

Henry KH: Nursing Administration and Law Manual. Rockville, MD, Aspen Systems, 1987.

National Health Publishing Editorial Staff: Director of Nursing Manual, Federal Regulations and Guidelines. Owings Mills, MD, National Health Publishing, 1980; annual updates.

Scalzi CC: Role stress and coping strategies of nurse executives. J Nurs Admin 18(3): 34–38, 1988.

Shortell SM, Kaluzny AD: Health Care Management: A Text in Organizational Theory and Behavior, 2nd ed. New York, Wiley, 1988.

Sullivan EJ, Decker PJ: Effective Management in Nursing, 2nd ed. Menlo Park, CA, Addison-Wesley, 1988.

Yager D: Long term facilities feel the nursing shortage, too. Am J Nurs 88(4): 450, 1988.

CHAPTER 28

The Role of the Psychiatric Clinical Nurse Specialist in the Nursing Home Setting

Patricia Grodin

Chapter Objectives
At the completion of this chapter the reader will be able to:

1. Discuss changes in the care of the chronically mentally ill.
2. Describe the evolution of the psychiatric clinical nurse specialist's role.
3. List functions of the psychiatric clinical nurse specialist in the nursing home setting.

Since the late 1960s the United States has witnessed a policy of deinstitutionalization of the chronically mentally ill from psychiatric hospitals. It could be argued, however, that this deinstitutionalization would be better defined as *reinstitutionalization,* since the number of nursing home residents with diagnosed mental health problems doubled between 1969 and 1973 alone, and has grown steadily since then (Linn et al., 1985). In fact, nursing homes have been described as the centerpiece of the national deinstitutionalization policy (Shadish and Bootzin, 1984), with 85,000 direct admissions from mental hospitals into long-term care facilities in 1974 (Goldman et al., 1981).

The National Nursing Home Survey of 1977 attempted to determine the number of nursing home residents suffering from mental illness. The results illustrated several key points:

- More than one-half of the 1.3 million nursing home residents had a primary or secondary diagnosis of mental illness.
- Twenty percent of those residents had a recorded primary mental disorder of depression, dementia, or psychosis.
- An additional 10% were estimated to have the potential for a diagnosable primary mental disorder of depression, dementia, or psychosis.
- Thirty percent were estimated to suffer from dementia without psychosis.

- The remaining 40%, though assessed as "mentally healthy," were considered "at risk" for subsequent mental disease or behavior problems (U.S. Department of Health and Human Services, 1981).

The limitations of this study, such as the failure of records to reflect accurate mental health diagnoses and the limited psychiatric diagnostic categories considered, suggest that the problem of mental illness in the nursing home population is far greater than the preceding numbers indicate.

Mental health services for nursing home patients have been desperately lacking despite the prevalence of psychiatric problems in this setting.

Although many nursing home residents possess psychiatric disorders, the mental health component of care in long-term care facilities has been desperately lacking. Harper and Lebowitz (1986) have identified five factors that have influenced the current status of mental health care in nursing homes:

- Lack of financial resources and staff.
- Lack of staff (professional and paraprofessional) who have been specifically prepared to care for the mentally ill.
- Presence of the myth that mental health problems reflect the normal aging process.
- Failure of the current reimbursement system (Medicare and Medicaid) to provide adequate coverage for mental health services.
- Failure of licensure certification standards to specify mandatory provision of mental health services to mentally ill nursing home residents.

Several additional factors may be added to this list:

- Absence of a strong advocacy group to promote the needs of this population.
- Lack of interest by most psychiatric professionals in treating a "doomed" nursing home population.
- Lack of interest by most psychiatric professionals in treating a population where the most common psychiatric diagnosis is dementia.
- Discomfort of acute care psychiatric units and resistance to providing "back-up support" for nursing home staff by aggressively treating referred residents.

Statistics clearly indicate that a significant number of nursing home residents possess mental health problems. With the continuation of the closure of mental hospitals, the increasing number of persons with histories of psychiatric disorders who are aging, and the greater number of individuals who are surviving to their eighth decade and beyond—where the risk of mental health problems increases—it can be safely predicted that the prevalence of psychiatric problems in the nursing home setting will grow. Caregiver competency to manage the problems of the mentally ill in the nursing home setting must increase to meet this growing demand. Of the many strategies that can assist in improving mental health care in the nursing home, the role of the psychiatric clinical nurse specialist holds promise in making a significant impact.

Evolution of the Role

In 1981, when she discussed the future of psychiatric nursing, Claire M. Fagin noted that in order to establish priorities for future development of the discipline, consideration had to be given to demographic changes in society, such as the anticipated increase in the elderly population. Despite this foresight and the well-documented mental health needs of the elderly, psychiatric nursing has barely scraped the surface of the needs of this population, particularly the segment of the population that resides in nursing homes.

Psychiatric clinical nurse specialists are appropriate resources and role models to assist nursing staff in improving the mental health care of nursing home residents. However, although the number of clinical nurse specialists has been rising rapidly, it is rare to discover these advanced nursing clinicians employed in long-term care facilities. A review of the literature through 1986 reveals only one article describing the part-time *consultation* services of a psychiatric clinical nurse specialist in the nursing home setting (Tierney et al., 1986) and none identifying a specialist directly employed by a nursing home on a full-time or part-time basis. In addition, it is interesting to note that only one article describes the relatively new specialist role in gerontology, and that specialist worked in an acute care setting, not a long-term facility (Wells, 1985). This paucity of literature reflects the absence of psychiatric nurse specialists in the nursing home sector.

Many long-term care facilities are recognizing the need for advanced nursing expertise to guide them in the care of mentally impaired residents and are challenging psychiatric nurse specialists to enter their care setting. Such was the case with a large long-term care facility in the Washington, D.C., area that offered the author the opportunity to implement this new role. The following discussion will describe how the psychiatric nurse specialist role evolved in that setting.

Implementation of the Role

In initiating the psychiatric clinical nurse specialist's role in a long-term care facility, three target areas for intervention can be identified: the resident and family, the staff, and the organization in general.

The Resident and Family

Nursing home residents are very complex because of their unique manifestations of the aging process and the consequences of medical problems. Superimpose psychiatric disorders, and the complexities further increase. In order to plan and deliver effective care, skilled assessment is essential. Holistic assessment of the resident includes a biopsychosocial history, physical assessment, mental status evaluation, medication review, and an in-depth chart review (especially of laboratory results).

Perhaps more than any other age group, the elderly clearly exhibit the interrelationship between physical pathology and behavioral/cognitive symptomatology. For example, the occurrence of a simple urinary tract infection in an otherwise medically stable and cognitively intact elder can result in severe confusion, hallucinations, delusions, mood lability, and physical aggression. Likewise, the side effects and interactions of medications can result in cognitive dysfunction. The nurse specialist can demonstrate assessment techniques and guide staff in exploring all of the potential causes of mental health problems.

The nurse specialist can serve as a role model to staff by demonstrating the unique skills used in mental health assessment and care planning.

Once mental health problems have been identified, the specialist can advise nursing staff about the range of treatment modalities and assist them in planning interventions appropriate for specific problems. For example, some residents may benefit from psychotherapy groups, while others may need specific behavioral modification approaches.

In many nursing homes a significant number of residents suffer from dementias. These individuals often benefit from a protective, structured environment and specific care approaches. In addition to helping staff gain expertise in caring for individual residents, the specialist may assist by facilitating the development of a special care unit that incorporates the basic principles of care for dementia victims—for example, alarmed exits, clocks, controlled stimulation, consistent care approaches, and wandering areas.

The specialist's knowledge of family systems therapy enables the specialist to assess family dynamics and recommend appropriate interventions that the staff may otherwise overlook. The specialist can advocate an active family role in the resident's care, and can further extend services by initiating support, education, and counseling groups for families who share specific problems, such as a support group for families of dementia victims.

Ideally, the specialist should have contact with every newly admitted resident to assess mental health and identify the need for special interventions. If such contact is not possible, the specialist can develop criteria for staff to know when the specialist should be called, such as for any resident who scores below a specific level on the mental status examination or anyone for whom psychotropics are prescribed.

The Staff

By far the majority of care rendered to the elderly in long-term care settings is delivered by nursing staff. More significantly, 80–90% of that care is provided by paraprofessionals, the nursing assistants, who have limited training in general and little or no preparation in caring for persons with psychiatric impairments. In addition, licensed staff members are often inexperienced in providing care for the mentally ill (Carling, 1981; Jones, 1975; More, 1977; National Center for Health Statistics, 1979).

Effective staff development efforts include the specialist's involvement with staff in direct care activities.

The specialist plays an important role in educating nursing staff in principles of psychiatric nursing care; however, this role entails more than presenting theory in a classroom setting. Staff want to know specifically what to do in response to individual behaviors: How do they approach a resident who attempts to strike anyone who comes near? How can they calm the Alzheimer's victim who is resisting a bath? What can they do to safeguard a resident who wanders? How do they respond to the resident who constantly directs derogatory comments to them?

By participating in direct care activities and role modeling the specialist can be effective in helping staff gain improved skills in working with mentally impaired residents. The importance of this "hands on" involvement in basic care activities cannot be sufficiently underscored. The specialist can demonstrate how therapeutic psychiatric interventions can be incorporated into daily routines—for example, promotion of self-esteem through facilitation of maximum level of independent functioning, utilization of reorientation techniques, aggression prevention by means of interpretation of environmental stimuli, and communication tips for the cognitively impaired resident.

High visibility of the psychiatric clinical specialist during the provision of daily nursing care produces several other positive outcomes, such as opportunities for the following:

- Evaluation of staff's baseline knowledge and learning needs.
- Incidental learning.
- Additional resident assessment.
- Evaluation of physical plant factors that influence caregiving.
- Confirmation of oneself as an authority and resource.

The last item on the list is an essential step in maintaining the viability of the specialist role because it establishes a power base of referent or professional authority upon which all interventions rely. This statement is particularly true for the specialist operating from a staff position in the organizational structure (Stevens, 1976).

The Organization

Effecting change that is instrumental in the promotion of an optimal level of function and quality of life for the mentally ill and cognitively impaired elderly in nursing homes cannot be limited to the clinical area. Historically, nursing homes were not designed for rendering services to this population. Policies, procedures, staffing patterns, state and federal regulations, and the physical environment of the facility were developed to serve a population far different from that which resides in long-term care facilities today. These facets of the general organization of the nursing home also require evaluation and revision. The psychiatric clinical nurse specialist is clearly capable of effecting the revisions in the organizational policy that are necessary to promote a high quality of care for mentally ill and cognitively impaired residents because he or she is

- Trained in systems, organizational, and change theories.
- Familiar with nursing process and standards.
- Knowledgeable with respect to the research skills necessary to collect and evaluate data in order to substantiate recommendations for change.

TABLE 28-1. Examples of Intervention of a Psychiatric Clinical Nurse Specialist in a Long-term Care Facility

- Development and implementation of a special care program for the moderately to severely cognitively impaired resident, including relocation of these residents to a unit designed to provide a safe, secure setting, alteration of the staffing pattern in recognition of the increased incidence of physical aggression among this population, initiation of a goal-directed unit-based activity program, establishment of a liaison with the Alzheimer's Disease and Related Disorder Association, and initiation of a family group.
- Development and implementation of a special care staff training program directed toward improving skills in caring for the cognitively impaired elderly and increasing sensitivity to and understanding of resident behavior.
- Introduction of formal mental status evaluations to the preadmission protocol, and instruction in the implementation of these tests.
- Development and implementation of a weekly psychotherapy group for residents suffering from selected psychiatric illnesses and capable of participating in insight-oriented therapy.
- Implementation of support groups for all levels of nursing staff.
- Development of a protocol for psychiatric emergencies.
- Provision of monthly experiential mental health in-service training for all disciplines and each shift.
- Formulation of "communication tips" guidelines for use during interactions with the cognitively impaired elderly.
- Development and implementation of unit-based seminars on such topics as death and dying, aggression prevention and management, and care of the "problem" patient.
- Alteration of the nursing assistant assignment from weekly to monthly rotations to facilitate education, promote accountability, and allow time for the development of a therapeutic working relationship between the resident and the nursing assistant.
- Collection of statistics for future research in such areas as the impact of the special care program on patient care outcomes and characteristics of referrals received for mental health evaluation and treatment.

Examples of some of the interventions of the specialist in a long-term care facility are highlighted in Table 28-1.

Evaluation of Impact

In an effort to validate the need for continued service of a psychiatric nurse specialist at the facility in which this role was implemented and to confirm that the staff perceived mental health services to residents as having improved as a result of the specialist's interventions, an evaluation survey was conducted. This survey took the form of a 39-item questionnaire that was distributed to all staff—nursing and nonnursing clinical staff. In addition to evaluation of job performance, several questions related directly to role function. A review of the feedback indicated benefits in four major areas:

Clinical services:

- More astute resident assessment.
- More individualized care plans.
- Better interpretation of data to caregivers.
- Improved interventions.

- More appropriate crisis intervention, especially with psychotic, suicidal, and physically aggressive residents.
- Improved medication assessment and utilization.
- Expansion of therapeutic programs.

Education:

- Effective training for nursing assistants.
- Informative and applicable education for all disciplines.

Support:

- Establishment of family groups.
- Effective staff groups in managing stress and conflict more appropriately.
- Advocacy for caregivers' needs.

Communication:

- Improved interdepartmental communication.
- More effective staff-resident and staff-family communication.

It has been stated that the "emergence of clinical specialism in nursing has had far greater impact on nursing practice than any other movement to date. Delivery of patient care has markedly improved because of the leadership and clinical expertise of the specialist" (Edland and Hodges, 1983, 500). Hopefully, this statement can be true of the psychiatric nurse clinical specialist in the long-term care setting. An abundance of opportunity exists for creating new roles and demonstrating psychiatric nursing's unique contribution in nursing homes.

REFERENCES

Carling PJ: Nursing homes and chronic mental patients: A second opinion. Schizophrenia Bulletin 7(4): 574–579, 1981.

Edland BJ, Hodges LC: Preparing and using the clinical nurse specialist. Nurs Clin N Am 18:500, 1983.

Fagin CM: Psychiatric nursing at the crossroads: Quo vadis. Perspectives in Psychiatric Care 19(3&4): 99–106, 1981.

Goldman H, Gallazzi A, Taube C: Defining and counting the chronically mentally ill. Hospital and Community Psychiatry 32:21–27, 1981.

Harper MS, Lebowitz BD (eds): Mental Illness in Nursing Homes: Agenda for Research. Washington, DC, U.S. Department of Health and Human Services, 1986. DHHS Publication No. (ADM) 86–1459.

Jones M: Community care for chronic mental patients: The need for reassessment. Hospital and Community Psychiatry 26:94–98, 1975.

Linn MW, Gurel L, Williford WO, Overall J, Gurland B, Laughlin P, Barchiesi A: Nursing home care as an alternative to psychiatric hospitalization. Arch Gen Psychiatr 42:544–551, 1985.

More MT: Education and consultation on mental illness in long term care facilities: Problems, pitfalls, solutions: An administrator's point of view. J Geriatr Psychiatr 10:151–162, 1977.

National Center for Health Statistics: National Nursing Home Survey: Summary for the U.S. Hyattsville, MD, 1979.

Shadish WR, Bootzin RR: The social integration of psychiatric patients in nursing homes. Am J Psychiatr 141(10): 1203–1207, 1984.

Stevens BJ: Accountability of the clinical specialist: The administrator's viewpoint. J Nurs Admin 9:30–32, 1976.

Tierney JC, Cronin A, Scanlon MK: . . . And don't send her back! Am J Nurs 86(9): 1011–1014, 1986.

U.S. Department of Health and Human Services: Care of the Mentally Ill in Nursing Homes: Addendum to National Plan for the Chronically Mentally Ill. DDHHS Pub. No. (ADM) 81–1077. Washington, DC, The Department, 1981.

Wells DL: Gerontological nurse specialists: Tomorrow's leaders today. J Gerontol Nurs 11(5): 36–40, 1985.

BIBLIOGRAPHY

American Health Care Association: Facts in Brief on Long Term Care. Washington, DC, The Association, 1984.

American Nurses' Association: Nursing: A Social Policy Statement. Kansas City, MO, American Nurses' Association, 1980.

Anderson G, Hicks S: The clinical nurse specialist—Role overview and future prospects. Austral Nurs J 15(8): 36–38, 53, 1986.

Baker C, Kramer M: To define or not to define: The role of the clinical specialist. Nurs Forum 9:41–55, 1970.

Blake P: The clinical nurse specialist—A nurse consultant. J Nurs Admin 7(10): 33–36, 1977.

Brown M: Nursing assistants' behavior toward the institutionalized elderly. QRB 14(1): 15–17, 1988.

Colerick E, Mason P, Proulx J: Evaluation of the clinical nurse specialist's role: Development of a dual purpose framework. Nurs Leadership 3(3): 26–34, 1980.

Gordon M: The clinical specialist as change agent. Nurs Outlook 17:37–39, 1969.

Hellman C: The making of a clinical specialist. Nurs Outlook 22(3): 165–167, 1974.

Kahut S, Kahut JJ, Fleishman JJ: Reality Orientation for the Elderly, 3rd ed. New York, Medical Economics Books, 1987.

Lipkin LV, Faude KJ: Dementia—Educating the caregiver. J Gerontol Nurs 13(11): 23–27, 1987.

Loomis M: The clinical specialist as change agent. Nurs Forum 7:136–145, 1968.

Menard SW: The Clinical Nurse Specialist: Perspectives in Practice. New York, Wiley, 1987.

Paremski A: A conceptual model for clinical nurse specialist practice. J Gerontol Nurs 14(2): 14–19, 46–47, 1988.

Parkis E: The management role of the clinical specialist, Part 2. Supervisor Nurse 5:49, 1974.

Shadden BB: Communication, Behavior, and Aging: A Sourcebook for Clinicians. Baltimore, MD, Williams and Wilkens, 1988.

Sparacino P: The clinical nurse specialist. Nurs Prac 1:15–228, 1986.

Tarsitano BJ, Brophy EB, Snyder DJ: A demystification of the clinical nurse specialist role: Perceptions of clinical nurse specialists and nurse administrators. J Nurs Educ 25(1): 4–9, 1986.

Whall AL: Therapeutic use of self. Gerontol Nurs 14(2): 38–39, 46–47, 1988.

Whiting SM: Managing care of a client with organic brain syndrome. J Gerontol Nurs 13(10): 18–24, 1987.

Williams LB, Cancian D: A clinical nurse specialist in a line management position. J Nurs Admin 15(1): 20–26, 1985.

Wyers MA, Grove SK, Pastorino C: Clinical nurse specialist: In search of the right role. Nursing and Health Care 6(4): 203–207, 1985.

Index

The letter *t* following a page number indicates tabular material. Figures are indicated by italic numbers.